Re-treating Religion

John D. Caputo, *series editor*

Contributors

Alena Alexandrova

Daniela Calabrò

Ignaas Devisch

Federico Ferrari

Ian James

Laurens ten Kate

Marc De Kesel

Michel Lisse

Donald Loose

Boyan Manchev

Jean-Luc Nancy

Anne O'Byrne

Frans van Peperstraten

François Raffoul

Aukje van Rooden

Kathleen Vandeputte

Hent de Vries

Theo W. A. de Wit

Edited by ALENA ALEXANDROVA,
IGNAAS DEVISCH,
LAURENS TEN KATE
AND AUKJE VAN ROODEN

Re-treating Religion

Deconstructing Christianity with

Jean-Luc Nancy

With a Preamble and Concluding
Dialogue by Jean-Luc Nancy

FORDHAM UNIVERSITY PRESS
New York ▪ 2012

Illustration on p. 290: Claudio Parmiggiani, fourth photograph in *Latte e sangue* (2007), from the catalog *Apocalpysis cum figuris* (Turin: Allemandi, 2007); reprinted courtesy of Claudio Parmiggiani.

Fordham University Press has no responsibility for the persistence or accuracy of URLs for external or third-party Internet websites referred to in this publication and does not guarantee that any content on such websites is, or will remain, accurate or appropriate. Fordham University Press also publishes its books in a variety of electronic formats. Some content that appears in print may not be available in electronic books.

Library of Congress Cataloging-in-Publication Data

Re-treating religion : deconstructing Christianity with Jean-Luc Nancy / edited by Alena Alexandrova, Ignaas Devisch, Laurens ten Kate, and Aukje van Rooden ; with a preamble and concluding dialogue by Jean-Luc Nancy.—First edition.
    pages   cm.— (Perspectives in Continental philosophy)
    Includes bibliographical references and index.
    ISBN 978-0-8232-3464-6 (cloth : alk. paper)
    ISBN 978-0-8232-3465-3 (pbk. : alk. paper)
    1. Nancy, Jean-Luc. Déclosion.   2. Deconstruction.   3. Philosophy and religion.
I. Alexandrova, Alena, editor of compilation.   II. Nancy, Jean-Luc.
B2430.N363D4337   2012
230—dc23
                                                                          2011048557

Printed in the United States of America
14 13 12   5 4 3 2 1
First edition

Contents

Preface

In the fall of 2005 a small research group was founded at an equally small institute for interdisciplinary religious studies: the Heyendaal Institute of the University of Nijmegen, the Netherlands. Its aim was simple: to start a series of meetings for study and debate that would contribute to the philosophical analysis of the relation between modern culture and religion. Right from the start Jean-Luc Nancy's project of a deconstruction of monotheism—and in particular of Christianity—became the central focus of the group. Its members were Alena Alexandrova, Ignaas Devisch, Aukje van Rooden, and Laurens ten Kate (coordinator). They presented the first results of their research at the 2006 conference of the International Association for Philosophy and Literature in Freiburg i. B., Germany;[1] soon they decided to initiate, prepare, and edit an international volume of critical studies on Nancy's rethinking of monotheism and its legacy in our secular times—the result is the present book. The editors are very grateful to have been able to collaborate with Jean-Luc Nancy from the beginning of the project, a collaboration that finds expression in the volume's Preamble and the Concluding Dialogue. The Preamble, originally written for this volume in a shorter version, was then reworked and extended by Nancy and published in French as "Au milieu du monde," the second chapter of *L'adoration: Déconstruction du christianisme, 2* (Paris: Galilée, 2010), 35–63. We include the final, extended version here.

Furthermore, the editors would like to thank the Heyendaal Institute of Nijmegen, and in particular its director at the time, Erik Borgman, for offering an inspiring context for the project, as well as financial support. The Departments of Theology and Religious Studies of the University of Nijmegen, and the Faculty of Humanities of Tilburg University equally deserve our gratitude for their financial contribution. A special word of thanks should be extended to those who translated and copyedited the texts: Caroline Ardrey, Christine Blackmore, Jeff Fort, John McKeane, Schalk van der Merwe, Ron Peek, and Massimo Verdicchio, and to Helen Tartar of Fordham University Press, who believed in this book from the start and kept us moving.

Alena Alexandrova, Ignaas Devisch, Laurens ten Kate,
and Aukje van Rooden
May 2010

Abbreviations for Works by Jean-Luc Nancy

References to Nancy's works appear parenthetically in the text, giving first the page numbers in the English edition (if it exists), then page numbers in the French edition. Where no English version exists, the translation is our own.

Occasionally, for economy of reference contributors use abbreviations for works by other authors. These abbreviations are defined in the first citation of these works in the footnotes to the contributor's essay.

Biblical translations are, in general, taken from the New Revised Standard Version (1989).

BP   *The Birth to Presence.* Trans. Brian Holmes et al. Stanford: Stanford University Press, 1993.

BSP *Being Singular Plural.* Trans. Anne E. O'Byrne and Robert D. Richardson. Stanford: Stanford University Press, 2000. Augmented with "Cosmos Basileus," which first appeared in *Basileus*, ed. Paul Minkkinen, http://www.helsinki.fi/basileus, March 1998. Orig. *Être singulier pluriel* (Paris: Galilée, 1996).

BT   "Between Story and Truth." Trans. Franson Manjali. *The Little Magazine* 2, no. 4 (Delhi, July-August 2001): 6–8. Orig. "Entre deux." *Magazine Littéraire* 392 (November 2000): 54–57. Later expanded as the first part of *UJ*.

C   *Corpus.* Trans. Richard Rand. New York: Fordham University Press, 2008. Orig. *Corpus* (Paris: Métailié, 1992; augmented ed.

2000). The English edition corresponds to the 2000 French edition and contains the French text of the title essay.

CC   "The Confronted Community." Trans. Amanda Macdonald. *Postcolonial Studies* 6, no. 1 (2003): 23–36. Orig. *La communauté affrontée* (Paris: Galilée, 2001).

Com   "La comparution/The Compearance, from the Existence of 'Communism' to the Community of 'Existence.'" Trans. Tracy B. Strong. *Political Theory* 20, no. 3 (1992): 371–98. Orig. "La comparution (De l'existence du 'communisme' à la communauté de l' 'existence')," in Jean-Luc Nancy and Jean-Christophe Bailly, *La comparution (politique à venir)* (Paris: Bourgois, 1991), 47–100.

CP   "The Calculation of the Poet." Trans. Simon Sparks. In *The Solid Letter: Readings of Friedrich Hölderlin*, ed. Aris Fioretos, 44–73. Stanford: Stanford University Press 1999. Orig. "Calcul du poète," in *Des lieux divins*, 2nd ed. (Mauvezin: Trans-Europ-Repress, 1997).

CSR   "Church, State, Resistance." Trans. Véronique Voruz. In *Political Theologies: Public Religions in a Post-Secular World*, ed. Hent de Vries and Lawrence E. Sullivan, 102–12. New York: Fordham University Press, 2006.

CW   *The Creation of the World, or Globalization.* Trans. François Raffoul and David Pettigrew. Albany: State University of New York Press, 2007. Orig. *La création du monde ou la mondialisation* (Paris: Galilée, 2002).

D   *Dis-enclosure: The Deconstruction of Christianity.* Trans. Bettina Bergo, Gabriel Malenfant, and Michael B. Smith. New York: Fordham University Press, 2007. Orig. *La déclosion: Déconstruction du christianisme I* (Paris: Galilée, 2005).

DI   "Dies irae." In Jean-François Lyotard et. al., *La faculté de juger*, 9–54 (Paris: Minuit, 1985).

DP   "Of Divine Places." Trans. Michael Holland. *IC* 110–51. Orig. *Des lieux divins* (Mauvezin: Trans-Europ-Repress, 1987; 2nd ed., 1997).

DS   *The Discourse of the Syncope: Logodaedalus.* Trans. Saul Anton. Stanford: Stanford University Press, 2008. Orig. *Le discours de la syncope I: Logodaedalus* (Paris: Aubier-Flammarion, 1976).

EF   *The Experience of Freedom.* Trans. Bridget McDonald. Foreword by Peter Fenves. Stanford: Stanford University Press, 1993. Orig. *L'expérience de la liberté* (Paris: Galilée, 1988).

EG   "Entzug der Göttlichkeit: Zur Dekonstruktion und Selbstüberwindung des Christentums." In *Lettre International* (Winter 2002): 76–80.

EM   "Entretien sur le mal." *Apertura* 5 (1991): 27–32.

FT   *A Finite Thinking*. Ed. Simon Sparks. Trans. Simon Sparks et al. Stanford: Stanford University Press, 2003.

GI   *The Ground of the Image*. Trans. Jeff Fort. New York: Fordham University Press, 2005. Orig. *Au fond des images* (Paris: Galilée, 2003) and *Visitation (de la peinture chrétienne)* (Paris: Galilée, 2001).

GT   *The Gravity of Thought*. Trans. François Raffoul and Gregory Recco. Atlantic Highlands, N.J.: Humanities Press, 1997; 2nd ed., 1999.

H   *Hegel: The Restlessness of the Negative*. Trans. Jason Smith and Steven Miller. Minneapolis: University of Minnesota Press, 2002. Orig. *Hegel: L'inquiétude du négatif* (Paris: Hachette, 1997).

IC   *The Inoperative Community*. Trans. Peter Connor. Foreword by Christopher Fynsk. Minneapolis: University of Minnesota Press, 1990. Orig. *La communauté désoeuvrée* (Paris: Bourgois 1983; 2nd, augmented ed., 1990).

LA   *The Literary Absolute: The Theory of Literature in German Romanticism*. Trans. and introd. Philip Barnard and Cheryl Lester. Albany: State University of New York Press, 1988. Orig. *L'absolu littéraire: Théorie de la littérature du romantisme allemand* (Paris: Seuil, 1978).

LP   "The Look of the Portrait." Trans. Simon Sparks. *M2* 220–47. Orig. *Le regard du portrait* (Paris: Galilée, 2000).

M1   *The Muses*. Trans. Peggy Kamuf. Stanford: Stanford University Press 1996. Orig. *Les muses* (Paris: Galilée, 1994).

M2   *Multiple Arts: The Muses II*. Ed. Simon Sparks. Trans. Simon Sparks et al. Stanford: Stanford University Press, 2006.

NM   "The Nazi Myth." With Philippe Lacoue-Labarthe. Trans. Brian Holmes. *Critical Inquiry* 16, no. 2: 291–312. Orig. *Le mythe nazi* (La Tour d'Aigues: L'aube, 1991; 2005).

NT   *Noli me tangere: On the Raising of the Body*. Trans. Sarah Clift, Pascale-Anne Brault, and Michael Naas. New York: Fordham University Press, 2008. Orig. *Noli me tangere: Essai sur la levée du corps* (Paris: Bayard, 2003) and *Au ciel et sur la terre* (Paris: Bayard, 2004).

PD   *La pensée dérobée*. Paris: Galilée, 2001.

PF   *Une pensée finie*. Paris: Galilée, 1990.

R   *Résistance de la poésie*. Bordeaux: William Blake & Co., 1997.

RM   "Rien que le monde: Entretien avec Jean-Luc Nancy." *Vacarme* 11 (2000): 4–12.

RP   *Retreating the Political.* Coedited with Philippe Lacoue-Labarthe. Ed. and trans. Simon Sparks. London: Routledge, 1997. Orig. *Le retrait du politique* Paris: Galilée, 1983.

SV   "Sharing Voices." Trans. Gayle L. Ormiston. In *Transforming the Hermeneutic Context: From Nietzsche to Nancy,* ed. Gayle L. Ormiston and Alan Schrift, 211–59. Albany: State University of New York Press, 1990. Orig. *Le partage des voix* (Paris: Galilée, 1982).

SW   *The Sense of the World.* Trans. with a Foreword by Jeffrey S. Librett. Minneapolis: University of Minnesota Press, 1997. Orig. *Le sens du monde* (Paris: Galilée, 1993).

UJ   *"Un jour, les dieux se retirent . . ."* Bordeaux: William Blake & Co., 2001. Partially translated in BT.

V   "Visitation: Of Christian Painting." Trans. Jeff Fort. *GI* 108–25. Orig. *Visitation (de la peinture chrétienne)* Paris: Galilée, 2001.

Y   "You ask me what it means today." *Paragraph* 16, no. 2 (1993): 108–21.

ZA   "Zwischen Zerstörung und Auslöschung." *Deutsche Zeitschrift für Philosophie* 41 (1993–95): 859–64.

Preamble

In the Midst of the World; or, Why Deconstruct Christianity?

JEAN-LUC NANCY

> MANDORLA
> In the almond—what dwells in the almond?
> Nothing.
> What dwells in the almond is Nothing.
> There it dwells and dwells.
>
> **—Paul Celan**

Why Christianity?

Why speak of Christianity?

In truth, I'd like to speak of it as little as possible. I'd like to move toward an effacement of this name and of the whole corpus of references that follows it—a corpus that is already mostly effaced or has lost its vitality. But I do think it is important to follow the movement that this name has named: that of an exit from religion and of the expansion of the atheist world.

This world, our world, that of what used to be called "Western" civilization, which can now be distinguished as such only by vestiges of language or by divisions in which the "orient/occident" distinction plays only a small part—it is no accident that this world was first built up as "Christendom" [*chrétienté*]. Christianity was much more than a religion: it was the innervation of a Mediterranean space that was searching for a nervous system after it had put in place the morphological and physiological system of law, the city, and reason. Indeed this ternary—law, city, reason (we can also include art)—was a translation of the disappearance, with which the ternary itself was faced, of any assurance [*assurance*] concerning the foundation of existence. That is to say, any assurance concerning what we can also designate as the presence of the gods. It was the Greeks who perceived the absence of the gods in the place of this presence.[1]

We can say this in a different way, in order to move toward an essential characteristic of Christianity. The Greco-Roman world was the world of mortal mankind. Death was irreparable there; and whether one tried to think about it in terms of glory or in terms of deliverance, it was still the incompatible other of life. Other cultures have always affirmed death as another life, foreign yet close by, strange yet compatible in various ways. Irreparable and incompatible death struck life as an affliction. Christianity, reinterpreting an aspect of Judaism, proposed death as the truth of life and opened up in life itself the difference of death, whereby life could know itself as immortal and "saved."[2]

That life can be saved, or better still, that its salvation should be a certainty has been interpreted in many ways—by martyrdom, by ascesis, by mysticism, by the mastery and possession of nature, by adventure and enterprise, by the search for happiness, by the "emancipation of mankind"—and we will come back to what this "salvation" [*salut*] might still mean to us, what it still has to tell us. The turning point of civilization that reenergized "the West" was played out around what was called "eternal life." However, *eternal life* is not life indefinitely prolonged, but life withdrawn from time in the very course of time. Whereas the life of ancient mankind was a life measured by its time, and the life of other cultures was a life in constant relation to the life of the dead, Christian life lives, in time, what is outside time. This characteristic seems to have an intimate rapport with what I am calling here adoration, which I could characterize as a rapport with the outside of time (with the pure instant, with the ceasing of duration, with truth as an interruption of sense). Because sense is made complete in its interruption: it is not made complete, it is not satisfied. Sense is a dissatisfaction, a permanent desire for sense.

But before coming back to the motif of salvation, we must lay out what is contained in this proposition: "Christianity" is life in the world outside of the world. Nietzsche (to invoke the best witness on this subject) understood it perfectly. This despiser of "backworlds" [*arrière-mondes*] knew that Christianity (at least in a version of it that no Gospel or Church ever truly conforms to) consists in being in the world without being *of* the world. This is to say that it does not limit itself to adhering to inherence, to what is given (whether this is taken as the "real" or, on the contrary, as an "appearance"). Two of Nietzsche's well-known figures illustrate what he sometimes claims to be the "experience at the heart" of Christianity: the tightrope dancer and the child playing with dice. Neither relates to the world as a given by which they are surrounded; on the contrary, they relate to that in the world which makes an opening, rift, abyss, game, or risk.

"Life in the world outside the world" is so far from being an exclusively "Christian" formula that it finds an echo [*répondant*] in these statements by Wittgenstein: "the sense of the world must lie outside the world" and "God does not reveal himself *in* the world."[3] Of course, Wittgenstein is not calling on any representation or conception of "another world": he is asking that the outside be thought and grasped in the midst of the world.

What is thus shown by Nietzsche and Wittgenstein could be shown by a thousand other references. The "spirit of Christianity" (to quote Hegel) is none other than the spirit of the West. The West (which—need it be said?—no longer has any distinct circumscription) is a mode of being in the world in such a way that the sense of the world opens up as a distancing within the world itself and in relation to it. This mode can be distinguished both from the mode in which sense circulates without discontinuity in the world—death as another life—and from the mode whereby sense is circumscribed in the narrow space of a life that death dispatches to insignificance (a dispatch that can shine with the brief splendor of tragedy). Of course, the Western mode brings with it the great danger of an entire dissipation of sense when the world opens onto nothing but its own chasm. But this is precisely what concerns us.

Where initially there had been an uninterrupted circulation between life and death, then a tragic celebration of mortal life, what was produced and put an end to this—an end to what we call "antiquity," which is to say, the first epoch of the "West"—was what a historian describes as "the huge divide which all late antique thinkers, pagan, Jewish, and Christian alike, saw between the 'upper' and the 'lower' world."[4]

For the moment, then, this: "Christianity" has developed and modulated the theme of this "immense fracture" and, on that basis, has engendered the intimate constitution of our "mundane," atheist civilization, with its indefinitely dispersed ends [*fins*]. We exited from Christendom long ago, but that only serves to confirm this particular constitution. It is not a question, then, of being somehow interested in Christianity for itself, or for some religious, moral, spiritual, or saving virtue in any of the senses that the professions of Christian faith have left us with. In order to end, we give what remains of Christianity its leave, and this is why we can maintain that it is deconstructing itself.

But in deconstructing itself, it dis-encloses our thinking: whereas Enlightenment reason, and following it the reason of the world of integral progress, judged it necessary to close itself off to all dimensions of the "outside," what is called for now is to break the enclosure in order to understand that it is from reason and through reason that the pressure, the drive (this *Trieb* of reason that Kant wants to uphold[5]) of the relation with the infinite outside comes about *in this very place*. Deconstructing Christianity means opening reason to its very own reason, and perhaps to its unreason.

ॐ

A few words more about the other branches of Western monotheism, as well as, in a more lateral way, about Buddhism.

What I am saying about Christianity does not confer any privilege upon it, nor does it place Christianity at the top of some list of honors. Rather, it comes down to indicating Christianity as the least privileged of religions, the one that retains the least well, with the most difficulty, the energy that is strictly speaking religious, that is to say, the energy of a continuous sense from life to death and back again. And it is no accident, if what I have said above is granted, that Christianity has desacralized, demythologized, and secularized itself in such a constant and irreversible way for at least six centuries—if not for far longer. (Should we not say: from the moment Christendom existed, it entered into deconstruction and dis-enclosure?)

"Christianity" is nothing more than a name here—and a highly provisional one—for "us": for what makes us the bearers of this being outside the world in the world. "We" who have borne the entire world to this "civilization" that not only knows "discontentedness" [*Unbehagen*; *malaise*], as Freud said, but henceforth recognizes itself precisely as discontentedness in the guise of civilization. Discontentedness: because we no longer know what makes us "civilized" or even what this word should indicate. Because we can no longer be sure that our civilization does not engender itself as barbarity.

During a certain period we believed that Christianity was the malady of the West. Not only did we think that reason would cure us of this malady, but we expected from reason the true flowering of what the Christian message had no sooner announced than betrayed: justice in fraternity, equality in the distribution of wealth and in a common destination, the election and the dilection of the singular individual and of everyone together. In truth, everything that we called "humanity"—using a word that named both the species of speaking beings and the ideal of rational beings—proceeded from Christianity insofar as it was an assurance that the other life was opened up in life itself and in its death.

What we can understand today is that, if there is malaise or malady, it was not produced by a religion which would have infected the Western body. It is this body itself that is ill, if there is illness, and the task of treatment belongs entirely to it—a body henceforth extended to all humanity, and further, to all heaven and earth—whether we are thinking in terms of healing, conversion, metamorphosis, grafting, or mutation. It is necessary to extract from Christianity what bore us and produced us: it is necessary, if possible, to extract from a ground deeper than the ground of the religious thing [*chose religieuse*] that of which religion will have been a form and a misrecognition [*méconnaissance*].

✧

This is why I am not setting up any competition between Christianity, Judaism, Islam, and Buddhism. Only Christianity produced itself as the "West," and it alone decomposed its confessional features and disintegrated its religious force in this West, for better or for worse. It is out of the question to deny the genius proper to each of the three other religions and their contributions to the thinking and splendor of mankind. What's more, one could say that all three have withheld themselves from the process of "civilization"—by engaging in it either not at all or very little, or, alternatively, by instilling vital energies that, as they became detached from their religious sources, came to give nourishment to civilization (such as Arabic science and philosophy, Jewish meditations on speech and on the flesh, the Buddhist discipline of detachment and compassion).

To become detached from the source and observance of religion was to become detached from all the ways of relating to death as the outside of life, or as its extension: it was to adopt the possibility that the other of life could open up within life itself and unto life itself—to the point of running the risk, as we do from now on, that all that opens up is a chasm into which life plunges. As a religion, Christianity delivered the message of this opening in an equivocal way: it promised a life found anew in the afterworld, and it also proposed frequenting the dead via the communion of saints. The Christian religion mixed together all the characteristics of religion—and the other religions are by no means wrong about its impurity, which they denounced and which was also denounced from within Christianity. In truth, Christianity unceasingly reforged the sacred link and religious observance, because its destiny as a *religion* depended on them (all the more so because Christianity had in fact invented the status of "religion" as an instance and institution of salvation, as distinct from civil religion as it was from philosophical atheism). There would be no end to a list of all the dogmatic contents and all the spiritual tonalities that reforge the link between life and death and turn away as much from "death opened in the midst of life"—another way of saying "life in the world outside the world"—as from incompatible (tragic) death.[6] Certain moments or aspects of Christianity enable us to see this, such as the Orthodox tradition or the most initiatory or magical aspects of the Roman Catholic tradition (sacraments, ecclesiastical authority), or even the various puritanisms. Here and there, in various ways, it has always been a question of the promise and/or the calculation [*calcul*] of another life, replacing and remunerating this one—and not of an irruption opening up this life, in an outside-the-world forming a gaping chasm in this world.

Let us define things carefully here: we speak with some familiarity of "this world" in the sense of this world here, this "down-here," this "mundane" world—but it is a way of speaking that is proper to the West. Whether with the biblical "flesh" or with the Platonic "sensible"—the differences between them being set aside here—the possibility that there should be two "worlds," two regions or regimes of a different nature, was given in a particular place (where "this world" is not completely "globalized"). In this place one only knew, or one still only knows, one ensemble to which heaven and earth belong, which is the dwelling of both mankind and gods, regardless of the distance that separates them. "This world" implies that there is another world: another order, another laying out of all things and of life or existence, rather than an "other life" beyond, at the distance of God or of devils. In a certain sense, with "this world" there is no longer any totality of beings or any internal distribution of the regions of the all: or rather, there is such an "all," but it is in itself open, it is at the same time entirely consistent in itself, without outside, and open. The beyond is within [*en deçà*].

⸭

It is therefore necessary simultaneously to follow to its last extreme Christianity's movement of self-deconstruction and to reinforce the symmetrical movement of the dis-enclosure of reason. We must not return to the spirit of Christianity, or to the spirit of Europe or of the West. On the contrary, we must refuse every kind of "return," and above all the "return of the religious"—the most threatening of all [such returns]—and go further into what brought about the invention of this civilization that from now on will be globalized and perhaps lost, that may be approaching its end but is perhaps also capable of another adventure. This invention is a world without God—without any assurance of sense, but without any desire for death.

Doubtless this also means: without Christ and without Socrates. But with what can be found at bottom in Christ and Socrates, and is more powerful than them: the faculty of being in the world outside the world, the force and tenderness necessary to salute [*saluer*] another life in the midst of this one. (*To salute*, not to save, that is what is at stake. It is Derrida's "Salut!")[7]

To salute a man other than the son of God—or his double, the son of man, the man of humanism. Another one, yes, opened in the midst of the same, another same man. And another same world. Or even salute an other than man, an other than the world.

But—to salute, here and now. For the outside of the world *in* the world is not "outside" according to the logic of a divorce, a rift, but according to that of an opening that belongs to the world, as the mouth belongs to the body. Better still: the mouth is, or is what makes, the eating and speaking body, just as other openings are what make it the breathing, listening, seeing, eliminating body. The outside traverses the body in all these ways, and this is how it becomes *a body*: the exposure of a soul. Our bodies are thus entirely, in their turn, openings of the world, and so are other open bodies, those of animals and plants. They can all salute.

Christian Atheism

The possibility of atheism, if by this we mean at least the denial of any kind of afterworld extending this world in order to console it, is inscribed at the source of Christianity, precisely insofar as in itself it is not (only) a religion, or rather insofar as from the outset it has disarranged or destabilized the religion that it was nevertheless creating. This possibility is marked in two ways.

1. On the one hand, Christianity is inaugurated in the affirmation of the presence "down here" of divine otherness or of the other life; not after death, but in death: this is the moment when Lazarus must rise again, now that Christ is rising again. Down here is not a place from which supplications or hopes can be addressed to the beyond. In all its tonalities, adoration is "of here" and opens the *here*—onto no elsewhere.

2. On the other hand, in this affirmation Christianity replays that of philosophy: the death of Socrates is indeed not a passage into another world but the opening of the truth of this world. Where the "world of ideas" was still able to take on a religious hue—and was indeed indicated as the world "of the god" (*ho theos*, a singular that was utterly strange to the Greek ear and that in Plato comes to strike out all the names of the gods along with all the mythology of their distinct sojourns). This "god"

in the singular is only metaphorically elsewhere: it depends on the "right here" [*ici même*] of whoever pronounces it.

In this sense, Socrates and Christ are the same: their deaths open up in the midst of the world, opening the truth of this world as the outside that presents itself right here, an outside that is "divine," if you like, that is in any case "true," that is to say, causing the failure of the indefinite pursuit of any final "sense" that would take place in some paradise or other dwelling of the beyond.[8]

There is nothing original about qualifying Christianity as atheist—nor about qualifying Judaism, Islam, and, of course, Buddhism as such (the latter is always described as a "religion without God," though it tends toward a divinization of the Buddha and his avatars). An entire tradition lies behind it, complex in itself and requiring long exposition. A vector of atheism does indeed cut across the great religions, not insofar as they are religious but insofar as they are all contemporary (to speak in very broad terms) with the exit from human sacrifice and with the Western turn in world history, and thus also in philosophy, which is atheism articulated for itself—these religions have witnessed a complete recasting of the "divine," a recasting whose deep driving force pushes toward the removal, if not of the "divine," then at least of "God."

Although this recasting is undeniable and the tradition of atheism or of the becoming-atheist of these religions is well documented, we persistently refuse to know anything about it. Moreover, most of the currently proliferating attempts to reanimate and reevaluate the religious element proceed by ignoring or bypassing this perspective. This is why I feel it is important to emphasize that *only an understanding and an accentuation of Christianity's becoming-atheist* (as well as that of the other religions, but I shall say why I am limiting myself to Christianity) *can give us access to a thought that I am indicating as a dis-enclosure of reason.*

I am therefore calling "Christianity" the posture of thought whereby "God" demands to be effaced or to efface himself. Undoubtedly, this definition leaves little room for the contents of the various expositions of theological and spiritual truths. However, there is nothing in it that does not originate in such expositions. Nothing—but on the condition that one is able to distill out of doctrine the salt that it carried along while covering it over, or even dissolving it. And it is indeed a question here of not allowing the *salt of the earth* to become insipid: that is, quite precisely, what gives flavor to this world and our existence in it: flavor, appreciable quality, a price, value, sense.

God who effaces himself is not only God who takes his leave, as he did of Job, or God who constantly refuses any analogy in this world, as for Mohammed. It is God who becomes man, abandoning his divinity to the point of plunging it into the mortal condition. Not in order to exit once again from death, but to reveal the immortality in it: very precisely, the immortality *of the dead*. In death, the definitive suspension of sense (of existence) eternally crystallizes the shattering brilliance [*éclat*] of this suspended sense. This does not reduce the pain of dying, even less that of seeing others die. It does not overcome mourning, resolve it as "work" that has been completed: but it does affirm the absolute singularity of the dead.

The man into whom God "descends" and "empties himself" (Paul's *kenosis*) is not rendered divine by this. On the contrary. God effaces himself in that man: he is this effacement, he is therefore a trace, he is an impalpable, imperceptible vestige of the emptied and abandoned divine. Man *is* the abandonment of God: the trace upon him, the trace that he is, constitutes him as a sign of this abandonment. A sign of this: that *the effacement of God is the sense of the world*. The effacement of the Name, of Sense fulfilled. The effacement of the singular name (and even the greatest of these tend to be doomed to effacement; this process is already at work as they become the names of works) contains the effacement of any name claiming to name the Unique (thus the hundredth name of Allah is silent).

Not effacement alone, however. Christianity wants more: not to dwell in the absence of God, in his infinite distance, but to affirm it "among us." That is to say, he is "himself" the *among*: he is the *with* or the *between* of us, this *with* or *between* that we are insofar as *we* are in the proximity that defines the world. The world = all the beings [*étants*] that are near to or neighboring one another, that hereby relate to one another, and to nothing else. "God" was a name for the relation among all beings— therefore, for the *world* in the strongest sense of the word.

In order for this to happen, "God" effaces himself in yet another way: in the *Trinity*. It is a question neither of three gods nor of a three-headed god. It is exclusively a question of this: God is relation. He is his own relation—which is not a reflexive relation, neither an aseity [*aséité*] nor an ipseity, one that does not relate *itself* but *relates* absolutely. The ternary structure or appearance goes from one of its aspects to the other via something that is other to each of them, which is the relation *between* them. What is other to each of them is breath, spirit: sense. (That each of the others should be "father" and "son" is not necessarily patriarchal, even though it has been: father and son means: one after the other, life and death, proximity and distancing—it is one way among many of saying ourselves all together and as we are, and what's more, not "we" men alone but all "we" beings, we the world, we the world without God.)

In a word: the Christian "god" is atheist. In fact, "atheist" signifies the nonpositing of "God," the deposing [*déposition*]⁹ of any god that can be posed as such—that is to say, as a "being" or "subject" to which one property or another is given (including the perfection of all properties): but the Christian "god," insofar as we can name him as such, is not posed, not even self-posed. There is neither a ground nor a space for this: there is neither world nor afterworld, but an opening of sense that produces the spacing of the world and its relation to itself.

It is thus an elsewhere, an outside that opens in the world, or rather opens it to itself, opens it as such, as *world*. But this elsewhere, this outside is here—*hic et nunc*—because it is the excess of this "here" itself over itself, that is to say, over its simple positing. The nonpositing of this God is also the nonpositing of the world or of beings [*étant*] in general: the world is not posited; it is *given*, given from nothing and for nothing.

Given/nothing or non-given—such is the opposition, and not given/giver, since the latter opposition sends us back toward a giving of the giver itself. As Lévi-Strauss writes: "The fundamental opposition . . . is . . . between being and non-being. A mental effort consubstantial with his history [that of man], and which will cease only with its disappearance from the stage of the universe, compels him to accept the two self-evident and contradictory truths which, through their clash, set his thought in motion."¹⁰ The first motion [*branle*] of thought is that of mythological constructions, which are Lévi-Strauss's concern here. But the aftereffect or *après coup* of myths that figured oppositions derived from a fundamental opposition (such as heaven and earth, night and day, etc.) leads toward a confrontation with this opposition as such: between the world—in our overdetermination of it in signs, systems, codes, and networks of artifacts—and nothing, a nothing in the provenance of nature and a nothing in the destination of technics. Between the two, our thought is set in motion [*s'ébranle*] once more.

It is important for us to take on this *from nothing and for nothing*: atheism, therefore, as the rigorous consequence and implication of what the Christian West has engendered and extended to the whole world (while dispersing itself in that world and losing its contours in it). A tremendous ambivalence: on the one hand, it can be nihilism; on the other, it can be sense itself, the sense of this: that sense is given outside.

Not Even Atheism

However, it is not enough to understand that Christianity has deployed in this way the possibility of this most daring and elating relation of sense, that which exposes us to the nonpositedness of the world and thus to nonentity [*né-ant*]: to what is not [*le non étant*], is not posited, but given, given by no one, by no giver, but is in itself entirely woven from the substance of the gift: gracious, generous, abandoned.

It is not enough to understand that Christianity by itself created its destiny of metamorphosis into atheism—its God having said everything or given everything from the moment that he opened this general deposing or de-positing [*déposition*]. We must understand that this movement goes beyond a metamorphosis. It is not an "ism" converting itself to another "ism."[11] There is neither post-Christianity nor any "renewal" of any sort. *There is not even "atheism"; "atheist" is not enough! It is the positing of the principle that must be emptied. It is not enough to say that God takes leave, withdraws, or is incommensurable. It is even less a question of placing another principle on his throne—Mankind, Reason, Society. It is instead a question of coming to grips with this: the world rests on nothing—and this is its keenest sense.*

It is on this point that Reason is most conspicuously called into play: atheism consisted essentially in substituting a Reason for a God. In fact, in substituting a reason—cause, principle, finality—of the world for a god who was himself conceived of as a reason, merely a superior reason, equipped with extraordinary properties of omnipotence and omniscience. The death of this God—and it is only that God who is dead, as Nietzsche himself says—is nothing other than the death of any Reason endowed with the attributes of necessity and of the completeness of the foundation-production of the totality of beings. This reason did not see that it was putting itself to death in erecting this idol of itself, which was nothing but a God for atheists.

At the same time, in the time of the triumph of this supposed Worldly Reason, the "principle of reason" demanded by Leibniz (everything must have its sufficient reason) came to deploy itself *and* encountered its own uncertainty, trembled on its own foundation.[12] One can even say: the "principle of reason" became an expressly philosophical demand because the model of rationality that had been constructed was already aware of its own limit, or was already touching it: Did not Newton imply this in his "I feign no hypotheses"—which is to say, I am constructing an order of rational physical laws, but there is no question of using them to provide a reason for [*rendre raison de*] the existence of the world as such?

Kant will draw a lesson from this, tracing the circumscription of what he names "understanding" (cognitive reason) and bringing down any imaginable rationality of a "proof of God," which is to say, of an evidencing of the first Reason of the world. From now on, a place was empty. It was occupied by many supplementary instances, for example, Hegelian Reason as a deployment of Spirit. But already with Hegel himself, and even more from his time to ours, what became manifest was that *the empty place must not be occupied.*

Materialisms, positivisms, scientisms, irrationalisms, fascisms or collectivisms, utilitarianisms, individualisms, historicisms, legalisms, and even democratisms, without mentioning all the relativisms, skepticisms, logicisms—all duly atheist—will have been attempts, more or less pitiful or frightening, to occupy this place, with greater or lesser dissimulation of the effort to do so, for one had, after all, become somewhat aware that this was not what needed to be done.

Such is still, and on a renewed basis, our responsibility: to keep the place empty, or better still, perhaps, to ensure that there shall be no more place for an instance or for a question of a "reason given" [*raison rendue*], of foundation, origin, and end. *Let there be no more place for God—and in this way, let an opening, which we can discuss elsewhere whether to call "divine," open.*

Israel—Islam

Having thus drawn Christianity out of itself and even beyond atheism, I may have given the impression that, though I have noted some converging traits of the two other Western monotheisms, I am placing them at a lesser level of power or interest in the enterprise that concerns me.

On the one hand, I hold—as should be obvious—that this triple monotheism, in its profound and secret unity, bears the certainty, paradoxical for a religion, that I have just formulated: "the world rests on nothing." No pillars, no turtle, no ocean, not even an abyss or yawning gulf: for the world is the gulf that swallows every type of back-world. The world is strangeness itself, absolute strangeness: the strangeness of the real, the quite tangible reality of this anomaly or this exception devoid of all attachment. Each god says this in his own way: he says "Listen!" or he says "Love!" or he says "Read!" Of course, this extreme triple contraction does not claim to provide a summation: it merely suggests that these three gods neither pose nor found, but essentially do something else. This triple God is not, first of all, he who made the world (and in any case, he makes it from nothing, which is to say without foundation or material: he does not make the world, he makes *there be* a world), rather, he is first of all, or even uniquely, he who addresses. He is the one who calls, who interpellates. He is a god of speech. Without entering further here into the implications of this formula, I will limit myself to saying: the nature and law of language is to be addressed, both well on the hither side and far beyond all signification. Adoration responds to this address, or rather, resonates with it.

On the other hand, and to the contrary, I hold that, of the three religions, only one has undone itself as a religion and has in some way transformed itself into an irrigation system for the culture of the modern world (its morals, its law, its humanism, and its nihilism). We must say it precisely, though I cannot linger on this point: only one of the veins of Christianity flowed in this direction. This was the Reformation and the part of Catholicism that took inspiration from it, as well as at least a part of Christian mysticism (particularly Eckhart) but not Catholicism *stricto sensu*, no more than the Orthodox churches. This is to say that the Christianity that I claim is deconstructing itself and entering into a relation of mutual dis-enclosure with modern reason not only is far from being one with the ensemble of dogmas, institutions, and sociopolitical behavior of the different churches, but that it even breaks with them. This break is not new; it doubtless opens from the beginning of Christianity (e.g., between James and Paul, but perhaps also in Paul himself, or else in the difference between John and the Synoptic Gospels), and it can be found down the ages (Anselm, Eckhart, Francis of Assisi, Fénelon, and, of course, the great Reformers up to Barth, Bultmann, and Bonhoeffer; more subtly, it traverses Augustine or Pascal—and these are only a few names at random). I do not wish to linger here: I only wish to emphasize that it is not the entirety of the Christian religion that is dis-enclosing itself, outside religion and outside Christianity. Not even, and in some way, the entirety of the reformed confessions, as certain conflicts (particularly around homosexuality) have shown. But the presence of this disposition is proper to Christianity, to what under the name of "Christendom" for a time structured what one could already have named "Europe," with its knowledge, its law, its expansion, its humanism, its art.

꒝

But comparison with the two other monotheisms interests us here. In a way, and starting with the least obvious thing, insofar as we are considering Judaism and Islam as religions, the disposition that I have just declared proper to Christianity is also present in the two other confessions. Doubtless each of them possesses a vein exceeding religion, that is to say, a vein that dissipates observance in adoration. More than one mystic from each tradition confirms this for us.

However, the Jewish and the Muslim religions remain religions, very rich and complex systems of representation and observance, and it is difficult to see how they could be "secularized" (whatever the precise concept of the word might be). This is because they have no reason to enter into tension or conflict with institutions comparable to those of Christian Churches. The absence of such "Churches" obviously plays an important role here, one that has often been commented upon. But there is a reason for this absence: Christianity hastened to build a Church—to conceive of itself as a Church—because from the beginning it understood itself as an "assembly" (this is the meaning of the word) distinct de jure from any other assembly in the world, and therefore first of all political or sociopolitical.

It is starting from this point that it seems to me most possible to elucidate the relations among the three monotheisms—of course, in two rigorously different ways.

First of all, the relation between Christianity and Judaism. If one does not forget that Christianity is by birth Judeo-Christian—and in a sense, as we shall see, does not cease to be that—then one must remember that the Jewish currents in which it was born were tending toward a radical difference between "kingdoms." Judaism was undergoing the experience—which, in truth, began in it long ago—of a separation between kingdoms, that is, an experience of the "not of this world" in the midst of the world.[13] On the one hand, this experience takes the Christian form that will become, in a few centuries, the ambiguous, eminently debatable form in which a Church that is quite distinct from any Kingdom or Empire will nonetheless mix up its destiny in a thousand ways with those of kingdoms and empires, at times (often) to the point of apostasizing itself by becoming a power in the world.[14] On the other hand, it takes the form of the dispersion of Israel, a *diaspora* that is precisely the carrying of this affirmation of the separateness of "kingdoms" into any possible place, whether kingdom or empire. (It is remarkable that, in certain respects, Paul should be the one who, on the one hand, suppresses the difference between Jews, Greeks, and "nations" in general, who is so strongly opposed to those who wish to withdraw into small formations that historians call "Judeo-Christian," and, on the other hand, who emphasizes in so many ways the congenital Judaism of Christianity, if only because he speaks of a "circumcision of the heart." With him perhaps emerges the first condition of possibility for what will much later provoke the Christian hatred of Jews, in what I shall attempt to characterize as a form of self-hatred.)

Much later still, in a history that has been transformed, "Zionism" will be invented and, after it, what led to the State of Israel as we know it. I will not enter into this history: I merely note that it originates at least to a large degree in the exacerbation of what one names "antisemitism."

What is antisemitism (extremely poorly named, since Arabs are Semites)? I hazard the following hypothesis: it is the hatred of Jews developed by Christians, for whom they represent an upholding of the distinction between the kingdoms, from which the Catholic, Reformed, and Orthodox Churches have constantly departed.[15] The Jew is the witness to what Christianity, in this respect, ought to be, and this respect is not indifferent, or a detail of theology, because it engages nothing less than the confusion, sometimes of the most hypocritical sort, between spiritual testimony and social and political domination. The hatred of Jews is a hatred because it proceeds from a conscience that is guilty about *itself,* and this hatred attempts to destroy the testimony of what Christians have a duty to be. This is also why, as history could show, the Christians who were least touched by games of power were also the least antisemitic. (What the hatred of Jews becomes with Nazism is not Christian in principle, although many did find precedents in the existing tradition. Yet Nazism is the affirmation par excellence of a unique and exclusive *Reich*: it does not wish to and cannot know anything of another "kingdom" opened in the midst of the world.)

It is not as a religion that Judaism provoked the hatred of Christians: it is insofar as this religion, but also at times a Jewish thought entirely withdrawn from religion, represents something that Christians were all too aware—and all too ready to deny—that they had elaborated from a Judaism coming detached from the kingdom of Israel, a Judaism that was deconstructing itself.[16]

⟅⟆

The case of Islam is obviously quite different. It came after Christianity, in a context where the latter could only appear completely linked to Empire—to the two Empires of the West and the East.[17] Thus from the beginning Islam took on a political as well as a religious figure, and the great division between Sunni and Shi'a proceeds from a political struggle, which removes nothing from the importance of their doctrinal differences. Still, the question of the caliphate, and of the distinction between a political power and a religious authority (never for its part taking on the form of a Church), has been posed more than once and in several ways. But this is not a subject that I can properly address.[18]

One must remark, however, that Islam implies, in a highly singular way, the coexistence of an intrication and a distinction between the profane and religious orders. On the one hand, everything is under the attentive gaze of God; on the other, his absolute incommensurability demands nothing of the believer other than to affirm it according to the forms prescribed to him, without mixing this with worldly affairs in any way. There is, in sum, neither one nor two kingdoms: there is the register of human affairs and that of the unique affair of the believer as such, which is to confess "the All-Powerful, the Merciful."

In a sense, Islam is dedicated to adoration, even as it deploys an empire. This is why Christendom ended up wanting to repel this empire, being a rival to the one it was beginning once again to develop. But even if this relation of political force is accompanied by the accusation of being an "infidel" and of large scale confrontations , never have Christians harbored a hatred for Muslims. The former did not see in the latter a mirror of their own malfeasance. On the contrary, the Christians who are most disengaged from the Churches can without difficulty recognize the proximity of their traditions with those of the great Muslim sufis, like Ibn Arabi, or those of mystics like Al-Hallaj.

Some sufis have even gone so far as to declare that nothing exists except God. Such an affirmation—seemingly quite Spinozist—obviously does not signify that only a unique "One" exists, which, resting only on itself, could also only collapse into itself, but on the contrary that everything only *is* in and according to its relation to who or what is thus named, to this unnameable incommensurable who or which is not, for his or its part (but he or it has no "part" that is apart) an existent, but rather the measurelessness of existing.

It remains that, for reasons different from those in the case of Judaism, but also in conditions quite other than those of the kingdoms, empires, or sultanates of long ago, Islam today forms states founded on a reference to religion. I shall not venture into this territory. One cannot, however, avoid remarking that, in a world that has emerged from a major transformation in the very midst of which there is at play what I have designated in the Christian mode as the "difference between the kingdoms," now understood as the opening of the world onto its own absence of a world beyond and as the necessary dis-enclosure of its reason—in such a world, one cannot be content with what until now has appeared self-evident regarding the relations between "religion" and "politics," whether they be relations of exclusion or inclusion. Everything in this regard will have to be reworked.

One World, Two Dimensions

I do not wish to take these suggestions any further, so I will stop with this: on the one hand, (Judeo-)Christianity—and, to a degree, Islam too—has deconstructed itself in a culture of science, democracy, and the rights and emancipation of mankind. But along the way it has never stopped making more opaque or more fugitive the identity of the "mankind" in question, which could, in fact, be rather close to asking itself if it is not from itself that it should deliver itself. On the other hand, and along the same path, triple monotheism—which is to say, this profound shock to the religious order or to the relation to the sacred, to the ground of sacrality itself,—has dis-enclosed itself by telling us that Reason cannot be satisfied with explanations or "reasons given" [*raisons rendues*] but pushes toward an incommensurable and an unnameable of sense—or toward a truth without concept or figure. If it fails to give this push or drive its due, reason wilts and sinks into general commensurability and an interminable nomination in which all names are interchangeable.

What remains of religion—Jewish, Christian, Muslim—can now provide only a formal testimony for this drive (which I am naming adoration). (I say nothing about the other religious forms in the world, those from Asia and Africa in particular. At times, some people evoke them as possible modes of recourse by invoking forms of meditation and mental exercise or spiritual practice: they forget that one cannot easily transplant cultural elements and that, for many reasons, we are not yet capable of reflecting on the possible or impossible relations such forms might assume with modern rationality. This is because in Asia, Africa, or Oceania either they have already been transformed or contact with the rationality that came from the "West" is still not, for certain portions of the population, sufficiently pronounced to allow us to judge.)

This is why my interest is not in gathering together some sort of remainder, neither of Christianity nor of the entire Western monotheistic complex. It is to understand how the civilization that propagated itself throughout the world in the forms of scientific, legal, and moral rationality has arrived at a sort of confinement both of reason and of the world that makes us despair of ourselves. For we know that this confinement is contrary to the drive—to the pressure, the élan, or, why not, the instinct—that searches, in us, for contact with the "open": because this open, we are it ourselves, language is it, the world itself is it.

(Saying "the open" is already an abuse of language. One ought to avoid this substantive as well as that which pulls it toward either a concept or a name. It [*ça*] opens up precisely at a distance from both.)

An open world is a world without myths and without idols, a world without religion, if we understand by this word the observance of behaviors and representations that respond to a claim for sense as a claim for assurance, destination, accomplishment. This does not mean that in what one calls "the religions" it should be a question only of myths and idols, nor that it should be easy to decide what is and what is not "myth" and "idol" in the critical sense of these words (senses that were decided, we must remember, in the send-off or *coup d'envoi* of Western history, between the Greeks and the Jews). At the very least, it is possible to say that what constitutes the myth and the idol in these senses has to do with the assurance that each one—the mythical tale [*récit*] or the figure as idol—assures a presence and responds to a demand. In other words, it "gives reasons" for [*rend raison de*] existence. In a paradoxical way, it is in its a desire to "rationalize," to provide a ground or account, to "give reasons" that religion can exhaust itself, becoming nothing more than mythology and idolatry. On the contrary, it can exhaust myths and idols—and it can do so in itself—from the moment when it no longer seeks to give reasons, or no longer claims to do so.

But this is just as much the affair of Reason itself,—of this pressure or drive (Kant's *Trieb*) directed toward the "unconditioned" or toward the unlocalizable outside of the world, in the world itself.

For this reason, the separation of the "kingdoms" or the "worlds" is decisive here.[19] It is not that one must be subordinated to the other—which would still be for one to reign over the other—nor is it that their reigning powers should be in opposition, which would put them in the condition of kingdoms "of this world." Rather they are to each other as vertical is to horizontal: heterogeneous, heterotopic dimensions, which cross at one point. This point, lacking dimension as do all points, forms the opening of the world, the opening of sense in the world. Through this opening, sense penetrates and escapes at the same time, in the same movement and in "making sense" just as much by the penetration as by the escape.

This opening is nothing other than the gaping that has been characterized as an "immense fracture" between a high and a low but that is equally at the common root of Western monotheism, what one can designate as "the prophecy of Abraham," which represents "a new conception of heritage and of history, a new filiation, a new definition of land and of blood"—for "the land of all the nations shall be the promised land for the sons of Abraham. A land without land, however, without divisible, assignable territories, without countries, without nations. It is a desert land where a son of Abraham can be born from every rock."[20] That from every rock could be born one who inherits the promise that promises nothing but this dis-enclosure of the territory and of all circumscription of sense, this is what the opening I am speaking of signifies—far beyond any religious or philosophical representation or conception.

To avoid misunderstanding, we must also emphasize that the point of sense does indeed belong to the world, to "this world here," just as the rock belongs to the desert and the point of intersection belongs to the horizontal as much as to the vertical line. Being in the world without being of the world—this condition that a certain Christian monarchism sought to incarnate—is not to live in the world while abstaining from it, holding oneself in some retreat, even if entirely "interior" and "spiritual." It is to think and feel the world according to its opening. Which is to say, first of all, according to an irreducibility to all relations defined by a common measure of forces and values. But it is to think a value and a force that are incommensurable, and consequently also to think an unfigurable form.

"A" force, "a" value—yes, in the sense that the monotheisms introduced the "one" not as a numerical index but rather as something external to all numeration, to any counting. This "one" embraces the multiple without unifying it. Its unity lies in the fact that it is essentially withdrawn from all that can posit equivalences—between beings, between forces, between forms. It is precisely the sort of unity that is that of *everyone* [chacun]: of each singular, whether one understands this as a "subject" or as any kind of discernable singularity, the leaf of a tree or the crest of a wave.[21]

With

Perhaps it is not impossible to bring together and focus the stakes by saying this: what has prevailed in triple monotheism, and in its finally "globalized" expression (which is to say, in the strong sense: what has been driven out of its birthplace to the point of both traversing the world and making itself a world, to the point of making itself the new age of the world and therefore of man) is the thought of a "God" who is *with* and not beyond or above. That God is with us is doubtless the most profoundly shared and constant thought of triple monotheism. It ultimately says this: that in the decomposition of his religious figures, above all of the Christian figure that opened this dissolution, "God" is nothing other—if we are dealing with a thing at all, and it is perhaps *the thing* itself—than this *with* itself.

There was "gods and mankind," then there was "God with us," there is henceforth "we among ourselves [*entre nous*]"—and to say it once again, this "we" becomes the pronoun of all beings, allowing what "mankind" is or does in the bosom of this universal coexistence to appear in a new—uncertain, disquieting—light. There is no "secularization" in this narrative, but instead transformations of the world's being world, which is not something given once and for all, but which replays and relaunches the *ex nihilo* that is its sharing [*partage*].

This is what must be understood in the motif of "revelation." The so-called "revealed" religions distinguished themselves from others only in this way: the sign of the infinite, which is itself infinite, sends itself of itself. It is certain that all religions are traversed by a motion, an élan of this sort. All religions and ultimately all kinds of knowledge, science, or philosophy: for we could not even be within the movement of any knowing whatsoever if the desire for the infinite did not impel us there. Finite knowledge is a kind of information, an instruction; it is not what opens itself to the inexhaustible bottom of things. If we are "finite" insofar as we are mortal, this finitude configures our access to the infinite. There are or there have been mythological, shamanic, esoteric, metaphysical, and gnostic configurations, as well as others. What "revelation" introduces is ultimately a disconfiguration. Revelation is not a doctrine. What is revealed is not concerned with content-based principles, articles of faith, and revelation does not unveil anything that is hidden: it reveals insofar as it addresses, and this address constitutes what is revealed. God calls Abraham, Mary, Mohammed. The call calls for a response, which is another call. It is not a question of learning a doctrinal corpus, but of responding. Call and response (which also means: the responsibility to respond) of all to all, of everyone to everyone, as if only to salute one another: nothing more, nothing less, but in this way clearing endless paths [*voies*] and voices [*voix*] between contingent existences.

Truth revealed is truth that contains no doctrine or preaching. It is not the truth of any adequation or of any unveiling. It is the simple, infinite truth of the suspension of sense: an interruption, for sense cannot be completed, and an overflowing, for it does not cease.

This is also why our world is the world of literature: what this term designates in a dangerously insufficient, decorative, and idle way is nothing other than the opening of the voices of the "with." On the same site where what we call myth gave voice to the origin, literature tunes in to the innumerable voices of our sharing [*partage*]. We share the withdrawal of the origin, and literature speaks starting from the interruption of myth and in some way in that interruption: it is in that interruption that litera-ture makes it possible for us to make sense.[22] This sense is the sense of fiction: that is to say, neither mythical nor scientific, but giving itself in creation, in the fashioning (*fingo, fictum*) of forms that are themselves mo-bile, plastic, ductile, and according to which the "with" configures itself indefinitely.

What we must say about literature in this way is valid for all that con-stitutes "art," all the irreducibly plural—singular/plural—ways of fash-ioning and exchanging sense outside of signification (for even the art of language and literary fiction do not signify: they carry significations away into another realm, where signs refer [*renvoient*] to the infinite).

ʓ

By way of a final cadence:

> Who knows who she was, his model that day: a woman from the street? the wife of a patron? The atmosphere in the studio electric, but with what? Erotic energy? The penises of all those men, their *verges*, tingling? Undoubtedly. Yet something else in the air too. Worship. The brush pauses as they worship the mystery that is man-ifested to them: from the body of the woman, life flowing in a stream.[23]

—*Translated by John McKeane, with Jeff Fort*

Re-opening the Question of Religion

Dis-enclosure of Religion and Modernity in the Philosophy of Jean-Luc Nancy

ALENA ALEXANDROVA, IGNAAS DEVISCH, LAURENS ten KATE, and AUKJE van ROODEN

A Return to Religion?

One of the most complicated and ambiguous tendencies in contemporary Western societies is undoubtedly the phenomenon usually referred to as the "turn to religion," "the post-secular," or, more generally, the "return of the religious." What at first sight appears to be a simple return to religious values, inspired by a critical rejection of the basic assumptions of modern secular culture, is in fact a refined dialogue with this culture, a dialogue in which religious and secular arguments often change places. This delicate relationship between religion and modernity manifests itself not only in daily practical discussions about the role of religion within our democratic societies but touches on philosophical questions regarding the historical and systematic bond between Western culture and its religious heritage. Numerous scholarly publications on the issue of religion mirror the urge to understand the rearticulation of its role within modern society.[1]

Certainly one of the most original thinkers in this field is Jean-Luc Nancy. In contrast to most of his contemporaries, Nancy neither advocates a turn or return to religion, nor proclaims or calls for the end of religion, nor attempts to reconcile secularism and religion in a so-called post-secular society. Instead, Nancy attempts to conceive monotheistic religion and secularization not as opposite worldviews that succeed each other in time but rather as views that spring from the same origin and that are intertwined to the point of synonymy. The dialogue between modernity and—especially Christian—religion is a recurring theme throughout Nancy's work and eventually culminated in a volume entitled *Dis-enclosure: The Deconstruction of Christianity*.

One of the remarkable gestures of this project is that Nancy attacks the very attempt to think of religion in terms of a possible or impossible "return." "The much discussed 'return of the religious,'" Nancy states, "deserves no more attention than any other 'return'" (*D* 1/9). Nancy thus immediately broadens the question of the religious within contemporary society, taking it to be a *philosophical* issue rather than a historical or theological one. Nearly a decade earlier, in "The Forgetting of Philosophy," Nancy was already indicating that this "logic of return" characterizes virtually the entire history of Western thinking. However varied the discourses that stem from this logic may be, according to Nancy they share one basic, highly paradoxical assumption: referring to a *return* or a *revival* implies that nothing has truly been lost. After all, the possibility of a return means that what was presumably lost or in crisis was only out of sight, but in the meantime has always been there, unchanged and unmistakably shining on the horizon, waiting to be rediscovered. (*GT* 10/ 13–14).

However, as Nancy continues in the opening of *Dis-enclosure*, "among the phenomena of repetition, resurgence, revival, or haunting, it is not the identical, but the different that invariably counts the most" (*D* 1/9). That is, because it is *returned*, the identical by necessity is not the same as it was, and therefore the contemporary "return of the religious" is more a demand to return *to* the religious than a sign *of* its returning (*GT* 20/27). If contemporary issues such as outbursts of religious fundamentalism or debates concerning the relationship between religious doctrine and democracy incite us to reopen the question of religion, we must first ask ourselves anew what the "religious" means and, in relation to that, the meaning of the "sense of the world," the "human," and "reason."

These questions do not have a ready-made answer, as the logic of return would have us believe, but can only be asked at the expense of new and unforeseen risks, because they question the basic assumptions of our existence. This is why Nancy's deconstruction of Christianity concerns philosophy far more than the historical reality of organized religion. This project articulates the need to reexamine the central concepts religion and philosophy share. As we shall see, such a reexamination, as Nancy states explicitly, in contrast to Kant's *Religion Within the Boundaries of Mere Reason*, should not be a matter of thinking religion within the limits of reason but, conversely, of "opening mere reason up to the limitlessness that constitutes its truth" (*D* 1/9). If religion is and always has been a modern question through and through, it is so because it questions the status of reason and of thinking itself.

The Deconstruction of Monotheism and of Christianity

This deconstructive analysis of religion, as Nancy calls it, involves first and foremost an understanding of *monotheism* and, more specifically, of Christian monotheism. Although Nancy's deconstructive analysis focuses mainly on Christianity, it is not a deconstruction of the Christian religion in itself but an exploration of the deconstructive elements that constitute this religion, elements that can also be found in Judaism and Islam:

> I will call "deconstruction of monotheism" the operation consisting in disassembling the elements that constitute it, in order to attempt to discern, among these elements and as if behind them, behind and set back from the construction, that which made their assembly possible and which, perhaps, still it remains, paradoxically, for us to discover and to think as the beyond of monotheism, in that it has become globalized [*mondialisé*] and atheized [*athéisé*]. (*D* 32/51)

The main thesis he wishes to develop is that Christian monotheism is an internally contradictory religion, which therefore *deconstructs itself.* Following Marcel Gauchet's dictum that Christianity has essentially been and still is a "religion retreating from religion,"[2] Nancy explores various ways in which Christianity questions and even exceeds itself as religion— that is, instead of *opposing* secular gestures, such as those minimizing, marginalizing, or even eliminating religion from individual and collective existence, Christianity, as Nancy demonstrates, seems, in part, to have taken such gestures *as its own premises.*

The most important premise in this respect is that of the unique monotheistic God being a God *in retreat from the world.* What characterizes the three monotheistic religions—Judaism, Christianity and Islam—in comparison with polytheistic religions is not the reduction of the number of gods but the mode of presence of this God. In monotheism, the divinity of the unique God lies not in his effective presence within the world or, more specifically, within certain objects or places but instead in his being *absent,* that is, unknowable and unpresentable. This retreat of God is not an incidental characteristic of monotheism; it is fundamental to its total configuration. One of the remarkable central theses Nancy develops is that monotheism therefore boils down to a form of atheism, insofar as the monotheistic God is completely deprived of his divine presence. As Nancy puts it, he has become the designation of a principle "that no longer has as 'divine' anything but the name—a name dispossessed of all personality, and even the ability to be uttered [*prononçabilité*]" (*D* 21/35).

One of the results, as we have seen, is that, instead of preceding secularism, religious monotheism is closely interwoven with, even constitutive of it. Monotheistic religion has spread "the news of God's death" from the beginning of its history, that is, from the Judeo-Greek beginning of what is called the West. By introducing this God into their different configurations and histories, the three monotheisms have thus radically displaced or converted our notion of divinity: "From a present power or person, it changes divinity into a principle, a basis, and/or a law, always by definition absent or withdrawn in the depths of being" (*D* 22/36). By creating a distance between the divine and the human world and by stressing humans' responsibility for their lives in the face of God's absence, monotheism gave rise to the possibility of critique and could even lead to the kind of radically individualistic understanding of religion that we find, for instance, in Augustine.[3]

Nancy's view of monotheism, and in particular Christianity, as a religion that anticipates modernity instead of opposing it raises some interesting questions. How can this monotheistic religious tradition, which fundamentally and continuously wants to "leave itself behind," still be religious? How can the critique of religion be an integral part of religion? And how can one relate to religion—to its complex heritage—without evoking a return of religion? Another question, undoubtedly the most fundamental for Nancy, is how religious monotheism relates to secular reason. By means of his deconstructive analyses, Nancy insists that reason is not only the key notion to go against the grain of the religious, as secularism generally has it, but that reason always keeps at its heart, and even depends upon, an element that exceeds it—the *a-logon*, the *allos*. In this sense, reason is not the main tool shedding light on an initially obscure religious understanding of the world, but something that maintains in itself an a-logical element, an element that is not itself religious, but that religion has understood and used.

This element consists of an opening—a *dis-enclosure*—of the self-prescribed limits of rational thinking. This opening points not to a transcendence of God but to the void, the absence of God as a giver of sense. Nancy's project as a whole is dedicated to examining the fine mechanics of this mutual overlap between philosophy, metaphysics, and religion. In *Dis-enclosure*, he engages with different aspects of the legacy of Christian monotheism in particular and demonstrates the initial openness, or even ambiguity, of its texts and traditions, as well as the traces of its continued presence within philosophy.

The Deconstruction of Christianity: Project and Key Themes

The groundwork for Nancy's deconstructive exploration of Christianity and modernity is already visible in his early works. First, they focus on the often hybrid and deinstitutionalized ways in which religion appears in our time, as in his reflections on "divine places";[4] in his discussion with Nietzsche, Heidegger, and Bataille about the role of the "sacred" in secular times; and, more generally, in the account throughout his work of the sacred and the divine as dimensions of the *distinct*.[5] Second, in critical analyses of art, literature, and the politico-religious myths of our time, Nancy develops key concepts in his innovative vocabulary: the *désoeuvrement* ("inoperation") of the sociopolitical community; *being in common* as opposed to the notion of a community with a communal identity; *partage* ("sharing" as well as "dividing"); the *cum* (*avec*, "with"), *in between* (*entre*); *ex-position*.[6] Third, Nancy's analysis of the concepts of *sense* and *world* as events that lack any external underlying ground or foundation are an important preparation for the deconstruction of Christianity.[7]

More explicit announcements of Nancy's project can be found—all in footnotes—in *The Sense of the World*, *Being Singular Plural*, and *La pensée dérobée* (*Concealed Thinking*).[8] In *The Sense of the World*, Nancy attempts a first definition of this future project. The deconstruction of Christianity would be:

> something other than a critique or a demolition: the bringing to light of that which will have been the agent of Christianity as the very form of the West, much more deeply than all religion and even as the self-deconstruction of religion, the accomplishment of philosophy by Judeo-Platonism and Latinity, ontotheology as its own end, the "death of God" and the birth of the sense of the world as the abandonment without return and without *Aufhebung* of all "christ," that is, of all hypostasis of sense. It will of course be necessary to come back to this. (*SW* 183n50/91n1)

In 1998, a first programmatic article appeared with the title "The Deconstruction of Christianity" ("La déconstruction du christianisme"), in which Nancy presents his project in a more detailed way. This text was first delivered as a lecture three years earlier and contains the theoretical groundwork *in nuce* for *Dis-enclosure*, which comprises a series of studies pursuing the same path. In it, Nancy presents daring new interpretations of: Christianity's concept of history; its doctrine of revelation; its experience of faith; its figure of the Son as the incarnation of God into humanness; God as name and the idea of the "passing God" in the later Heidegger; resurrection; consolation; prayer as an interruption of myth; and Christianity's relation with Judaism. With these interpretations, the author engages in dialogue with thinkers such as Jean-François Lyotard, Gérard Granel, Roland Barthes, Maurice Blanchot, Michel Deguy, and, in particular, Jacques Derrida.

Because Nancy conceives of Christianity as a religion that turns away from itself, or rather, beyond itself, a deconstruction of Christianity as he understands it is at the same time an "analysis of Christianity" and the "displacement . . . proper to Christianity" (*NT* 108n4/10n4). Nancy's investigations into the deconstruction of Christianity may well, therefore, be named a deconstruction of *modernity*. Christianity's deconstruction is not a *historical* exploration in the proper sense. His detailed analyses of historical features of Christianity, such as its narrative and dogmatic tradition, its art and ritual, do not concentrate on the historical itself, but *displace* it by showing its topicality, by destabilizing any rigid distinction between past and present. Only, for instance, insofar as a deconstructive study of the figure of Christ and the dogma of the Trinity contributes to thinking the (post)modern configuration of secularism is such a study useful to Nancy.

If modernity is not a liberation or emancipation from Christianity, but rather Christianity evolving out of itself and thus being itself, then Nancy urges us to rethink the paradigm of secularization, that is, of what is often seen as a historical process of development toward our "secular age."[9] In "The Deconstruction of Christianity," he already mentions two main precepts for fulfilling this task. In response to a thesis by Luigi Pareysson, he indicates that "(1) The only Christianity that can be actual is one that contemplates the present possibility of its negation. . . . (2) The only thing that can be actual is an atheism that contemplates the reality of its Christian origins" (*D* 140/204–5). Although Nancy uses the words *actual, possibility*, and *reality*, he insists that Christianity has come to its end, that it no longer makes *sense* in the meaning he gives to this word. It no longer founds and forms our horizon of thinking and acting in the world. However, as the second precept tries to clarify, neither does atheism, or a certain atheism—that is to say, the idea that a modern understanding of the world was and is only possible by destroying Christianity. This means that secularism is only possible *within* and not *despite* Christian monotheism.

As a religion that has come to its end, Christianity is still an actual reality, and if we wish to understand what secular modernity—or atheism—really means, we must rethink the Christian traces of this reality. In the chapter "A Deconstruction of Monotheism," Nancy indicates the need to question and ultimately leave behind a particular version of one-sided rationalism, according to which modernity develops as a movement away from Christianity and its "own obscurantism." He insists, however, that the " 'ills' of the present-day world" cannot be "cured" by any return to religion and that we should ask ourselves in the end what "would open upon a future for the world that would no longer be either Christian or anti-Christian, either monotheist or atheist"(*D* 34/54).

The answer is to think *existence itself* as opened, as opening. Christianity, Nancy writes, may be summarized as "living in this world as outside of it" (*D* 10/21), where this outside "is" no being but must be understood as what Heidegger defines as the *Ek-sistenz* and *Erschliessung* of being: being opened toward the world; or, in other words: *déclosion, dis-enclosure.*[10] In French as well as in English, these concepts are neologisms. Nancy extends the Heidegger's interpretation of *aletheia* as "dis-closedness," in which things give themselves, to Christianity as an opening up of the sense of the world. Or rather, in Nancy's view, Christian monotheism teaches us that the sense of the world must itself be conceived as an opening.[11] Monotheism affirms that *being* is nothing but being opened toward the other of itself, as is also indicated by Spinoza's *deus sive natura*. The divine is thereby reduced to a premise, a logic of dependence on the world (cf. *D* 20/34).

One of the important consequences of this dynamic of dis-enclosure is that the *sense of the world* should be thought of as beyond the notion of a divine giver, as presupposed in a mythological worldview. The monotheistic notion of God implies a retreat from mythology and from the mythological representation of the divine. According to Nancy, the modern world does not *have* sense—that would still presuppose a duality of sense to be given to the world and a giver—but already *is* sense. Consequently, sense is not something humans have, give, or are given, but something they *live* or live in. This means that there is no preexistent sense offered to the world, either in God or in the human subject. According to Nancy, Christianity and modernity coincide precisely in the absence of a principal sense giver, and therefore of an absolute first or last sense. Sense is always there but never fully given, and is therefore *poetical* rather than mythological. In the end, the sense of the world resides in nothing but the opening of being to an otherness, in its dis-enclosure. Nancy stresses the poetical dimension of this gesture because poetry can be seen as an emergence of sense that is without principle or that serves as a foundation. Instead of expressing an absolutely given sense, poetry expresses the very act of the emergence of sense, its creation.

The theme of creation ex nihilo is an important motif in monotheism. If we follow Nancy's analyses, it centrally reveals the movement of Christianity's self-deconstruction. Nancy discusses this concept extensively in *The Creation of the World*, and it occurs frequently in *Dis-enclosure*. However, perhaps his clearest exposition is the brief formulation in "In Heaven and on Earth," a lecture given to an audience of children (*NT* 71–99). He points out how the theological interpretation and the mystical traditions in monotheism always had at their heart an interpretation of creation that implies subverting (or indeed deconstructing) the very notion of creator or of a pregiven principle. Thus, according to Nancy, creation should be understood as the opposite of a project of production or fabrication. Yet it should not be understood as a "miraculous apparition" (*CW* 52/55) out of nothing. The ex nihilo of creation signifies precisely the double absence of a producer, a principle, and "nothing" as the very matter of creation. Theology used the concepts "nothing" and "God" at once to signify and to conceal the fact that the world is as it is, without a reason, without a producer, or, for that matter, without another world: "The idea of *creatio ex nihilo*, inasmuch as it is clearly distinguished from any form of production or fabrication, essentially covers the dual motif of an absence of necessity and the existence of a given without reason, having neither foundation nor principle" (*D* 24/39). "Ex nihilo" refers not only to the absence of any pregiven principle but to emptying "nothing" of its quality as a premise. Creation is, according to Nancy, not one act of God among others, but his only feature: God "is" the act of his creating the world.

If in Nancy's interpretation creation deconstructs the relationship between creator and a creature—the formula "in the image of"—then the *incarnation* is the idea in Christianity that makes explicit the tension between the creator and his image. The idea that God empties himself of divinity to become human—the idea of *kenosis*—is the continuation of the ex nihilo. Incarnation cannot be understood as representation; the body does not represent God. It is neither an "image of" nor a mere container for a higher "something," a soul. As Nancy points out, Christian theology has always maintained that the divine *itself* became flesh, or was engendered as flesh. One can understand such an internal paradox or tension within Christianity (God is human) as a way of introducing an important nuance in the biblical formula "in the image of," for it gives a body to the absence or withdrawal of God. As Nancy puts it, humans are created "in the image of that which has no image" (*GI* 30/64), therefore in their own image.

The theme of incarnation, studied in *Corpus*,[12] recurs several times in Nancy's treatment of *kenosis*,[13] through which "God empties Himself and lays aside His divinity, in order to enter the human state" (EG 78). The death of God through becoming human is immediately pursued in the death of the human into whom He had entered: that is, in the death of Christ. It is not God's becoming human as a unique "historical" event that is at stake here, but the fact that "the divine in humans becomes a dimension of retreat [*retrait*], of absence, and even of death" (EG 78). In *Noli me tangere*, which contains an analysis of John 20:17 (the famous "Noli me tangere" addressed by Jesus to Mary Magdalene) and of its representation in painting, Nancy specifies this retreat by highlighting the distance created between Christ and those who witnessed his death and resurrection. Another example of Nancy's decision to comment on Christian painting as a means of articulating the way Christianity deconstructs itself is "Visitation: Of Christian Painting." In this text, Nancy suggests that Christian images are at the heart of that self-deconstructive movement and that Christian painting *is* Christianity, "or something of Christianity in painting or as painting" (V 122/44). He suggests that, if monotheism centers on the withdrawal of gods and real presence becomes "the presence that is par excellence not present" (V 123/46), then Christian painting becomes in itself a repetition, and not an illustration, of that formula.

The Philosophical Context of Nancy's Project: Polemics, Differences, Connections

Questioning the Secular

Nancy states that the modern rejection of religion—considered as something that hinders humanism, freedom, progress, and emancipation—is a continuation of a rejection that the Jewish and Christian traditions carried in themselves from the outset. Nevertheless, secular humanism, in its Renaissance and modern form, is often defined as an emancipation from the Christian era. Two important twentieth-century thinkers of modern secularization, Karl Löwith and Hans Blumenberg, have both, in different ways, tried to demonstrate the limitations of this model of emancipation.[14] Their positions represent a rich tradition of philosophical thought about the secular status of modern culture, a tradition that seems to have originated *within* the Enlightenment; it goes back, for instance, to Kant's and Hegel's reflections on the relation between religion and reason, and it proceeds via Nietzsche, Schmitt, and Heidegger to postwar research on the topic. Next to Löwith's and Blumenberg's work, one may also mention Charles Taylor's investigations.[15] At stake in this tradition of thought is always a certain reserve concerning the emancipatory model. Nancy's deconstruction of Christianity partly feeds on this tradition, although he does not refer explicitly to Löwith and mentions Blumenberg only a few times and very briefly.[16]

Both German philosophers state that modernity cannot be understood if one thinks it primarily as a historical negation of and liberation from a previous period. The uniqueness and proper, "new" character of the *Neuzeit* disappears from sight if one considers it to be only a history of secularization and emancipation.

Blumenberg wants to determine this unique "legitimacy" of modernity by disconnecting it radically from the Christian era; the "modern" consists of a series of historical processes that cannot be reduced to the Christian legacy, or to the protest and resistance against it. Löwith, by contrast, sees the singularity of modernity in its being a unique, secularized continuation of Christianity. If one pursues this idea to its radical consequences, one must consider Christianity and its Jewish roots to be the "inventors" of modernity instead of its enemy, and modernity to be the achievement, fulfilment, and radicalization of Christianity, at a moment in history—the decline of medieval societies in Europe, the Renaissance, the Reformation, the rise of early capitalism, the development of the sciences, and so on—when this became historically possible. Michel Foucault defends a similar position when he points out how the modern way to treat and experience sexuality has been stamped by the Christian experience of shame and guilt, which transforms sexuality into a scene of limitation and transgression.[17]

Nancy clearly takes the same starting point as these thinkers, that of a critique of the emancipatory model. Then, not unexpectedly, in the way he develops his deconstruction of Christianity he first appears to join Löwith's and Foucault's positions, stressing a continuity between Christian and modern history. As he suggests, the marginalization and dissolution of Christianity is far too easily "assumed to be the effect of the modern transition toward a rationalized, secularized, and materialized society. So it is said, but without having any idea why that society has become what it is . . . unless that is because it has turned away from Christianity, which merely repeats the problem, since the defined has thereby been placed within the definition" (*D* 143/209). But Nancy, with Blumenberg, also inquires into the specific "legitimacy" of modernity, and hence the *dis*continuity and the tension between the "premodern" and the modern, between the Christian and the secular. The question is whether this legitimacy, this singularity of modernity, should be equated with and reduced to secularism:

> Opposing Schmitt, Blumenberg states that the emergence of the modern world should be read not as a mere transcription [of Christianity] but as the opening of a new space in which new modalities of sense, thought, and truth have developed. [Modernity] had to ground and legitimate itself, instead of finding its legitimation in a secularized version of divine transcendence. I do not think this solves the question of what, then, this legitimacy can be. But the question has been formulated correctly by Blumenberg. (EG 79)

Alongside these critical twentieth-century thinkers of secularization, those who advocate a renewed focus on the *theologico-political* in twentieth-century philosophy underline the fact that modern societies and their political institutions have actively been modeled on "the religious."[18] The work of Marcel Gauchet is of central importance here, and Nancy expresses his "overwhelming agreement" with his work when he formulates one of the "axioms" of a deconstruction of Christianity:

> Christianity is inseparable from the West. It is not some accident that befell it (for better or worse), nor is it transcendent to it. It is coextensive with the West qua West, that is, with a certain process of Westernization consisting in a form of self-resorption or self-surpassing. This first axiom presupposes—as does a good portion of what I propose here—my overwhelming agreement with the work by Marcel Gauchet, *The Disenchantment of the World*, particularly with the part related to Christianity, titled "The Religion for Departing Religion." (*D* 142/207; cf. 146/213)

Gauchet demonstrates that the disenchantment of the modern world should be traced back to the monotheistic religions of the West, which have put the religious itself into question by rejecting any divine "enchantment" of the human world, that is, by negating divine power over our lives. The monotheistic God is always a distant, or even an absent God: one who has "departed" from our social and political existence, leaving an empty place.

According to Gauchet, this specific "revolutionary" feature of, for example, Christianity has affected modernity's political experiments and inventions, including the procedures and mechanisms of democracy, since, in the empty place of the departed divinity, new, secular forms of sovereignty and transcendence were tried out and installed.[19] Living in a society "after" and "outside" religion, "we continue to explain ourselves through it, and always will":[20] "The wholesale reconstruction of human space under the influence of God's paradoxical absolutization/withdrawal is the hidden source behind the expanding, fragmented components of our democratic, individualizing state-based, historical, technological, capitalist world, which seem contradictory, but are essentially unified."[21]

Questioning the Post-Secular

The traditions of thought discussed so far treat the history of modernity—its singularity or "legitimacy," as Blumenberg names it—as a *dual history*.[22] In this history, the secular and its other—religion—are both active within a complex cultural and sociopolitical configuration, so active that their opposition becomes problematic. Duality (in the sense of ambiguity and indecidability) challenges chronology here. There is no historical development or even progress: from presecular to secular and on to a post-secular era. Nevertheless, the term *post-secular*, has become important for all we have attempted to think the "return of/to religion" in the last decade. The proclamation of a post-secular society by an increasing number of scholars, artists, and politicians is informed either by a criticism or even a rejection of secularism in favor of a certain rehabilitation of religion—from traditional monotheistic religion to new, individually created forms of spirituality—or by the recognition that a secular world cannot simply be atheistic, so that "something," whether the religious or the nonsecular, must be given a place within it in order to render it viable in our time.

Although he does not deny that the return of religion is "a real phenomenon," Nancy distinguishes his project sharply from the proclamations of what we will provisionally call a post-secularist current in recent philosophy. "It is not a question of reviving religion. . . . It is not a question of overcoming some deficiency in reason. . . . It is not our concern to save religion, even less to return to it" (*D* 1/9). Although post-secularism is part of the philosophical context for the deconstruction of Christianity we are exploring, Nancy's attitude toward it seems predominantly critical.

According to Jürgen Habermas, the philosophical designer of post-secularism, the "consciousness of a post-secular society" is not something that has come into being in recent decades but dates back to the work of Friedrich Schleiermacher and his famous *On Religion* (1799).[23] Habermas emphasizes that Schleiermacher's plea for "the continued existence of religion in an environment that is becoming progressively more secular" has not lost any of its relevance in the twenty-first century.[24] Unlike Schleiermacher, however, Habermas's perspective remains that of secularism and of the secular state, to which "something" must be added. Habermas does not embrace religion as some forgotten value; instead, he looks for ways to incorporate it within a secular configuration. Facing the difficult reality of a "pluralism of worldviews" characteristic of our time, Habermas states that the citizens of present-day Western societies should "realize what the secular grounds for the separation of religion from politics in a post-secular society actually mean."[25]

Nancy disagrees with the hypothesis that modern societies should return to religion in its positive form, rehabilitating it in a presumed post-secular world. Nor does he adopt Habermas's attempt to reconcile secularism and religion in the post-secular society he proclaims.[26] Instead, the deconstruction of Christianity aims to reexamine—re-treat—the way these societies rearticulate, in many cases critically, their complex relationship to religion. His investigation focuses on their inability either simply to remain secular or to abandon secularism and enter the new era of a *post-seculum*; in other words, he focuses on today's simultaneous retreat from *and* resurgence of religion *and* secularism. One can neither retreat to the former domain of the secular nor take refuge in some post-secular as a "new" condition.

Questioning the "Theological Turn in Phenomenology"

The philosophical debate concerning the secular status of modernity, as well as the appeal to, if not the desire for, a post-secular condition, is not new. It is implicitly present in at least two centuries of modern philosophy, dating back, as Habermas rightly states, to the early Romantic criticism of rationalism (Schleiermacher). In contemporary thought, the search for a return to and rehabilitation of religion can be encountered in such thinkers as Gianni Vattimo and Alister McGrath,[27] but its most striking example can be found in the so-called theological turn in phenomenology.

Jean-Luc Marion, Michel Henry, Jean-Louis Chrétien,[28] and, in less explicit ways, Emmanuel Levinas, Paul Ricoeur, and Jean-François Courtine are among its proponents. They were criticized from a radically secular and neo-humanist perspective by Dominique Janicaud in his "The Theological Turn of French Phenomenology" (orig. 1991), which called attention to this development within the phenomenological tradition.[29]

Nancy shares an interest in what these advocates of a theological turn in phenomenology see as phenomenology's blind spots, as well as with the deconstructive approach to philosophy in general. Heidegger's critical revision of the principles of phenomenology in Husserl's work is a strong influence here. By these blind spots they mean, first, the "unapparent,"[30] the "nonappearing," or, as Nancy would say, absence as opposed to, or as a "remainder" of, the apparent, of the appearing in presence and, second, the other person, others as well as the Other of transcendence—God—all of whom are tacitly marginalized or even negated by phenomenology's preoccupation with the ego and its presence to self. Nancy, together with those advocating a "theological turn," does not disagree with phenomenology itself. Rather, they seek to establish a turn within phenomenology, bringing it toward and maybe even outside its limits.

However, Nancy disagrees at a fundamental and methodological level on the issue of how to deal with the *theological* in that turn. Those who advocate the theological turn are dealing, broadly speaking, with the non-apparent—a key feature of the other/Other, of transcendence, and ulti-mately of God—as belonging to the realm of phenomenality. This "appearing of the nonapparent," in a phenomenal mode, is not of the order of the simple presence of things. Rather, it should be thought of as an event, an act of *giving*: donation. By giving itself and by giving what is then "given" for us (the world of presence, of things), it invests itself in the phenomenal world without loosing its transcendence, its absoluteness, and its irreducibility. Rethinking the nonapparent, the remainder of ab-sence, or transcendence as a feature of phenomenality involves rethinking and rehabilitating the religious as a feature of phenomenality: religion, religious experience, and religious practice are conceived as a special cate-gory of phenomena, and creation, incarnation, salvation, and rituals like prayer or confession are also all rephenomenalized in this way. Marion, for instance, aims to "examine . . . the phenomenological figure of philos-ophy and the possibility it keeps in store for God."[31]

According to Nancy, however, the nonapparent—what can be called God, the gods, or the divine—can never end in a reconciliation, however subtle its form, with phenomena. Absence can never stop being the blind spot of presence, of phenomenality, and thus of phenomenology. In other words, phenomenology cannot be "improved" or "completed" by making it theological, by adding God (*theos*) to its field of inquiry, or at least to its language or vocabulary. The question of God, Nancy states, is "no longer one of being or appearing" (*D* 111/165). The inclination toward a re-presentation of the nonapparent by the thinkers of the theological turn resembles the paradigm of a return to religion, which Nancy rejects. One may even speak of an apologetic tone here, where (aspects of) Juda-ism (Levinas) or Christianity (Henry, Marion, Chrétien) are revitalized and defended against modernity's negation or suppression of them. The corollary of the attempt to reintroduce religion in a modern context, that is, to reintroduce absence into presence, bringing the nonapparent toward a new state of appearing, is the attempt to defend something that was "lost" but must be found again. It is the inevitable second nature of any "turn," let alone a "theological" one, to be apologetic in its self-legitimation as well as restorative in its practice.

By contrast, the path Nancy seeks to enter is entirely different. It combines critical-philosophical and historical methods, in order to explore the way religion and secularism, theism and atheism are still entangled in our time. What we need is not a re-presentation and rephenomenalization of religion, of God but an understanding of how, why, and to what extent religion, God, is still "present"—albeit, maybe, *as* absence—in our secular societies and lives.

The More Immediate Context: The Philosophy of Deconstruction

These fundamental reservations about the theological turn in phenomenology indicate the philosophical context to which Nancy clearly belongs: that of *deconstructive thinking*, but at the same time a thinking *of* deconstruction. Nancy's preoccupation with a deconstruction of Christianity coincides with a certain recurrence of religious and theological motifs in the later writings of Derrida, that is, from the 1980s until his death in 2004. This coincidence of trajectories is an important context for Nancy's work on Christianity. It led to a productive exchange between the two thinkers, addressing the issue of the (im)possibilities of a deconstruction of Christianity.[32]

One of Derrida's most innovative and influential contributions to the debate concerning the meaning and presence of religion in the twenty-first century is "Faith and Knowledge: The Two Sources of 'Religion' at the Limits of Reason Alone" (1996).[33] Part of the chapter "On a Divine Wink" in Nancy's *Dis-enclosure* is devoted to this text. Hent de Vries's *Philosophy and the Turn to Religion* takes "Faith and Knowledge" as a starting point for many of its analyses. De Vries formulates the stance from which Derrida works in this text in a way that can easily be applied to Nancy's project as well. Derrida, de Vries states, directs us toward "the persistent conceptual and analytical necessity for discourse to situate itself at once close to and at the farthest remove from the resources and current manifestations of the religious and the theological, their traditional and dominant figures, their cultural practices, and the basic tenets of their ethics and politics."[34]

One should distinguish authors who try to use Derrida's writings to rethink the task and the scope of systematic theology from the deconstructive approach to religion represented by Derrida himself.[35] Both Derrida and Nancy offer many meticulous analyses of biblical passages; of Christian doctrine, art, and practices; of the writings of the Church Fathers (e.g., Augustine's *Confessions*); of mystical traditions from Pseudo-Dionysius to Angelus Silesius; and of general Judeo-Christian themes such as testimony, prayer, circumcision, confession, and forgiveness. Yet their goal is never to establish new, "postmodern" meanings of Christianity or to formulate a new theology or, more generally, a new future for religion on the basis of its presumed return. Rather, as de Vries rightly says, they open a perspective in which we can ask, particularly for the modern situation: "Why is religion a relevant philosophical or theoretical topic at all?"[36] We see this question as lying at the heart of Nancy's deconstructions. He combines this question about the philosophical relevance of religion today with a meticulous rereading of the Christian legacy and of its oldest sources, in order to determine how and why this cultural, social, and political legacy has exhausted itself in modernity, and how and why we are witnessing its persistence.

Nancy and Derrida share this approach with some other contemporary thinkers who all, despite many differences, have turned their attention to their own particular, implicit variations on a deconstruction of Christianity, although none of them would apply the term *deconstruction* to their thought. We will mention four of them, very briefly, in the hope that our remarks will encourage further research comparing Nancy with these thinkers: Alain Badiou, Giorgio Agamben, Slavoj Žižek, and Peter Sloterdijk.

In his essay on the biblical letters of Saint Paul, Badiou involves himself in a deconstruction to the extent that he searches for the "unheard-of" in Paul's theology. He locates this in Paul's concept of truth and universality, grounded in a "paradoxical connection": that "between a subject without identity and a law without support."[37] Badiou argues that Paul presents a new vision of the human subject: it bears a paradoxical, universal truth *as* a singular event and, in the end, coincides with this event, while defying the truths of his time—those of Judaic Law and of the rationality of Greek *Logos*. The Pauline subject rejects the order of the world without withdrawing from it into some individual realm; he refuses the world by proposing a new one, totally different in "nature" and "being": the world not as infinite substance but as infinitely finite event. This subject is outside and inside the world at once, in a crucial double bind that is also thought by Nancy as the kernel of Christianity's self-deconstruction.

Agamben, by contrast, rejects this universalist key to Paul's writings, claiming instead that Paul's concept of time—*kairos*, as the moment interrupting the present *as* present—escapes any form of the universal and opens a "remnant" (*reste*), in which any identity, any vocation is negated.[38] In this attempt to think time and event beyond a structure of identity and identification, Agamben remains close to Badiou and Nancy, however. Later, in *The Kingdom and the Glory*, Agamben attempts a genealogy of modern economy by deconstructing the early Christian notion of *oikonomía* as it is present, for instance, in the divine economy expressed in the doctrine of the Trinity. Following this path, Agamben states that "secularization," seen as "the conceptual system of modernity, is a signature that refers it back to theology."[39]

In *The Fragile Absolute*, Žižek underlines, as does Badiou, an unheard-of and even subversive feature of Christianity, which he ascribes above all to Saint Paul. It is, as he states in *On Belief*, the Christian discovery, or rather invention, of God's imperfection, as represented in the story of the crucifixion, paralleled in Christian notions such as love and belief, which, according to Žižek, are nothing other than forms of a basic "attachment to the Other's imperfection."[40] Žižek's daring interpretations of the doctrine of incarnation are clearly reminiscent of Nancy's view that the Christian God—in Christ—retreats from himself *within* himself, opening up a space where presence and absence become entangled. Žižek does not speak of a retreat, but of a separation: "in the figure of Christ God is thoroughly separated from himself."[41] According to Žižek, monotheism's, and particularly Christianity's, emphasis on the general separation of humanity from a radically distant God originates in this internal separation of God and man *in* God. Yet this separation also "unites us with God" in the twofold nature of Christ. Like Nancy, Badiou, and Agamben, Žižek presents the deconstructive analysis of this structure of separation and unification in monotheism primarily as a new perspective on modernity, referring positively to Kant:

> We are one with God only when God is no longer one with himself, but abandons himself, "internalizes" the radical distance which separates us from him. . . . Kant claims that humiliation and pain are the only transcendental feelings: it is preposterous to think that I can identify myself with the divine bliss—only when I experience the infinite pain of separation from God do I share an experience with God himself (Christ on the Cross).[42]

In his trilogy *Sphären*, Sloterdijk argues that modernity cannot be considered without taking its Christian foundation into account. He even takes one normative step further. Modern humans need protective "spheres" they can experience as virtual but nonetheless meaningful and reassuring "spaces" that distinguish them from and immunize them against the infinite, spaceless, fragmentary world in which they must live: the globe called Earth. Religion, and particularly Christianity, as Sloterdijk deconstructs its historical meanings, has invented numerous "tools" to form these temporary spheres, which, like foam on a beach, momentarily come into being and then pass away. However, according to Sloterdijk, in a certain phase of its history, that is, in the scholastic period in late medieval theology and doctrine, the Christian religion detached itself from this vital role by transforming the intimate God of early Christianity into an "infinitized" God. Whereas the God in Christ of the incarnational narrative formed a topos in which humans could live (the community of Christians is "*in* Christ"[43]), the late medieval God is a radically distant God, representing an infinite void in which humans are left to themselves, exposed to nothingness. Sloterdijk considers this condition of exposure to be a Christian prefiguration of secular modernity.[44]

About This Volume

Re-treating Religion aims to engage in dialogue with one of the central themes in Nancy's oeuvre. Since it is the first volume to address the topic of the deconstruction of Christianity, it seeks to treat its subject in a way at once introductory and exhaustive. Its parts concentrate on four specific aspects of the subject. Apart from this general introduction, which sets out the aim of the deconstructive project and the preparations for it in Nancy's earlier work, each part is preceded by a short Intermezzo, outlining the questions and topics of the ensuing part and introducing its contributions and contributors.

Part I—"Christianity and Secularization; or, How Are We to Think a Deconstruction of Christianity?"—starts with a general discussion of the status of Nancy's project. It elaborates his view of the relationship between Christianity and modernity and discusses in what way this view results in a critique of the paradigm of secularization. It also attends to the politico-theological aspects of the deconstruction of Christianity. Part II deals with Nancy's analyses of monotheism (especially in its Christian and Jewish forms), and focuses in particular on the way he deals with the concept and the name of "God" in monotheism. Part III, "Creation, Myth, Sense, *Poiēsis*," relates the question of a deconstruction of Christianity to Nancy's view of myth and poetry, as elaborated in earlier work as well as in *Dis-enclosure*. It proposes seeing poetry as a way of challenging the mythological aspects of religion, doing justice to Nancy's emphasis on the groundlessness and plurality of sense. Part IV, "Body, Image, Incarnation, Art," explores different aspects of the way Nancy conceives the doctrine of incarnation as a central self-deconstructive aspect of Christianity, his radical rethinking of the status of the body, his analysis of the concept and the figure of touch, and his writings on art and the image. It proposes that art and the image do not illustrate religion, but rather provide sensible articulation of the internal destabilization of the religious mode.

Re-treating Religion is not only an exploration of the work of Nancy but also a discussion with Nancy himself. To begin with, Nancy has contributed an extensive Preamble, in which he explains what is at stake in his deconstructive treatment of Christianity. The volume concludes with a dialogue between him and the editors on the issues brought forward by a deconstruction of Christianity. Yet all the explorations in this book are in dialogue with Nancy and his project. They enter the difficult path of what deconstruction actually is: a way of philosophizing that prefers questions to answers, dialogue to lessons. In deconstructing Christianity as well as modernity, the religious as well as the secular, this book avoids giving sense; rather, it interrupts sense, since "philosophizing starts precisely where sense is being interrupted" (*UJ* 13). In tracing the complex history of Western culture and the legacy of monotheism, it also aims to trace the history of this interruption—in order to illuminate its immense relevance for the twenty-first century.

PART I

Christianity and Secularization; or, How Are We to Think a Deconstruction of Christianity?

Intermezzo

We often take for granted that Western modernity has brought about a secularized, atheistic world, in which religion no longer dominates the public sphere. We are equally convinced that a world once ruled by heteronomy and faith has been developed into a world of autonomy and rationality—in other words, a world whose sense lay outside the world is thought to have given way to a world whose sense is situated within it. Indeed, one cannot deny that religion no longer plays the foundational and regulative role it once did, nor that society is no longer based (at least formally) on its ideas, imagination, and judgments.

We will begin with the observation that God is no longer present in the world or, at least, in society. Since we are undertaking a deconstruction, not a sociology, of Christianity, the question that concerns us is less today's atheism than the how we can think the renewed relationship between Christianity and the modern world. This is both a practical issue and a profound philosophical problem. It is practical in that it involves the problem of how to organize a society that configures religion as a private matter. Many contemporary debates about tolerance or multiculturalism are concerned with the (im)possibility of this kind of "public atheism." Yet this practical question is at the same time a fundamental problem. At a philosophical level, it is not a matter of being pro, contra, or neutral toward atheism and of deciding how to organize these different opinions within the public sphere. Instead, we must ask how we can "think" atheism and secularization, or whether this is even possible. From what point of view, from which position in the world would it be possible to articulate a secularized worldliness? These questions may seem to be rhetorical, but their stakes are high. Does modernity not show how difficult it is and has been to detach oneself from religion without accomplishing this detachment in a religious way? Can the gesture of "leaving religion behind" be an atheistic one, or is it, on the contrary, the religious gesture par excellence? And, in consequence, is the question not how to *re-treat* religion, rather than how to leave it behind and confirm its retreat into the past? Following the line of thought Nancy sets out in several of his books, such as *The Sense of the World*, *The Creation of the World*, or *Globalization*, and especially *Dis-enclosure*, these questions place us in a complex field of aporias. The issue of the retreat of religion is not only related to the way one understands secularization or religion, it also challenges modern thought to create a new ontological vocabulary indicating what we mean by "world," "sense," "foundation," and so forth. Thus, what at first sight seems to be a simple gesture—leaving religion behind—becomes a very complex one. If we want to think secularization and atheism within modernity, we must investigate it with Hegel's "ruse of reason" at our side: at the very moment we are convinced that the problem is behind us, we may be embracing it more tightly than ever before. The structure of "leaving behind," which seems to inspire most modalities of secularization, is a particularly tricky one. Nancy seems to be aware of this. In contrast to the paradigm of secularization, he thinks modernity as something that has evolved out of Christianity, and thus as a process in which Christianity has turned away from itself. Or, to be more precise: his thesis is that the movement of turning away from oneself may in itself be Christian.

Christianity is a religion that deconstructs itself. Hence modernity is not primarily a liberation or emancipation from Christianity, but Christianity evolving out of itself and thus "being itself." The process of secularization must be rethought, and so too must the logic of "the end of" or "leaving behind." Whether and how we may be able to do this is one of the foremost questions with which this first part deals: How are we to think a deconstruction of Christianity?

The first contribution, by François Raffoul, addresses this question by examining what it means that Christianity should deconstruct itself. Raffoul then explores the implications of this self-deconstructive dynamic. A deconstruction does not criticize Christianity, nor does it obtain any restoration. Raffoul looks for an answer to the most basic question one can pose: How are we to think a Christianity that is supposed to deconstruct itself?

Second, Marc De Kesel critically comments upon Nancy's approach to deconstruction in general and to the deconstruction of Christianity in particular. He offers a reading of *Dis-enclosure* and *Noli me tangere*, then suggests that Nancy's deconstruction of Christianity might be seeking a truth of Christianity in a rather contradictory gesture. De Kesel argues for a deconstruction of Christianity that would aim to discover how the truth of Christianity is sustained by and sustains "untruth." If there is a truth to be found in Christianity (or monotheism in general), it lies in the fact that it is both a religion and a critique of religion.

Ignaas Devisch and Kathleen Vandeputte reflect upon an idea Nancy expresses in *The Sense of the World*: "There is no God because there is the world." They ask: If there "is the world," then how are we to understand it? In other words, how are we to think the secularized world we live in? What do we mean by "sense" or "world"? Christianity introduced the notion of infinity and thereby indirectly paved the way for the infinite modern world. It installed a remarkable relation between finitude and infinitude, between measure and excess. God was not only the maker of earthly things, he also added a cosmic dimension with his promise of another Kingdom from which evil will be banished. But with the retreat of God in the modern era, creation is more and more thrown back on itself. Lacking any criterion or limit point, it becomes its own measure. Is this then the secular world we face "after" the deconstruction of Christianity? Or is this what we have to think if we want to deconstruct Christianity in the first place?

Finally, Theo de Wit examines the relationship between the deconstruction of Christianity, secularization, and modern politics. In "Church, State, Resistance," Nancy summarizes a series of attempts to introduce an affective dimension into the heart of the modern "autonomous" political bond: Rousseau's *religion civile*, the *fraternité* of the French Revolution, Hegel's "love" as the principle of the State, and so on. De Wit analyses this affective dimension of political bonds and raises the question of how politics and "being in common" relate to one another. The model according to which Nancy conceives of politics and community in a secularized world is an affective one, de Wit states. Therefore, a dimension of heteronomy is active within and between both spheres, without one sphere subordinating or instrumentalizing the other. This implies a new modesty with regard to politics: not everything is politics, and politics is only one aspect of being-in-common.

—*Ignaas Devisch*

The Self-Deconstruction of Christianity

FRANÇOIS RAFFOUL

Jean-Luc Nancy often insists on the necessity of understanding the expression "deconstruction *of* Christianity" as a subjective genitive: the deconstruction of Christianity would be—in a still enigmatic sense—a self-deconstruction. Commentators have often taken "deconstruction" to be an external intervention by a sovereign interpreter, as a gesture performed, often violently, on a text or some other object of thought. However, what would it mean for our understanding of deconstruction if it were, as Nancy insists (following Derrida himself), a self-deconstruction? What would the deconstruction of Christianity mean if it were, first and foremost, the self-deconstruction of Christianity and not another attack on Christianity? No one, Nancy says in *Dis-enclosure*, "can imagine being confronted today by a Voltaire-like philosopher, having at Christianity in an acerbic tone—and doubtless not in the best Nietzschean style" (*D* 141/206). Nancy clearly emphasizes that, given the title *Deconstruction of Christianity* (an expression whose very terms display the intertwining of Christianity and Western metaphysics or, in Nancy's words, "already bring together philosophical and religious features"),[1] it is not an issue of a "belated attack" *on* Christianity, nor can it be a matter of defending Christianity. Such projects are "simply out of season" (*D* 141/206), because Christianity as such is surpassed (*dépassé*), already in the process of being overcome: "Christianity, *as such*, is surpassed, because it is itself, and by itself, in a state of being surpassed [*en état de dépassement*]" (*D* 141/206). Now, this state of being surpassed is a self-surpassing (*autodépassement*); in this passage Nancy speaks not of overcoming but of self-overcoming. Thus, it is not an issue of deconstructing Christianity in the sense of attacking Christianity, because in a deeper fashion, in a way that is "very profoundly proper to it," in its "deepest tradition" (*D* 141/ 206), Christianity is in a *state of self-overcoming and self-deconstruction*. What would this reflexive mean for an understanding of deconstruction, of a deconstruction of Christianity? In this essay, I will pursue that question in the hope of deepening our understanding of deconstruction as self-deconstruction. As Nancy writes, "it is this transcendence, this going-beyond-itself that therefore must be examined" (*D* 141/206).

Thinking at the End of Christianity

Nancy's reflections on Christianity, on the end of Christianity, and on its self-deconstruction are rooted in an analysis of our present time, a need to reflect on how it has come into being and on the historical trajectory of the West that has led to a point where sense itself has come into question. It is thus in the context of a disintegration—indeed, a (self-) deconstruction—of sense that Nancy seeks to engage that history. This disintegration of sense—of the sense of the world—can be seen in the phenomenon of globalization, in which the West has both established dominance and exceeded itself (to the point where the "West can no longer be called the West"; *D* 29/48) to take the form of the global. Now, the global is not the worldly; in fact, it is the disintegration of the sense of the world. In *The Creation of the World, or Globalization*, Nancy's reflections on the world, on "the being-world of the world," are developed in a play between two French terms that are apparently synonymous, namely, *globalisation* ("globalization") and *mondialisation* ("world-forming"). Although at first glance the two terms seem to be interchangeable, converging in the designation of the same phenomenon, that is, the unification of all parts of the world, in fact they reveal two quite distinct, if not opposite, senses. "Globalization" is a uniformity produced by a global economic and technological logic, "a global injustice against the background of general equivalence" (*CW* 54/63). It leads to the opposite of an inhabitable world, which Nancy calls the "the un-world [*im-monde*]." Globalization, far from being a world-forming, leads to a proliferation of the un-world.[2] In short, "The world has lost its capacity to 'form a world' [*faire monde*]: it seems only to have gained that capacity of proliferating, to the extent of its means, the 'un-world'" (*CW* 34/16). The profound nihilism of the logic of globalization is here revealed, for,

Nancy concludes, "everything takes place as if the world affected and permeated itself with a death drive that soon would have nothing else to destroy than the world itself" (*CW* 34/16). The question, henceforth, becomes: "can what is called 'globalization' give rise to a world, or to its contrary?" (*CW* 29/9). Nancy will oppose to the un-world a "creation" of the world, a process I will analyze in terms of a self-deconstruction of Christianity.

Nancy's reflections on the deconstruction and self-deconstruction of Christianity begin with the fact that the world destroys itself. This is not hyperbole, the expression of a fear or anxiety, nor is it a hypothesis to be reflected upon. It is, according to Nancy, a fact, indeed, *the* fact in which any reflection on the sense of the world must originate: "The fact that the world is destroying itself is not a hypothesis: it is in a sense the fact from which any thinking of the world follows" (*CW* 35/17). Noting briefly the features of this destruction, Nancy highlights the shift in meaning of the papal formulation *urbi et orbi*, which has come to mean, in ordinary language, "everywhere and anywhere." This "everywhere and anywhere" consecrates the disintegration of the world, because it is no longer possible, since this disintegration, to form an orb of the world. The orb of the world dissolves in the nonplace of global multiplicity. In consequence, parts of the world loose their distinctiveness—for instance, the urban in relation to the rural. Nancy calls this hyperbolic accumulation "agglomeration," in the sense of the conglomerate, of the piling up, of a "bad infinite" (*CW* 47/46) dismantling the world: "In such a *glomus*, we see the conjunction of an indefinite growth of techno-science, of a correlative exponential growth of populations, of a worsening of inequalities of all sorts within these populations—economic, biological, and cultural—and of a dissipation of the certainties, images, and identities of what the world was with its parts and humanity with its characteristics" (*CW* 34/14–15).[3] The accumulation of globalization accentuates a concentration of wealth that never occurs without the exclusion of a margin that is thrown into poverty. Nancy thus notes the correlation of the process of technological and economic planetary domination with the disintegration of the world, that is, the disintegration of the "convergence of knowledge, ethics, and social well-being" (*CW* 34/15). The access to totality, in the sense of the global and the planetary, is at the same time the disappearing of the world. It is also, Nancy emphasizes, the end of the orientation and the sense of the world. Globality does not open a path, a way, a direction, or a possibility; rather, it furiously turns on itself and on its own absence of perspective and orientation, thereby exacerbating itself as blind technological and economical exploitation.

The world no longer makes sense as world. The world, Nancy writes, "no longer acknowledges itself as holding a world-view, or a sense of the world that might accompany this globalization." The world is reduced to a world market and the sense of the world identified with a mere "accumulation and circulation of capital" (*D* 30/48). At a time when the West has become globalized, and for that reason no longer possesses a sense of the world, when sense itself is reduced to the domination of the general equivalence of values and the accumulation and circulation of capital, in an indefinite technological growth deprived of recognizable finality, always increasing the gap between the powerful and the have-nots, it becomes urgent, Nancy argues, to come back to (*revenir sur*) what he calls the *provenance* of our history, to reengage the history of the West in which this process of disintegration or decomposition of sense has occurred. "Our time is thus one in which it is urgent that the West—or what remains of it—analyze its own becoming, turn back [*se retourne sur*] to examine its provenance and its trajectory, and question itself concerning the process of decomposition of sense to which it has given rise" (*D* 30/49). In such a history of the West, Christianity occupies a central and determining place, and it thus becomes what must be questioned above all. However, this return or revisiting of (*retour sur*) Christianity must not be confused with a simple return to (*retour à*) Christianity, and Nancy clarifies in the very first lines of *Dis-enclosure* that his goal is not to revive religion, "and even less to return to it" (*D* 1/9). A return *of* or *to* religion, Nancy writes, could only worsen the dangers that are inherent in it. Indeed, Nancy had already distanced himself not only from the idea of a return to Christianity but also from the very motif of the return in philosophy, for instance, in "The Forgetting of Philosophy."[4] This is why he explains that the "much-discussed 'return of the religious,' which denotes a real phenomenon, deserves no more attention than any other 'return'" (*D* 1/9), for what matters in such returns is the return not of the identical but of the different: "the identical immediately loses its identity in returning" (*D* 1/9), all the more so if the return is to the *resources* of Christianity, which can only have remained other to and ignored by Christianity. It will be a matter of reopening a possibility—a "resource"—that, *within and yet beyond Christianity*, would no longer belong to Christianity, but would nonetheless have made possible both the West and Christianity: "In other words, the question is to find out whether we can, by revisiting [*en nous retournant sur*] our Christian provenance, designate in the heart of Christianity a provenance of Christianity deeper than Christianity itself, a provenance that might bring out another resource" (*D* 143/208).

This movement of reopening a resource defines what is at stake in a "deconstruction of Christianity."

In "The Deconstruction of Christianity," Nancy associates the overcoming (*dépassement*) and self-overcoming (*auto-dépassement*) of Christianity with the destiny of the West, asserting that "Christianity is inseparable from the West" (*D* 142/207), "co-extensive with the West qua West." The very motif of an overcoming refers to the fate of Western metaphysics, as approached both in Nietzsche's genealogy of our history as a history of nihilism and Heidegger's history of being. The term *dépassement* refers unmistakably to the French translation of Heidegger's "Overcoming Metaphysics.⁵ In Heidegger's later work, the early problematic of a *Destruktion* of the history of Western ontology was pursued in terms of an *overcoming* (*Überwindung*) of metaphysics and further understood as *appropriation* (*Verwindung*) of its essence.⁶ *Destruktion* is explained by Heidegger in his 1949 introduction to *What Is Metaphysics?*: "The thinking attempted in *Being and Time* sets out on the way to prepare an overcoming of metaphysics [*Überwindung der Metaphysik*]."⁷ Nancy writes that such an overcoming could not mean a simple passing beyond, following Heidegger on this point: What, Heidegger asks, does it mean to overcome or surpass? It means "to bring something under oneself," and consequently "to put it behind oneself," that is, as something that no longer has any actuality or "determining power."⁸ In overcoming or surpassing, there is an attempt to go against something, a pressure or a sort of attack employed against what is to be overcome. The project of an overcoming thus still retains the element of power and will constitutive of the West, which was precisely what was to be overcome. Hence Heidegger writes, in *On Time and Being*, that to think being without beings means: "to think Being without regard [*ohne Rücksicht*] to metaphysics. Yet a regard for metaphysics prevails even in the intention to overcome metaphysics. Therefore, our task is to cease all overcoming, and leave [*überlassen*] metaphysics to itself."⁹ What is required is not an overcoming that reaches higher but a "descent," as Heidegger would write in his "Letter on Humanism," into the poverty of essence. Thinking does not overcome metaphysics by "climbing still higher, surmounting it [*übersteigt*], transcending it somehow or other"; rather, one overcomes metaphysics by "climbing back down [*zurücksteigt*]" into the poverty of its essence. The descent "is more arduous and more dangerous than the ascent."¹⁰

Nancy echoes this powerlessness or poverty of a deconstruction that does not surpass or reach higher by stressing our *abandonment* to the end and exhaustion of Christianity. He thereby gestures toward a certain void or empty place at the heart of Christianity. Indeed, the very task of thought, he says, is to attend to such a void, as it were unclaimed (*en déshérence*), to gather "the void of the opening" (*D* 2/10; trans. modified).[11] The presence of this void indicates the extent to which deconstruction must be understood as a self-deconstruction: from such a void, Christianity is in a constitutive state of self-deconstruction. It is in this ending, in this place of exhaustion, that Nancy situates his problematic of a deconstruction of Christianity. This exhaustion does not signify that we would be "done with Christianity," and its overcoming does not amount to our existing beyond it. As Heidegger shows, to overcome metaphysics does not mean that metaphysics itself is being "passed by" or belongs to the "past," understood as about to "perish and enter what has been."[12] Metaphysics has "passed," but its passing continues, for its end *lasts*: "metaphysics is . . . past in the sense that it has entered its ending [*Verendung*]. The ending lasts longer than the previous history of metaphysics."[13] For Nancy, we have entered the end of Christianity and exist in it: we exist *in* such an exhaustion, and just as Buddha's shadow "remains for a thousand years before the cave in which he died," in turn, "We are in that shadow" of Christianity. In fact, far from moving beyond Christianity's shadow, "it is precisely that shadow that we must bring to light" (*D* 142/207). Overcoming is not a simple passing beyond, if that means acceding to another sphere. Similarly, for Nancy overcoming and self-overcoming "do not mean that Christianity is no longer alive" (even though it "has ceased giving life [*il a cessé de faire vivre*]"; *D* 141/206). It continues to have a hold on us; we exist in its "nervation," to the point that "*all* our thought is Christian through and through. Through and through and entirely, which is to say, all of us, all of us to the end [*jusqu'au bout*]" (*D* 142/207–8; trans. modified). "To the end" (rather than "completely," as the English translation proposes) because the issue for Nancy is to show that we are still Christian all the way *to the end* of that history: we are held in and by Christianity through its end, which is an extremity. This is why the question for Nancy is: "We must try to bring to light how we are still Christian," that is, "to ask ourselves 'how we are still Christian' takes us to the very end, to the ultimate extremity of Christianity" (*D* 142/208). The overcoming of Christianity, its deconstruction, signifies that Christianity has reached its end and that in such extremity we are held.

Consequently, for Nancy the deconstruction of Christianity means accompanying the movement that takes the history of the West to its end, "end" being taken to be an extremity of sense, where sense can both end and arise: at the place where Christianity and the West would have to let go of themselves in order to be what they are, or still be something of themselves beyond themselves. In this letting go of oneself, one can read a self-deconstruction of Christianity, as Nancy writes that "this [letting go] is what I think properly and necessarily gives rise to a deconstructive move" (D 143/208). Such a letting go of oneself, or self-deconstruction, is not a shedding of one's old skin, a dropping of one's tradition; rather, in letting go one encounters what comes to the West or Christianity from further than itself, that is, one encounters its other as what has remained concealed in its origin. In letting go, one opens to what Nancy calls the *provenance* of Christianity, a provenance that is "deeper then Christianity itself" and that therefore, to the extent that it has remained other to the Christian tradition, "might bring out another resource" (D 143/208)—a resource that would be neither a weakened version nor a dialectic rehearsal of Christianity. There is no overcoming of Christianity, no deconstruction, except as an entry into such provenance, if one understands that by "provenance" Nancy does not simply mean the past, but that which from the past, as its unthought resource, is still to come. This is why he states: "Now, 'provenance,' here as elsewhere, is never simply a past; it informs the present, unceasingly producing therein its own effects" (D 32/50; trans. modified).

Nancy insists that such a provenance structures our history *jusqu'au bout*, "to the end," including its modern period, and that Christianity "is present even where—and perhaps especially where—it is no longer possible to recognize it" (D 33/53). A classic representation tends to contrast the Christian age with the modern atheistic period, a schema that Nancy rejects. It is a matter of being "done once and for all with the unilateral schema of a certain rationalism, according to which the modern West was formed by wrestling itself away from Christianity and from its own obscurantism" (D 34/53). Instead, one needs to understand that Christianity has structured the West through and through. In this sense, the "only atheism that can be actual is one that contemplates the reality of its Christian provenance" (D 140/205; trans. modified). This is why Nancy insists: "Let us therefore, very simply but very firmly, posit that any analysis that claims to find a *deviation* of the modern world from Christian reference forgets or denies that the modern world is itself the unfolding of Christianity" (D 143–44/209; trans. modified). One finds, for example, in the Kantian corpus both the denial of the Christian reference (modernity itself is built, according to Nancy, upon such a denial of Christianity within it) and at the same time the maintaining of Christian motifs (such as the universal, law, human rights, freedom, conscience, the individual, reason, etc.). Regarding the persistence of Christian motifs in our modern age, one could also include here the relation to nature and the reference to the intimate certainty of the heart in Rousseau, the dimension of eschatology and the salvation of man in Marx, the call of conscience and original "being-guilty" in Heidegger, and so on. Relying on what he calls a "deconstructive" knowledge, Nancy stresses that the most salient features of the modern understanding of the world—"and sometimes its most visibly atheist, atheistic, or atheological traits"—must be approached "in their strictly and fundamentally monotheist provenance" (*D* 32/50). This phenomenon—both heritage and its denial—points to a conflict within Christianity, more specifically between a fundamentalism (*intégrisme*) and its disintegration or "dissolution by adaptation to a world" ("modernity"; *D* 144/210). We will discover shortly how such a conflict harbors a distention or difference within Christianity—the difference *of* Christianity—a difference that would have to be understood in terms of the opening and provenance of Christianity as such, allowing for its self-(de)construction.

Let us for now note the secret and intimate affinity between atheism and Christianity. In the chapter "Atheism and Monotheism," Nancy attempts to show that the opposition between atheism and theism—which is, in one sense, undeniable by the very fact that a-theism is the negation of theism—nevertheless conceals the profound belonging of atheism to theism. A-theism is the negation of theism, "but we should not overlook to what degree this negation retains the essence of what it negates" (*D* 16/29). This statement needs, however, to be reversed: if atheism harbors a deep dependency on theism, Nancy shows how "monotheism is in truth atheism" (*D* 35/55), how it deconstructs itself as atheism, a still-enigmatic formulation that we will attempt to clarify in terms of a self-annihilating of God in his creation. What is nonetheless beginning to appear here is the co-belonging of atheism and theism, atheism not being the simple refutation of theism, and theism somehow leading to atheism in an essential way. (Nancy thus explains that Christianity "shelters within itself—better: more intimately within itself than itself, within or without itself—the principle of a world without God"; *D* 35/55). This atheism, or rather absentheism, as Nancy calls, a world without God, is the true meaning of both atheism and Christianity.

Deconstruction as Self-Deconstruction

Nancy stresses the co-belonging of Christianity and Western metaphysics. In fact, as we noted above, he asserts that not only is Christianity "inseparable from the West" (*D* 142/207), rather than some accident that befell it, but it is "coextensive with the West qua West." Indeed, he speaks Christianity as the "nervation" of the West. He explicitly assumes the definition of metaphysics (in its onto-theo-logical constitution) proposed by Heidegger, stating that metaphysics designates the "representation of being [être] as beings [en tant qu'étant] and as present beings [étant présent]" (D 6/16), that is, he establishes being as a *foundation* of beings. Nancy thus assumes the Heideggerian conception of metaphysics as onto-theological, that is, as the foundation of beings in a supreme being. "In so doing," Nancy continues, "metaphysics sets a founding, warranting presence beyond the world" (D 6/16), enclosing beings in their beingness and consecrating what he calls the enclosure of metaphysics (*clôture de la métaphysique*). Due to this onto-theological structure of metaphysics, Christianity for Nancy must thus be considered to be a "powerful confirmation of metaphysics" (D 7/16): it accentuates the reduction of being to beingness through the establishment of "a supreme, arch-present, and efficient Being," and thereby the enclosure of metaphysics.

However, such enclosure—and on this everything turns—"amounts to an exhaustion" (D 6/16), and the accomplishment of metaphysics amounts to the twilight of its idols. The foundation of beings, precisely insofar as it is the foundation, is itself without foundation, and thus the ground, as ground, constitutively deconstructs itself (as Heidegger has shown in his *Principle of Reason*[14]). Nancy stresses in *Dis-enclosure* that metaphysics "foments in itself the overflowing of its rational ground" (D 7/17). Here one can glimpse what Nancy means by the disclosure or dis-enclosure (*déclosion*) of the closure of onto-theology: closure dis-enclosures itself from within: "it is from within metaphysics itself that the movement of a destabilization of the system of beings in their totality can take shape," so that, literally: "The closure invariably dis-encloses itself" (D 7/17). It dis-encloses itself constitutively, that is, from within metaphysics itself. This is why Nancy includes as an example of such self-deconstruction Kant's notion of the unconditioned in pure reason, an excess of reason with respect to itself, for deconstruction is not some phase that would follow a monolithic history, but the excess of closure that inhabits (as excess) and haunts metaphysics.[15] Such excess is also manifest in the Heideggerian *Destruktion* of ontology, in Jacques Derrida's *différance*, or in Gilles Deleuze's lines of flight. Metaphysics deconstructs from within. (Otherwise, Nancy asks, how could the destabilizing of this supposedly monolithic system have arisen?) Therefore one must state that *deconstruction is a self-deconstruction*: "In truth, metaphysics deconstructs itself constitutively, and, in deconstructing itself, it dis-encloses [*déclôt*] in itself the presence and certainty of the world founded on reason" (D 7/17). What does deconstructing Christianity mean from this perspective? Not an external intervention into an object, but simply "accompanying [Christianity] in the movement by which philosophy displaces, complicates, and undoes its own closure" (*D* 10/21; trans. modified), that is, by grasping in it the movement of a self-deconstruction. The deconstruction of Christianity (objective genitive) is the accompaniment—and the revealing—of Christianity's deconstruction (subjective genitive).

Where would that movement lead? To what does it give access? Not to some original givenness of being, as Heidegger may have wished, nor to some supra-essential being lying beyond our world, but rather to "the disjointing and dismantling [*désajointement*] of stones," with a gaze directed "toward the void (toward the *no-thing* [chose-rien]), their setting-apart" (*D* 11/21).[16] Let me clarify this sense of deconstruction. In section 6 of *Being and Time*, Heidegger writes of the *Destruktion* of the history of ontology. That term has been reformulated in Derrida's work as *déconstruction* (although the Vezin translation renders it as *désobstruction*).[17] Although deconstruction has become identified with the thought of Derrida, its provenance is decidedly Heideggerian, and Nancy explicitly refers to that history in *Dis-enclosure*. However, Nancy understands "deconstruction" in a way quite different from Heidegger, and it is important to make this difference explicit. Seeking to clarify how he understands deconstruction ("Let me specify what the operation of 'deconstruction' means"; *D* 148/215), Nancy recalls the history of the term, the tradition to which it belongs, for as he states, deconstruction "belongs to a tradition, to our modern tradition." If deconstruction (de)structures the history of the West, its name appeared as a philosophical concept in Heidegger ("if we look back at its origin in the text of *Being and Time*"; *D* 148/215), where it has the sense of a reappropriative dismantling of our tradition. Heidegger indeed stresses the positive intent of *Destruktion*, aiming to retrieve original experiences of being that have become concealed by our obscuring and alienating tradition. He thus meant by *Destruktion* an ontological reappropriation, while assuming a certain hermeneutic violence directed at the concealment of phenomena, as this passage from *Being and Time* makes clear:

> Thus the *kind of being* of Da-sein *requires* of an ontological interpretation that has set as its goal the primordiality [*Ursprünglichkeit*] of the phenomenal demonstration *that it be in charge of the being of this being in spite of this being's own tendency to cover things over.* Thus the existential analytic constantly has the character of *doing violence* [*Gewaltsamkeit*], whether for the claims of the everyday interpretation or for its complacency and its tranquillized obviousness.[18]

Destruktion in the Heideggerian sense seeks to reappropriate the original being of Dasein, countering (this is where the negative aspect of *Destruktion* comes into play) the concealment of phenomena in our (fallen) tradition. Here is where Nancy marks his difference: he does not aim to reappropriate the proper of human existence and original Dasein, nor to return to origins ("I don't want to take out the gesture of 'returning to the sources' and of 'puri-fication' of the origin"; *D* 58/84), for, according to him, to deconstruct means instead "to take apart, to disassemble, to loosen the assembled structure in order to give some play to the possibility from which it emerged but which, qua assembled structure, it hides" (*D* 148/215). Nancy's gesture shares with Heidegger's a positive intent: he notes that Heidegger explicates his move as an *Abbau*, a dismantling or "taking apart" of the concealments that cover over being—a deconstruction—and not as a *Zerstörung*, or "destruction." It thus has a positive intent, and is neither a destruction in order to rebuild nor a perpetuating. However, for Nancy deconstruction gives access not to an originary proper domain, to "being" or to *Ereignis* (it is not "a return to the archaic"; *D* 44/68), but rather to a sheer *case vide*, an "empty slot" (*D* 149/217), a gap or void without any substantiality or integrity of its own. That gap would play the role of a hyphen, the *trait d'union* of a distension.

Deconstruction thus will not lead to any reappropriation of the proper. It is not something existing or subsisting outside the structure; it is not access to another domain but simply the *differential gap in the construction*, the delineation of the structure itself, the lines of construction, and the structure of the edifice. Nancy stresses in "The Judeo-Christian (on Faith)" that deconstruction "thus belongs to a construction as its law or its proper schema: it does not come to it from elsewhere" (*D* 44/68). Any construction supposes a gap within it, and that gap delineates the contours of the construction, marking its limits, its exposure to the void, and already its self-deconstruction. This is why Nancy writes, in relation to the deconstruction of monotheism: "I will call 'deconstruction of monotheism' the operation consisting in disassembling the elements that constitute it, in order to attempt to discern, among these elements and as if behind them, behind and set back from the construction, that which made their assembly possible" (*D* 32/51). Between or among these elements, the differance of a dis-, deconstruction has nothing that is proper to it and exhibits nothing but the construction itself in its own assembling. It is as if deconstruction was or came to pass "even before construction, or during construction and at its very heart" (*D* 58/84). Deconstruction as the law of the construction, as its logic, and also as the space or spacing, the "space through which the con-struction is articulated [*s'ajointe*]" (*D* 44/68), a sort of com-position, as one speaks of a painting, which is as much a dis-position. The *com-* of this com-position is a difference, and any construction, as thus dis-posed and com-posed, harbors or contains "at its center a gap [*un écart*] around which it is organized" (*D* 44/68).[19] The Latin *cum-*, the *trait d'union* ("hyphen," but literally the "mark of union," connecting mark), Nancy states, "passes over a void that it does not fill" (*D* 44/68): The dis- of disposition and the com- of com-position do not fill the gap but simply organize it as a construction, for the com- includes "constitutively the voiding of its center or its heart" (*D* 44/68). That void calls for a deconstruction of the structure, and in turn it is what deconstruction manifests. "But this deconstruction—which will not be a retrocessive gesture, aimed at some sort of morning light—henceforth belongs to the principle and plan of construction. Deconstruction lies in its cement: it is in the hyphen, indeed it is *of* that hyphen" (*D* 58/84). To that extent, both construction and deconstruction are undecidable, as Nancy suggests when he states that the "com-" designates both construction and deconstruction "taken together" (*D* 48/ 73). This undecidability allows Nancy to understand deconstruction strictly as the differential structure of construction, out of a void. He thus proposes as the general law of any construction, itself harboring the principle of a deconstruction: "the construction in question, like any construction, according to the general law of constructions, exposes itself, constitutively and in itself, to its deconstruction" (*D* 48/73). This deconstruction belongs to "the principle and plan of construction" (*D* 58/84), although in the construction of Christianity it is neither a merely formal "empty slot" nor the *case vide* of the structuralists. The deconstruction of Christianity reveals a void at its heart that is for Nancy an *opening*, which he will approach as the resource of sense, of a sense as the opening of sense and to sense, empty of all content, all figure and determination. "Thus everything brings us back again to opening as the structure of sense itself" (*D* 156/226). Ultimately, the nothing that is here revealed points to a kenosis by which God empties himself (self-deconstructs) in his creation.

The gesture of deconstruction consists in approaching the places where constructions are made possible out of a void, an opening. Deconstruction thus is the reopening of the opening. Nancy stresses this sense, for it is not simply a matter of disassembling or loosening a structure but in fact of revealing the play of its possibility, of the "to-come."[20] The gesture of deconstruction lies in the attempt to "reach, at the heart of the movement of integrality's self-distension, the heart of this movement of opening. My inquiry is guided by this motif of the essence of Christianity as opening:

an opening of self, and of self as opening" (*D* 145/210). This opening, as Nancy stresses elsewhere, is never pure but is always the opening *of a closure*, always an opening made possible by a "contour," the drawing of a form and of limits. The open, he explains, "is not gaping infinitely," and there is no infinite opening. An opening "requires its contour in order to open itself," as a mouth opens and gives or forms its contour.[21] The opening is always the opening of a distension, and the disassembling is the distension of an opening, for indeed "it is only from within that which is in itself constituted by and setting out from the distension of an opening that there can be a sense to seek and to disassemble" (*D* 148/216), which reveals once again that deconstruction is ultimately a self-deconstruction, and that the deconstruction of Christianity as objective genitive adjusts itself to Christianity's deconstruction as subjective genitive. This is how Nancy makes that claim: "In engaging in a 'deconstruction of Christianity,' in the sense I have specified, we find first this, which will remain at the center of every subsequent analysis and represent the active principle in and for every deconstruction of monotheism: Christianity is by itself and in itself a deconstruction and a self-deconstruction" (*D* 35/54–55).

This represents the very destiny of Christianity, for Christianity is as such the movement of its own distension, out of a void that is both its possibility and its self-deconstruction, in the sense of the aporetics of the possibility of the impossible spoken of by Derrida.[22] What makes history possible (the void) is also what deconstructs it. Nancy thus speaks of the profound ambiguity of Christianity, of "the entire self-destructive or self-deconstructive ambiguity of Christianity" (*D* 157/226): on the one hand, the empty slot "makes the structure work" (*D* 149/217), but on the other hand, it also disassembles it. This is why Nancy speaks of the Open "as horizon of sense *and* as a rending of the horizon," as that which "assembles/disassembles the Christian construction" (*D* 156/226).

The Self-Deconstruction of Christianity, or God's Absentheism

That opening and that spacing are in the end what Nancy calls the eclosure (*éclosion*) of the world, the eclosure of eclosure itself, a creation of the world without given but properly ex nihilo, in which the creator annihilates itself—deconstructs itself—in its creation. This is what the self-deconstruction of Christianity gives us to think: the self-deconstruction of God in his creation, the absenting of God in the world. What is peculiar to the very notion of creation for Nancy is precisely that it is not a production, from a given and by a transcendent producer. Nancy engages this motif of creation to the exact extent that he takes leave of all reference to a given ("the withdrawal of any given thus forms the heart of a thinking of creation"; *CW* 69/91): nothing is given, all is to be invented, to be created, and the world "is created from nothing: this does not mean fabricated with nothing by a particularly ingenious producer. It means instead that it is not fabricated, produced by no producer" (*CW* 51/55). Thus, Nancy writes that if "creation means anything, it is the exact opposite of any form of production" (*CW* 51/55), which supposes a given, a project, and a producer. This is why Nancy insists on thinking the "eclosure of the world" in all of its radicality (or rather, since there is no question of roots here, in its *béance*, its void and gap): "No longer an eclosure against the background of a given world, or even against that of a given creator, but the eclosure of eclosure itself" (*D* 160/230). To that extent, creation deconstructs the reference to an author or creator. In *Being Singular Plural*, within the context of a discussion of his notion of a "creation of the world," Nancy explains that the concept of a creation of the world "represents the origin as originarily shared, spaced between us and between all beings. This, in turn, contributes to rendering the concept of the 'author' of the world untenable" (*BSP* 15/34). What creation shows is that the "creator" becomes indistinguishable from its "creation." If creation is ex nihilo—as it must be, since it is not a production from a given[23]—that means not that the creator starts from nothing but that the creator *is* the *nihil* and that this *nihil* is not prior to creation, so that "only the *ex* remains" (*BSP* 16/35). That *ex* is a distributive, as the origin is the disposition of the appearing, and creation is nothing but the ex-position of being.

In *The Creation of the World*, Nancy shows that the question of the world was or has formed "the self-deconstruction that undermines from within onto-theology" (*CW* 41/32). Nancy argues that the world emerged as a proper philosophical problem against the background of a self-deconstruction of onto-theology. He characterizes the becoming-world of the world as a "detheologization," insofar as the God of metaphysics has merged with the world, indeed, has become the world. This is why, for Nancy, the God of onto-theology, in a peculiar kenosis, or self-emptying, was "progressively stripped of the divine attributes of an independent existence and only retained those of the existence of the world considered in its immanence" (*CW* 44/39), which amounts to saying that the subject of the world (God) disappears in order for the world to appear *as subject of itself*. The becoming-world of the world signifies that the world loses its status as object (of vision) in order to reach the status of subject (previously occupied by God as independent existence).

Henceforth, there is nothing but the (immanent) world as subject of itself. The world is a relation to itself, which does not proceed from a ground or a basis; it is an extension of itself, relating to itself from its proper extension as world. The God of religious representation as subject of the world, as self-subsisting and self-sustaining substance of the world, will be thought of as emptying himself in the opening of the world.

Following this understanding of kenosis in divine creation,[24] Nancy explains: "The God of onto-theology has produced itself (or deconstructed itself) as subject of the world, that is, as world-subject. In so doing, it suppressed itself as God-Supreme-Being and transformed itself, losing itself therein, in the existence for-itself of the world without an outside (neither outside of the world nor a world from the outside)" (*CW* 44/39). God thus disappears, but He disappears *in the world*, which immediately means that we can no longer speak meaningfully in terms of being *within* the world (*dans-le-monde*) in the sense of what is contained within something else, but only in terms of being *in* the world (*au-monde*). The preposition *au*, "in," explains Nancy, represents in French what best encapsulates the entire problem of the world. This shift from "within" to "in" indicates the radical immanence of the world: everything now takes place in the world, that is to say, right at the world, *à même* the world.

To think the world outside representation, that is, outside of onto-theology ("A world without representation is above all a world without a God capable of being the subject of its representation"; *CW* 43–44/38), nothing could be more appropriate, according to Nancy, than to appeal to the motif of creation, that is, a creation ex nihilo understood in a non-theological way. Creation would even be, in its content and its logic, a nontheological notion, if it is the case that creating can only be ex nihilo, emergence from nothing, and not from a transcendent producer. This is why " 'Creation' is a motif, or a concept, that we must grasp outside of its theological context" (*CW* 50/54). Nancy even characterizes creation as the nodal point in a deconstruction of Christianity, precisely to the extent that it resides in the ex nihilo. "The idea of creation . . . is above all the idea of the *ex nihilo*" (*CW* 51/55). The creation of the world is ex nihilo, letting the world appear as nothing given, because "neither reason nor ground sustains the world" (*CW* 102n20/47n1). From the theological understanding of creation as the "result of an accomplished divine action," one moves to an understanding of it as an "unceasing activity and actuality of this world in its singularity (singularity of singularities)" (*CW* 65/82), that is, creation as *mise-en-monde* or *mise-au-monde*, a bringing or coming into the world.[25] That creation is without a creator, without a subject, for the world does not pre-suppose itself but is "only coextensive with its extension as world, with the spacing of its places between which its resonances reverberate" (*CW* 43/36, trans. modified), and is a resonance "without reason" (*CW* 47/47).

The world is thus an abandonment (not held by an author or subject but surrendered without origin to itself), an abandonment by and to: the world *is* poor. This poverty (which is not misery but being abandoned as such[26]) is the nothing that the world manifests: coming from nothing, resting on nothing, going to nothing, the world is, writes Nancy in a striking passage, "the nothing itself, if one can speak in this way, or rather *nothing* growing [*croissant*] as *something*" (*CW* 51/55). Noting the etymological links between "growing" (*croissant*), "being born" (*naître*), "to grow: (*croître*), "to be born, to grow" (Latin *cresco*), and "to make something merge and cultivate a growth" (Latin *creo*), Nancy connects creation with growth as movement of the world: "In creation, a growth grows from nothing, and this nothing takes care of itself, cultivates its growth" (*CW* 51/55). Thus, in this sense, poverty grows. "If the world is the growth of/from nothing [*croissance de rien*]—an expression of a redoubtable ambiguity—it is because it only depends on itself, while this 'self' is given from nowhere but from itself" (*CW* 51/56). The world is created from nothing, that is to say, as nothing, not in the sense of nothingness, but in the sense of nothing given and nothing of reason. The world emerges from nothing, is without precondition, without models, without given principle and end. Coming from nothing signifies the presentation of nothing, not in the sense of a phenomenology of the unapparent or of negative theology but in the sense where "that *nothing* gives *itself* and that *nothing* shows *itself*—and that is what is" (*CW* 123n24/97n1).

Creation lies entirely in the ex nihilo and not in the position of a theism, not simply an a-theism but an *absentheism*: a world without God, a world without another world: "At the end of monotheism, there is world without God, that is to say, without another world, but we still need to reflect on what this means, for we know nothing of it, no truth, neither 'theistic' nor 'atheistic'—let us say, provisionally, as an initial attempt, that it is *absentheistic*" (*CW* 50–51/54). God is *absent* in the creation of the world and disappears in the world, and Nancy clarifies that "absentheism" as designating "an absent God and an absence in place of God" (*CW* 120n23/54n1). A creation no longer referred to theology, but to the ex nihilo, without a transcendent creator (in which the creator disappears and self-deconstructs in his creation), a creation immanent to itself, a creation of itself and from itself.

This creation of the world deprived of a subject becomes an unpredictable appearance, an irruption of the new, an absolute beginning, a dis-posing openness (the *ex* of *ex nihilo* as *différance*). Ultimately, the self-deconstruction of God *is* the opening of the world, its eclosure: "the creator necessarily disappears in the very midst of its act, and with this disappearance a decisive episode of the entire movement that I have some-times named the 'deconstruction of Christianity' occurs, a movement that is nothing but the most intrinsic and proper movement of monotheism as the integral absenting of God in the unity that reduces it in and where it dissolves" (*CW* 68/88). To that extent, the nothing of creation ex nihilo "opens in God when God withdraws in it (and in sum *from* it) in the act of creating. God annihilates itself [*s'anéantit*] as a 'self' or as a distinct being in order to 'withdraw' in his act—which makes the opening of the world" (*CW* 70/93). The self-deconstruction of God is the opening of the world ("the opening of the world in the world is the result of a destitu-tion or a deconstruction of Christianity"; *D* 78/120), so that self-deconstruction now means the "opening" of the world, out of a void, that is, an ex-appropriative opening: this is one of the most significant aspects of what Nancy has addressed as the deconstruction of Christianity, that is to say, its self-deconstruction:

> The unique God, whose unicity is the correlate of the creating act, cannot precede its creation, any more that it can subsist above it or apart from it in some way. It merges with it: merging with it, it withdraws in it and withdrawing there it empties itself there, empty-ing itself it is nothing other than the opening of this void. Only the opening is divine, but the divine is nothing more than the opening. (*CW* 70/93)

Deconstruction or Destruction?

Comments on Jean-Luc Nancy's Theory of Christianity

MARC DE KESEL

Nancy's *Noli me tangere: On the Raising of the Body* focuses on Christ's enigmatic words to Mary Magdalene at the moment when she is the first to meet Him after His resurrection: *mē mou haptou* (Greek), *noli me tangere* (Latin); "Do not touch me" (John 20:17). According to Nancy, this sentence reveals the entire self-deconstructive truth operating at the heart of Christianity:

> We could just as well understand that it [Christ's body] must not be touched because it cannot be: it is not to be touched. Yet that does not mean that it is an ethereal or immaterial, a spectral or phantasmagoric body. . . . But it does not present itself as such here. Or rather, it slips away from a contact that it could have allowed. Its being and its truth as arisen are in the slipping away, in this withdrawal that alone gives the measure of the touch in question: not touching this body, to touch on [*toucher à*] its eternity. Not coming into contact with its manifest presence, which consists in its departure. (*NT* 14–15/28)

How does Nancy therefore interpret the "essence," or "truth," of Christ's resurrected body, which is the core of Christian doctrine? Not as death's destruction but as its affirmation. For him, "resurrection," acknowledges that the human body—the human bodily relation to the world—is eternally marked by death. Neither Christ nor we will ever have full access to

63

the body that ex-poses us to the world and to others. Our body will for-ever continue to be marked by a kind of alterity—another name for "death"—that remains forever immune to any attempt at appropriation. The "essence," or "truth," of Christ's resurrected body is to be found only in the withdrawal occurring in the very act of its appearance. That withdrawal concerns not the spirit but the body or, which amounts to the same thing, the bodily nature of Jesus' appearance. It marks the "resurrec-tion of his body."

This, in a nutshell, is the main thesis of Nancy's program of the decon-struction of Christianity, as elaborated in *Noli me tangere* and more ex-haustively in *Dis-enclosure*. In this essay, I shall examine whether the notion of deconstruction is applied correctly. I shall argue that Nancy's approach is far more a (Heideggerian) *Destrukion* of Christianity than its (Derridean) *deconstruction*. This distinction is not without important consequences for what is at stake in Christianity and its (self-)critical potential.

Christianity's Derridean Deconstruction

In "Faith and Knowledge: The Two Sources of 'Religion' at the Limits of Reason Alone," an essay reflecting on the religious revivals at the end of the twentieth century, Jacques Derrida unfolds the double-bind logic that both constructs and deconstructs religion's performance.[1] On the one hand, religion posits things as safe and sound, as sacrosanct, sacred, un-touchable: as something "known with certainty," (*savoir*). This, however, requires the sacrifice, in a sense, of the thing one attempts to save. This "sacrificial logic" comes into play when many religions—as well as many nonreligions—postulate the absolute value of life. Inevitably, they risk sacrificing the very life they want to save by reducing it to a mere idea, a dead fetish: to something for which one would give one's own life or that of another in order to defend it. "Life" thus becomes something for which life can be "sacrificed."[2]

This is why, on the other hand, performing something as sacred and untouchable requires the assistance of another "fiduciary" or "testimonial logic."[3] To be what it is, the sacred must be recognized as such by others and therefore testified to by me. I must not only believe in the sacred value I put forward (here, the logic is sacrificial), I must also believe I *will be believed* (here, the logic is testimonial). I need faith in the faith others will have in what I declare to be sacrosanct.[4] This "fiduciary" faith (*foi*) in the testimonial capacity of my message, however, necessarily hands over the sacred to a public space full of uncontrolled communication, where, inevitably, the sacred message is open to profanation, desecration, violation, et cetera. To be valued as sacred and untouchable, life must be handed over to a public field of communication where anyone can touch this sacred value and use or misuse it in the most unholy ways.

Thus, the construction of the sacred is impossible by means of its own sacrificial logic alone (reducing a presumedly authentic value to an inauthentic fetish). Such logic must be supplemented by a testimonial logic, in which it is no less infected (deconstructed) by an unavoidable possibility of profanation. Similarly, the sacred message meant to be heard by all must perform itself as being touchable by no one, as immune to the very audience by which it must be received. The sacred can only be performed—and thus exist—as supported by, and vacillating between, these two logics, between the sacrificial and the testimonial. It is only possible thanks to a double-bind relation that unites both construction and deconstruction without ever sublating the radical difference separating them. No construction works without the secret and inappropriable assistance of some deconstructive supplement. Nor does a deconstructing operation ever work without simultaneously constructing the entity or identity it subverts.

Does this mean that, for Derrida, nothing is sacred, that sacredness is phony? Certainly not. There are, and always will be, sacred things, but they will never really and fully be what they claim to be. They will always already be contaminated by the nonsacred supplement of a profaning testimonial logic indispensable to their own performance as sacred. Similarly, there never will be a world definitely delivered from anything sacred or sacrosanct, a world where each value or message can be exchanged for any other value or message whatsoever. The logic of communicational exchange is impossible without the supplementary logic treating the value or message concerned as safe and sound, unhurt, sacred, sacrosanct.[5]

Even without an extensive elaboration of Derrida's reflections on current religious revivals and the double-bind logic they obey, it should be clear that, according to him, construction and deconstruction, however logically incompatible they may be, nonetheless operate together; that the *de*construction of Christianity at the same time constructs it. The construction side of deconstruction is certainly not a restoration, since the deconstructing operation is inappropriable, by definition anarchistic and incurably subversive. But precisely as such it is fully part of the construction.[6]

Nancy's Approach to the Destruction of Christianity

Does this fit with Nancy's ideas on the deconstruction of Christianity? According to him, is Christianity building up itself by deconstructing, as in the narrative of "Noli me tangere," for instance? Not at all. Again and again, as Nancy states, the discovery of Christianity's self-deconstructive move does not save, restore, and thus (re)construct Christianity.[7] Its self-deconstruction goes in one direction only: under its metaphysical and religious narrative, it reveals a persistent, nonreligious truth. It is true, for Nancy, that the religious narrative is itself the deconstructor of its metaphysical constructions. Again, however, the direction is one way: from construction to deconstruction, and not vice versa, as is the case in Derrida.

In a passage from *Noli me tangere*, Nancy hesitates before using the word *erection* as a term that can indicate the nonreligious truth of "resurrection." He describes the latter as the emergence—the "raising or uprising [*relèvement ou soulèvement*]" (*NT* 18/33)[8]—of death within the realm of life. Referring to the raising of Lazarus (John 11:1–44), Nancy writes

> In the Lazarus episode, the dead man leaves the tomb bound in his bandages and wrapped in a shroud. This is not a scene out of a horror movie; it is a parable of the lifted and upright stance in death. Not an erection—either in a phallic or monumental sense, although these two could be taken up and worked with in this context—but a standing upright before and in death. (*NT* 18/34)

Nancy describes resurrection as the uprising of death within life. In the case of Lazarus, it is the other way round: as life's "lifted and upright stance in death [*statue droite levée au sein de la mort*]." For Nancy, however, it amounts to the same thing: it indicates the moment where the dead say "I am dead," thus expressing the impossible moment of non-coincidence with oneself—the impossibility that makes presence with oneself possible. "'I am dead' (an impossible statement) and 'I am resurrected' say the same thing," Nancy writes a few lines later (*NT* 19/35). However, why does he hesitate in applying the term *erection* to "resurrection"? Because, he argues, the term has the connotation of being "phallic," as well as being "monumental." He immediately adds that, if reworked, both connotations, as well as the term *erection* itself, may well be useful.

Are both connotations—being "phallic" and being "monumental"— different from one another? Not that much. The phallus, not being the penis, is literally its monument, its blown-up representation, carried around in Dionysian processions. It is a monument representing the fertility of male potency. So why does Nancy hesitate to use "erection" as an explanatory name for "resurrection"? Not because of its sexual character, but because of its connotation of "monument" and thus of representation, that is, of representation's capacity to appropriate the fullness of presence. Resurrection's truth—that is, the affirmation of death as the inner core of life, the affirmation of absence as the inner condition of possibility of presence—cannot be fully appropriated, sublated by the erection of a monument representing its truth (read: reducing its truth to the limits of a representation).

But can the "erection" of such a "monument" be avoided? Can one name the impossibility of being present to oneself without representing it, without sublating that impossibility in the very act of naming it? Derridean deconstruction answers this question in the negative. In "Faith and Knowledge," Derrida dishes up a *phallus theory* precisely in order to explain this.[9] What, therefore, is a phallus, according to Derrida? It is the signifier naming the vitality of life par excellence. It raises human sexual energy to something sacred, sacrosanct, untouchable, carried around in a religious, Dionysian procession. Erected to the level of the sacred, however, the phallus turns life's sexual potency into something "more than life," that is, into a dead fetish. The strange thing is that only if the erected phallus were to "fall down" would it really show what it claims to show: life.

Here it becomes clear why Derrida's reference to the phallus and its erection/fall illustrates the double-bind logic revealed in the performance of religion (and other discourses): an erect phallus is already contaminated by coming fall, just as, conversely, the "fallen" phallus is already infected by the erection to come. Both eclipse one another in a kind of elliptic logic.[10] This phallic construction contains its deconstruction as its inner condition of both possibility and impossibility. Thus its deconstruction contains construction as its inner condition of both possibility and impossibility. Deconstruction is not only part of the construction, construction is also always at work already in deconstruction.

Deconstruction Constructing Christianity

Like Nancy, therefore, Derrida puts forward a kind of quasi-transcendental truth at work in religion's performativity—as it is in the performance of so many other forms of human culture. Unlike Nancy, however, Derrida comprehends that this truth can never appear *as such*. The appearance or performance of this truth is itself contaminated by the double-bind structure it reveals. In order to appear or to be performed, this truth requires an establishment or erection, which is always already infected by the "bad things" it is unmasking at that very moment (such as untrue fantasies, wrong beliefs, etc.).

What does this imply for the Mary Magdalene pericope in John 20, as interpreted by Nancy? That it is the untouchable itself—the very "Noli me tangere"—that has always already been touched, not only in the way the transcendental structure of touching is revealed (as Nancy contends) but also in the way that this revelation has always already been contaminated by a less transcendental touch, by the banality of untrue touching. The clear opposition between the transcendental and the empirical touch, between the phenomenologically unrepresentable truth of touching and its representation, is never not already deconstructed at the level of the most authentic revelation of truth. Even at this moment, we have always already appropriated the inappropriable, and we do so in a way that makes the choice between appropriation and its opposite forever undecidable.

Is the unambiguous difference, therefore, between religion and nonreligion or between religious and nonreligious truth that Nancy postulates tenable after all? Following the line of Derridean deconstruction, one must admit that this opposition, too, is in the end deconstructed by its inner undecidability. The nonreligious truth has always already been infected by the truth that religion claims, not so much at the level of content as at a formal level (the nature of nonreligious truths cannot definitely be separated from that of religious truth). This is to say that nonreligious truth has always already been infected by the myths, fantasies, magic stories—in short, the representations and monuments—on which religious truth relies.

Is this to say that there is no outside of religion, according to Derrida? That would be too rapid a conclusion, if only because we do not really know what *religion* is. The only thing we know is that, despite centuries of the most intelligent religious critique, a certain revival of religion occurs. Without knowing precisely what it is, we observe that the thing *called* religion, imagined as having been paralyzed and neutralized by ages of criticism, suddenly "revives." It is not quite certain, however, whether the thing reviving is the same as the thing that was supposed to have died. Rather, it is the opposite, Derrida states. Since difference precedes essence, since repetition precedes identity,[11] the very repetition of religion makes it change in each "retake" or even turn into something other than religion. History is not a matter of identities, which begin by existing on their own and then, in a logical second step, undergo changes. It is a process of changing, a game of differences that secondarily appeal to so-called identities—identities that above all repress the abyssal and undecidable character of the "dissemination" of difference and repetition that constitutes history.

There is no outside to this disseminating realm of difference and repetition. Or, to express it with reference to one of the leading themes in Derrida's oeuvre: "*There is nothing outside of the text*" (there is no outside-text; *il n'y a pas de hors-texte*),[12] that is, no outside to the world open to us as a text, as a "textile" woven with endlessly exchangeable signifiers and written in a "writing [*écriture*]" characterized by a double-bind logic. Within the limits of that condition, to ascribe something an identity is both to separate it from the rest of the "text" and to deliver it to the intertextuality of a disseminating realm of references. Constructing something as an identity is impossible without relying on some "originary supplement" that deconstructs it at the same time—which is to say that, precisely because of this, any deconstruction inevitably sustains the construction it undermines.

This is Derrida's way of redefining the core of what, after all, thinking is, including critical thinking. We owe to Plato our traditional idea of criticism as separating truly real things from false representations, from mimesis. We must find the way out of our cave full of shadows to true reality. For Derrida, however, there is no outside to the mimesis in which we live. The world is a generalized representation, a construction made of representations that, inevitably relying on some supplementary logic, deconstructs the representational logic and prevents it both from arriving at some supposed "real" world outside and from closing in on itself. Within the limits of this condition, critical thought will still be possible and greatly needed, but it will never be able to claim a truth that is located outside the mimesis, outside the representation, in a realm of authentic presence. Mimesis will still require criticism, but that criticism will no longer be able definitively to liberate us from that very mimesis.

If there is a self-deconstruction at work in monotheistic religion, it must be defined within the limits of that condition. Monotheism is not the religion of belief or faith, as the post-Kantian approach has always stated. According to the main monotheistic texts, belief and faith are put forward, not as the aim of the religious life, but as a problem it must overcome. Again and again the Old Testament prophets repeat that people believe *all too easily*. They have faith too quickly in the idols they assume to be God. Too eagerly they forget that only God is God, a God who Himself is unknowable and of whom they know that, compared with Him, nothing is true. In a way, monotheistic religion is based less on trust than on distrust. Of course, God grants a kind of trust, but it is above all a trust that enables me to distrust both my own and others' religious aspirations. The monotheistic message is by definition suspicious about people's inclination to believe, since God is not what they believe God is, for only God is God.

Monotheistic religion is critical to the core.[13] Its very essence is criticism and, even, *religious critique*. The God to whom monotheism refers is radically abstract, and it has no defined idea of who He really is. But it has very accurate ideas about false gods, idols. This is why, from a strictly religious perspective, monotheism is rather poor. The core of its content is that God is not its first concern, that is, that people should not fantasize about who He is. To honor God is to be obedient to his word, that is, to the Law He has given, which tells us, in particular, how to deal with our neighbors, how to do justice to the "widow and the orphan" and to other brothers and sisters with no rights. In the name of God, we should be preoccupied not with God himself but with justice for his creatures. This is why monotheism is critical of typically religious concerns and largely reduces that dimension of its practice to critical attacks on man's inclination to venerate all kinds of false gods. Atheism in this sense is not per se contradictory to monotheism, as Nancy rightly states.[14] Atheism and monotheism in fact share the same criticism of man's "natural" inclination to believe. To combat it is the central mission of both atheism and monotheism.[15]

Yet it is crucial here to recall that monotheistic criticism, however close it may come to atheism, considers itself to be fully religion. It is true that, at its core, it is nothing but religious critique, attacking anyone who pretends to have insight into what is behind the face of a God who, in His very appearing, withdraws—a God who, in His presence, is always already absent. But it nonetheless fully admits to being a religion. However paradoxical this may be, it is interesting to note that in this way monotheism acknowledges that it is not radically different from the thing it criticizes. It admits to sharing the same nature as the thing it nonetheless criticizes to the core.

This is perhaps why the paradox of monotheistic religious critique is not so inconsistent with the condition in which deconstructionist criticism finds itself. Is deconstruction not aware that its critical move belongs in full to the construction of what it criticizes? And is its point not that criticism is nonetheless possible because no construction can fully appropriate the deconstructive move it feeds? In that sense, deconstruction is indispensable, even if it cannot offer a nondeconstructible truth, for any construction must recognize and acknowledge the inner gap or deficiency that makes it deconstructible. It is the task of any modern criticism *actively* to make this happen. It cannot offer an alternative to the system being criticized—this is what the tragedy of twentieth-century ideological critique has shown—but it nonetheless has to hold open the system, whose nature is to come full circle and to repress or deny its own inner openness.[16]

Here, monotheism, in its quality of age-old critical religion, can offer an instructive point of reference for contemporary criticism, including Derridean deconstruction. It displays a criticism aware of its inability to offer a radical alternative to what it criticizes.

The reference to monotheistic critique, however, also confronts deconstructive thought with the inner weakness—and thus the danger—of its own critical gesture. The fact that criticism—or, more precisely, self-criticism—has always been its core business has not prevented monotheism from claiming access to absolute truth and acting as if it were legitimate to use (and abuse) absolute power—just as the high tradition of critical thought in the nineteenth and twentieth centuries has been used and misused by totalitarian and other disastrous trends in political and social life.

"But That Is Not Our Purpose Here"

In the "Opening" of *Dis-enclosure*, Nancy explicitly refers to Christianity's dark pages, telling the history of its manipulations, exploitations, and other kinds of abuse of power. He does this, however, in order to declare this issue "superfluous" and immediately to leave it behind:

> It seems superfluous to repeat all the grievances that can legitimately be leveled against Christianity, from the divestiture of thinking to the ignoble exploitation of pain and misery. We should even push the accusation farther—indeed, farther *than* mere accusation—to interrogate the conditions of possibility of a so powerful and durable religious domination exerted upon a world that, simultaneously, almost never stopped outmanoeuvering and deposing this domination, and that found in it weapons to be used against it (freedom, the individual, reason itself). But that is not our purpose here. (*D* 9–10/20)

Neither an investigation of how Christianity's immense and lasting abuse of power "in God's name" has been possible nor a reflection on the fact that Christian doctrine itself has supplied the "weapons" to be criticized for that is part of Nancy's deconstruction of Christianity. Of course,

Nancy admits that such investigation must be done and that these self-critical tools must be taken seriously—but nonetheless, it "is not our purpose [*objet*] here."

Do we read this correctly? Christianity supplies itself with the tools by which it can be (and has been) criticized and deconstructed; does Nancy declare this to be the "purpose" of its deconstruction? These "weapons" of Christian origin—"freedom, the individual, reason itself"—are they not a perfect illustration of how Christianity itself possesses the equipment for its own deconstruction? Therefore, why does Nancy refuse to take into account that, in spite of centuries of the hardest (self-)criticism—and thus, in a way, self-deconstruction—Christianity has held its dominion and at times even strengthened its abuse of power?

The problem here is not only Nancy's refusal to discuss the dark history of Christianity's power. The crucial point to be made is that, declaring the issue to be of less importance, Nancy leaves undiscussed the possibility that both power and the abuse of power may be sustained *even by Christianity's (self-)critical tendencies*. The true side of Christianity may be as responsible for its dark pages as its false ones. This is an extremely important hypothesis, which a so-called deconstruction of Christianity cannot simply dispense with in a single sentence. It touches the heart of the entire deconstructive project. In fact, Nancy misses the opportunity to consider the possibility of an inner and dangerous weakness, which may be characteristic of all modern religious criticism, *including his own deconstruction of Christianity*. What if the "weapons" with which one fights against the abuse of power can turn into that criminal power's most efficient instruments? What if the deconstruction of Christianity's dark side is at the same time useful in its construction? In leaving Christianity's dark history aside, Nancy avoids a confrontation with the possible dark sides of his own deconstructive thought. "But that is not our purpose here," he writes, and adds that: "For the moment, one remark must suffice, but it is essential. Christianity designates nothing other, essentially (that is to say simply, infinitely simply: through an inaccessible simplicity), than the demand to open in this world an alterity or an unconditional alienation. However, "unconditional" means not undeconstructible. It must also denote the range, by right infinite, of the very movement of deconstruction and dis-enclosure" (*D* 10/20). Nancy's "remark" is indeed an "essential one." In fact, it is too essential to be simply a remark, for it recounts nothing less than the main argument and the central thesis of *Dis-enclosure*, even of his entire project of a deconstruction of Christianity. Apparently, therefore, only the essential *core* of his theory suffices here to neutralize the problem averted in the paragraph above, that is, the problematic inner weakness of deconstruction and other kinds of modern criticism.

As I would rephrase Nancy, the "demand to open in this world an alterity," "an unconditional alienation," is the truth of Christianity. But has the long history of criticism (and self-criticism) of Christianity's violence and corruption not demanded precisely an opening up of an alterity within Christianity itself, as well as within the world in general? How could such openness have ever had a chance if not in the shape of "all the grievances [*griefs*] that can legitimately be leveled against Christianity," that is, in the shape of critical questions, questions originating within Christianity itself and therefore organizing its self-deconstruction? It is bizarre that Nancy considers this to be "not our purpose here," as if ages of (self-)criticism were not the way par excellence to get in touch with the "unconditional alienation" to be opened by Christianity as well as by modern thought.

One can even wonder whether Nancy is serious when he writes that here "unconditional" refers to the deconstructibility of the "alienation" or "alterity" that are to be opened by Christianity ("However, 'unconditional' means not undeconstructible"). Is the line of Nancy's reasoning not simply the other way round? Is "alienation," openness toward its own inner openness, not the final aim of Nancy's deconstruction? And is it not simply logical to conclude that this openness or "alienation" is *un*deconstructible in itself? That it incessantly deconstructs the system without being deconstructed itself? In the note accompanying this sentence, Nancy seems to admit this. There he writes that the "undeconstructible" can only have the shape of the "active infinite [*infini actuel*]" present in experiences such as "death, the truth, birth, the world, the thing, and the outside" (*D* 196n12/20n2): these are all shapes of the inner openness revealed and realized by the incessant self-deconstruction at work in Christianity. Again, however, is that openness, that "alienation" or "alterity," not *in itself* undeconstructible? Even the terms *alienation* and *alterity*, of course, will surely finally become too much of a representation covering the "infinitely simple" experience of being's openness. However, if I understand Nancy correctly, that experience *as such* is not to be deconstructed. It is the very raison d'être of any deconstruction. According to Nancy, Christianity has a truth (not in the ontological but in the phenomenological sense of the word), a truth that is unconditional and, in that sense, *un*deconstructible. Or, to put it in the terms of the next sentences in Nancy's essay: within the closing universe of the *logos*, Christianity saves the *alogon*. And this *alogon*—or so one must conclude, against

Nancy's own assertion—cannot be deconstructed; it is the "*un*deconstructible" that any deconstruction wants to save, to behold, and to restore:

> In other words, Christianity assumes, in the most radical and explicit fashion, what is at stake in the *alogon*. All the weight—the enormous weight—of religious representation cannot change the fact that [*ne peut pas faire que*] the "other world" or the "other kingdom" never was a second world, or even a world-behind-the-worlds, but the other of the world (*of every world: of all consistency tied up in beings and in communication*), the other than any world. Christianity can be summed up, as Nietzsche, for one, knew well, in the precept of living in this world as outside of it—in the sense that this "outside" is not, [or] not an entity. It does not exist, but it (or again, since it) defines and mobilizes ex-istence: the opening of the world to inaccessible alterity (and consequently a paradoxical access to it). (*D* 10/20–21)

In the "most radical and explicit fashion," Christianity "assumes . . . what is at stake in the *alogon*" of the human *logos*, in the openness constituting the world, an openness toward what does not exist but "defines and mobilizes ex-istence" (i.e., human *Dasein*, which for Nancy is always *Mitsein*)[17] as being open to an "inaccessible alterity." All this repeats what has already been explained above. The summarizing idea he puts forward is not very new either: "Christianity can be summed up, as Nietzsche, for one, knew well, as the precept of living in the world as outside of it." It is Heidegger's famous idea that, as human beings, we are in a sense outside the world of beings, since we are not simply being (*seiendes*) but *Dasein* and *Mitsein*, having its locus in the world's "inner outside" or, more precisely, coinciding with (*being* with) that inner outside.

The Subject of Deconstruction

Yet here a peculiar implication of Nancy's thesis comes to the fore. The kind of inner outside he mentions does not simply name the *object* of Christianity's deconstruction; it names its subject position at the same time or, more generally, the truth of the human subject position as such. It indicates the position from where we take part in the world—which is the position from which we take part in Christianity's self-deconstruction, as well. Being *in* the world, we are not *of* the world, as early Christianity defined it.[18] Christianity's inner outside, which throughout its history has been more and more the object of "unconcealment," indicates the subject position, the locus from where we relate to the world.

This locus or subject, however, is far from being unproblematic. The question is whether, in our condition of modern subjects, we have made this position *as such* ours. Have we knowingly and consciously assumed this position? Not at all, Nancy would answer. For that, we are still too heavily captivated by metaphysical and representational logic. That is why Christianity is still to be deconstructed and to be acknowledged in its self-deconstructive move. And that is why modernity, too, still has to deconstruct itself by deconstructing Christianity.

Once Christianity is deconstructed, however, and we fully embrace its inner self-deconstructive move, will we then be able to assume this inner outside position and make it properly ours? Or is the question rather: Can we make this position ours *at all*? Can we *appropriate* it? The only answer possible according to Nancy is that we cannot. Such presumed appropriation denies the inappropriable alterity of that very position. Every authentic response of a *Dasein* to the injunction proceeding from that inner outside position affirms this. It acknowledges the impossibility of appropriating its own position, of getting "settled" in its own inner outside.

This, however, is only one side of the coin, for it is also a question of whether one is able *not* to appropriate this position. Has *Dasein* not always denied the impossibility of a self-appropriation, has it not "initially and for the most part"—*zunächst und zumeist* (to use the idiom of Heidegger's *Being and Time*)[19]—covered up being's openness with representations, and is it not from this "inauthentic" position that it is susceptible to the injunction of authentically taking its *Dasein* upon itself?

"All the weight—the enormous weight—of religious representation cannot change the fact that the 'other world' or the 'other kingdom' never was a second world, or even a world-behind-the-worlds," Nancy writes. This kind of second world or after-world is fictitious and distracts attention from the world's inner alterity or inner openness. Is the opposite claim, however, not equally valid? Is it not also the case that all the world's inner alterity cannot ensure that it will be covered up by the "enormous weight of religious representation"? Is the inner openness in which human existence is grounded not necessarily as fatally doomed to be covered up by inauthentic, phantasmagorical, "religious" representations?

Affirming that we are "in, but not of the world" consists in affirming our subject position as mere openness toward the world, as an open space within it. Yet at the same time it consists in acknowledging that we can never definitely escape from repressing or covering up this openness. We will never be definitely freed from supposing that we belong to a world separated from the one whose openness we *are*, that we inevitably start from the supposition of being free subjects independent of the world, and that we will never be able to leave that starting position finally behind. To put it in Heideggerian terms: the pretension to be beyond everyday life mentality (*Altäglichkeit*) is the best definition of this mentality. To take on the impossibility of going beyond is part of *Dasein*'s *authentic* mode of being. Affirming that we are in, not of the world implies affirming the impossibility of really getting settled in that way of being. Such a position is never conquered; it is, again and again, *to be* conquered. No one is ever definitely able to overcome its false starting supposition.

The risks inherent in the ambiguous side of the human subject position—to know we are being's openness and to know that this very knowledge is not able to appropriate this openness—can be illustrated by the way this being in, not of the world functioned in the early ages of Christianity. What is more: in the light of this Christian subject position, a kind of disposition to perversion comes to the fore and lays bare an intrinsic possibility, if not of the subject position in general, at least of the one the *modern* subject is in.

As we all know, "Christians" was a term for those who believed in Jesus as the Messiah, that is, as the one in whom God was incarnated in order to put an end to the existing creature corrupted by time, sin, and death, and to open up a new creature, a heavenly world of eternal life. At least, this was what Christians soon assumed to be the case. For now, this had happened to Christ alone. He was still the only one who had made the step from the old to the new creature. As the Gospels recount, the resurrected Christ had to return to his Father but was soon to come back in order to complete what he had started: the *eschaton* and its apocalypse, that is, the end of time going hand in hand with the entire revelation of God and his mysteries. In the meantime, the old creature was living in the *interval*, in the time between the instant time's end had *started* and the moment of its *definite end*. The coming of the Messiah had completed God's revelation (apocalypse) and destroyed death and sin (*eschaton*). By means of his faith in Christ, the Christian shared the realm of accomplished revelation and was delivered from sin and death. In that sense, he was already part of the other, newly created world. Yet, he did so *only in principle*, for in fact he was still living in the old world, since the Messiah was still *to come* (back) in order to finish his mission, that is, to finish the act of definitively finishing what he alone had started. So, indeed, the Christian was—and still is—*in* the world, all the time being no longer *of* the world (because of already belonging to the new creature).

This messianic phantasm underlying the Christian position defined as being in, not of the world had far-reaching consequences. One is that it enabled the tricky way in which Christianity succeeded in claiming absolute power and abusing it, as all too often has been the case in history. Is this specific subject position not Christianity's best guarantee of having the truth *always* on its side, whatever side it is forced to take? Already sharing the Messiah's new creature and the completion of revelation, Christianity is able legitimately to claim the absolute truth, that is, to speak in the name of a truth not affected by time, sin, or death. When, by contrast, Christianity takes up a standpoint in the world, where it cannot claim any truth or is itself attacked by hostile truths, it can always legitimately criticize the adversary by saying that the Messiah is still to come, that the absolute truth is still not revealed, and that no one, therefore, is yet able to speak in its name.

This is the double-bind logic enabled by Christianity's central phantasm: messianic expectancy is acknowledged as being both fulfilled and unfulfilled *at the same time.* On the one hand, Christianity can claim that the existing world is still under *apocalyptic reservation* and that it is therefore still to be criticized. This is the *critical* aspect of Christianity, which, in its capacity as a monotheistic religion, is, as it were, its core business. On the other hand, however, it considers itself at the same time to be the holder of the apocalyptic truth *without any reservation* and claims permission to criticize the entire world from a point of view that is itself beyond any possible criticism.

Modernity can be defined as a break with a world dominated by Christian doctrine. Yet if modernity has nonetheless inherited some aspects from Christianity, its formal subject position of being in, not of the world is certainly one of them. It is the so-called neutral position of the modern scientist observing reality from a point supposed to be radically separated from the investigation's object—from a point *outside in* the world. It is the position of the modern bourgeois, being engaged in social life from a point supposed to be free, that is, to be free from what binds me to society and enables me to have an open relationship with that society.[20]

With this subject position, modernity has taken over the possibility of a perverse double bind-logic enabling the modern subject always to have right on his side. The modesty of science lies in the fact that it relates to reality from a neutral position, renouncing any subjectivity; yet it is precisely from this empty and neutral position that modernity embraces reality with an historically unseen omnipotence, which shows its dark side in its capacity, for instance, to destroy man and the world by means of nuclear weapons. Similarly, the point from which a modern bourgeois takes part in the world is, on the one hand, an extremely modest point forcing him to declare he is equal to—and equally as free as—anyone in the entire world, which makes him really someone *of* the world. On the other hand, however, he is able at the same time to assume that he is free of that world, flirting with the idea of spending his life far from the turbulence of social life or, another possibility, of criticizing—and even revolutionizing—that social world. The double-bind logic is at its clearest in the so-called post-modernist position. Claiming all grand narratives to be dead and truth to have become an empty pretension, the postmodernist subject in fact tells the truth about everyone who dares to claim truth. He claims nothing less, in fact, than the absolute truth, the truth about all truths and, in that sense, the apocalyptical and eschatological truth we met in Christian doctrine—apart from the fact that postmodernity lacks any kind of eschatological reservation.

Precisely because Christianity is responsible for the absolute pretension of modern man's apparently most modest position, the history of both Christianity's power claims and the critical questions attacking these claims genuinely belongs to a so-called deconstruction of Christianity. Unlike Nancy's statement, these critical questions are to be taken up by any deconstructive thought, for they have opened Christianity to its own inner openness, to the openness of being what it preaches and is. The crucial point, however, is that these questions deconstructing Christianity's metaphysical doctrine from within have also enabled its abuse of power. These questions—as well as these answers—were at least attacking *and* sustaining at the same time the pretensions to power of Christian imperialism.

The deconstruction of Christianity (or of monotheism) is not about finding the truth at work in the phantasmagorical discourse of that religion, as Nancy postulates. It is instead about discovering the way in which even that truth is sustained by—as well as sustains—"untruth." It lays bare the way in which the criticism unmasking the falseness of its object is never itself without contamination by that object, including its falseness. If there is a truth to be found in Christianity (or monotheism in general), it lies in the fact that it is both religious criticism *and* religion. It is, as it were, a religion, a critical religion. Its core mission states that nothing of what man calls God is God, for only God is God. It performs its God as a fundamental critical paradigm, attacking the human inclination to create gods and to feel based in divine sacred values. However, this basically atheistic mission of monotheism does not prevent it from declaring monotheism to be a religion.

This is why monotheism can be revealing for modern criticism. The former can shed some light on the impasse in which the latter finds itself. Contemporary criticism is in fact in a shape similar to that in which monotheism once was: having convincingly unmasked the great ideologies of our time, it must acknowledge that ideology still remains the horizon within which modern man operates. What is more, it must acknowledge not only that it has no real alternative to the ideology criticized but that it is itself unable to operate entirely outside ideology, that it is itself never really nonideological. This is why its ideological critique could not avoid being (mis)used by ideology itself. This, however, does not mean that ideological critique is impossible or senseless. It only emphasizes the necessity and even ethical duty of such critique. It only emphasizes deconstruction as an ethical injunction, as an absolute and absolutely undeconstructible, untouchable imperative.[21]

Sense, Existence, and Justice; or, How Are We to Live in a Secular World?

IGNAAS DEVISCH AND KATHLEEN VANDEPUTTE

> The generalized secularization of the West is an indisputable fact. However, the evocation of this fact does not resolve the philosophical issue.
> —Bernard Flynn, *The Philosophy of Claude Lefort: Interpreting the Political*

The World from a Secular Perspective

From a Christian perspective, the world is a place whose sense lies beyond it: a position Wittgenstein also seems to share in statement 6.41 of his *Tractatus Logico-Philosophicus*: "The sense of the world must lie outside the world."[1] If secularization is our perspective, the most logical option seems to lie in a mere immanentization of this otherworldly sense. Were this logic still to inform the thought of Jean-Luc Nancy in *Dis-enclosure*, his stance would be highly repetitive: Have we not been saying this for centuries now?

In fact, Nancy tries to tell us something different: unless we want to inhabit a negative version of Christian thought, if we want to live in a secularized world, if we want to be "atheists," we must look at sense in a completely different way.

For this reason, Nancy enters into dialogue with Wittgenstein in *The Sense of the World*, if only very briefly. Sense is not something that we "the secularized," as the successors of God, now confer upon the world ourselves. If we could do so, that would merely confirm the Christian idea that the world represents an absence of sense or an object whose sense is given from the outside by some subject or other. What remains as our horizon is the world and nothing but the world. Sense is thus nothing other than co-existence itself. Being secularized is being radically exposed to sense, to the world as such. At no moment is the meaning of the world given by a Creator. But if there is only this world, and it is no longer founded in and through otherworldliness, does Nancy not seem to confirm the classical thesis of secularization? Whereas, for a religiously founded world, the sense of the world would lie in an instance beyond the world or acquire an otherworldly status, in a secular world, sense would be located purely immanently in the world.

It is precisely this idea that Nancy questions and nuances. His relation to Wittgenstein's claim that the sense of the world must lie outside the world offers an interesting angle on how he proceeds. Wittgenstein regards the world as a given facticity, a plain and simple state of affairs. To this world, sense can be granted from outside it. But this "place" "outside the world" is thus also a place outside the totality of all places, a place without place, as it were. The question then is: How, today, can we think such an outside? According to Nancy, Wittgenstein's "outside the world" still partially operates as the continuation of a Christian concept of the world whose sense lies outside itself. (See *SW* 55/91.) If we want to account for the "world as such," we must approach it from another direction:

> As long as we do not take into account, without reserve, the worldly as such, we have not gotten rid of demiurges and creators. In other words, we are not yet atheists. Being an atheist is no longer a matter of denying a divine instance that has reabsorbed itself into itself (and this can perhaps therefore no longer be called "atheism"). It is a matter of opening the sense of the world. (*SW* 158/239)

In other words, Nancy appeals to a rather Heideggerian move: if we are always "thrown" into sense and that sense places us in a being-open(ed)-to, in a being-toward, then sense is always being-toward and it is this that constitutes co-existence, being toward the world as such. Any comprehension or understanding of sense thus already takes place from within the opened horizon that the world is for us and to which we are always already exposed. That the world *is*—the global spacing or taking place as such—is what sense is for Nancy:

> As soon as the appearance of a beyond of the world has been dissipated, the out-of-place instance of sense opens itself up within the

world to the extent that it would still make sense to speak of a "within." Sense belongs to the structure of the world, hollows out therein what it would be necessary to name better than by calling it the "transcendence" of its "immanence"—its *transimmanence*, or more simply and strongly, its existence and exposition. (*SW* 55/91)

That there *is* something means that the world arises. The origin of the world, Nancy claims at several places in his work, takes place everywhere, over and over again in every singular act of sense, always momentary and local. *World* is always a plurality of worlds, an infinite passage of phenomena. The world is structured as being-toward, as a relation—in all possible connotations of the word. The "singular plural origin" of the world is what comprises our co-existence. It is the naked structure of our "we-ness" in a world that is nothing but world. As the "trans-immanent" structure of sense, such an origin of the world does not lie outside the world, but each and every arising of the world takes place as exposure, as transcendence in the world. Ultimately, the sense of the world is thus a tautology. The world is structured as sense, and sense is structured as world: "If we are toward the world, if there is being-toward-the-world in general, that is, if there is world, there is sense. The there is makes sense by itself and as such. We no longer have to do with the question, 'why is there something in general?' but with the answer, 'there is something, and that alone makes sense'" (*SW* 7/18). The world is the name for the sense that "there is." If the world *is*, and if existence no longer has sense but is sense, then there is no senselessness in this name, and man cannot declare its existence null and void. Nihilism and idealism sublate one another at this point (*SW* 79/127). The bankruptcy of the concept of the world as deriving from a first cause or an Idea thus does not cast us into an abyssal or rudderless world. It is not because the world no longer permits itself to be represented in a sense-bestowing totality that existence has become senseless or abyssal.

The world seen from a secular perspective can only be sense (and vice versa) if it has no sense (to lose). Sense is there just as the world is there: without any questioning why. Sense stands for existence itself, for the fact that one is opened to existence and to the world. That we are sense, that there is sense and that we are here—this is the radical demand and consequence of the opened space that the global world has become for us. Being in the world comprises the sense of our existence. To the extent that the world stands in relation to a creator outside the world, a God or a Subject, it can have sense. If want to live in a secular world, this (relation with a) creator has to fall away. The world then no longer has sense: it is sense. This is why Nancy can write:

If the world is not the work of a God, this is not because there is no God, as if this were an annoying circumstance, a privative condition to which one had to accommodate oneself as best one could. (As if, in the final analysis, the world were not complete, as if the causal or final part of the totality had been simply amputated. Often, atheism has not known how to communicate anything other than this.) But there is no God because there is the world, and because the world is neither a work nor an operation but the space of the "there is," its configuration without a face. (*SW* 156/236)

The Incommensurable

"There is no God because there is the world." But if there is the world, how are we to understand it? More exactly: How are we to think the secularized world we live in? Let us quote from the "Opening" to *Disenclosure*:

> The West was born not from the liquidation of a dark world of beliefs, dissolved by the light of a new sun—and this no more so in Greece than during the Renaissance or the eighteenth century. It took shape in a metamorphosis of the overall relation to the world, such that the "inaccessible" in effect took shape and functioned, as it were, *precisely as such* in thought, in knowledge, and in behavior. There was no reduction of the unknown, but rather an aggravation of the incommensurable (which was no accident, if the solution to the mathematical problem of "incommensurables"—the *alogon* that is the diagonal of the square—furnished the emblematic figure of the birth of true knowledge and, with it or in it, the modeling or mathematical regulation of philosophy). (*D* 8/18)

The sentence that fascinates us in this quote is "There was no reduction of the unknown, but rather an aggravation of the incommensurable." It fascinates us not only because of its content and its presence in other texts of Nancy's oeuvre but also because it relates the problem of secularization, including *sense* and *world*, to that of *justice*. For Nancy, justice is above all connected with the fact of our co-existence, with what is unique about every existence in its co-existence with other creations. He addresses juridical issues as religious problems or vice versa: issues such as the day of judgment, being judged and judging, being summoned, the law, the covenant, right and justice, or being responsible. Nancy treats these issues in a way that enables him to demonstrate their "religious" origin.

In a small text called "Cosmos Basileus," included in *Being Singular Plural*, Nancy discusses this topic by means of a reflection on the unity of the world. He states that the unity of the world is nothing other than diversity and, hence, the world's nonunity. A world is always a plurality of worlds. Existing begins with exposure to plurality and to sharing. The sharing of the world, or co-existence, is, according to Nancy, thus also the "law of the world." The world has no other law than this; it is not subject to a sovereign authority. The world always means co-existing, being shared and divided; and it is never a unity or a totality. Therefore the law of the world cannot be equated with the accomplishment of one or the other unity or totality. On the contrary, already in the opening sentences of the essay Nancy describes the *nomos* of the world as the dissemination, the division, and the allocation or sharing of everything.

Nancy's elaboration of this is just as brief as his description of it. Things to be disseminated can be places in which we live, but just as well portions of food or rights and duties. To the question of the just measure (of such a distribution), Nancy answers that the measure of covenant, of law or of absolute justice, lies nowhere other than in this sharing itself and in the exceptional singularity of everyone with everyone offered by this sharing. This means, according to our interpretation: because the world is not given once and for all, because there is no God Who offers the Measure of the world, there is no perfect division in which everyone would be assigned a fixed place. On the contrary, because the world arises in and through the taking place of every singular plural appearance, its division and its divide are at stake time and time again, that is, within every one of us, with every appearance, and each time something or someone appears. Sharing or division is thus precisely that which connects the theme of the world, or existence, and that of justice. In this way, the covenant is also nothing other than co-existence. Co-existence is not something added to existence, as a phenomenon in itself. Co-existence is existence existing *as dividing-sharing*. In consequence, justice means doing justice to what belongs to every unique, singular creation in its coexistence with other creations. Justice is not primarily a matter of a singularity and only secondarily the relation of this singularity to others. That which makes the singular unique is simultaneously that which puts it into relation. To do justice to the singular absoluteness of one's proper being is thus simultaneously to do justice to the plurality of the singular.

To do justice does not mean that we can dream of a world without injustice. In a world that tries to think itself as secular, there is no answer to the question of *why* there would be injustice. The theological instances that attempted to explain or justify this have disappeared. Justice no longer enters from outside the world to recuperate the world's injustice or to sublate it; rather, it is something given with the world, as the law of its act of donation. The world is itself the supreme law of justice—not the world as it is, but *that* the world is, that it always surges forth again, always singular plural.

This brings us back to the issue of the "incommensurable," to which Nancy refers in the paragraph from *Dis-enclosure* quoted above. Already in *The Experience of Freedom*, Nancy offers an illuminating statement about the incommensurable. Justice, he writes, can no longer be that of a right environment presupposing a given measure. (See *EF* 75/101.) By this Nancy refers to the ontological order of an (ancient) world that gave a central function to the idea of a just measure.

The collapse of the idea of a just measure and its environment refers implicitly to Aristotle's doctrine of the mean. In the *Nicomachean Ethics*, Aristotle describes the task of the excellent person as discovering the right mean and keeping just measure.[2] All excellence or virtue lies in the middle of two extremes, and it is necessary to abide midway between too much and too little in order to retain the middle. The right mean is not the arbitrary choice of a free individual but a pressing task. To act virtuously is to act in accordance with the stable order of being: one must do good in accordance with the good that is being. Holding to the middle path is therefore never just an individual matter. As a polis, citizens must strive together for the mean and comply with the superior structure that is the cosmos. The right mean and just measure are never purely moral matters but always questions of being. Every digression from the right mean is a detour from the unfolding of being and therefore always an ontological excess. The (right) mean is, as it were, the covenant of finite beings, of the closed cosmos of the ancient world. Or, put differently, justice (*dikē*) is a question of the right modality of being.

Because Christianity introduced the notion of infinity, and thereby indirectly paved the way for the infinite modern world, things changed substantially. Christianity instituted a remarkable relation between finitude and infinitude, between measure and excess. Insofar as creation is created, its mode of being is one of finite dependence, but insofar as creation is the result of a Creating Act that comes into being ex nihilo, its covenant is that of incommensurability and infinity. What the finite creature measures itself against is the universe, the All, the infinite expansion of the universe that induced such turmoil in Pascal. Nevertheless, such a notion of infinity still maintained a supreme theological limit, by which every right and wrong was finally to be judged. God was not only the maker of earthly things, He also added a cosmic dimension with his promise of another kingdom from which wrong would be banished. But with the retreat of God in the modern era, creation increasingly is thrown back on itself. Lacking any criterion or limit point, it becomes its own measure; but this means only that all measure, as something limiting human life from outside, is absent. Consequently, measure is constituted by nothing but excess. Creation can measure itself against nothing other than itself. One can therefore no longer speak about creation proper: it is now pure being that is its own measure. For this reason, all former measures no longer hold. Aristotle's world of right mean and just measure is miles away.

The Incommensurable as a Modern Excess

Six years later, Nancy's suggestion in *The Experience of Freedom* acquired greater specificity in the essay "Human Excess" (1994).[3] Its point of departure is the idea of keeping measure, and in it Nancy reflects on a form of excess or immeasurability that would be proper to a modern and thus secularized order.

First of all, Nancy describes modern time as a period of vast numbers. Of course, one hardly needs Nancy's help to make this claim. Modern time obviously feeds on enormous numbers, imposing records, and dizzying figures. These immense numbers initially seem to refer to a form of immeasurability or excess proper to our time. Everything goes faster and faster and is expected to grow exponentially. Optimists tell us that we should to be fascinated by this immeasurability; pessimists warn us about the uncanniness of it all. But these alternatives are precisely what Nancy puts into question.

Both positions, one can infer from "Human Excess," fail to make a crucial step when thinking the place of this excess in modernity. According to Nancy, excess is not to be found in larger and larger numbers. Although certain things seem immeasurably large, we still can measure them and express the results as figures. One can, for example, measure how many millions of grains of sand there are in a handful, how many inches of books there are in a shop rack, or how many individual letters can be found in the collected works of Hegel. In our modern era, the immeasurable can always be measured: hence there is no measure given a priori from which the immeasurable is said to diverge. Excess, therefore, does not lie in huge numbers. Whether the world population is now twenty or thirty million makes no difference to the excessive. There is no fixed criterion against which we could measure these twenty or thirty million, and precisely the lack of this criterion shows how excess lies elsewhere. The ever-greater dissemination of vast numbers in our culture, such as computer memory or the price of a nuclear submarine, indicates less an aberration from certain established measures or norms than an exponential growth in our responsibility for the world and for existence. Numbers that measure the stock market or the world population point to a certain connectedness or commitment: an engagement. The risks and consequences of the growing impact of multinationals on our economy or of the ever-increasing world population, for example, reveal an urgent responsibility to act without any pregiven criterion. The excess of these figures lies less in the size and degree of their divergence from some criterion than in the responsibility that conceals itself precisely in the lack of such a criterion (*BSP* 179/207)

In a secularized era, the *humanitas* of man reveals excess and immeasurability to be the measure of all things; because of this, man must measure himself. This implies a *different ontological order*, a different status of what is. It is not without significance, for Nancy, that figures of genocide and other forms of extermination have become the semantemes or signifiers of modernity. Six million is, for example, inseparably linked with the six million victims of the Shoah. This number, six million, does not simply mean "a lot" or an "immeasurable amount." The figure is in itself not immeasurable and does not indicate that a specific limit has been transgressed. Furthermore, how do we measure the deaths of ten Jews, or the extermination of hundreds of thousands of Armenians? Rather than a sort of excess, this sort of figure indicates a specific order, a proper register of engagement and responsibility. Extermination is literally an exhaustion of numbers, the counting out of a people to its existence as a totality.

With this, Nancy indicates the modern tendency to posit the excess of numbers of our world population as an absolute fact, as something that exists fully in itself; consequently, he calls for another covenant of being. More precisely, excess is its own proper covenant. The world is measuring itself, that is, as excess; it forms the measure of an unheard-of measure. That the world measures itself means that it is engaged as a whole. Nancy gives the example of the Big Bang, which, for him, is not a matter of something very large but of a certain greatness (*grandeur*), in the sense of being its own measure. There is no measure against which the being of the Big Bang could be measured.

The magnitude that is its own excessive measure indicates at the same time the criterion for an absolute responsibility. Once we take the measure of the Big Bang, our responsibility for the universe is total and immeasurable. The Shoah, for example, is usually regarded as a form of excessive violence, but it no longer suffices to name the correct measure from which this excess would diverge. Responsibility must take on the posture of a similar excessiveness.

In this way, human beings receive their proper measure as an absolute, limitless responsibility. Such responsibility has no pregiven measure that would precede it. That is also indicated, for example, by the population explosion. The question is not only how many people the earth can sustain, it is also which people, and which existences. The grandeur of the number turns into a moral grandeur: "the size [*taille*] of humanity becomes indissociable from its dignity" (*BSP* 180/208).

Justice

The problem Nancy lays before us is how justice is to be thought in a secularized world that has become its own measure and is thus simultaneously without measure. This perspective leaves us open to an engagement without measure, and that constitutes our existence. Here we resume our opening question, that of *sense*. We saw that Nancy claims that it is no longer a question of whether the world has a meaning or makes sense, but that the world *is* meaning, is (as) sense. In the same way, the world in which we live no longer has a measure, but *is* measure. The new way of being demands a new covenant. Furthermore, the world itself becomes that which institutes what is just and what is not. Justice does not come into the world from outside—the world lacks nothing—and is not given as a fixed measure: a secularized world has no foundation or overall aim. The world is itself the sharing and the dividing of justice and injustice such that justice is no longer a matter of a "(theo- or socio-)dicy" or *dikē*, Nancy writes in *The Sense of the World*:

> "Neither *dikē* nor *dicy*": this is a call neither for despair nor for hope, neither for a judgment of this world nor for a "just world"— but for justice *in* this world, for justice rendered *unto* the world: that is, for resistance, intervention, compassion, and struggle that would be tireless and oriented toward the incommensurability of the world, the incommensurability of the totality of the singular outline, without religious and tragic remuneration, without sublation, and thus without discourse. (*SW* 148/225)

Precisely because *dikē* and *-dicy* have vanished, one needs a reflection on justice, sense, and world if one wants to think the secularization of the world. Something has appeared at the level of existence itself and could profoundly influence our view of justice. In light of this, "Cosmos Basileus" begins with a reflection on the unity of the world (*BSP* 185). For

Nancy, this unity or totality is not a whole but a co-existence that as such *is* not (has no substance), but that comes into being through the plural co-existence of singularities. This is why justice is that which must be awarded to every existence "according to its unique, singular creation in its coexistence with all other creations" (*BSP* 187). This is also why Nancy speaks of a total responsibility that, once there is no longer any single *-dicy* or *dikē* to measure or limit it, precedes all laws. In *The Experience of Freedom*, Nancy describes this total responsibility as "an established or prevailing 'just measure' in the name of the incommensurable" (*EF* 75/ 101). By this, Nancy understands the fact that our responsibility does not stem from a just measure or from a self that is responsible only for its own legal obligations. Archi-responsibility precedes all measures and laws and even exceeds every self. This does not mean that one has to bear, always and for all time, ontically, an unlimited responsibility, nor that political, moral, or juridical responsibility is not to be assessed in concrete situations. This assessment is also a responsibility, but once the measure for it is no longer given in advance by a *-dicy* or *dikē*, all assessment of responsibility already starts from this archi-responsibility.

The Day of Judgment

Nancy's strategy in his discussion of secularization and justice does not differ from the way he approaches other questions. He takes a number of already-existing motifs or concepts and gradually "unpacks" them, so as to introduce them into his own vocabulary with new meanings or changes in their meaning. His presupposition is that these concepts deconstruct themselves.

It is particularly interesting for the theme of the deconstruction of Christianity that, when Nancy discusses justice, the motifs he draws upon are frequently of religious origin: the day of judgment, being summoned or put on trial, the (second) coming, the absolute other. As in his treatment of the sense of the world, Nancy expands these religious motifs to existential matters, to the ontological conditions of possibility of existence. These conditions are central to his oeuvre in its entirety. Nancy's emphasis, in the context of justice as in all the other cases, is on the real multiplicity within which our existence takes place.

Existing, he emphasizes, consists not only in being open but also in being responsible. To be responsible means that we are always in relation to something. We are always already thrown into existence and must always answer for our existence. In this responsibility, we are judged because we come to appearance in the sharing that we are with and in respect to others. This structure of our responsibility and our being judged "simply" arises from the fact that we are *compearance* (Com 372/51).[4] We appear as *com*, and through this we are summoned by the co-existence that we must be. We advene, and such an arrival is never on its own but is always both a sharing and a dividing, that is, a shared and divided being singular plural. According to Nancy, we are always already exposed to existence, always already summoned. I am already responsible even before I assume my responsibility. I must always already answer for my existence. This archi-responsibility summons me; I am exposed to it as a result of co-existence. The day of judgment is thus not a final judgment but, as Nancy puts it in "La comparution/The compearance: From the Existence of 'Communism' to the Community of 'Existence,'" conveys one's being exposed to existence at every moment of every day:

> There would thus no longer be a court to which we should compear. However, we find ourselves still in judgment. The Day of Judgment—*dies irae*, the day of divine wrath—is no longer a day at all. . . . This day is thus an instant always in suspense, always a deferred judgment that cannot be appealed. This judgment (justly) reaches a verdict in the name of the *end*. This is not an End set up as an Idea on the horizon; it is rather how we approach our own *final* horizon and how we do (or do not do) justice to that horizon. This is a simple judgment, without appeal; it is not subject to any superior law [*droit*] for it proceeds from that which precedes law. Have we done right [*droit*] by that which still has no right? Right by our existence itself—or since this word is subject to misuse in the singular—by our existences, by their community? Before this law without law we have never ceased to compear. *In the end* we compear there naked. (Com 372/50–51)

Once again, co-existence is the central point of reference. Here too, Nancy begins from the radical idea that we can no longer think on the basis of any *-dicy*. With respect to justice, this means the bankruptcy of the idea of justice as a final settling of accounts: the undoing of all evil or injustice in an ultimate destination or aim. Such a conception of justice is, moreover, an indirect justification of today's evil and suffering. The ambition of such justice is infinite in the sense that its aim lies in an order beyond every finite order, whether as a transcendent *civitas Dei* or as the realization of a free society in the future.

In order to avoid thinking justice in the sense of an infinite *-dicy*, Nancy explicitly conceives of it on the basis of a finite order of existence. What one, in an infinite vision of society, still regards as a final judgment or ultimate destination is, in Nancy's thought, reduced to the ever-present and eternally arriving judgment within the finite horizon that is our existence. Indeed, not only has this infinite society become bankrupt, but the entities that formerly summoned us and functioned as the supreme law-giver, together with this society, have likewise lost their social ground and legitimacy.

One might say: to think as an atheist would thus also mean first and foremost being finished with every ontological foundation or principle that justifies evil. This is why Nancy speaks of a naked justice that no longer strives for the teleological sublation of all injustice in a society yet to come. The day of judgment takes place within the finite horizon of co-existence and is therefore always a judgment without a summoning entity (be it God, We, or the Other). This does not mean that henceforth all criteria for justice lie in me, in the sense of stemming from a literally autonomous subject that separates good from evil. If it did, Nancy would be just another defender of an accomplished humanity, whereas his critique is directed precisely against this position. Nancy grants theoretical primacy not to a law-making subject but to existence, to being exposed, to our appearance to and with others in the world.

Put differently, *nomos* is not the entity that founds the *autos* and its existence but, on the contrary, the law to which every *autos* is exposed. Such exposure means being summoned and judged, *hic et nunc*. Or again: there is no longer any theological judge before whom we must appear. *Dies irae*, the day of judgment, is not a day that could ever occur in history but the tribunal of co-existence before which we appear at every moment. Being exposed to co-existence is the law without law before which we continuously appear. The law without law is the command literally to do justice to the co-existence that is ours, a criterion before all criteria (Com 372/51; see *FT* 146/*ICa* 24 and *FT* 169/*ICa* 58). In responding to it, in the archi-responsibility in which we are always placed, we must do justice to existence, although it is never existence in general but always singular existences to which one does justice (or injustice). It is precisely by not reducing the law without law and co-existence to an ultimate (infinite) day of judgment that we do justice to a secular existence. Living in a secular world means living in a world that is sense, a world that has become responsible for itself but never closes in on itself.

Between All and Nothing

The Affective Dimension of Political Bonds

THEO W. A. DE WIT

An Ancient Value, Dissolving Like Smoke

A striking example of what Jean-Luc Nancy calls the (self-)deconstruction of Christianity was already given by Ernst Kantorowicz in 1951. In his article "Pro Patria Mori in Medieval Political Thought," he discusses a fundamental difference of opinion between two cardinals that occurred at the beginning of the Great War.[1] As Belgium was being occupied by German troops in the summer of 1914, Cardinal Mercier, the primate of Belgium, published a pastoral letter entitled "Patriotism and Endurance." In it, he defended the position that Belgians were justified in experiencing their patriotism as "consecrated" and the German violation of their national dignity as a kind of sacrilegious profanation. More specifically, his letter responded to a pastoral-theological question that had been put to him by a member of his flock, namely, whether a soldier who fell in the service of a just cause ("and that ours clearly is") should be regarded as a martyr or not. Mercier answered that a soldier who died arms in hand could not be termed a martyr in the theological sense of the word, for, after all, the Christian martyr does not resist his executioners. However, at the same time Mercier had no doubt that a soldier who, in order to avenge violated justice, laid down his life in honor of his fatherland could be assured of eternal salvation:

> The soldier who dies to save his brothers, to protect the hearths and the altars of his country, fulfils the highest form of love. . . . We are

justified in hoping for them the immortal crown that encircles the foreheads of the elect. For such is the virtue of an act of perfect love that of itself alone it wipes out a whole life of sin. Of a sinner it instantly makes a saint.

A few months later, Cardinal Billot, his French counterpart, responded with severe disapproval: "To say that the mere fact of dying consciously for the just cause of the Fatherland 'suffices to assure salvation' is to substitute the Fatherland for God . . ., to forget what God is, what sin is, what divine forgiveness is."[2] For Billot, positing any politico-theological link between God and fatherland, between the forgiving of sins and the imperative of patriotic duty, is *theologically* indefensible and therefore in need of a reprimand. *Dieu différent!*[3] Today's theologians would echo him, and many believers today, especially in Europe, would probably be inclined to view the positing of any link whatsoever between God and the political (dis)order—that which binds or separates us as citizens—as blasphemous, for we have, as Marcel Gauchet puts it, "in a metaphysical sense, become democrats."[4] The "end" of theologico-political thinking, Nancy stated in the early nineties, comes "from out of its own interior and out of its own past" (*SW* 92/146). All the same, even today Mercier's comforting words have not entirely lost their appeal, for perhaps he understood his besieged nation's feelings and needs somewhat better than had his French colleague.

For Kantorowicz, the cardinals' difference of opinion is cause for launching a historical investigation into the whole notion of *pro patria mori*. As he says, "if two eminent Princes of the Church disagree so profoundly on a fundamental matter of life and death, and of life after death, we may be sure that the reasons for such a basic disagreement are to be sought in a distant past and that the whole problem has a long history."[5] He shows that in Greek and Roman classical antiquity great esteem first came to be attached to the act of falling in the service of one's community—for *patria* here read "city" (*polis*), and all the city stood for. In feudal times, mainly as a result of the influence of Christianity, this notion of laying down one's life for the good of the city gradually lost its emotional and (semi)religious significance. Augustine already argues that Christians should fight and fall not for the sake of earthly fame but rather—as martyrs—for the invisible *patria eterna*, the heavenly Jerusalem. Only in the twelfth and thirteenth centuries did the temporal notion of *patria* (now framed in terms of national territory or kingdom) regain its emotional appeal, and thus, in a manner of speaking, return from heaven to earth. A precedent for the contrasting positions of Mercier's politico-theological link and Billot's theological reservations can be found in a much earlier debate, namely, whether participation in a crusade contributed to a crusader's salvation or not. Although the Council of Clermont (1095) clearly established that participation absolved a crusader from outstanding churchly penances (e.g., prescribed fasting, almsgiving, and prayers) but did not simply absolve him of all sin (*remissio peccatorum*), in political and churchly practice this distinction was effectively ignored. As a result, it was understood that any crusader who fell in defense of the Holy Land automatically gained martyr status and direct access to paradise.[6] In the early fifteenth century, at the height of this development toward an emotive valorization and sacralization of the fatherland (France constitutes the paradigm here: *la doulce France, Francia Deo sacra*), some authors even started to draw a parallel between the martyr's death or that of the crusader and the act of sacrificing one's life in defense of the *corpus mysticum* of the fatherland: both were regarded as acts rooted in love (*caritas*).

Kantorowicz concludes that both the positions of Mercier and Billot, each in its own way, therefore find vindication in tradition: Mercier's pastoral patriotism follows a long-established tradition of ecclesiastical and political thinking, whereas theological dogma is on Billot's side when he admonishes against the substituting the fatherland for God. Of most relevance to us, however, is Kantorowicz's concluding remark: "it may be left to the reader to figure out all the distortions which the central idea of the *corpus mysticum* has suffered by its transference to national, party, and racial doctrines in more distant and in most recent times."[7] As examples he mentions the "Tombs of the Martyrs" that the National Socialist Party erected in Munich and the gigantic banner proclaiming *Chi muore per Italia non muore* ("Whoever dies for Italy does not die") that was draped over the façade of the Milan cathedral as a backdrop to the 1937 Christmas service held in commemoration of the Italian Fascist divisions fallen in the Spanish Civil War.

For Kantorowicz, these "distortions," together with the progression of the "disenchantment of the world," signal that "the ancient ethical values, miserably abused and exploited in every quarter, are about to dissolve like smoke." Given the "cold efficiency" during and since the Second World War, on the one hand, and the fear of today's individual that he may fall into the trap of religio-ideological "illusion," on the other, it would seem that the days of the traditional religious and ideological "superstructure" are numbered. The result, Kantorowicz suspects, is that

> human lives (are) no longer (being) sacrificed but "liquidated." We are about to demand a soldier's death without any reconciling emotional equivalent for the lost life. If the soldier's death in action—

not to mention the citizen's death in bomb-struck cities—is deprived of any idea encompassing *humanitas*, be it God or king or patria, it will be deprived also of the ennobling idea of self-sacrifice. It becomes a cold-blooded slaughter or, what is worse, assumes the value and significance of a political traffic accident on a bank holiday.[8]

To reformulate Kantorowicz, I would describe as follows the new constellation to which he points: by instrumentalizing ancient traditional values (such as that of *pro patria mori*), the great twentieth-century totalitarian movements, which Walter Benjamin characterized as the "slave revolt of technology,"[9] made politically very relevant a certain theological or eschatological reservation that had always been present within Christianity. It is the reservation about a strong affinity or "cohesion" with political-military power. In the wake of the wholesale slaughter of two world wars, Europeans have learned from bitter experience that all bonds between religion and nationalism need to be severed and that churches should refrain from lending their weight to the exaltation, the "praising to the skies," of dying in war. In addition, an imperative to die for the fatherland, whereby a confrontation *ad mortem* with the enemy would become a prerequisite for eternal salvation, is inseparable from an imperative to kill for the fatherland.

But the loss of what Kantorowicz indicates as an "idea encompassing *humanitas*" also points to a void that had come into existence, one I would describe as the *loss of the affective dimension of society as political community*. Especially during the past few years, Western politics, both inside Europe and abroad, seems once more tugged back and forth between a bleak and defensive liberalism (Kantorowicz's "anti-ideological individual"), rational management, and a purely formal notion of citizenship, on the one hand, and, on the other, a longing for a (greater) sense of community and a turning toward what many see as the kind of populist, charismatic, and sacrificial politics that Eric Voegelin termed "political religion"—that is, toward the sacralization of collective identities such as state, nation, or race and the dissolution of self within them.[10] It is no coincidence that in many European countries today—not least of them my own, the Netherlands—an at times fierce debate is once more raging regarding the proper relationship between religion and politics, on the one hand, and, on the other, the bond between democratic citizenship, national identity, and loyalty.

As I will demonstrate, this problematic concerning the affective dimension of co-existence and the "communality" of the political community is also raised in a number of Nancy's texts—albeit framed in his own vocabulary. As a point of departure, I will take two texts in which this problematic is prominent. Both refer to notions of sacrifice and sacrificial logic—notions that, as Kantorowicz established in 1951, still persisted after the Second World War.[11] The first text, "Politics II," in *The Sense of the World*, dates from the early 1990s and offers a perspective on the linking of fundamental political concepts such as sovereignty, citizenship, community, and subject. The second text, "Church, State, Resistance," is more recent and is dedicated to the problematic of the (un)coupling of politics and religion.[12] In both texts he indicates a significant tension within traditional political thinking. The two texts are linked by a conviction derived in part from a remark by Gérard Granel, "the 1930s lie before us," meaning that they still remain possible—a dictum that eloquently expresses Nancy's enduring intellectual disquietude (*D* 3/11).[13] I will conclude by discussing Nancy's suggestion regarding a way out of the impasse to which dominant politics has given rise.

The Politics of Self-Sufficiency

A significant aporia in traditional political thinking comes into focus once one realizes that all known combinations of the four fundamental concepts of citizen, (metaphysical) subject, community, and sovereignty ultimately lead to various configurations of political autarchy or political self-sufficiency. This is Nancy's thesis in "Politics II," an intellectual exercise on the concept of the political written in 1993, that is, not long after the fall of the Berlin Wall and Fukuyama's proclamation of "the end of history."

Let us start with the concept of the citizen. The citizen is preeminently defined as someone who, invested with rights and duties, dignities and virtues, shares the public space (the space of the city, the polis) with other citizens. The "Greek" city, for example. comes across to us as something completely autotelic. The Aristotelian notion of citizenship is neither the expression of a more fundamental private sphere nor is it tied to what we may term a "nation." In this Greek political space, religion seems to have been relegated to the realm of the private or to the realm of the supra-civil. This type of citizenship is therefore formal, contractual, without "interiority," and already virtually global—in the same way that the French citizen of the French Revolution was conceived as also being international and cosmopolitan. At first glance, all of this seems diametrically at odds with a *politics of the subject*, which, according to Nancy, is "always religious politics" (*SW* 105/166). But precisely herein lies the ambiguity of the French Revolution: on the one hand, it broke with politico-theological tradition; on the other, it demarcated the beginning of secular theology (*théologie laïcisée*)—one of the people, of history, even of humanity—and therefore of politics in the modern sense, a politics of the subject and sovereignty. Typical of this secular religion is the appropriation of the constitutive exteriority of the city (the polis) in the function of a meaning, an identity or a substance that either precedes the political space of the city or constitutes its proper destiny, as may be expressed in terms of an organic people or a nation. Politics and citizenship thus become a way of self-becoming, an increasing revelation and unraveling of meaning, a movement into which politics needs to incorporate its own negativity, that is, become violent and sacrificial. In this conception, politics is therefore founded upon a preexisting bond, *one that is already given*. The bond may be constituted in originary violence but may just as well be that of the original fraternity, of "race," or of love.[14] Such a bond makes ex-istence superfluous, because essence is already given.[15]

While the *citizen* in the politics of the *subject* therefore comes to (re)-present definitive meaning, the conception of *community* changes from that of an inappropriable public space to an interiority in need of completion, whereby sovereignty becomes transformed from the simple indication of the autojurisdiction of a political unit into the highest expression of the essence of the community. In an article that Nancy wrote a few years earlier, following the first Gulf War, he discusses at length the most rigorous theory of sovereignty in this sense—that of Carl Schmitt, including its manifestly sacrificial logic.[16] War in this theory, Nancy concludes, is "the monument, the festival, the somber and pure sign of the community in its sovereignty" (*BSP* 122/148), in which the individual death of the citizen is sublimated into the destiny of the community. Indeed, it is no coincidence that Schmitt affirmatively quotes Emile Lederer's description of the day Germany mobilized in 1914 as "the moment in which society [*Gesellschaft*] revealed its essence as community [*Gemeinschaft*], as political unity."[17] In Nancy's summary: politics here brings about a final meaning, it "*must* be destiny, must have history as its career, sovereignty as its emblem, and sacrifice as its access" (*SW* 89/141). That this type of politics and sovereignty, partly rooted in Hegel,[18] has become sterile and exhausted in 1993 appeared to Nancy most clearly in the wars in the Balkans—wars in which "the communal" (*le commun*) was *being realized* by means of ethnic cleansing.

Yet Nancy does not intend to play formal citizenship, contractual community, and purely juridical sovereignty off against their appropriation by a politics of the subject, to counterpose the nothing of sovereignty as autojurisdiction to the all-absorbing sovereignty conceived by someone like Schmitt. On the contrary, he suspects that this nothing and all are fundamentally *related*, for both are (leftist or rightist) configurations of political self-sufficiency, of politics conceived as autarchy—one by means of the excessive realization of meaning in subjectivity, the other through atomization, whereby democracy remains an empty shell, devoid of *demos* and *kratein* (*SW* 108/170). Nancy fears that, as had happened in the 1930s, the latter could easily reverse into the former . . . Here we may also recall one of classical Marxism's critiques: in a world appropriated by a simultaneously powerful and empty "subject"—that of capital—a purely formal notion of citizenship becomes insufficient, forcing one to shut one's eyes to extreme inequality and injustice.

As we have seen, this tension between a "nothing" and an "all" is already present in Kantorowicz's concluding remark concerning the loss of ancient values such as that of *pro patria mori*. In the absence of any "idea encompassing *humanitas*" (which, especially in the twentieth century, leads to an all-devouring subjectivity), only a self-centered liberalism would seem to remain. Contemporary liberalism can conceive the act of falling in battle—and in a country such as the Netherlands this is bolstered by the abolition of conscription—only as the potential outcome of an individual choice of a high-risk profession. Such a death—one that might befall any Dutch, Canadian, or French soldier in the current war/ peacekeeping mission in Afghanistan, no longer has any real public significance. The oft-heard reaction "those guys have freely chosen it" is typical of a liberal society that no longer recognizes, or may not even be capable of comprehending, duty in any supra-individual form.[19]

The political community then approaches nothing, for it can have only an *instrumental* meaning for the individual, conceived as ideally living an autarchous life without any exposure to/within a community. Thomas Hobbes, undoubtedly one of the sources of this kind of liberalism, already clearly had difficulties in establishing a foundation for the traditional virtue of courage. After all, "the Obligation of Subjects to the Soveraign, is understood to last as long, and no longer, than the power lasteth, by which he is able to protect them. For the right men have by Nature to protect themselves, when none else can protect them, can by no Covenant be relinquished."[20] After all, Hobbes's entire philosophical construction of the state here seems to tumble into ruins, for when the state is in mortal peril, a calculating individual would feel no obligations toward this "failing" state.

The Longing to Celebrate Community

In a recent article on the (history of the) relationship between religion and politics, Nancy returns to this problematic of a tension or even dialectic between a "nothing" and an "all." Referring to the Roman example of a civil religion, that is, an attempt to conjoin the Greek tradition of democracy—essentially conceived as the domain of autonomy and of the free discussion of political matters pertaining to justice—with a religious dimension that would pertain to everyone, Nancy asks, "To which longing does this correspond?" In its very conception, the Aristotelian idea of democracy resists the idea of any regime of heteronomy, and thus of theocracy. And yet without some form of civil religion, politics seems destined to shrivel up into a mere matter of "administration" or "police" (CSR 105). Thus, for Marx emancipation from religion marks the onset of society's becoming autarchous in its emancipation from state and politics—things that are destined to wither away as soon as society realizes its immanent authenticity.

Schmitt also regarded this connection as valid, although that fueled his wish to defend both (Catholic) political theology in its nineteenth-century counter-revolutionary version and the state and the political (*das Politische*). "In a good world among good people [such as Marxian society once it had realized its authenticity], only peace, security, and harmony prevail," writes Schmitt. "Priests and theologians are here just as superfluous as politicians and statesmen."[21] This German jurist thus had a sharp intuition of the "death of God" (in the sense of an end to the politico-theological complex) that was in the offing. While Marx strove toward "nothing" (the autoproduction of society without religion and politics), Schmitt—after 1933, at any rate—defended an all-consuming sovereignty and a "total state" in which all is politics.[22]

Between these two extremes lies the regime with which Europeans today are most familiar, one that has probably found its clearest expression in France: the separation of the political and religious orders and their respective spheres of law. Nancy rightly points out that this heterogeneity of the two orders (or realms, cities, etc.) is rooted in Christianity and Jewish messianism—a heterogeneity at odds with national civil religion (as Cardinal Billot stated at the beginning of the First World War).

All the same, the call for a civil religion also recurs under modern conditions. Whereas an absolute monarchy derives its authority from itself (insofar as its political legitimacy is essentially independent of any religious endorsement) and the modern sovereign state may be termed profane and autonomous, civil religion in some form or another is needed to compensate for or to mend the weak point of the modern political bond. This weak point lies in the *instrumental* character of the social contract and the state. We have already seen it in the example of Hobbes's calculating citizen: the moment the state becomes unable to defend the citizen effectively, it ceases to be of any interest to him and may even cease to exist in his eyes. To sacrifice his life out of love for the political community would strike him as irrational, insofar as the natural right of self-preservation would have primacy over any ethical imperative based on natural law or virtue.

In "Church, State, Resistance" and elsewhere,[23] Nancy summarizes a series of attempts (most of which never got off the ground) to introduce an affective dimension into the heart of the modern "autonomous" political bond: Rousseau's *religion civile*, the *fraternité* of the French Revolution, Hegel's "love" as the principle of state, American civil religion, constitutional monarchies in a number of countries, Habermas's "constitutional patriotism" (*Verfassungspatriotismus*), but also philosophical concepts such as friendship, solidarity, and even responsibility and justice—all of which can never completely be stripped of some affective charge. Thus French *laïcité* has not only the negative meaning of repelling religious intervention in the political domain but, as is often argued,[24] also the positive one of a civil religion. Nancy's rejoinder to those who would detect a "vague fascism" in the whole notion of an observance and celebration of the values, symbolism, and signs of recognition that attest to everyone's adherence to the community is that the historical forms of fascism and communism indeed knew how benefit from modern democracy's "unutilized desire to celebrate community" (CSR 109). Even today it holds true that the state cannot be merely a space of tolerance.

Perhaps the current crisis of multiculturalism and of the culture of tolerance in Europe—especially in the Netherlands, until recently regarded as a small but stable stronghold of plurality and tolerance—constitutes the most spectacular example of what Nancy has in mind here. New populist and nationalist political parties and movements represent the desire to restore to democracy a national civil religion, or perhaps even a prepolitical national identity, which would go beyond merely integrating immigrants toward *incorporating* them. Here a politics of the unraveling of a "given bond," including the sacrificial logic necessary for its rescue or execution, is once more overwhelmingly present, and in two variants, in each of which one can easily discern one of the two twentieth-century totalitarian traditions distinguished by Nancy.[25]

The first variant is that of national authenticity or identity, in which the state is sometimes once more conceived and defended as an organism or a *corpus mysticum*. In its *defensive* nature (thus, e.g., in the title of Roger Scruton's article "In Defense of the Nation"), one can descry doubt in this nostalgia for self-presence without an "outside" (especially one without foreigners or aliens).[26] In the name of national unity, some politicians today even explicitly ask that certain civil liberties (such as religious freedom for the Muslim part of their populations) be sacrificed in order dialectically to rescue *freedom as social order*.[27]

The second variant is that of the rationalist and universalist politics of teleological unraveling. It has once more become visible in international politics, especially in the legitimation of the war against Iraq, which has been cast—for example by the Bush administration—in terms of a "peaceful expansion of Western Reason, using its police forces to combat, contain, and convert the many Empires of Evil."[28] It concerns a rationalistic liberalism that once again (like communism in the past) provides reason with a historico-philosophical narrative. Stanley Fish succinctly describes the problem this "liberal orthodoxy" runs up against. "Liberalism," he writes:

> requires a universal enemy so that its procedures of inclusion and exclusion can be implemented in the name of everyone. If, however, there is no universal enemy but only enemies (mine or yours), procedures will always be invoked in the name of some and against some others. The unavailability of a universal enemy is something liberal thinkers are always running up against. They respond typically either by just stipulating someone's enemy as universal . . . or by giving up the attempt to identify an enemy and regarding everyone as potentially persuadable to the appropriate liberal views.[29]

It now also becomes clear why some, in reaction to this hunt for "the enemy of humanity," think back longingly—just like Schmitt—to the "classical" (state-centered) concepts of friend and enemy, and therefore also to the classical politics of the subject.[30]

A Heteronymous Affect in Politics and Society

These topical examples emphasize how difficult it is for us to conceive of politics, struggle, and community without some aspect of unraveling or completion (*finition*) in an essence or destiny—that is, to dispense with all religious or secular political-theological schemes. And yet this is exactly what Nancy proposes: taking seriously an important rupture in our history, for "we are in the midst of a shift [*déplacement*] that is suspending the dominant meanings of our culture, and which is simultaneously a loss and a new beginning" (RM 5).

Although, as we have seen, he recognizes the affective dimension of the political bond and "the longing to celebrate community," Nancy does not advocate the political adoption of some kind of civil religion—he is skeptical about the idea of even a "moderate" version. Nancy defends the separation of church and state: there should be no appropriation of the state by an existing religion, nor any politics that would appropriate the gathering (*rassemblement*) of social affect, no politics that, in the words of the German philosopher Hermann Lübbe, would carry out an act of "legitimatory self-service."[31] Rather, says Nancy, we must reconceive "the affect according to which we co-exist" (CSR 109).

Nancy's position with regard to a longing for community within modern democracy is novel, for he does not defend any secular or religious civil religion, or any variant on the "communitarian" style of thinking,[32] nor does he advocate a liberalism that would prefer to relegate everything "affective"—especially the religious impulse—to the private sphere in favor of the monopoly of reason. His position is, moreover, subtle, for, in order to ensure that politics does not shrivel up into mere technocratic control, he seems to regard as necessary a certain heteronomy or transcendence *within* (autonomous) politics. This is, for instance, evident in a remark in "Church, State, Resistance," where he states that democracy "at birth" is both too Christian and not Christian enough: "too Christian" for having accepted the separation of the two realms too completely; "not Christian enough" for failing to rediscover within its own secular realm the "power of affect," despite recurrent indications that restricting the political order to managing the useful and rational is untenable (CSR 110). According to Nancy, we become fully aware of the current constellation and the risks we face only once we realize that secular democracy's opposite pole—the Christian *ecclesia*, the religious "realm"—has a tendency to dissolve itself as social religion, and thus as religion tout court, thereby tending to take with it all other religions. Once the tension or mutual resistance between religion and politics threatens to disappear, either one can tend to become fanatical and to absorb the other. Once more all surfaces as an answer to nothing, to the emptiness of democracy or a culture of tolerance. In *Dis-enclosure*, Nancy, somewhat like a contemporary Cassandra, sounds a warning against a "(sur-)religious threat" (D 3ff/11ff). For my part, I think the threat of nationalist or populist "immanence" in Europe is far greater.

Nancy's texts on this theme extend a continuous and sometimes—as after 9/11—heartwrenching plea to refrain from bandaging the "wound" (the exhaustion of the thought defined by the One and by a unique destination of the world) with "the usual tatters of worn-out finery: god and money, petrol or muscle, information or incantation, which always ends up signifying one form or another of all-powerfulness and all-presence" (CC 24/15). To Nancy's list I would have liked to add "culture," in the emphatic, polemical sense it has assumed since 9/11. The rhetoric concerning culture has been summarized and criticized by Wendy Brown: "We [the superior West] *have* culture, while culture has 'them,'" meaning nonliberal, barbarian peoples; or "we are a democracy, while they are a culture."[33]

For Nancy, instead of trying to avert these old or new "finalities," we must, as he states in "The Confronted Community," come to terms with our nihilism and take our departure from it from within this nihilism itself. In that essay, he pleads for preventing the (always heteronymous) affect to which we are exposed in that co-existence that constitutes our condition from changing over into new, violent affirmations of the omnipotence and omnipresence of a familiar "fool's gold." Looking back on the important motif of the community in the thinking of Georges Bataille and Maurice Blanchot, as well as in his own, Nancy talks of the "uncoupling of the political and being-in-common [*l'être en commun*]," an uncoupling with which Bataille had come to terms in his thinking after the Second World War (CC 29/34). The separation of church and state in a politico-philosophical sense thus implies that the state is no longer the destination or expression of the community or the people, while this community or people should no longer be conceived as a substance or a value in itself with any such (Christian) connotations as fraternity and the spiritual kinship it may imply.

Nancy points out a double tendency, both for the homogeneous "people" that supposedly found its destination in the nation-state to disappear and for the rise of the civil society that relativizes the state (CC 29n5/34n).[34] This undermines the traditional doctrine of *pro patria mori*. In a book analyzing what she refers to as the current struggle with the boundaries between territoriality, sovereignty, and citizenship, Seyla Benhabib notes that since 2003 a considerable number of the American soldiers who have fallen in Iraq would not, for lack of the necessary documents, have been eligible to vote in the United States.[35] These soldiers therefore fell without having been citizens, for a country that could not be called their *patria*, in a war that was not even being called a war, but a noble-minded mission serving democracy and security. It would hardly be possible to think of a better example of the self-undermining and deconstruction of this ancient value.

The Secret We Share

But once they have been decoupled and separated, how do politics and being in common (*être en commun*) relate to one another in their mutual resistance? This seems to be the model according to which Nancy conceives of politics and community: an affective and therefore heteronymous dimension active in both spheres, but without the subordination or instrumentalizing of either pole by the other. This also implies a new modesty with regard to politics: not all is politics; politics is but one aspect of co-existence (*être en commun*), for Nancy, especially the aspect pertaining to power and justice. To some extent, in "The Confronted Community" Nancy also raises the question of their precise relationship when he asks about the relationship between the two parts of Blanchot's essay *The Unavowable Community*, in which Blanchot responds to his *The Inoperative Community*.[36] Whereas the first part of the essay reflects upon and reacts to Nancy's philosophical study of community, the second part treats Marguerite Duras's novel *The Malady of Death*.[37] Is there any point of intersection between these two parts—and therefore between the experience of community in the sociopolitical order and that in the order of love and intimacy, a point of intersection that Blanchot himself indicates with the term "inavowable [*inavouable*]," "not to avow or to name"? Nancy writes that, at some point it would be advisable "to conceive the enigma of intensity, of eruption and of loss, or abandonment, which allows simultaneously plural existence (birth, separation, opposition) and singularity (death, love). But the unavowable is always entailed in birth and death, love and war" (CC 33/46–47).

At the beginning of the second part of his essay, Blanchot ties the two parts of his diptych together. Here he discusses the "sovereignty" of the "people" or—perhaps a better term—of the masses, which are neither the state nor the fabric of society but rather the "instinctive refusal to accept any power."[38] Blanchot gives an example of this type of sovereignty of the people. The first sections of his second part are entitled "May 1968" (also for Nancy the beginning of a new way of co-existence[39]) and "Presence of the People." He draws his example from that time: the masses are described as an "immobile, silent crowd . . . gathered . . . to walk in procession for the dead of Charonne." They are "a power supreme, because [they] included, without feeling diminished, [their] virtual and absolute powerlessness."[40]

The masses, then, are aware that "sovereignty is nothing"—in Bataille's phrase, so often quoted by Nancy.[41] This seems the essence to me. In Nancy's own words: the "grandeur" of the "we" is precisely that "it is condemned never to find *its own* voice" (CC 32/45).

Perhaps herein also lies an answer to the question of how we today may honor the fallen in our wars that are no longer wars (such as that in Afghanistan): through a gesture of a society of co-existing singularities, of masses, rather than through contemporary politics' ever more hollow-sounding avowals of security, progress, and humanity.

Naturally, Blanchot continues in his essay, a gulf exists between this powerlessness of the people and the "antisocial society" of friends and beloved, between *sovereignty* and *intimacy*.[42] But they also have some characteristics that bring them together. If it is possible to state of the masses or the people that they may be equated, in the words of Régis Debray, with the "arid solitude of anonymous forces," then one may also note that "this is precisely what justifies comparison with what Georges Bataille has called 'the true world of lovers'": "the unfelt, uncertain torment of those who, having lost the 'intelligence of love' (Dante), however still want to tend toward the only beings whom they cannot approach by any living passion."[43] The heteronymous affect that takes possession of us is indeed excessive, and Nancy thinks this affect as an exposure to its own limit.

By way of conclusion, I would like to add that among the instrumentalizations and sacrificial schemes that have marked our history, the heteronymous affect made possible the horrors of the 1930s. Yet sharing the secret of a world that exists "for no reason," that, no longer the handiwork of a God or a secular subject, has become sovereign in itself, holds the potential to prevent a repetition or even a destructive surpassing of these horrors, though not by disavowing the heteronymous affect, and most certainly not by subjecting it to a new (global) giver of meaning. What would the departing from nihilism "from within" that Nancy advocates actually mean? In a few texts in which Nancy reflects on Nietzsche's diagnosis of nihilism and how it may be overcome, he establishes that a number of Nietzsche's phrasings still bear a religious character and attest to a sacrificial logic. Thus the antinihilist and Anti-Christ in Nietzsche appears as some kind of messianic figure who has come to deliver us from nihilism—a religious will that has come to save us from religion (*religion salvatrice de la religion*). Nihilism may thus be viewed as a "sacrificial nihilism, the matter of Nietzsche's entire sacrificial dramatology" (ZA 863).[44] We therefore must transcend nihilism without delivering ourselves from it, complete it without transitioning out of it and thus relapsing into recourse in a (willing) subject and a sacrificial logic. "TO ESTABLISH A SENSE [EINEN SINN HINEINLEGEN]," as Nietzsche's capitalized phrase would have it,[45] would then have to be uncoupled from any thought referring to a subject of power, the creator of a world, an end to history, and also from the destruction or production of "nonsense" (as in contemporary funda-mentalism) or "nothing"—in short, uncoupled from any "finality [*fin, but*]."[46] "Sense," or its opposite, would even cease to be something in which man can "believe," becoming instead something that happens un-ceasingly in our affectively charged exposure to the existence we share.

—Translated by Schalk van der Merwe

PART II

Monotheism, God

Intermezzo

In the previous part of this book, the deconstruction of Christianity has been presented as an analysis of the complex relation between modern culture and religion. As Nancy carries it out, this analysis is not simply a form of "deconstructive activity"—deconstruction as a means to investigate an object—but an examination of Christianity's self-deconstruction. The interplay between religion and modernity brings to the fore a dynamic of self-deconstruction, in which both are involved in a constant process of "turning away from themselves" and "leaving themselves behind." This retreat from self, Nancy suggests, may be a movement that is as such Christian, though it has been intensified by modernity. If so, the paradigm of secularization becomes problematic.

In the second part of this book, contributors treat the way in which Nancy connects the theme of the self-deconstruction of Christianity with a broader focus on the meanings of monotheism and of the monotheist God. Self-deconstruction, according to Nancy, is a central aspect of monotheism. The standard interpretation of monotheism, a key structure, though in quite different forms, of the so-called Religions of the Book, is that God constitutes himself as a single, unique presence, eliminating the "old, other gods" of polytheism. By contrast, in Nancy's view, the oneness and unicity of God consist in the paradoxical fact that such a god "absolutely excludes its own presentation" (*D* 41/62–63). Nancy mentions several examples of the way this strange "God without being"—to invoke the expression by Jean-Luc Marion—has been shaped: in Judaism, as the one who is in exile and diaspora or who has retreated from his creation; in Christianity, as the one who incarnated himself in the human world, becoming human, or who is fragmented as the three-in-one of the Trinity; or, in Islam, especially in its mystic traditions, as the one who has infinitely withdrawn himself, having no equal and being the absolutely distant God, forbidding any image of himself. Hence, Nancy states that, since the monotheistic God interrupts any thinking of presence and being in the onto-theological sense, while identifying the "presence" of divinity with absence and disappearance, monotheism is an atheism.

Starting from these new analyses of monotheism, Nancy's deconstructions show how the place of God has become an ambivalent topos precisely because of this monotheistic heritage. In monotheism the place of God, or "divine place(s)," as Nancy analyses this notion in "Of Divine Places," an earlier text that, in a way, paved the way toward the later project of a deconstruction of Christianity, is left "wide open, and vacant, and abandoned" (DP 137/33). The contributors to Part II raise the question of what the connection can be between this general theme of the empty place of God and the modern, secular condition. Moreover, this question will be connected to the way Nancy embeds his account of "Christian atheism" and of the "atheist God" in an interpretation of the themes of the incarnation and of kenosis, to be found throughout Nancy's works pertaining to the deconstruction of Christianity. Here, the relation between Judaism and Christianity will be a focal point as well.

First, Hent de Vries analyzes the paradoxical topos of the monotheist God as a place where his only gesture and only "language" can be that of the *wink*, the "nod": before any logic of being and nonbeing, presence and absence comes into play. He gives an extensive reading of "Of Divine Places" and of the way Nancy enters into dialogue with Hölderlin and Heidegger. De Vries demonstrates that the analysis of the divine topos in monotheism should involve an analysis of modernity, of modern art and poetry, and of the way they stand in monotheism's legacy.

Laurens ten Kate pursues this analysis by stressing the importance of the "Mosaic distinction," introduced by Jan Assmann, for a deconstruction of monotheism. He shows how this distinction is at the same time a connection or relation, entangling presence and absence, and offers a reading of some texts in *Dis-enclosure* that, continuing the path of "Of Divine Places," rearticulate the ambivalence of the divine topos as a place of the *wink* and of passage.

Frans van Peperstraten then asks whether the way monotheism deconstructs itself in this topos belongs to the composite character of all monotheistic religions, or is, rather, a specific feature of Christianity and its doctrine of incarnation. Opposing Nancy's thought to that of Jean-François Lyotard, he discusses the relation between Judaism and Christianity, basing himself on a reading of the chapter "The Judeo-Christian" in *Dis-enclosure*. At the end of his analysis, van Peperstraten explores the proximity of Lyotard's concept of estranged *aisthēsis* and Nancy's concept of inadequate praxis.

Donald Loose concludes this part with a discussion of the view of and relation to the absolute, to the nothing that is characteristic of monotheism, on the one hand, and modernity, on the other. Loose observes the continuity as well as the differences here, asking whether the modern transgression and exceeding of the self by the self as a self-critique and rational critique (Kant) and the self-deconstruction of monotheism are not an excess of the same movement. If this is so, then a radical critique of transcendence and of religion, as articulated by Nancy in his deconstruction of monotheism, is nevertheless linked to the given figure and the complex historical assemblage (*D* 149/216) of religion. Does a certain return to such a given religion and its history—despite Nancy's resistance in this regard (*D* 1/9)—not form an unavoidable part of deconstruction as its first and lasting condition of possibility?

—*Laurens ten Kate*

Winke

Divine Topoi in Nancy, Hölderlin, and Heidegger

HENT DE VRIES

> . . . und Winke sind
> Von Alters her die Sprache der Götter . . .
>
> **Friedrich Hölderlin, "Rousseau"**

That Hölderlin's poetry revolves around certain notions of the divine, of gods, and of the holy is almost a commonplace, though it does so in a manner very different from the discourses on the coming god familiar from the Romantics through the later Heidegger.[1] The notion of the divine is often introduced in Hölderlin in a language that invokes topological images, theophanic heavens, and semigodly rivers, each of which seems to mark a specific manifestation or presence that is at once ineluctable and elusive, inscribed on the face of the earth and the sky but also "immediate" in an utterly undialectical and nonidealistic sense of this word. This immediacy does not let itself be reduced to that of mere empirical reference, biographical detail, or material inscription. Such refusal is obvious in that it finds no better expression than in the figure of the "nod," the signal or gesture of the *Winke*. Hölderlin says that this figure has from early on (*Von Alters her*) been the language of the gods (*die Sprache der Götter*). This phrase and the constellation it evokes cast surprising light on the problem of divine names—or the lack thereof—that pervades the history of Western philosophy, apophatic theology, and mysticism. Hölderlin's poetry, in ways all too often overlooked by many of its most insightful readers, in the first place Heidegger, liberates the question "What is God?" (*Quid est deus?*) from the dilemmas of linguistic ineffability, of the sayable and the unsayable, and reorients our thought—our gaze, to be precise—in more than one direction at once. In what follows, I will attempt to substantiate this hypothesis by establishing an interpretative context for a few relevant lines, taken from "What is God?" and "In Lovely Blueness . . . Blossoms."

Of Divine Places

First published in a Festschrift entitled *What Is God?*, Nancy's "Of Divine Places" prepares the ground for his later project of the deconstruction of Christianity by rethinking the monotheist God as a *passing*, "winking" God—a rethinking that refuses any positive answer to the question "What is God?" and that, in fact, problematizes this question altogether. In that essay, Nancy engages the question of whether—and, if so, where—there is still a place for the divine, for its experience and its "presence." This question opens an inquiry into the concepts, the names, the tropes, and the topoi of the divine, one quite different from most other discourses about difference and the "Other," which often reduce this problem to that of linguistic insufficiency or ineffability. These apophatic discourses—ranging from Pseudo-Dionysius, to Meister Eckhart and Angelus Silesius, to the atomistic premises that led to the conclusion of Wittgenstein's *Tractatus Logico-Philosophicus* and beyond—presuppose another, more challenging suspension, retreat, or dispersion, one that Nancy pursues across his essay's fractured topology. In fact, "Of Divine Places" is nothing less than an attempt to elucidate and to situate a historial and epochal displacement that resembles a relentless *Dei paralysis progressiva.*[2]

It has often been claimed that in the modern epoch the question and the naming of the divine takes the form of an ongoing reduction, a continuous process of erosion, a *reductio perennis*. This process, Nancy writes, has irrevocably diffused the divine, well beyond the scattering of the deity and the gods as separate and significant entities, whether immortal, eminent, or infinite:

> "God," the motif or theme of God, the question of God, no longer means anything to us. Or else—as is all too obvious to an unbiased eye—what the theme of God might mean to us has already moved or been carried entirely outside of him. Is there any statement about the divine that can henceforth be distinguished, strictly speaking, from another about "the subject" (or its "absence"), "desire," "history," "the other" [*autrui*], "the Other," "being," "speech," "the

sublime," "community," and so on and so forth? It is as if "God" were in fragments, an Osiris dismembered throughout all of our discourse (indeed there are those who will now continue to speak of the divine in terms of explosion, dispersal, suspension, etc.). As if the divine, God, or the gods formed the common name or place— common and as such erasable, insignificant—of every question, every exigency of thought: wherever thought comes up against the furthest extreme, the limit, against truth, or ordeal, in short, wherever it thinks, it encounters something that once bore or seems to have borne, at one time or another, a divine name. (DP 112/3–4; trans. modified)[3]

Distanced from everything else, from beings and Being—even, as it were, from "itself"—the religious and theological notion of "God" loses all specificity and thereby all relevance:

Far from being rediscovered, God disappears even more surely and definitively through bearing all the names of a generalized and multiplied difference. Monotheism dissolves into polyatheism, and it is no good asserting that this polyatheism is the true word and the true presence of God in his distance from the supreme Being of metaphysics. For the infinitely absent god . . . should no longer be termed "God," nor be presented in any way as "God" or as divine. . . . There is no theology that does not turn out here to be either ontological or anthropological—saying *nothing about the god* that cannot immediately be said about "the event," about "love," about "poetry." (DP 113/4)

On the one hand, this implies that the language of "modernity" subtracts the privilege of speaking of "the Other, the Infinitely-other, the Other-infinite" from the jurisdiction of theology: the proper negativity of our present and future thoughts seems to enable us to address the "*absconditum*" (DP 113/5) that was formerly reserved for esoteric discourse alone. And yet, on the other hand, this secularization or, rather, becoming-exoteric of the absolute places thought in a paradoxical situation. Nancy describes this aporia in no uncertain terms:

In baptizing our abysses with the name of God, we are guilty of at least two errors or incoherencies: we fill in the abysses by attributing a bottom to them, and we blaspheme . . . the name of God by making it the name of *something*. On the other hand, the most subtle— and most theological—error would doubtless consist in *believing* that the infinite cannot provide a bottom and that naming a person [for example, "God"] is not naming a sort of "thing." (DP 113/5)

Not only does this aporia belong to the very nature of theological discourse, but its slippage and, indeed, blasphemy are as old as Western thought. Here, we encounter the unavoidable and, in a sense, transcendental illusion of all discourse, whether written or oral. The word and the notion *god* is always accompanied by a dual temptation: the seduction to baptize all experiences of the limit of our world with a divine name, and the desire to protect this name and the obscurity of our experience from idolatry and superstition. This double yet incoherent allegiance to two types of naming, of ascription and of apophasis, cannot be resolved as long as one continues to move within the horizon of reference, that is, of positive and negative attribution alone. If "god," as Nancy insists, is neither "a manner of speaking" nor some "ultimate truth of mankind" (DP 142/40), then the uses and abuses of this name—which is not a concept, a term, or a figure, properly speaking—are no longer governed by any semantics or metaphorics.

Given the inconsistencies of any discourse *on* or *about* God (*de Deo*), whether ontotheological or not, whether coming *from* God or not, it clearly no longer suffices to ask: "What is God, if He is?" The question *Quid est deus?* could very well "turn out to be the surest means of falling short of the question (if indeed it is a question, if it still hides or still reveals a true question), for God has perhaps become everything (or nothing); perhaps he has become, potentially at least, every true question, exigency, or furthest extreme of thought" (DP 114/5–6). Instead, "Of Divine Places" emphasizes the question of *place* and *space*, with a remarkable turn of thought and an intensity that at once seems close to Heidegger's thought of the site (of the *Ort*, the *Erörterung*, as well as the *Situation* of which *Being and Time* speaks) and moves far beyond the confines of the thinking of (*Andenken*) as well as the prerogative of (the one) Being. Writing of divine places, Nancy interrogates the being one, the being indivisible, of the place and the determination of whatever place or space as a site of gathering Being and beings, divinities and mortals, heavens (the sky) and Earth. Thus, rather than asking whether or what "god" *is* or *names*, we should, Nancy claims, raise the more central question: "*If there is a place* for god, if there is still room [*place*] for him: that is, a place where he does not become indistinguishable from something else, and where it is consequently still worth calling him by the name of *God* . . . could we then in fact be dealing with a question of place, of distinct location [*lieu*] and not with a question of being?" (DP 114/6). The very title "Of Divine Places" thus stands for a fragmentary and partial, indeed *local* and *topical*, exploration of the gods and their places; of the places they have abandoned and of those where they hide; of gods without hearth or home, of nomadic gods; of the *here* where the gods are *also*; of the common places of God; of the gods common to all places, to some places, to no place; of God: in what way he is *topos*; topics and atopics of the divine; of gods and places: treatise on divine paronomasia; where is God to be found? in what place? (DP 114/6)[4]

For all the subtlety of his rephrasing of a traditional question, Nancy retains, if not the question *quid est*, then at least the form of the question and of questioning as such. Here, the question "Where, if anywhere?" (or "Is there any place, somewhere, where . . .?") is substituted for—takes the place of—the ontological interrogation "What is *X* in its very essence and existence?" Remarkably, Nancy refrains from putting into question the principle of identity in this context. The very exclusion of a third possibility beyond the alternative *X* or not *X* (*tertium non datur*) regulates the basic assumptions on which "Of Divine Places" is based. For the notion "god" to be meaningful and not a mere *flatus vocis*, an empty word or sound, it should, Nancy maintains, have some *differentia specifica*, some distinctive feature. This is not to say that the word *god* should have a stable semantic reference (it has none), nor that one ought to be able first to answer the question of God's existence and essence by proving that and how the substance called "divine" must of necessity have all perfect properties and can therefore, by implication, be said to exist eminently. Clinging to the principle of identity—that the notion and word *god* must refer to some "presence" *here and now* in order to make sense at all, that "god" is either "god" or "not-god," without there being any third possibility—Nancy rephrases the traditional questions of whether "god" exists (*an sit*) and, if so, what he is in essence (*quod sit*) by introducing the more topical and timely question of *where* he is, not in fact but, again, in essence (*quo sit*). To ask where and *when* his essence can be said to exist comes down, Nancy asserts, to posing the question of "how he withdraws from existence, how he *is* not where we expect him to be" (DP 133/29).

In the same vein, Nancy reiterates in his essay "The Calculation of the Poet" that: "The god is only the place [*Le dieu n'est que le lieu*], the place is the place of departure and return, of the coming that withdraws and thus makes sense" (CP 63/76). Far from cultivating a Romantic imagery, far from nostalgic and irresponsible desire for lost or coming gods, to read Hölderlin *here and now* means paying attention to the metric precision with which in his writing what is without measure is captured. Nancy formulates it almost apodictically: "Poetry: material calculation of this atheistic passage" (CP 63/76). One might wonder, of course, why, if the name *God* can no longer be taken to refer to the highest or the supreme Being, the first cause of all as well as of himself—*causa prima* and *causa sui*—this notion and the very "presence" that it evokes should be distinguishable from something else at all. Why should there be a specific difference where, precisely, a certain indelible sublime indifference vis-à-vis finite differentiations is at stake? How, in other words, could one not sacrifice the specificity of God, even or precisely while one claims to speak *to* him, *about* him, let alone *away from* him and *without* him? Is not this what the *à dieu*, the invocation or denial of an absolute witness as the condition of all claims to truth, to truthfulness—in short, of all utterances made in good *and* bad faith—expresses economically and provocatively? Why should presence at or in a certain locus or locution provide the divine with a distinctive feature or a discriminatory marker? Would not a confusion and transgression that is always possible—an idolatry or blasphemy—constitute "God's" or "the god's" unpredictable occurrence, if and wherever he (or it) occurs? Is not every epiphany characterized by a transposition that in its very *transcendere*—in its movement upward *and* downward, in its *transascendance* and *transdescendance*, to cite Emmanuel Levinas, who in the opening pages of *Totality and Infinity* cites Jean Wahl's *Treatise on Metaphysics*—retains something (of the) undecidable? It is on both sides of the same line at once, as if this line, which is supposed to set apart not only the finite and the infinite but also two different forms or experiences of the infinite, were in itself infinitely divided. That is to say, it is not divided in any determinable measure or randomly but by being haunted at any given point by a necessary possibility of the intervention of chance.

Instead, in "Of Divine Places" Nancy recalls the Hölderlinean motif of the lack of holy or divine names, here and now, in this place, where we are, and opposes it to the at bottom metaphysical preoccupation with the inexpressible, the ineffable, the unsayable beyond any ontic or ontological determination, *epekeina tes ousias*, beyond essence. In our days, Nancy writes, "God" is not

> unnameable in the metaphysical sense of that being that is inaccessible to all names . . . including the name of being itself, according to an unbroken tradition that is the very tradition of ontotheology. God is not unnameable in that sense, because in that sense unnameability is the result of an overflowing of names and language, whereas the unnameability of the god to whom I address myself (if I can) results from *the lack of a name*. . . . There is no impotence on

the part of names in general to express or refer to God (just as, conversely, the unnameable is neither necessarily nor exclusively divine. . . . In fact it could well be that the "unnameable" is never divine, and that the divine is always named—even if it is *for want of a name*. (DP 117–18/10; my emphasis)

Nancy alludes to the last strophe of Hölderlin's elegy "Homecoming"— "es fehlen heilige Namen [holy names are lacking]"—a classic topos for the retreat and want of the divine name. Heidegger also traverses this topos in his exegeses or elucidations of Hölderlin's poetry, or rather— more emphatically—*Dichtung*.[5] Neither Nancy nor Heidegger reads this lack against the background of the tradition of negative theology.[6] The apophatic way, Nancy suggests somewhat surprisingly, was always more obsessed with the difficulty of using *concepts* rather than the singular designators called *names* when speaking of God, of his hyperessentiality, or, more precisely, his abode. He holds that the lack of which (or from which) Hölderlin speaks in "Homecoming" cannot be interpreted as a merely empirical—historical, cultural, biographical, or even linguistic— absence, as if names were lacking in the sense of not or no longer being ready at hand (or *vorhanden*):

No doubts are cast, in Hölderlin, on the possibility of divine names. On the contrary, the assertion of a lack of sacred names implies that we know what such names are—names, as Heidegger's commentary puts it, "which are commensurate with the sacred (or the holy) and which themselves cast light upon it." These names are thus not only proper to the divine, they bring it to light, they make it known as the divine that it is. These names are the manifestation of the divine, they are thus perhaps not far from being the divine itself. It is simply . . . that these names, here and now, are lacking. (DP 118/11; trans. modified)

I will argue that this lack is not a loss or negativity that would make itself available to a dialectics and thus—Nancy assumes, following a long tradition of engagement with Hegelianism—to metaphysical substantialization or ontologization. Hölderlin's thought here—as it can be read through the prism of Nancy's *theotopography*—is less nostalgic, classicist, or Romantic mourning than a mourning that is impossible and, in that sense, a paradoxical affirmation. In order to demonstrate this claim, let me first sketch the horizon from (within) which Nancy departs.

The Failing God: Heidegger's Reading of Hölderlin

In "The Lack of Holy Names," published in the 1974 *Denkerfahrungen* (*Experiences in Thinking*), Heidegger illustrates the Hölderlinean notion of the *Fehl*, or "want," in heavily charged sentences that—at least typographically, in their very verse form—are reminiscent of poetic prose, of a writing that neither is philosophy strictly speaking nor, in its aspiration to further thought, claims to be *Dichtung* in the limited, let alone the Hölderlinean sense. If *Dichten*, "to poeticize," and *Denken*, "to think" (and, let us not forget, *Danken*, "to thank") go hand in hand, they nonetheless belong to distinguishable spheres and follow different regimens. According to Heidegger, a situation of need and distress, namely, the persistent deferral of the divine, solicits the poet's utterance: "What urges the poet into [his] Saying, is a distress. It hides itself in the deferral of the presence [or presencing] of the divine." This need insinuates itself throughout Hölderlin's mature and late poetry and is expressed in his at once "simple," "illuminating," and "mysterious" word. Heidegger holds this to be how "holy names are lacking." He hastens to point out, however, that only those who are granted an insight (*Einblick*) into the "experience" of the "origin" (*Herkunft*) of this lack can understand its singular meaning (*das Eigentümliche*). That origin lies concealed in a "reserve" (*Vorenthalt*) of the "Holy." In Hölderlin's universe, Heidegger surmises, the "reserve" of the Holy and ultimate meaning of Being withholds itself and thus (but why and how, precisely?) holds us mortals back from access to holy names or (which is hardly the same) from appropriately naming this divine.[7] For Heidegger, to make or write poetry—that is, *Dichten*—is to let oneself be addressed by the pure call of the presencing of Being, which gives itself only *in* and *as* its retreat and thus never without reservation: "To poeticize—this means here: to let oneself be said the pure call of presence [or presencing] as such, and be it only and first of all a presence [or presencing] of withdrawal and reservation."[8] In so doing, poetry is at odds with the primacy of "method" in the technological age. *Dichtung* forges a path, leads the way forever underway toward a "clearing." It proceeds, as it were, without "procedure" (*Verfahren*), without "proof" and without "mediation" (*Vermitteln*).[9] Only the thought that follows this path, which has the character rather than merely the form of the path, can hope to prepare the "experience of the lack" (the *Fehl*) and thus help the poet—the sole figure who can and must put this lack into words through his saying (*sagen*)—to understand. Not that it helps him make the distress and the necessity—the *Not*—of the lack intelligible or understandable. Instead, it helps him to exist in or, rather, to *stand out* and *stand through* the *Not*. This happens in an original and originary sense: the poet's *ausstehen* of *die Not* concerns first and foremost the earliest and primal *Not*, that of the forgetfulness (*Seinsvergessenheit*) and the self-concealment (*Sichverbergen* or *Lethe*) of Being. This self-concealment is the proper feature of Being's presence or essence (its essencing or *Anwesen*) and the "source" or "domain" from which the present *Not*, the *Not des Fehls* "*heiliger Namen*," stems. Originating in the forgetfulness of Being, the need for holy names eventually might also leap away from this source. The understanding of thought that could help the *Dichten* does not imply, then, making this *Not* "understandable" but persevering in it.

The forgetting in question, Heidegger adds, should not be identified with an all-too-familiar privative sense, as if we were dealing with a lack in the sense of *Mangel*, of something that should not have been, a fault that could have been prevented, a mistake, an omission, an *Unterlassung*. On the contrary, Heidegger continues, the word *Seinsvergessenheit* names the sending of Being in the very essence of its clearing, which can only manifest itself if this clearing—that is to say, if its truth, its *Aletheia*— *retains* or withholds itself, if it keeps to itself or keeps itself in reserve for thought, as it has done from (and, Heidegger writes, *as*) the very beginning of Western thought, all the way through the different epochs of the history of Being up until now, that is to say, the present technological age (*technologische Weltalter*).

Yet, as this forgetting has turned into the—forgotten—principle of thought, it has become increasingly difficult or even impossible to understand it properly. Consequently, the lack of divine (sacred or holy) names cannot be experienced in its own right,[10] that is to say, in its origin or *Herkunft*. More than ever, we seem removed from the "possibility" (the *Möglichkeit*) of gaining insight (*Einblick*) into this situation and assessing the appropriate task of thought.

Heidegger leaves no doubt that this task consists in a turn, a turning away, from the dominance of method (the following of a path, *methodos*, of sorts) in favor of a different, less secure but more demanding path. Underway to whatever is given thought to think, we might come to learn (again?) that in the retreat and the reserve that characterize the dominion of *Lethe*, the epochal forgetfulness of Being, there reigns "a proper mode of presence (or presencing)," one that is *constitutive of*, that opens, enables, insight into the anxious situation of the *Fehl* "*heiliger Namen*." Only our staying (*Aufenthalt*) or dwelling in the openness of the primary domain (*Gegend*) guarantees the possibility (*die Möglichkeit*) of overcoming our present blindness and seeing what, here and now, somehow *is*, even though, or precisely insofar as, it is lacking.[11] What is lacking *is*, somehow, if not somewhere, if not at some given moment in time and space. And this *is*, Heidegger implies, grounds the very possibility of an insight.

As so often in Heidegger, there is thus an emphasis on the ontological or epochal primacy of the possible, as well as on the grounding, the localization, of lack in the *Lethe*, that is to say, in the presencing, the *Anwesen*, of Being insofar as it absconds itself from the present. This preoccupation directs Nancy's reading. He asks whether or to what extent Heidegger's thought still reserves for itself the possibility of an ontological or dialectical "reserve," and, if so, whether the *Fehl heiliger Namen* becomes secondary to a supposed primacy of the *Lethe* at the bottom of *Aletheia*. Might this "lack" (*Fehl*) and the "reserve" (*Vorenthalt*) that Heidegger thinks it signals and presupposes be understood as the overture to a new and other beginning or to a return—a re-turn as much as a "rerun," a turning up again—in which the gods once more might make their appearance?[12] And would the poet—especially der *Dichter* par excellence, Hölderlin—have a decisive role to play here? Is that how Hölderlin understood his poetry and himself? Or, to avoid interpreting the poet *e mente auctoris*, is that how he is most fruitfully or plausibly read? Does Heidegger's later thought measure up to the difficulties of Hölderlin's text, or should we attempt a more complex reading, a *lectio difficilior*, that resists the possibilities of hermeneutic understanding and, indeed, the very premises of the possibilism on which such understanding ultimately rests? If Heidegger's *Erläuterungen* somehow miss the mark, what help, if any, do Nancy's more elliptical observations offer?

The Topos of *Fehl*: Back to Nancy

By transcribing and displacing Heidegger's account of the topos *Es fehlen heilige Namen*, Nancy to a large extent reassesses the situation as well as the situating of thought it evokes. He maintains that the lack is not tied to a cut, to a being cut off, marked by the caesura or circumcision of language that comes with baptism into a given community. The want of names is constituted not by the lack of this or that name but by the (temporary or perpetual) absence or cessation of the gesture of naming, that is, of appellatives, of invocation or prayer. This allocation has not merely been historically or historially displaced. The lack of names unsettles and uproots address in a more radical sense than by simply transporting it into a different context. It decontextualizes or eradicates the very *hic et nunc* of saying or praying (or is it cursing?)—*mon dieu!*—This "apparent possessive" is the basis of the sublime destitution and abandonment that Nancy sees at the origin of the divine topoi.

This view might seem to allow one to hold at a distance, at least philo-sophically or with regard to the task of "thought," the all-too-familiar, naive, and dangerous attempts to explore and exploit a supposed renais-sance, resurrection, or *réveil* of the religious. It would seem that the death of God is irrevocable, and that gods return only as idols and idle kitsch. Yet the presupposition underlying this confident distance, the assumption that for want of prayer there can only be a parody of re-citation, is vulner-able in terms of Nancy's own analysis and is, I would suggest, anything but convincing. Just as the validity of the concepts of the "idol" and "idolatry" are based, as Nancy rightly points out, on the silent presuppo-sition of the *Idea* of which they are thought to reflect a merely distorted—anthropomorphic and profane—image, so also the suspicion of *mere* recitation makes sense only in view of the ideal of direct and pure address, of a full speech, as it were, that is unequivocal and present to itself, here and now. In its very purity, however, this address can never exist or be given as such. This is what resonates in Hölderlin's phrase about the lack of holy names. What matters most is neither nature nor culture but how, as Hölderlin puts it in the second letter to Böhlendorff, "the living rela-tionship" and "destination" (*das lebendige Verhältnis und Geschick*), of which nature and culture are the "abstract elements,"[13] manifests or re-veals itself only, *if at all*, in relation and *as* relation to its other, and thus, as we shall see, both *im-mediately* and *inflected*. For us moderns, it assumes the form of the immeasurable, of a sacred pathos or a fire from heaven. Far from mimicking the classicist—supposedly Greek—ideal, this is, in fact, its other.

If one holds to Nancy's terms, faith must be taken as "entirely an out-ward act of presence [*une comparution à l'extérieur*]," one, moreover, that resembles "turning one's face toward the manifest heavens" (DP 140/37). This comparison should make us pause since it invokes a remarkable Höl-derlinean topos that cannot be easily situated or elucidated (as Heidegger would say, *erörtert* or *erläutert*). While we seem to be dealing here with a *topos aistheton* rather than a *topos noeton*, this distinction inaugurates and constitutes the very project of a metaphysical cosmology that is no longer pertinent to understanding Hölderlin's hint. "Turning one's face toward the manifest heavens," Nancy holds, has much more to do with the singular "phenomenon" of an "idea" being inscribed on—and playing around—the face of an "idol."

"What is God?": The Question Questioned

Hölderlin, too, asks "What is God?" That is the question "Of Divine Places" starts out to discuss, if only to raise doubts about its topicality.

The question figures prominently as the title and *incipit* of one of Hölderlin's poetic writings, taken as the point of departure for Heidegger's elucidations. In it Hölderlin poses and answers the question "What is God?" by pointing to the aspect or the face of the sky, the *Angesicht des Himmels*, its "lightnings," which strike mortals and signal a divine visitation, an appearance and a shining of the divine, a theophany. The poem, also cited in Heidegger's ". . . Poetically Man Dwells . . .," reads as follows:

Was ist Gott?
Was ist Gott? unbekannt, dennoch
Voll Eigenschaften ist das Angesicht
Des Himmels von ihm. Die Blitze nämlich
Der Zorn sind eines Gottes. Je mehr ist eins
Unsichtbar, schicket es sich in Fremdes. Aber der Donner
Der Ruhm ist Gottes. Die Liebe zur Unsterblichkeit
Das Eigentum auch, wie das unsere,
ist eines Gottes.

What is God?
What is God? Unknown, yet
Full of his qualities is the face
of the sky. For the lightnings
Are the wrath of a god. The more something is
Invisible, the more it destines itself to what's alien. But the thunder
The fame is God's own. Love for immortality
is the property, also, like ours,
of a god.[14]

While Heidegger's commentary starts out from the question "What is God?" his reading takes its lead from a passage in "In Lovely Blueness . . . Blossoms," whose authenticity has been disputed but which for Heidegger, in its "substance" (*sachlich*) and its time, belongs to the same "ambience" (*Umkreis*)[15] of the poem "What is God?"

Ist unbekannt Gott? Ist er offenbar wie der Himmel? Dieses Glaub'
ich eher. Des Menschen Maass ist's. Voll Verdienst, doch dichter-
isch, wohnet der Mensch auf dieser Erde. Doch reiner ist nicht der
Schatten der Nacht mit den Sternen, wenn ich so sagen könnte, als
der Mensch, der heisset ein Bild der Gottheit. Giebt es auf Erden
ein Maass? Es giebt keines.

Is God unknown? Is he manifest like the sky? This rather I believe.
It is the measure of man. Full of acquirements, but poetically, man

dwells on this Earth. But the darkness of night with all the stars is not purer, if I could put it like that, than man, who is called the image of God. Is there a measure on Earth? There is none.[16]

This late fragment confronts us with the difficult problem of the interplay of poetry or poeticizing and topology, topography, and theophany: a relation that is not one relation among others, but provides the measure for all these others. How, if at all, can it be thought? How, if at all, is it experienced?

Heidegger interprets the first lines taken from "In Lovely Blueness . . . Blossoms" as saying that the divine, while retaining its invisibility and unknowability, is made manifest (*offenbar*) by the heavens, sending, dispatching, or destining itself in the appearing of the world, which nonetheless remains completely foreign to it. However, in doing so, he also takes the risk of reducing the modality of this manifestation to a logic of absence and presence, revelation and concealment. Here, in other words, the divine epiphany is still thought, Nancy suspects, in terms of an Idealist alternative, as the manifestation of a god who does or who does not wish to be "close to us" (DP 123/16). Yet he urges us to ask, "Can we still be content to go on conceiving of God, with or against Hegel, with or against Augustine, as a form of extreme intimacy? Will a day not come when we shall have to confront a god outside, exposed in the open sky, nowhere hidden and internal to nothing?" (DP 123/16).

Nancy proposes another, in my view far more provocative, reading of the lines cited above. The poem, he claims, maintains less that God is revealed "by means of the heavens" than that "the god" is only "as manifest as the heavens": "The face of God is as manifest as the *Angesicht* of the heavens" (DP 123/17).[17] This means that, for Hölderlin, the heavens are not the mere appearance, reflection, mirror image, or projection screen for a god whose existence (or presence) and essence ought to be located elsewhere, beyond this surface, or who would jealously retain some space, some reserve, some *Vorenthalt*, for himself. What alternative do we have for thinking divine manifestation as an occurrence that takes places *either* in interior (psychological or, rather, spiritual) enlightenment *or* that draws on the resources of an outer nature (from, say, "elements of the cosmos," *stoicheia tou kosmou*, through the created universe, to the Pascalian infinite voids of infinitely extended and infinitely divided spaces filled by divine grace alone): "The invisible divine lets itself be seen resting, itself, upon the face [the *Angesicht des Himmels*], or woven into it, sent or destined therein, but as another face that lets itself be seen *here, without 'here' serving as a mediation for it*" (DP 124/17). For lack of a better word, Nancy speaks here of the "im-mediacy" (*im-médiateté*) of the divine, the "*im-*" implying neither negation, privation, nor mere indifference but rather a relation or a state that has absolved itself from that of both mediacy and immediacy, and, we should add, concerns man alone.

He discusses this relation, whose terms absolve themselves from every possible mediation—and thereby from the very mediation that is kept in reserve by every possible, whether transcendental, virtual or real—extensively in his *The Experience of Freedom*. There he notes that "immediacy"—this time around, the immediacy of "freedom"—should not be confused with "sensuous immediacy":

> Nor is it an absence of mediation in the intelligible. It is neither a sentiment nor an intellectual given. . . . This might resemble what we could call the specific pregnancy of the "feeling of reason," which for Kant is the *respect* for the law of freedom. . . . The immediacy of this experience [the "passion" of freedom] must . . . be understood as *the affective im-mediacy of freedom in existence insofar as freedom affects existence from an infinite distance*. (*EF* 195–96n6/131n1)

One should not, therefore, confuse im-mediacy with "temptation itself, the cunning abdication of thought into [that other] immediate, into the 'lived,' into the ineffable, or into the praxis and art designated as the others of thought," as it can be found, for instance, in the well-known reference, in Hegel's *Phenomenology of Spirit*, to the image of the young girl who "presents the outstanding products of ancient art and the divine places that the gods have left" (*EF* 156/200). Rather, Nancy insists, "immediacy," as that which enables and characterizes freedom, calls for a "returning of praxis to thought," and in this turn, he adds, a central element from Marx's writings "resonates" with "something from Heidegger" (*EF* 157/200).

The "im-mediate" of which Nancy speaks in "Of Divine Places" gives a hint man can follow up on, or not. It is all too easy to miss the point, the pointer, which is nonetheless somehow *there*, out there, but "in," if one can still say so, a "there" that cannot be fixated—indeed, pinpointed—with the help of the usual coordinates. What the heavens and the god have "in common" is neither a common measure—"Giebt es auf Erden ein Maass? Es giebt keines"—nor an *analogia entis*, but "the sovereign interplay [*jeu*] of darkness and radiance [*l'éclat*], of radiance withdrawn into darkness and of darkness as manifest as radiance" (DP 126/19) From this Nancy draws a dazzling conclusion. Seen in this light, against the background of this radiance, revelation can be thought neither as "presentation" nor as "representation," since it is not the conveying of some message, but merely as "the evidence of the possibility (never the necessity) of a *being-unto god*" (DP 124/17). The "radiance," in its very indeterminacy, is itself as such the revelation, though it reveals nothing but a possible. It reveals a pure relation or relatedness from which the terms (addresser and addressee) have withdrawn or *absolved* themselves completely and irrevocably: "What there is revelation of is not 'God,' as if he were something that can be exhibited . . . , it is rather the unto-God [*l'à-dieu*] or being-unto-god. Or more exactly, it becomes manifest that such a being-unto-god is possible" (DP 124/17–18).

These formulations expose the fragility of Heidegger's suggestion that the divine is made manifest *by* the heavens, that the presence-absence of the gods should be projected against the screen of Being's manifestation and concealment, that the Hölderlinean "time of need" (*dürftige Zeit*) should be taken as the time in which the gods have fled while the god is still to come. These are all premises of a reading that enables Heidegger *in advance* to "extract" a future "positive" out of a past and present, supposedly nonprivative and nondialectical, "negative."[18] Indeed many, if not all, of Heidegger's formulations that seek to determine the relation between Being and the highest Being, between the holy and the gods, between the gods or the holy and the Christian God (the others, we have seen, are either kept in reserve or not to be mentioned, let alone taken serious, at all), are deeply ambivalent in this respect. One example must suffice here to illustrate this claim. Heidegger writes, in *Elucidations of Hölderlin's Poetry*: "by providing anew the essence of poetry [*Dichtung*], Hölderlin first determines a new time. It is the time of the gods who have fled *and* of the god who is coming. It is the *time of need* because it stands in a double lack and a double not: in the no-longer of the gods who have fled and in the not-yet of the god who is coming."[19]

Here, the doubled "not" already has the structure of a lack that calls for and calls forth a presence, if only by opening a space, by ending or, rather, closing an epoch, marked by the flight of the gods. These gods, in turn, serve, if not as the medium, then at least as the signs and the mediators of *the* god (*der Gott*): "The divine [*die Göttlichen*] are the nodding [*winkenden*] messengers of the god [*Göttheit*]. Out of their holy ruling [*Walten*] the god appears in his presence or hides in his retreat [*entzieht sich in seine Verhüllung*]."[20]

How are we to understand these words? Do they confirm the basic tenets of Nancy's suspicion? Does not the thought of Being from the very outset prejudge the eventuality and the very modality of the coming of gods, by framing this coming or not coming in terms a of a possible and associating the present lack—the *Fehl* "*heiliger Namen*"—with a with-holding or keeping itself in reserve, with a *Lethe* at the bottom of *Aletheia*? This question has far-reaching implications, not the least of which would be to problematize a common reading of the relation of Being and the divine topoi.[21]

The *Wink* of God: Nancy's Rethinking

Nancy's question posed to Heidegger's reading of the Hölderlinean manifest heavens, his rethinking of this figure as a mere "possible" or as the "possibility of a possibility," is itself open to question. This attempt to frame the relationship between Being and the heavens, gods and mortals, in terms of a—possibilizing—dimensionality remains steeped in the ultimately metaphysical presupposition of the existence, the deontological force, and the aesthetic value of dispositional capacities (that is, *Möglichkeit* identified with a *Vermögen*, a *dunamis*, a *potentia*). Such forms of thought can no longer satisfy, because in any thought of possibilization, what is supposedly made possible is *ipso facto* also made into what it is not. It is *screened* in all senses of the word: projected onto and limited by properties, the openness of the *there* (*Da*), albeit in light of a horizon deemed most proper to its ownmost being or the Being—again, the *Dimension* of Being—that opens it up while folding it back into the One, the simplicity that for Heidegger, following a long tradition, remains the *index veri*. Indeed, as Jean-François Courtine has noted, in the *Beiträge zur Philosophie* (*Contributions to Philosophy*) Heidegger's attempts to delineate a new, postmetaphysical concept of and space for the transcendence or epiphany of the divine that departs from the "prolonged Christianization of God [*des Gottes*]."[22]

Only when he reinscribes Heidegger's problematic formulations into the Hölderlinean topos of the divine *Winke* does Nancy efface the last remnants of the ontotheological legacy discernible in the restriction of thought to the openness to a possible being unto God. Reading Heidegger against Heidegger; Nancy proposes that a better name for the peculiar modality of the "presence" of "God," "god," "the god," and "the gods," as they are revealed and manifest *like* the heavens, would be that of the *Wink*, the divine "nod" or "sign." The divine does not signal something; it signifies nothing in particular, nothing that exists, nothing phenomenal, not even the radiance of the heavens. But if the divine "glory" is said to be "open, offered, dazzling like that of the heavens and effaced like them" (DP 121/19), then this appears to mean, if anything (since the order of meaning and appearance is precisely what is displaced or erased here), that it has the "nature," the "mode," or the "quality" of a *Wink*, of a *Wink*, moreover, that in its elusiveness ambivalently evokes joy and fear at once,[23] thereby recalling the formal features of the sublime, and not only in a Kantian sense. The god, Nancy writes, translating Heidegger's words *im Vorbeigang*, is only "in passing" (*de passage*; DP 115/7), and, to the extent that all departure entails some sort of death, has always already passed away. This theme of the passing God is an essential element in Nancy's recent explorations into the deconstruction of Christianity, or in a more precise sense, the deconstruction of the monotheist God. It is treated substantially in *Dis-enclosure*, particularly in the chapter "On a Divine *Wink*." But, as we have seen, the theme is already strongly present in his earlier work, especially in "Of Divine Places."[24]

Let me make two observations here. First, for all its continuity with the interpretation of *kairos* in Heidegger's early lectures on the phenomenology of religion, notably in his reading of St. Paul, the "passage" in question here no longer has the character of a parousia.[25] As Courtine notes, we should seek the source of Heidegger's concern with the specific modality of the "passage" and, indeed, the *Wink* in his dialogue with Hölderlin. Here, Hölderlin's "Celebration of Peace," "The Only One," and "Patmos" would be particularly revealing.[26] Second, the divine *Wink* thus found is, in Heidegger's view—and here he may come close to Hölderlin—intrinsically linked to an understanding of finitude, which it radicalizes or pushes to its extreme.[27] Important differences, however, remain intact.

Citing Hölderlin's passage on divine *Winke*, Heidegger comments:

. . . and nods are
From time immemorial the language of the Gods.

The poet's saying is the intercepting of these nods, in order to pass them on [*winken*] them to his people. The intercepting of nods is a receiving, and yet at the same time, a new giving; for in the "first signs" the poet catches sight of [*erblickt*] what has been completed, and boldly puts what he has seen [*Erschaute*] into his word in order to foretell what is not yet fulfilled. Thus

. . . the bold spirit flies, like the eagle
Ahead of the thunderstorm, prophesying
The coming of his gods.[28]

Nancy emphasizes the double reading that these words allow. Hölderlin's verse does not presuppose that the realm of the profane has the ability to gesture toward the sacred. No analogical continuity surmounts the abyss between appearance and essence, the many and the One, the mortal and the divine. And yet, he adds, this does not exclude the possibility that "to 'give a sign' is perhaps always—divine" (DP 115/7).[29]

To be sure, the relation between the different modes of giving a sign while signifying nothing in particular, between the *Wink* that is a divine gesturing and gesturing that is a *Wink*, is hardly symmetrical, despite a secret correspondence. Not every giving of signs, calling, seducing, and so on can pretend to present us ipso facto with the divine. For Hölderlin no less than for Heidegger, only poets function as the heralds—and, perhaps, the very *Winke*—of the *Winke* called "divine." Yet the privilege accorded their words can hardly be attributed to the semantic or metaphorical potential of poetic speech, just as the lack of divine proper names cannot simply be ascribed to a supposed "metaphysical surfeit of the thing over the sign, of the real over language" (DP 119/12). On the contrary, if the lack of names is the absence of a *Wink* that is or evokes a gesture of naming, then the want of a name has nothing to do with some "signifying capacity" or lack thereof. As a result, the lack of divine names "cannot be judged in relation to sense" (DP 119/12), and precisely this circumstance and not some "dispositional capacity" may enable all names, in principle and in fact, to address—or name—the divine.

In the text "Winke," dated 1941, Heidegger describes the *Winke* in terms that circumscribe their status while "forging a path" between the supposedly separate domains of poetry and thought, aesthetics and philosophy:

> The "nods" [again, Heidegger speaks of his own "Winke"] are not poems. Nor are they "philosophy" put into verse and rhyme. The "nods" are the words of a thought that in part needs this expression [*Aussagen*], but does not fulfill itself in it. This thought finds no anchor [*Anhalt*] in being[s], for it thinks *das Seyn*. This thought finds no example in being, since what is thought thinks being [*das Seiende*]. The saying of thought is other than the word of poetry without image [*bildlos*]. And where there seems to be an image, it is neither the poeticized of a poem nor what is intuited by a "sense" [or "meaning"], but only the desperate anchor of an attempted but failed abstinence from any image [*Bildlosigkeit*].[30]

Here and elsewhere, the word *Winke* retains an intimate relationship with the manifestation and the revealability of the essence of Being, that is to say, of Truth. None of this, however, is assumed in Hölderlin's poetry or in the commentaries on which we have been focusing. On the contrary, the quintessence of the interrogation of the relationship between the poetic, on the one hand, and the thought of Being and (its) Truth, on the other, consists in questioning the primacy of the latter over and against the former.

How, then, can Hölderlin's "poeticizing"—the writing, reading, or recitation of his "poem" as well as the simple *aisthesis* of the heavens of which it speaks—signal the turning of a possible being-unto-the-god, without at the same time returning this relation to the order of signification and of aesthetic representation? And where, if anywhere, does the *Wink* touch upon art? Nancy's demarcation between the two modes of manifestation seems to leave no room for confusion. Apodictically, "Of Divine Places" upholds a clear-cut distinction between the presence without (re)presentation of the divine, on the one hand, and presentation of/ as representation of art, on the other: "God . . . comes in the ruin of all appearing [*le paraître*]. Art, on the contrary, infinitely incises the edges of appearance [*l'apparaître*], but keeps it intact" (DP 130/25).

At least three traditions seem to cross paths here, one of which is passed over in silence: the one that relies on the New Testament figure of the *hoos mē* ("as if not"), which forms an important key to understanding Heidegger's "exegeses," not of Hölderlin, but of St. Paul. Nancy identifies the two remaining ones as two particular modes of the sublime, each of which seems to have left its imprint in the very texture of his essay:

> There is the sublime in art, going from Kant to Benjamin and from there on to us. It signifies: to feel the fainting away of the sensible, to border on the furthest extreme of presentation. . . . And there is divine sublimity, that in terms of which Hegel seeks to characterize the Jewish moment in religion. . . . The coming of God reduces the phenomenon to nothing. Here the sublime is no longer to be found at the furthest extreme of presentation where presentation is transformed into offering. It is in a presence that ruins all presentation and all representation. It is no longer the gesture of offering, it is the imposition of glory. It is no longer the limit of forms and figures, it is the light that disperses the visible. (DP 130/25)

Nancy tries to capture the difference between these two sublime modes of signifying at the limit of and beyond the phenomenal world, at the limit of and beyond art, in the fragmentary form of presentation adopted in "Of Divine Places." Its most significant stylistic feature is that of "juxtaposition," without explanatory connectives, less of grammatical or syntactical elements (as in the parataxis of Hölderlin's late poetry), than of structures of argumentation or elucidation. It takes the form of a fragmented topology or, rather, topography. It allows of no gathering, no *Versammlung*, no *logos*. It does not let itself be folded into any *Einfalt*, nor does it limit the domain (the *Gegend*) of thought to any fourfold (*Geviert*), folded, in its turn, into one.

"Of Divine Places" demonstrates—in its propositions as much as in their performative structure—that the sublime modes of the divine and the aesthetic are fundamentally *irreconcilable*. They cannot be translated into each other, for they have no common measure. And yet, Nancy writes, each mode can offer the other: each can offer itself *to* or *as* the other:

> Between the "thing" of sublime art and the sublime "thing" of the divine, there can be said to be that infinitesimal (and in its turn sublime?) difference that lies between presentation at the limit and naked presence: it follows that each can offer the other, but also that it is impossible to confuse one with the other. (DP 130/25)

One might argue that the reverse must equally be true. Given the "infinitesimal" difference and distance between the two sublimes, neither one of them can ever hope to offer the other, strictly speaking. Nonetheless, it is impossible *not* to take the one for the other. One cannot but keep them apart *and* confuse them. On both counts, the infinitesimally small but lasting difference or distance between the limit(ed) and the limitless regulates their impossible yet inevitable relation. Or so it seems. One hints at the other, as its other, its *Wink*.

God Passing By

Presence and Absence in Monotheism and Atheism

LAURENS ten KATE

> I hold . . . the apprehension of God . . . to be an obstacle in the movement
> that carries us to the more obscure apprehension of the *unknown*: of a pres-
> ence which is no longer in any way distinct from an absence.
> —**Georges Bataille,** *Inner Experience*

The Mosaic Distinction, the Mosaic Connection

The central characteristic of monotheism may be, not the exclusive ac-
knowledgement of a single God, but something that Jan Assmann recently named the "Mosaic distinction."[1] This distinction is twofold.

According to Assmann, it primarily designates the discordant difference between true and false religion, and between a true and a false God.[2]
Assmann demonstrates how this distinction turned the natural and obvious presence of religion itself into a *problem*. Religion had to interrogate
its truth instead of simply coinciding with it—"being" its own truth—
and in this way its presence was no longer guaranteed, nor was that of its
God: their presence had to be affirmed by man. God could just as well be
absent, or even nonexistent.

Assmann illustrates this monotheistic distinction by referring to the famous first and second commandments in Exodus 20:3–4: "Thou shalt
have no other gods before me" and "Thou shalt not make unto thee any
graven image." He steers the definition of monotheism into a new direction by focusing not on the number of Gods but on the claim that only

one God *among many* should be worshiped: "I call "the Mosaic distinction" the idea of an exclusive and emphatic truth that sets God apart from everything that is not God and therefore must not be worshiped, and that sets religion apart from what comes to be shunned as superstition, paganism, or heresy. This idea finds its clearest expression not in the phrase "God is one!"but "no other gods!""[3]

A second feature of the monotheist distinction is touched upon in monotheism's iconoclastic program. The ban on the representation of the divine by means of images intensifies the presence of God *as a problem*, which establishes itself *within* the "true" religion. This problem articulates the difference in distance between God and humans, and monotheism thereby breaks away from polytheism.[4] The ban on images proclaimed in the Jewish Torah is a plea for—a hint at—distance, difference, and distinction.[5] Because the image bridges the distance by *representing* God, it must be destroyed.[6]

The Mosaic distinction shows that the "truth" of the monotheistic religions *is* this problem of presence and absence. It is played out in various opposing couples of concepts: divine-human, transcendent-immanent, outside-inside, Other-self, infinite-finite, etc. Monotheism's claim to give *sense* to the world and to humanity derives from this complex and contradictory truth. One can see the "deconstruction of monotheism" carried out by Jean-Luc Nancy as a rephrasing of Assmann's distinction in these terms: the terms of a tension between presence and absence, and of a discussion of the problem of the sense of the world. The truth of monotheism is hence a very modern truth: sense is never available, never "given," never stable, never a founding or grounding basis for the world. Sense is *in* the world—not underneath it, bearing it—and it is in the world as something that "happens" time and again, announcing, "assuring" itself, and then disappearing, "withholding itself" again. Following Nancy's line of thought, from the monotheistic distinction we progress to its complex truth and then to its modality of unstable sense—to modernity. That is the central movement, or rather, the "space" of the West analyzed in the chapter "A Deconstruction of Monotheism" in *Dis-enclosure*:

> I will call a "deconstruction of monotheism" that inquiry or search consisting in disassembling and analyzing the constitutive elements of monotheism, and more directly of Christianity, thus of the West, in order to go back to (or to advance toward) a resource that could form at once the buried origin and the imperceptible future of the world that calls itself "modern." After all, "modern" signifies a world always awaiting its truth of, and as, world [*sa vérité de monde*],

a world whose proper sense is not given, is not available, is, rather, in project or in promise, and perhaps beyond: a sense that consists in not being given, but only in being promised. . . . In Christianity, the promise is at once already realized and yet to come. (But is this not a theme that runs through all the monotheisms?) Is such a paradoxical space not that in which the presence of sense is at once assured, acquired, and always withheld, absented in its very presence? (D 34–35/54)

Let us return to our account of the Mosaic distinction. It does not simply divide two realms of being, but rather poses their mutual relation as a problem: as an unstable relation of tension and desire. The God who retreats from the world is at the same time the God who "presents" himself as such, as the "absent." As an ungraspable, distant force, the monotheistic God forces himself onto the people: that is the remarkable paradox in the "monotheistic revolution," as Assmann calls it, expressed, for instance, in the well-known scene of Exodus 19 and 20, when God gives his Torah (in its concentrated form of the Ten Commandments) while remaining absent. Here, the God who distinguishes himself from gods *and* humans asserts himself by bringing his absence proper into presence. The distinction plays itself out by blurring itself as soon as possible and becoming a *connection*. The scene is rephrased in Deuteronomy: "Then the Lord spoke to you out of the fire. You heard the sound of words but saw no form; there was only a voice" (Deut. 4:12).

The problem monotheism addresses and in a way enacts ("performs") in its narrative, ritual, doctrine, and art is this impossible connection.[7] The "living God," as the authors of the Jewish bible often call Yahweh, is not the God of presence, but he who "lives" in the interval between absence and presence. Assmann refers to this dynamic as a constant shift between "hiding and revealing": "The 'living God' hides and reveals himself as he chooses and forbids any attempt at a magical summoning of his presence. This is the political meaning of the prohibition against images."[8] Whereas Assmann still seems to keep open the possibility of understanding "hiding and revealing"as two alternating types of presence (hidden versus revealed), Nancy argues that one should complicate the monotheistic problem even further. How can one think and experience, how can one "live" presence *as* absence and the reverse? How can the monotheistic God be outside-in/inside-out the world at the same time? How can the distinction be a connection, a relation, albeit an impossible one? How can the impossible be a possibility? These questions bring us to Nancy's explorations into the deconstruction of monotheism and of

Christianity in particular, as carried in *Dis-enclosure* and many other recent works.[9] Indeed, the instability of the Mosaic distinction, letting religion oscillate between distinction and connection, between its own destruction ("religion without God") and construction ("religion *of* the without-God"), designates monotheism's complex character: that it is a constant process of self-deconstruction. It is this self-deconstructive drive that is, in Nancy's view, the unthought, unheard of, unexpected aspect of monotheism; and it is this aspect of monotheism that has persisted in a radical form in modernity. The deconstruction of monotheism is a deconstruction of modernity.[10]

Outside, Inside: Monotheism's Self-Deconstruction

Nancy adds to the definition of his "inquiry" in "A Deconstruction of Monotheism" several other descriptions, for example, in an interview with the German magazine *Lettre International*. It is, he states, the determination of "something" in Christianity that would have "made it possible" but that, at the same time, would be the "unthought" of Christianity: that is to say, something *in* Christianity that at the same time "is not Christianity proper" and "has not mingled with it" (EG 76).

Then, in the next sentence, Nancy adds to these rather complex formulations an even more difficult one. He states that the unthought of Christianity should be understood as something that can be grasped only in its "coming."[11] The outside[12] is something contaminating the inside *from within*, yet the inside can only be understood as something opening itself toward an outside described as its condition ("making possible") and its movement ("in coming"). One should speak here of a continuous "opening of possibility," of an active and dynamic "making possible," in other words, of a beginning or starting point that "begins time and again" rather than of a stable and preexistent "condition." Considered this way, the "condition" is part of the movement ("coming") instead of preceding it; it is an unconditional condition.[13] In is never in, and out never out. Surely, this complex and open structure of the unthought neither coincides with Christianity's "construction"—its historical traditions, doctrines, and institutions—nor transcends or even destroys it; the unthought, in other words, is neither simply present in nor radically absent from (beyond) Christianity, but it de-constructs the latter's construction from within its nucleus.

However, this unthought inside and outside Christianity, as Nancy thinks it, is not the hidden essence of the Christian religion leading eventually to its fulfilment in time. Rather, it refers to Christianity's *exhaustion*

(*D* 71/102). It is not of the order of an origin or of a destination, but belongs to a logic of self-undermining or, as Nancy puts it, of "self-surpassing" (*D* 39/59). In turn, this logic parallels the logic of what Nancy describes as the "entire structure of Western civilization" (EG 76): both Christianity and Western culture as a whole are characterized by a dynamic of self-exhaustion, which, according to Nancy, achieves its radical form in modern, secular times. In this sense, Christianity's unthought, which keeps "coming" *to* and *from* it, makes us aware of how closely it is interwoven with modernity—aware of how much it is a modern religion.

Granted that the emergence of modern time puts an end to the "Christian era" in a historical sense (the end of the political power of clergy and nobility, the marginalization of religious institutions and traditions in social and cultural life, the beginning of capitalism, etc.), it nevertheless continues the other, unthought "end" Christianity bears within itself. This structural ambivalence is mirrored in the way Christianity's history oscillates, from its earliest through its medieval to its modern phase, between an affirmation of sense outside of and inside the world. The life of the Christian receives powerful fulfillment as a form of care for oneself in the here and now and as responsibility for the earth—as, for example, Augustine teaches in his *Confessions* and Erasmus in his *Enchiridion*, but an equally forceful fulfillment is found in the longing for a life and sense outside the self and this world, as has been evoked by the chiliast movements, by numerous mystical traditions, or by early modern puritanism.

The Presence of Retreat, or How God Wants to Get Rid of God

Thus the Christian religion has itself, and from its very beginning—which should be traced back beyond the beginning of Christianity, in its Egyptian, Jewish, and Greek roots—a double relation to the possibility, or rather, to the event of sense. This relation to sense is parallelled in Christianity's experience of its God—caught up as he is in the ambivalence of distinction and connection. On the one hand, it is almost obsessively occupied with the here and now of sense, that is, the intimacy of our personal relation with Christ and his flesh and blood; here, no outside is necessary, for the outside is inside. The unthought that is "in coming" is in and since Christ always already there. On the other hand, Christianity remains totally devoted to the experience of a sense that is not of this world and transcends time and history: God's heavenly Kingdom is only one of the relevant metaphors here. In this second sense, the outside is so radically transcendent that no relation to it is possible: only an experience of distance and of waiting remains. In sum, the Christian God is "so close and yet so far."

In a parallel way, the Christian concept of the *parousia*, of Christ's appearance and subsequent presence in the world, with and among humans, is thought by Nancy in a double meaning. Though many believers would find this highly unorthodox, he points out that parousia should be thought in its literal meaning of a presence that falls short of being present: of a presence (*ousia*) that remains close but at a distance (*par-*). God's presence in Christ is a presence of *retreat*:[14] retreat from being as the only possible "mode" of being. (EG 80). This deconstruction of the doctrine of parousia is remarkably consistent with its traditional use, however. Christ's parousia refers both to his presence in the world, close to us, and to his coming presence—his presence *as* coming—outside the world, that is, when he will finally gloriously return at the end of time. The first meaning of parousia is usually associated with the story and symbolism of the cross, the second with the apocalyptic visions evoked in the last book of the New Testament.

But a double parousia can never be a full presence. The continuous deregulation of the oppositional scheme of presence and absence, inside and outside, and of the dualism of an innerworldly and a nonworldly sense results in a religion that, first of all, enacts the death of God: the Christian God dies in the intimacy of his becoming human in Christ, as well as in the infinite distance of his absence. The retreat consists in proximity *and* distance. In other words, *because* Christianity cannot choose between a present God and an absent God, this religion challenges the idea of a religion proper.[15]

The deregulation of the opposition between presence and absence forms a recurring theme and argument throughout Nancy's works on the deconstruction of monotheism and of Christianity.[16] The specifically Christian doctrine of incarnation is one of the prime examples here. In the chapter "*Verbum caro factum*" in *Dis-enclosure*, Nancy argues that, in the heart of early Christian dogmatics, after long debates on the "nature" of Christ, a creed was developed that rejected the idea that God would have temporarily (from outside) entered the flesh of a human (inside), but "*became*" and "*engendered itself*" as flesh (*D* 81—82/126). The problem of the two different natures of Christ, divine and human, with which the early churches wrestled at least shows that they wanted to avoid leaving any dualism of presence and absence intact. In Christ, both natures coincide (the dogma of the *homo-ousios*), meaning that the logic of "two natures" deconstructs itself (one cannot speak of natures anymore); in the flesh of Christ, the "disappearance of presence" "takes place"—and, I would add, presents itself in an impossible way, presents its absence and "absents" its presence. In Christ, as God, God becomes "not-of-god," "*a-theos.*" This "not" does not mean "the immediate self-sufficiency of man" but is, in fact, precisely the divine: the divine as a "place," a *topos* between the divine and the human at which presence loses its "founding" character:[17]

> In this sense, the Christian (or even the monotheistic) god is the god who *alienates himself.* He is the god who *atheizes himself* and who *atheologizes himself,* if I may for the moment forge these terms. (It is Bataille who, for his own purposes, created the term *atheological.*) Atheology as a conceptualization of the body is the thought that "god" made himself "body" in emptying himself of himself (another Christian motif, that of the Pauline *kenosis*: the emptying-out of God, or his "emptying-himself-out-of-himself"). The "body" becomes the name of the *a-theos* in the sense of "not-of-god." But "not-of-god" means not the immediate self-sufficiency of man or the world, but this: no founding presence. . . . The "body" of the "incarnation" is therefore the place, or rather the taking place, the event, of that disappearance. (*D* 82–83/127)

In "Between Story and Truth" one finds another explicit example of the deregulation we are analyzing here. "One day, the gods retreated. On their own, they retreated from their divinity, that is to say, from their presence. They do not simply absent themselves: they retreated from their own presence: they absented themselves inside [*dedans*]" (BT 7/UJ 7).[18] The idea of an absence *within* presence is crucial.[19] The text continues: "What remains of their presence is what remains of all presence when it absents itself: what remains is what one can say about it." Moreover, one should note that the type of retreat between presence and absence Nancy attempts to think here is formulated as a movement: he speaks of *to absent oneself* in stead of abstract absence. This movement is that of "passing by," to which I will return.

A similar structure of thought informs Nancy's account of the mono-theistic notion of faith (*foi*), which is an "act" in itself and not a belief (*croyance*) in some "kind of assurance, of a postulated certainty, . . . of some anticipation risked toward an end" (*D* 54/79). Faith, Nancy states in his commentary on James in the chapter "The Judeo-Christian (on Faith)," has no object, but is an act that does not conceive but receive.[20] It is a gift in which the entanglement of presence and absence, inside and outside is enacted or, so to speak, performed: "this faith . . . must come from the other, this faith must come from outside, it is the outside opening in itself a passage toward the inside" (*D* 54).[21] Again, this movement of an opening of absence within presence (and the reverse) is depicted as a "passage," not in the sense of a crossing, but of a passing by in a split second. It is the passing by of the retreating God evoked in "Between Story and Truth" and treated more elaborately in the chapter "On a Divine *Wink*." The entire deconstruction of Christianity, as envisaged by Nancy, may be a wink toward this passing by.[22]

Monotheism and Modernity: Ontology as Kenotic Retreat

Retreat as a mode of being—as the monotheistic mode—thus implies a fundamental distinction between presence and absence *as well as* their connection. God can never be presence, he is absence, but as absence he is presence. This is the formulation of an ontology of retreat. Such an entanglement of presence and absence is, as we have seen, monotheism's problem, but since monotheism has contaminated modernity far beyond the historical "end" of Christianity, modernity has intensified this problem immensely. In *Dis-enclosure* Nancy relies on Gérard Granel to address and analyze this entanglement of presence and absence as the modern development toward a radical "end" of a metaphysics of substance and essence: of being as presence to self, closed presence, that is, presence without absence. In a reading of Granel's "Far from Substance: Whither and to What Point—Essay on the Ontological Kenosis of Thought since Kant,"[23] he shows how Granel determines the "point" modern thought has reached as the awareness of the "void of being" or "the emptying out [kenosis] of being" in a single "event" (*Ereignis*) in which it "empties itself of all substantiality" (*D* 64/93).[24] "Granel asserts that this emptying out gives us the red thread of modern thought, from Kant to Heidegger and passing through Husserl" (*D* 64/93). Being rethought as event is in fact being retreating from itself qua being (qua substance) and opening itself to absence. It is important to notice that this event, as expressed in Granel's—and if he is right, in all modernity's—ontological event-ualism, is a never-ending dynamic *between* absence and presence, for the absence being opens itself to is precisely its "own" being. In retreating from itself, in emptying out, being opens itself to itself and not to some outside alterity. Retreat and kenosis coincide here. In this way, the "red thread of modern thought" parallels the monotheistic problem that is the legacy of modernity.[25]

An example of this modern inheritance of the monotheistic problem can be found in the tension between deconstruction and phenomenology in twentieth-century philosophy. A new concept of and a sensibility to presence, that is, to the impossible connection between presence and absence, is at stake here.

In many ways Nancy follows the path of a deconstructive analysis of the phenomenological tradition Jacques Derrida set out in *Speech and Phenomena*.[26] He observes and questions the phenomenological tendency to think the constitution of meaning and sense as an intentional act of the ego, which thereby would constitute its presence to self and reduce phenomenality to conscience.[27] Equally, for Nancy the idea that this act can and will lead to the appearance (*phainomai* in Greek, from which "phenomenon" is derived) of a full, pure, immediate and, in Husserl's words, "original" presence, should be deconstructed to the extent of losing its self-evidence. Nancy joins Derrida in attempting to demonstrate how phenomenology, in its strict methodological and egological Husserlian form, in its existential, ego-critical Heideggerian form, and in its postwar developments in, for instance, Sartre's, Ricoeur's, or Levinas's work, "touches upon its limit, and exceeds it" time and again. (*BSP* 200n53/ 83n1; trans. modified). This limit is reached in the difference between presence and absence, as Derrida points out, but also, Nancy adds, in the difference between the "I" and the other, in co-existence in time and space, which Husserl touches upon in the *Cartesian Meditations*.[28] The emphasis in Nancy's discussion of phenomenology lies on the structural analysis, fed by a certain wonder and fascination, of this limit—an analysis *in* and *with* the phenomenological traditions, and only as such *against* them.

Contrary to the "theological turn in phenomenology," which tries to give God a place in the phenomenal world, reactivating his phenomenal status as the "nonapparent," Nancy does not adopt a restorative approach with regard to the problem of God's presence/absence. Already in "Of Divine Places," one discovers that in his work the question of the (non)-presence of God does not receive a phenomenological response (telling us something about his presence, however outstanding, however transcending all being), but a historical one: how and why have the gods, has God disappeared, and how and why does he persist, lingering on in our societies, our lives, *as what has disappeared*?

"The gods went away long ago," said Cercidas of Megalopolis, in the third century B.C. Our history thus began with their departure, and perhaps even after their departure—or else, when we stopped knowing they were present. They cannot return in that history—and "to return" has no sense outside of that history. But where the gods are—and according as they are, whatever the present or absent mode of their existence—our history is suspended. (DP 145/43)

The question of God, Nancy states, is "no longer one of being or appearing" (D 111/165). The logic of being, of appearing, of phenomenality should be challenged by a "dynamic of passing," by a dynamic of the moment and the momentary touch, always taking place in some place.

Passing By

Let me finish by briefly investigating the possible meanings of such a topological dynamic, in which absence and presence are constantly entangled, in which God "is" only in "passing": passing by and passing on or even away, seen as two modes of one and the same moment. As a crucial movement, one that defines the "divine" in Nancy's outlook (the divine does not pass, as a subject of the act, but it *is* the act of passing) this passing requires, *as* movement, a place, a *topos*. It is always a passing toward, in, and away from a place that is "almost nothing," just a meeting point, a touching point, or, as Nancy depicts it in "On a Divine *Wink*," just a wink of the eye (D 104–5/156–57).[29] It is in this chapter that Nancy develops an account of this dynamic of passing, starting from a reading of a formulation in Heidegger's *Beiträge zur Philosophie* (*Contributions to Philosophy*).[30]

> The god is therefore not the designated but only the designating, the making-a-sign. There is no passage of the god, but this is the passing of the passage, the passage of whoever makes a sign. The passage of the one passing by—whose coming becomes more distant in the instant—makes the gesture that hails from afar and that at the same time puts the distant itself at a distance: the ever-renewed distancing of the other in being, and of the absent in the present. (D 114/168–69)

We observe here that Nancy thinks the gesture of passing—metaphorically juxtaposed with winking, hinting or "signaling"—as the dynamic that names and conceptualizes the dynamic between absence and presence. Passing is always coming and leaving at the same time, as in a twinkling of the eye: absence in/as presence and vice versa. The interplay between the Mosaic distinction and connection, that is, the monotheistic problem proper, is addressed here by using a term in Heidegger: *Vorbeigang*, "passing by." Then, in a next step, still close to Heidegger, the "name God" (*D* 115/170) is applied to the gesture of passing. Heidegger speaks of the *Vorbeigang des letzten Gottes* ("passing by of the last God").[31]

The way to speak of the monotheistic God, if we follow Nancy, is by speaking of a "passerby." This name can only indicate the "unnameable," since it does not make sense in the ordinary way: its sense is that it hesitates between being and nonbeing, between absence of sense and presence of sense. In this fundamental, dynamic hesitation it can never be a "stabilized" substance but refers us back to the "presence of retreat" treated in the previous section as a "retreat from presence." Let us notice now that this retreat is equally a retreat from absence: both retreats follow on each other continuously—that is the dynamic of hesitation.

> Whatever the unnameable nonmeaningful may be, the retreat of being into its différance,[32] the bearer of the name, signals it. . . . It signals it in passing, since it cannot be stabilized in a presence. He who signals in passing is the passer himself. The passer passes, and in order to pass, is someone. Some *one* who passes, is but the tread of the passing, not a being who would have passing as an attribute. One should not speak—Heidegger himself should not—of the passing *of the* god: but God is in the passing. God is the passerby and the step of the passerby. This step is his gesture, which, in passing, *winkt* and differentiates itself from itself. (*D* 115–70)

The structure of presence and absence we encounter here, mediated by the gestures of retreat and passing (both gestures involving the sequence of coming, arriving, and leaving), is what Heidegger calls the event (*Ereignis*). In other words, it is an event structured by presence in absence, absence in presence: "the onset and absence of an arrival . . . flight of the gods that are past" and so are absent, but still are present in "their hidden metamorphosis."[33]

Of the three monotheisms, one can describe Christianity in particular as a religion staging this passing event and introducing its God as a passerby. The incarnation is the narrative of the coming, passing, and leaving of God, told not as a historical but as an infinitely repeating event: God in Christ *is* this passing movement, problematizing the distinction between humans and God, because he is neither of the two and both at the same time. The unique staging of this passing event is replayed in numerous scenes and stories in the gospels: from annunciations, in which the angel announces the coming of God and his simultaneous conception in the Virgin Mary, through the many "passings" of Jesus when calling—

beckoning—his disciples, to Christ's passing by the travelers to Emmaus after his death, lingering between absence and presence (Luke 24:13–49). The fourfold, complex narrative of the incarnation, developed later on into the centerpiece of Christian doctrine, is the story, told in endless variations, of "an alterity that passes through, and throughout, the world, an infinite separation of the finite" (*NT* 47/78):

> Likewise, it follows that the "divine" henceforth no longer has a place either in the world or outside it, for there is no other world. What "is not of this world" is not elsewhere: it is the opening in the world, the separation, the parting and the raising. Thus "revelation" is not the sudden appearance of a celestial glory. To the contrary, it consists in the departure of the body raised into glory. It is in absenting, in going absent, that there is revelation. (*NT* 47–48/78)

However, thought within the context of a deconstruction of monotheism, this event is most of all a modern event: it is the event of modern sense in its instability and groundlessness. Modern sense is without a transcendent Giver, who would be outside this world; it simply "happens" in a moment, in a place, caught up between presence and absence. The event of sense in its modern, aporetic condition mirrors the event of the passing God who is no longer simply outside nor inside—who deregulates the opposition between outside and inside. Because he is no longer the external Giver of sense, Heidegger can speak of the "last God." Nancy lucidly formulates this issue in "Atheism and Monotheism." The last God is the monotheistic God, who "dissolves the very essence of the divine," and in this way he "figures" the *Ereignis* of modern man, that is, his "disappropriation" from himself as substance, identity:

> That god, that "last god," as he [Heidegger] puts it elsewhere—that "god," insofar as every god is the "last one," which is to say that every god dissipates and dissolves the very essence of the divine—is a god that *beckons* (*winkt*). That means, it makes a sign without sense, a signal of approach, of invitation, and of departure. This god has its essence in *winken*. And that sign-making, that blink of the eye comes to pass, starting from and in the direction of the *Ereignis*—the appropriating event through which man, appropriated to or by being, may be disappropriated [*ent-eignet*] of an identity closed in on its humanity. (*D* 27/43)[34]

One can only conclude that the modern problem of sense parallells and even repeats the problem of monotheism and of its complex God—that is, the problem monotheism *is* and wishes to be. In this way, the God of monotheism is the "last God," the one who persists within modernity and participates in its *Ereignis*. Again we discover how the deconstruction of the modern problem—the "void of being" analyzed by Granel and recast by Nancy, or the differential structure of an entanglement of presence and absence that is at stake in Nancy's discussion with phenomenology— must coincide with a deconstruction of monotheism.

We are still very close to Moses—to his distinction, to his connection, to the impossibility of these two. We are still close to his strange God, who passes by "in a dense cloud" (is he present? is he absent?) in order to give Moses his "words" as a series of winks and hints. We are still close to the Torah announcing the retreat of religion.

> Then the Lord said to Moses, 'I am going to come to you in a dense cloud.' . . . Then God spoke all these words. . . ." (Exod. 19:9 and 20:1)

Thinking Alterity—In One or Two?

Nancy's Christianity Compared with Lyotard's Judaism

FRANS VAN PEPERSTRATEN

Recent political problems in some European countries are once again strongly associated with religious differences within their populations. From within one religion, another religion or the absence of religion is experienced as alterity. At the same time, religion is in itself a way of experiencing alterity, namely, the alterity usually indicated with the word *God*.

Nancy discusses both kinds of alterity in *Dis-enclosure*. He refers to the first, for example, in discussing the complex relations between Judaism, Christianity, Islam, and Greek philosophy and to the second when he remarks, in the "Opening": "Christianity designates nothing other . . . than the demand to open in this world an alterity or an unconditional alienation" (*D* 10/20). It is important to examine how Nancy considers this alterity or alienation. According to Nancy, the second kind of alterity sheds light not only on the nature of Christianity or religion in general but also on the relationships between religions, or between religion and a nonreligious culture.

Unfortunately, Nancy has not yet paid much attention to the relationship between Christianity and Islam. However, in—"The Judeo-Christian (on Faith)"—he does address the relation between Christianity and Judaism.[1] This essay is closely connected to the preceding essay in *Dis-enclosure*, "A Deconstruction of Monotheism," which makes clear that Nancy does not distinguish fundamentally between the deconstruction of Christianity and the deconstruction of monotheism in general.

Against this backdrop, I want to address two questions.

First, what does Nancy mean by "deconstruction"? On the one hand, he argues that deconstruction results from the composite character of all monotheistic religions. On the other hand, in his analysis of the Epistle of James in "The Judeo-Christian," he appears to associate deconstruction with a certain "inadequation" in existence. How do these two focuses in Nancy's thinking of deconstruction relate to each other?

Second, how does the deconstruction of Christianity, as Nancy considers it, relate to Judaism? Here I will call upon Jean-François Lyotard's sketch of Judaism and of its relationship to Christianity, especially in *The Hyphen: Between Judaism and Christianity*.[2] I will therefore also be comparing Nancy and Lyotard.[3] Nancy himself invites his readers to draw this comparison, for he introduces his theme in "The Judeo-Christian" by quoting Lyotard's statement about the hyphen in the composite term *Judeo-Christian*: "the most impenetrable abyss that Western thought conceals" (D 42–43/66).[4]

Both Lyotard and Nancy appeal to texts that originated during the period when Christianity was still more or less a part of Judaism. Lyotard refers to the apostle Paul's letters to the Christian communities in, among other places, Corinth, Galatia, and Rome. Nancy bases "The Judeo-Christian" on the epistle of James, which, according to Nancy, occupies a position between Judaism and Christianity.

Nancy on Composition

Nancy explains in various ways how Christianity is to be regarded as a composite. In the early development of Christianity, both the Judaic religion and Greek and Roman philosophy played an important part. Christianity belongs, together with Judaism and Islam, to the three religions "of the Book," all of which recognize Abraham as a common forefather. In Nancy's view, these three religions can be seen as three attempts to redefine monotheism, and in every attempt a new association and disassociation of the Jew, the Christian, and the Muslim has been at stake (D 33/52). Furthermore, it is clear that each of these religions has broken up into a multitude of currents or forms (D 43/67).

The composite character of the three monotheistic religions within a historical perspective is connected with their compositeness in terms of dogma. The differences between these religions and their diversity of currents always result from different interpretations of the "covenant" between God and Man. The Christian idea of incarnation is rejected by both Judaism and Islam, but pardon for sins also appears in Judaism and the resurrection in Islam. In all these cases, the question is how God, although unique, "divides himself," Nancy writes (D 38/59). That is, God divides himself not only in himself but also over Man, as a redistribution of the divine and the human.

In "A Deconstruction of Monotheism," this composite character of Christianity appears to determine Nancy's notion of deconstruction. In at least two instances he expressly gives a definition of deconstruction, though I shall quote only the first: "I will call 'deconstruction of monotheism' the operation consisting in disassembling the elements that constitute it, in order to attempt to discern, among these elements and as if behind them, . . . that which made their assembly possible and which . . . it remains . . . for us . . . to think as the beyond of monotheism" (D 32/51).[5] What should we think of this definition? Is it sufficient to say that deconstruction consists in disassembling, understood according to the classical idea of "ana-lysis": one considers something to be a composite and dissolves this composite in order to recognize what elements there are and how they were connected?

The way in which, at the outset of "The Judeo-Christian," Nancy appeals to Lyotard agrees quite well with this definition. From Lyotard's statement on the hyphen (*trait d'union*) in the expression "Judeo-Christian," Nancy infers that this is a "*trait d'union* that holds this composition together or de-composes it at its core—which makes of its center a disunion." Nancy also calls this "the enigma of this uncomposable composition." He then refers to the various elements in this composite, such as Greek philosophy, so that "Judeo-Christianity" is also "Judeo-Greco-Christianity" (D 42–43/67). According to Nancy, compositeness as such has come to be the general character of the West: "the Judeo-Christian composition thus conceals or stimulates what we could call the general dis-position of the West" (D 44/67).

Nancy does not limit himself to merely providing a genealogy of this Western composition, he also indicates how it should be considered as such. He argues that the "Judeo-Christian composition" is structured according to a schema that plays a significant role "in our entire tradition of thought," namely, the schema of the *coincidentia oppositorum*. He explains that variations of this schema keep on reappearing—for instance, in the oxymoron, in Kantian schematism, in Hegelian dialectics, and in mystical ecstasy (D 44/67). Elsewhere in the volume, Nancy supplements this list by adding—among others—the dialogues of Plato, Derrida's aporia, and Kant's antinomies of pure reason. Moreover, Nancy adds here an element with a very broad field of application indeed: "the *sic et non* of all types" (D 131/192). These examples on their own do not add up to a defined whole. Fortunately, however, Nancy also provides a more detailed definition of the *coincidentia oppositorum*. Its most general law, according to Nancy, is "to contain at its center a gap [*un écart*]." Nancy immediately applies this idea to the hyphen and thereby to "uncomposable composition," with which he had already brought it in connection. He concludes: "The hyphen passes over a void that it does not fill" (*D* 44/68). Thus we have a construction or a composition by means of a hyphen and therefore, at the same time, a deconstruction, which is a decomposition. Nancy refers to a "com-position that would carry within itself, in its *cum* itself, the law of a deconstruction." The question is: "What is there beneath the hyphen and in the hollow of the assemblage?" (*D* 45/69).

When the composite is understood according to the model of the *coincidentia oppositorum*, deconstruction can indeed consist in a disassembling. In this case there are two, or, in a sense, three elements, namely, the two opposite terms and the void between them, the void that is also (bridged by) the hyphen. However, as we shall now see, in his reading of James, Nancy elaborates a model of deconstruction that works on one element, which does not coincide with itself and therefore can also be said to comprise two elements.

Nancy on the Inadequation of Praxis

James is for Nancy an outstanding example of a Judeo-Christian because it is impossible to decide whether his epistle falls under Judaism or Christianity.[6] The epistle attributed to James was incorporated into the Christian canon of the New Testament only "at the price of remarkable doubts and resistances," Nancy notes (*D* 45/69).[7]

Nancy has substantial reasons to consider James as a transitional figure between Judaism and Christianity. In his reading of James, Nancy highlights, among other things, the issues of work and of the relationship between God and Man.

Work

James wonders: "What good is it, my brothers, if a man claims to have faith but has no deeds? Can such faith save him?" (James 2:14). Nancy observes that James, to the extent that he calls for an active affirmation of faith, places less emphasis on its content. In a sense, James does not present us with any theology at all, or at least we encounter in his epistle "a retreat of theology," or "a theology in retreat." Therefore we can say that

James occupies a position *between* two theologies, between two religions, between Judaism and Christianity (*D* 48/73).

The subtitle of Nancy's essay is "On Faith." The apparent paradox here is that this could just as well have read "On Works." However, Nancy's statement echoes that of James: to talk about faith is to talk about deeds, or works. (Writing in Greek, James uses the word *ergon*.) James does not simply oppose faith and works, Nancy observes. On the contrary, works are faith itself. James puts it somewhat polemically: "Show me your faith without deeds, and I will show my faith by what I do" (James 2:18). To Nancy, the meaning being assigned to the word *works* here is of the utmost importance. In the preceding verse (2:17), James says: "Thus also faith by itself, if it does not have works, is dead." A little further on (James 2:20), in a similar passage, he uses the word *argē* instead of "dead"—according to Nancy, *argē* is a contraction of *aergos*: "without works," "ineffective." Now, if "without works" means dead, we may conclude that, inversely, "works" are life, or rather, existence: "the *ergon* here is existence," Nancy says. Works, then, entail not producing something but rather being effective, not the *operari* of an *opus* but its *être-en-acte*. This means that we should reorient our customary framing of the word *works*. It is no coincidence that in James the word *ergon* is sometimes translated as "practice." Thus, in Aristotelian terms, "works" can better be assigned to the category of *praxis* ("action, deed") rather than to *poiēsis* ("creation, making"; *D* 51/77). Bringing all the relevant Greek terms together, Nancy suggests that James implicitly maintains the following definition: "*pistis* (faith) is the *praxis* that takes place in and as the *poiēsis* of the *erga*" (*D* 52/77). From this, Nancy draws several conclusions.

1. Because faith is "praxical," *poiēsis*, the making of works, cannot be adequate to itself. "If I wanted to write this in Blanchot's idiom," Nancy continues, "I would say that faith is the *désoeuvrement* that takes place in and as the work." The work "unworks" itself; it is no longer a question of the traditionally "closed" work (*organon*), in which all the parts are in tune with one another, but rather a notion of work in which the work opens itself up and becomes "disorganized."

2. The concept on which the work might be based is being transcended. *Praxis*, according to Nancy, "is in every work and it is *ek tou ergou*, that which exceeds the concept of it."

3. This "praxical excess" provides the working subject with the possibility of being more than what this subject is in itself and for itself. However, according to Nancy, it also means that neither the faith nor the work of the subject can be regarded as the property of the subject (*D* 52/78). Nancy points out that the most important works referred to by James—

the love of one's neighbor, the rejection of wealth, speaking truthfully—all require an exposition to what cannot be appropriated (*D* 55/78).

4. That such a faith transcends the concept—and comprehension in general—means, according to Nancy, that faith must be distinguished from belief: "faith [*foi*] cannot be an adherence to some contents of belief [*croyance*]" (*D* 52/78). To be sure, faith cannot be separated entirely from the order of *logos*—the words *faith* and *foi* are, after all, derived via the Latin *fides* from the Greek *pistis*, which is in turn derived from the Greek *peithō*: "to convince." But the faith James has in mind is based, Nancy writes, upon "the inadequation of its own *logos* to itself." There are no "reasons" to believe. "Faith is not argumentative; rather, it is the performative of the commandment." The truth (*la vérité*) of faith, as Nancy puts it, requires first and foremost a "making-true," a "verification" (*D* 53/79).

5. Because the "agent," or the "acting entity," "*makes itself* exceed itself," faith as work also opens up the alterity qua other person, it is a "being-unto-the-other." At the same time, the persuasion or assurance of faith cannot come from the subject as such: "this faith . . . must come from the other, this faith must come from outside, it is the outside opening in itself a passage toward the inside" (*D* 54).[8]

The word Nancy uses here several times is *inadequation* (at one point explained by the added "or incommensurability"; *D* 58/85). One thing can be inadequate to another; for instance, Nancy calls Abraham's action (of offering Isaac up) inadequate to its concept or "sense" (to immolate his son; *D* 54/79–80). But something can also be inadequate to itself. According to Nancy, that happens here to *logos*. Thus it appears that deconstruction now focuses less on compositeness than on this inadequation.

God and Man

In "A Deconstruction of Monotheism," Nancy already claims that in monotheism—contrary to polytheism—the relationship between God and man is characterized by an absence of the god, or rather, by "the withdrawal of this god away from presence" (*D* 36/55). In his reading of James, Nancy indicates more precisely how to think of this absence. Several of James's wordings are relevant. First of all, James states that God "engendered us as the first-born of his creatures" (James 1:18). Furthermore, James repeats what is said in Genesis 1:26–27, that "man is made in the image of God" (James 3:9). The original Greek used by James is *kath' omoiôsin*: "likeness," "similitude," or "resemblance," rather than the narrower term "image." Nancy concludes that it is this resemblance that makes man the first-born of creation. Nancy interprets the term *first-born* as a distinguishing mark, as a "trace." That man has been engendered in the likeness of God means that he is "the mark or the homogeneous trace that dedicates the world to its creator." At the same time, the created world is less a produced world than "a marked world, a world traced" (*D* 49/74). However, a trace signifies a withdrawal from being present. Therefore, the likeness does not entail some kind of mirroring of God and Man, of two worlds in isolation from one another; rather, it entails that within his existence man is "equal" to something that is not present.

James also states that "every good and perfect gift is from above, coming down from the Father of the heavenly lights" (James 1:17). God is first and foremost a giver, the giver of light—not of the light reflected from the things in the world, but the light in which these things are possible. Such a gift is akin, Nancy argues, to "the grace God gives the humble" (James 4:6). Nancy points out that James opposes this giving of light and grace to a logic of lack and appropriation in which: "You covet and you have not. . . . You ask and you receive not, because you ask wrongly, in order to spend for your sensuous pleasures" (James 4:2–3). God's giving does not assume the form of a concrete gift, that is, what is being given does not belong to the order of appropriable goods. The logic of the gift, Nancy states—in reference to the other James, "the other Jacques" (i.e., Derrida)—is that the giver-God abandons (*s'abandonne*) himself to the gift (*don*).[9] Here Nancy remarks that the *homoiosis* can also be understood as a *homodosis* (which means "giving equally"; *D* 49–50/74–76): "To be in the image of God is therefore to be asking for grace, to give oneself in turn to the gift" (*D* 50/76).

And Jesus? Is he the mediator between two separated worlds? First of all, Nancy points out that James only *mentions* Jesus, as nothing more than a proper name. Because of the absence of a specific theology, Nancy infers, this proper name does not turn into a concept. It is only a name that "puts faith to work," as Nancy says. The only *description* James gives of "the Lord Jesus" is that he is "anointed with glory" (James 2:1), *christos tēs doxas*, as the Greek text says—which can be understood both as the glorious Christ and as the glorious Messiah.[10]

According to Nancy, what is important here is that "anointment with glory," like receiving grace, refers to the fact that faith "is faith in the inappropriable." Jesus is the name connected to glory, but glory (also "splendor," shining) is what accompanies appearing, and this in an inappropriable way—glory is not gold. Therefore, Nancy concludes, "*Jesus* is thus the name of this appearing . . .: the proper name of the inappropriable." And, because James stresses in the same verse that we may not "take account of persons," which means that we cannot even take account of the person of Jesus, Nancy concludes that "it is thus a name for any name, for all names, for the name of every other." The anointment, whether specified as Christ or as the Messiah, does not *represent* what is sacred (*sacré*) but signifies the withdrawal of the sacred. As appearing, the anointment (Jesus) consists in "the exposition of the world to the world," and at the same time in "the very withdrawal of the divine" (*D* 58/85).

For Nancy, these references to the inappropriable mean that in faith inadequation is at work (*D* 57/84). By now the reader might wonder whether in Nancy deconstruction means less disassembling something than demonstrating that something comprises an inadequation. However, when the meaning of Jesus is at stake, Nancy brings these two explanations of deconstruction together. First of all, he writes "Jesus-Christ," with a hyphen. This is because James connects Jesus as a name with the anointment with glory. Nancy concludes: "Deconstruction lies in its cement: it is in the hyphen, indeed it is *of* that hyphen." But then Nancy says that this hyphen is a conjunction in which "each of the edges, exceeding the other, remains incommensurable with it." And in this line of thought he concludes that the name Jesus is "the *proper* name of the *inappropriable*" (*D* 57, 84; my emphasis). Now, therefore, the hyphen does not connect two "edges" separated from each other but represents one thing full of tension, for we do have proper names, we do appropriate what is not appropriable. And this is why Nancy can say that the name is "always the name of an other, even if it were my own" and that "glory is the exposition of inadequation or incommensurability" (*D* 58/85).

The Compositeness of Praxis in Nancy

I think one can best summarize Nancy's argument in "The Judeo-Christian" by distinguishing two strands: one in which religion (that is, the complex assemblage of Judaism and Christianity) as such is at stake and one that is logical. In both strands, important shifts occur in the course of the essay.

Shifts in Nancy's Treatment of Religion

Initially, Nancy takes the expression "Judeo-Christian" to indicate a historical composite, in which Judaism, on the one hand, and Christianity, on the other, are brought together. A first shift, however, now appears in his argument. Because James is, so to speak, in the middle of this historical composition, Nancy examines James. However, Nancy also presents James as representative of Christianity. Thus our attention shifts from the composite "Judeo-Christian" to the composite "Christianity" as such, as if the composition A + B is equal to the composite nature of B in itself. Moreover, Nancy equates Christianity (B) with both monotheism and modern Western culture as such. Although he does not claim that this compositeness is a trait exclusive to Christianity or Western modernity, he does emphasize that the notion of a composite community has always been fundamental to Christianity, and that Christianity first introduced the notion of the "pleroma of peoples" into Western culture, or into Western-ness (*occidentalité*) as such (*D* 45/69). In this line of thought, it comes as no surprise that Nancy does not analyze Judaism but only takes up some issues in which Judaism and Christianity are not too far removed from each other, such as the emphasis laid on work.

When Nancy speaks about these issues, a second shift in his argument appears. At a certain point in his essay, Nancy leaves the question of the historical composite and turns toward existence. In his view, existence is primarily praxis. The primacy of praxis in Nancy does not mean that he has recourse to an empirical pragmatism, to the idea that only the "tangible" quality of action counts for anything. Neither does he appeal to the other extreme, that is, to an "intangible," supra-sensible, "other" world. Nancy assigns to praxis—as existence, as a mode of being—a transcendent involvement with the world. Thus he refers to "having, in the world, the experience of what is not of this world, without being another world for all that" and of opening "within the world an outside that is not a beyond-the-world, but the truth of the world" (*D* 78 and 79/120 and 121).[11] He calls this a "transcendence without a transcendent," a "transcendence immanent to our immanence" (*D* 136/198). In Nancy's view, praxis refers to the immanence of ordinary life, in which, however, transcendence is also at stake. For praxis transcends every defined entity we may feel tempted to recognize within it: the "closed" work, *poiēsis*, the concept, *logos*, or the subject. And therefore praxis is always something composite. Every action has—inseparably tied together—aspects of both the immanent and the transcendent. Thus we see that Nancy has equated the composite nature of Christianity and the composite nature of praxis or existence. Taken together, the two shifts go from "Judeo-Christianity" to practical existence.

Shifts in Nancy's Logic: From Coincidentia Oppositorum
to Inadequation

Closely connected to these shifts regarding the substance that Nancy presents, one also finds a shift in his logic. Initially Nancy explains the notion of composition by means of the model of the *coincidentia oppositorum*, as we have seen. He presents this model as starting from two elements plus a void traversed by a hyphen. The second half of his essay, however—that is, from the moment he focuses on the issue of works in James—is characterized by the frequent use of the term *inadequation*. Now this term could cause some confusion, because in philosophy, from Aristotle on, this term has normally been used when speaking about an accordance between two things that remain separated from each other (for instance, thing and word, or fact and sentence). However, Nancy's "inadequation" does not mean the absence of such an *adaequatio* between two things remaining in two different worlds. In Nancy's logical model of "inadequation," there is only one thing, in one world, which holds in itself a tension and therefore consists of two poles. In the passages I have quoted, Nancy attempts to articulate this twofold nature of one and the same thing as "an outside . . . not beyond the world," a "transcendence immanent to our immanence," and so on.

I am myself not convinced that one can actually convert the first model into the second one. But this is what Nancy does. When, as we discovered above, in the beginning of his essay he discusses the hyphen in the expression "Judeo-Christian," he calls upon the model of the *coincidentia oppositorum*. Later in the essay, however, when he places a hyphen in "Jesus-Christ" he stresses instead that this hyphen refers to an inadequation within one and the same entity. The latter thought results from the point of departure of Nancy's philosophy: being is positing, or positioning, such that it is also a spacing out. Thus every positing is a placing next to something else, every positing of one thing is at the same time a compositioning of two things. In Nancy's view, the hyphen is such a spacing out. Thus the meaning of the term *composition* shifts in the course of Nancy's essay. It no longer refers to the encounter between two opposite terms but to the positing of one term.

Clearly, it is the second model that really interests Nancy. What interests him is a critique of the "mono-" in order to show that it comprises in itself something else, an alterity. Pursuing this critique of the "mono-," Nancy repeatedly suggests that monotheism as a religious phenomenon, on the one hand, and the general equivalence of value in modern Western economy as uncovered by Marx, on the other, are related to each other.

Nancy analyzes and deconstructs the tendency, essential to the West, to limiting sense to "unidirectionality" (*sens unique*), founded in either God, value, or man (*D* 31/50). In the "Post-Scriptum" to "A Deconstruction of Monotheism," written after 9/11, Nancy refers to "the motive of the One," dominant in both economy and religion. At the same time, with regard to monotheism, Nancy observes "that the 'one' of the 'god' is not at all Unicity qua substantial present and united with itself" (*D* 41/62). Nancy's question, then, is: "What secret, ambivalent resource lies hidden within the organizing scheme of this mono-?" In his view, this "resource" would at the same time "open upon a future for the world that would no longer be either Christian or anti-Christian, either monotheist or atheist or even polytheist, but that would advance precisely beyond all these categories (after having made all of them possible)" (*D* 34/54). Here, one may conclude, the critique of the "mono-" shifts toward an affirmation of it.

Connecting the two threads I have distinguished in this section, one can perceive what Nancy has in mind with this resource: the transcendent immanence of praxis. Praxis that is the one that is two. And, according to Nancy, this is the real lesson monotheism teaches us.

Lyotard on Judaism and Christianity

Starting at the end of the 1960s, when, after his period of activism, he returned to philosophy, Lyotard repeatedly and intensively explored Judaism. For Lyotard, Judaism represents a counterpoint to, or within, Western culture. While his more detailed analyses of the relationship between Judaism and the West bear witness to the shifts that occurred from 1968 to 1998 in his thinking in general, the central thrust of his evaluation has remained constant: Judaism contains the necessary critique of an *illusion* that has profoundly determined Western culture. This can be defined as the illusion of presence, fulfillment, and totality: "May I confide in you here that, under the name 'Jew,' I am looking for that which tarnishes and leaves in mourning (and indeed must do so) this Western accomplishment?" Lyotard writes in *The Hyphen* (*TH* 57).

We see that Lyotard and Nancy criticize the same characteristic of Western culture: the illusion of fulfilled presence. However, Lyotard bases his critique on Judaism. He appears to treat Judaism, Christianity, and Western modernity as three completely different positions in history. Briefly, one could say that he sees Judaism as the religion in which man has a relationship of *estrangement* with God, Christianity as the religion in which man appropriates the *presence* of God, provided that he is prepared to disappropriate himself into God, whereas modernity holds that one can be freed from all dispossession and indebtedness to the other (*TH* 3–4/122). Nancy, by contrast, aims to find a ground on which to base his critique of Western culture in Western culture itself, insofar as this culture corresponds to the monotheism of both Judaism and Christianity (and Islam). The West is only *one* position for Nancy. And, in a certain sense, Nancy's idea of the West is ahistorical (there are no fundamental turning points or ruptures in Western culture, at any rate not after the era of myth and polytheism), for the (self-)deconstructive character of Christianity finds its manifestation already in James, or, in other words, monotheism and deconstruction coincide right from the start.

What is, according to Lyotard, the nature of Judaism? How can a critique of Western culture be derived from it?[12] Gershom Scholem tells us some interesting stories in this regard: What exactly happened when the Ten Commandments were revealed on Mount Sinai?[13] Put more precisely: what was being heard—by Moses, on the one hand, and by the people of Israel, on the other? To be sure, all would have heard the divine voice. But there is the story that the people of Israel heard only the first two Commandments, namely: "I am the Lord your God" and "You shall have no other gods before me." This experience already exceeded the people's faculties of comprehension; only Moses was therefore still able to "endure" receiving the remaining Commandments. Another story takes this even further: the people of Israel heard nothing but "the *aleph* with which in the Hebrew text the first Commandment begins, the *aleph* of the word *anochi,* 'I.' " "In Hebrew this *aleph* is just the glottal stop that precedes a vowel at the start of a word (like the *spiritus lenis* in Greek): so it's the source of all articulate sound. To hear the *aleph* is to hear nothing, but at the same time, the aleph is the spiritual root of all the other letters of the alphabet."[14] In other words, the people heard the initial impetus to what they were supposed to understand, but they did not know *what* they should have understood.

Lyotard's sketch of the starting point of Judaism in *The Hyphen* is analogous to this story about the aleph: a Voice (Lyotard uses a capital *V* here) has left behind letters on the stones of the desert. No vowels are to be found among these letters, and the letters themselves are as yet unvoiced. A people, Lyotard explains, becomes constituted by taking upon itself the obligation to act out these letters, that is, to vocalize them, to give voice to them, to track down their meaning and carry it out. In Lyotard's view, the Voice leaving behind these letters opens up a peculiar kind of historicity. What is relevant here is not the mythical history or the story in general, where the end is identical to the beginning, or at any rate "rhymes" with the beginning. Of just as little relevance is modern consciousness and its ambition to constitute the three modes of time from within itself. After all, the beginning—that is, the Voice—arrives in, but does not find itself within current time. To act upon the letters in current time implies that the Voice "itself" has withdrawn. Reality, as it has been given with the letters, is unfulfilled, which causes the people to go in search of justice. Thus, according to Lyotard, the people interrupt the mythical and invent the ethical (*TH* 13/136).

Again we can notice some points of agreement between Lyotard and Nancy. Both emphasize in Judaism (Lyotard) or (Judeo-)Christianity (Nancy): (1) a withdrawal from presence; (2) a demythologization (*D* 36–37/55–57); and (3) the importance of works instead of doctrinal creed. On the last point, to be sure, Lyotard thinks that Christianity, unlike Judaism, does base itself on doctrinal creed, but one might argue that this perception arises from the fact that he does not take James but Paul to be representative of Christianity.

However, we also get a first indication of an important difference between Lyotard's Judaism and Nancy's Christianity. In Lyotard's view, the Jewish community constitutes itself in working on the already given alterity of the Voice, whereas for Nancy alterity—which is also the alterity of the other person, being in community—only comes about *in working*.

Lyotard reads in the story of Abraham's sacrifice of Isaac a message not mentioned by Nancy. According to Genesis 22, God instructs Abraham to sacrifice his son. But after he has already tied up his son and placed him on the sacrificial altar, Abraham is told by an angel that he should do the boy no harm, for he (Abraham) had been tried sufficiently. By drawing an analogy between the bonds around the body of Isaac and the "bond" that ties the signifier to the signified, Judaism, according to Lyotard, concludes from this incident that the bond with which the letters are tied to their meaning is also unstable—insofar as it can be severed by God at any moment. The text may always turn out to mean something different from what it was thought to mean, and therefore it has to be reread continuously. This is why Judaism attaches such enormous importance to the endless work of interpretation (*TH* 10–11/130–31). This is all the more so, Lyotard points out, because in the tradition of Judaism one type of meaning is discerned (among other types) that is supposed to remain secret and inaccessible: *sod* in Hebrew, translated by Lyotard into French as *estrangé*. In Lyotard's view, interpretation is work, and work is interpretation. What is more important, however, is that both are evoked by the Voice but cannot overcome its estrangement.

According to Lyotard, Paul does not accept this relationship with a definitively estranged Voice. For this reason, Paul appeals to incarnation and transfiguration. The incarnation in Jesus Christ means that the Voice has become flesh and has come among us "once and for all" (Rom. 6:10). In transfiguration the bread and wine become signifiers of the actual presence of Christ. According to Paul, the bond with the signified is thereby guaranteed, which leads Lyotard to the conclusion that Paul dismisses the endless work of interpreting the letters as having become superfluous.[15] This introduces a dialectic of love, upon which, according to Lyotard, Christianity has been founded: here I am, in the flesh (*TH* 23–24/149–50). With this dialectic Paul *transforms* Judaism, insofar as this posits an incompatibility between the law (Torah; *nomos*) and the flesh (*sarx*). The flesh is abject in relation to the law; it is unsuitable as its subject and cannot be subordinated to the law. The law curses the flesh. Hence the numerous prescriptions and markings with regard to the flesh, such as those concerning diet and circumcision. By contrast, Paul makes it clear to his readers that the true nourishment is the body of Christ—"Now you are the body of Christ, and each one of you is a part of it" (1 Cor. 12:27)—and that true circumcision is spiritual in nature (Rom. 2:29). The crucial meaning of the flesh is spiritual, it is the Spirit (*pneuma*). Therefore in Paul's view, Lyotard observes, this incompatibility has in principle been resolved (*TH* 19–20/143–45).

Lyotard opposes this dialectic with which Paul sought to transform death into life, reading and interpretation into love, and thus Judaism into Christianity. The language of the Other, writes Lyotard, is marked not by death but by strangeness. This *estrangement* needs to be respected. The letters must be deciphered, vocalized, put into rhythm and sung, interpreted and translated. But their figuration is forbidden, as is incarnation and yielding to the temptation to render the Voice itself audible and visible (*TH* 24/151) There should be no transfer onto the imaginary of presence (*TH* 60).

Lyotard on the Estrangement of *Aisthēsis*

Where Nancy speaks of "inadequate" and "inadequation," Lyotard uses the words *estrangé* and *estrangement*. It may be assumed that Lyotard has deliberately chosen these uncommon alternatives to *aliéné* and *aliénation* ("alienated, alienation"). These more common terms are normally employed in dialectical thinking, where alienation is conceived as something that can in principle be resolved—or, to put it in Hegelian terminology, sublated—through an act of reappropriation. By choosing the word *estrangement*, Lyotard indicates that Judaism recognizes that the "strange," the "alien," is something irresolvable.

As a consequence, in Lyotard's understanding, Paul's epistles place a hyphen between two separated terms: *Judeo* and *Christian*. This hyphen is dialectical in nature. Its model is given in Paul's statement that the Jew becomes truly realized in the Christian. Therefore Paul speaks of both "rejecting" and "accepting" the Jews (Rom. 11:15; TH 22). For Paul, it is clear that Jews ought to convert to Christianity. Lyotard argues that Paul's *trait d'union* represents not the connecting of two things of equal worth but a dialectical trait from law *to* faith, and from Abraham *to* Jesus Christ (*TH* 15/138–39). Lyotard concludes that Judaism as such is no longer present in the Pauline *trait d'union*; the hyphen "itself" is Christian. Judaism is "taken along" by the hyphen only by means of being rejected or repressed. The "line" (*trait*), says Lyotard, crosses out a "blank space" (*un blanc*) (*TH* 13/135). In Lyotard's view, this blank space is to be seen as an abyss. Thus, according to Lyotard, Paul fails to appreciate the abyss that separates Judaism from Christianity. Lyotard's thesis is "that the text of the Gospels, the Acts of the Apostles, the Letters, and Revelation is not of the same literal, 'literary,' and thus ontological regimen as that of the Pentateuch" (*TH* 25/152).

On examining why Judaism and Christianity are so different, one arrives at a second abyss Lyotard appears to have exposed. There is not only the abyss between Judaism and Christianity as such, but also the abyss lying at the very foundation of Judaism. Lyotard elucidates this abyss by referring to the distinction between the Voice and its voiceless letters on the stones of the Sinai desert, the distinction between the letters and their meaning, and the distinction between the law and the flesh. When speaking of *estrangement*, Lyotard has this fundamental abyss in mind.

From other texts written by Lyotard in the same period, it becomes clear that this *estrangement*, as he sees it, is an inevitable aspect of *aisthēsis*. After the publication of his major work, *The Differend*, Lyotard gradually became a thinker of *aisthēsis*. He uses this Greek term, for it conjoins the meanings of perception and feeling. Man is always affectively touched in perception; his feeling indicates that something has taken place, but this feeling cannot be expressed by an articulated statement, susceptible to knowledge and communication, without becoming distorted. A complete articulation is impossible because, according to Lyotard, there is no *aisthēsis* without anaesthesia. *Aisthēsis* is a bolt of lightning, a shock paradoxically desensitizing us to what we are feeling. We are always trailing behind *aisthēsis*; we are forever trying to get a grip on what it was that had touched us. That with which a*isthēsis* started remains beyond reach, and therefore we can call it both *estranged aisthēsis* and the *aisthēsis* of *estrangement*. Lyotard encounters this estranged *aisthēsis* in Judaism as its starting point.

As we have seen, Lyotard refers to "the most impenetrable abyss that Western thought conceals." In my view, Lyotard indicates here the second abyss I have just described, which in fact is the primary, more fundamental one: the abyss or the *estrangement* felt in *aisthēsis*. Only insofar as Judaism recognizes this primary abyss and Christianity does not, an abyss also exists as a secondary phenomenon between Judaism and Christianity. This abyss between Judaism and Christianity is clear enough, whether it remains as a blank space or is traversed by a hyphen. But what remains concealed is a deeper abyss, namely, one that opens up where "Jewish" *aisthēsis* commences. It is this abyss that is impenetrable to Western thought, for Western thought has mainly opted for knowledge and communication, and therefore has never taken *aisthēsis* seriously, nor the estrangement it entails. According to Lyotard, the same is true of Paul, for Paul wants to base himself on a dialectic of truth. Whereas this dialectic—albeit with a blend of rejection and acceptance—could still come to grips with the abyss between Judaism and Christianity, it is completely irrelevant where the primary abyss, that of *estrangement*, is concerned. Consequently, Lyotard concludes his thinking on *aisthēsis* with an adage against dialectics: "there is some unsublatable [*il y a de l'irrelevable*]" (*TH* 58/79).

No Conclusion

A comparison of the views of Lyotard and Nancy appears to be simple. What Lyotard says about what I call the secondary abyss, that is, the superficially identifiable difference between Judaism and Christianity, fits in very well with what Nancy says about the abyss as a model of the *coincidentia oppositorum*. The only difference is that Lyotard's view of the hyphen as traversing this abyss is negative, whereas Nancy's is positive. However, Lyotard has not stopped here, and neither has Nancy. What if we bring into account Lyotard's notion of estranged *aisthēsis*, and Nancy's view of inadequate *praxis*?

Nancy gives no indication that he realizes Lyotard was actually referring to the more fundamental abyss felt in the estrangement of *aisthēsis*. Moreover, it appears that Nancy would prefer to nip such a train of thought in the bud. Evidence for this can be found in his *Being Singular Plural*. There he states that alterity should not be conceived of as an

Other. We should not conceive of it as an origin, as any *outside* the world, or as a stranger opposed to the self—thus, not as an *aliud*, *alius*, or *alienus*, but as an *alter*, as *one* among many, as everyone every time, as something that every time transforms the world *from within*. This means, according to Nancy, that one should not assume that there is an abyss beyond which lies something prohibited or concealed, or an alienation that needs to be reappropriated—as always happens when, again according to Nancy the Other is referred to in philosophy (*BSP* 11–12/29–30). In a footnote (*BSP* 196n14/29n1), he explicitly criticizes Lacan for this. As a matter of fact, Nancy's extremely brief commentary on Levinas fits the same bill (*BSP* 199n37/52n1). What Levinas understands as "otherwise than being" is, in Nancy's view, precisely what is most characteristic of "being." Thought does not start from an opposition between the other and being, because being itself is plural right from the start: as an event, after all, of *positing*, being is at the same time a spacing out and a being with (*BSP* 28–32/48–52). Insofar as being should thus be conceived only as co-existence, Nancy can see no difference between the ontological and the ethical (*BSP* 99/123). Without actually referring to Levinas—but clearly in opposition to his work—Nancy states that no ethics is possible apart from ontology and that only the ontological can be ethical (*BSP* 21/40).

It is in these basic views that Nancy also differs from Lyotard. Lyotard draws much of his inspiration from Lacan (specifically, Lacan's theorem of the Thing, the Real) and Freud—that is, from psychoanalytic theory in general. In addition, he draws heavily on Levinas and Jewish thinking in general. Lyotard's *Heidegger and "the jews,"* in particular, provides a clear attempt to combine both sources.

Does Lyotard's account of Jewish thinking imply the notion of the Other or outside challenged by Nancy? At first glance, he seems to do so in introducing the Voice, which does not allow itself to be made present. At the same time, however, we have seen that Lyotard starts from the idea that this estrangement operates within the sphere of life: it is felt and inspires works, first of all, the work of interpretation. Understood in this way, the Other is at least an alterity as well, which is effective *in* this world. Lyotard remarks: "Jewish listening must remain strained between the inaudible voice of the Other and the entire imaginary realm of the flesh, included in the pact as excluded" (*TH* 64). Even if Lyotard writes the Other with a capital letter, "Jewish listening" does not coincide with the Other as such but is situated in the space in between two extremes, between the Other and the imaginary. The fact that estrangement cannot be resolved does not preclude humanity from relating to it. And this is, according to Lyotard, what the Judaic conception of work is about.

Can Lyotard's estranged *aisthēsis* be integrated into Nancy's inadequation of *praxis*? And vice versa? Perhaps. I can draw no conclusion. I content myself with observing that what is at stake in Lyotard is an alterity that *presents itself* to us in *aisthēsis*; in Nancy it is an alterity that is *made* in praxis (in existence), an alterity that is posited by existing. This also means that Lyotard's alterity is there before our time, comes from "outside time," whereas Nancy's alterity is there *in* our time, or rather, in our being as "spacing" or spacing out" (*espacement*). Is a decision possible? Yes—if *we make* the decision. But what if the de-cision has always already been there?

The Excess of Reason and the Return of Religion

Transcendence of Christian Monotheism in Nancy's Dis-enclosure

DONALD LOOSE

Limits, Limitlessness, and the Problem of Delimitation

"It is not a question of reviving religion." The first sentence of the "Opening" of *Dis-Enclosure* is very clear in this regard. Further on in the same section, Nancy writes: "It is also not a question of repainting the skies" and "It is not our concern to save religion, even less to return to it" (D 1/9).

If not, then what *is* our concern? Nancy provides an answer by referring to Kant's *Religion Within the Boundaries of Mere Reason*: "It is, however, a question of opening mere reason up to the limitlessness that constitutes its truth" (D 1/9). Whereas for Kant reason could still conceive religion "within the limits" that delimit such reason, thus enabling it to comprehend and delimit religion as rational religion (*Vernunftreligion*), Nancy suggests that such reason itself is opened up in turn. Kant's ambiguous heritage lies in making "room for a rational faith" (D 2/10).[1] This should not be understood just in the sense of reason's being able to offer room for faith, insofar as reason—within its limit—defines faith. Nor should it be merely seen as reason being able to provide a space for practices that transcend reason or for beliefs to the extent that these serve rational faith. It also indicates that reason itself has a religious dimension: a "faith of reason" according to Nancy's original formulation (*foi de la raison* and not *foi rationelle*). For Nancy, Kant's "rational religion" simultaneously appears as a faithful reason: a reason that is confronted with its limits and excess.

In this context, the excess of rational religion is not that which falls outside such limits, which—as *parerga* of historical or institutional religion—is still given its true meaning by rational religion. The excess of rational religion must be understood not as something "outside" rational religion but as an intrinsic exteriority: rational religion is also an excess to itself. The transcendental movement of reason in relation to the understanding is repeated by reason in relation to itself. However, this reflexive return of reason upon itself is not a closed circle. Here, reason understands that it is unable to close the circle of its own rational foundation, being forced to leave an opening for what can only be described as having faith in its rational self:

> a critique of reason, that is to say, a demanding and non-complacent examination of reason by reason, makes unconditionally requisite, within reason itself, an opening and e-levation of reason. It is not a question of "religion," here, but rather of a "faith" as a sign of the fidelity of reason to that which *in and of itself* exceeds reason's phantasm of justifying itself [*rendre raison de soi*] as much as the world and man. (D 28/44–45)

In other words, "thinking . . . can think—and indeed, cannot not think—that it thinks something in excess over itself" (D 11/22).[2] A key notion in Nancy's definition of such excess is that of an *opening of* and *within* reason, thought as dis-enclosure (*déclosion*) of such reason. In particular, a dis-enclosure oriented toward an alterity that defies further signification or definition: a radical "outside" that is nothing but the endless movement of dis-enclosure itself. This movement ultimately dis-encloses reason itself, but also all sense, as given:

> But faith? . . . Should it not form the necessary relation to the *nothing*: in such a way that we understand that there are no buffers, no halting points, no markers, no undeconstructible terms, and that dis-enclosure never stops opening what it opens. (D 12/24)

> to open rationality to the dimension appropriate to the absolute, or again, to a "higher reason" (our translation of Hölderlin's *höher Besinnen*). (D 2/10–11)

This opening of rationality is the meta-critical[3] dimension that critical philosophy also generates in relation to itself: "The closure invariably dis-encloses itself: such is the precise sense of the demand for the unconditioned that structures Kantian reason" (D 7/17). But is there still a "precise sense" of "the unconditioned"?

The Self-Deconstruction of Christianity

According to Nancy, religion, especially monotheistic religion and in particular Christianity, points to this meta-critical dimension of reason, its faithful dimension: "Christianity designates nothing other, essentially . . . than the demand to open in this world an alterity or an unconditional alienation" (*D* 10/20). Christianity is inherently characterized by a movement that points beyond itself. Predominantly because of Platonic influences and the mystical tradition, the construction of dogmatic theology has time and again been forced open in the direction of an *absolutum* beyond all essence. In *On the Divine Names*, Dionysius the Areopagite pointed to the fact that all names for God must both be denied and affirmed, but also indicated that the negation itself needs to be negated, thereby making its meaning virtually incomprehensible to humans. God is beyond both affirmation and negation. Notwithstanding what we may claim about God, he himself will always be beyond such claims. In a certain manner, transcendence also signifies that which no longer "is" beyond the totality of all being, and not just the integral fulfillment of being at the highest level. For Dionysius, this movement transcends even the logical principle of noncontradiction. This *coincidentia oppositorum* is interpreted by Nicholas of Cusa as beyond all our thought, since it involves concepts whose meaning transcends our thinking in an absolute sense.[4]

As such a dis-enclosure of itself, Christianity has also always been a dis-enclosure of the faithful Christian self. It creates a subject that is seen as a dis-enclosure of itself. Augustine stumbles upon the open question that seems to entail the answer to a faith in God as such: "What then do I love when I love my God?"[5] In Nancy's words, this implies an intrinsic opening in Christianity's "assembly" or "assemblage," a "distension" and "surpassing" of itself.

However, such a demand for an unconditional transgression of itself does not mean that the demand would itself be undeconstructable, as Nancy claims. The "demand to open . . . an alterity or an unconditional alienation" raises the question of which elements are constitutive of the *assemblage* in monotheism and which force it to open itself. These elements consist of the following:

—The particular nature of the revelation, which ultimately proves to be nothing more than the revealed character of self-revelation;
—The evangelical message, which in essence is merely the announcement of the proclamation;

—The infinite distance to philosophical terms that are applied to proclaim the message within a dogmatic theology and which force such an infinite openness.

To quote Nancy: "For the idea of Christian revelation is that, in the end, *nothing is revealed*, nothing but the end of revelation itself, or else that revelation is to say that sense is unveiled purely as sense, in person, but in a person such that all the sense of that person consists in revealing himself. Sense reveals itself and reveals nothing, or else reveals its own infinity" (*D* 147/214).

Deconstruction of monotheism also involves "the operation consisting in disassembling the elements that constitute it, in order to attempt to discern, among those elements and as if behind them, behind and set back from the construction, that which made their assembly possible" (*D* 32/51). In other words, it is "that inquiry or research consisting in disassembling and analyzing the constitutive elements of monotheism, and more directly of Christianity, thus of the West" (*D* 34/54), but which also entails "to take apart, to disassemble, to loosen the assembled construction in order to give some play to the possibility from which it emerged but which, qua assembled structure, it hides" (*D* 148/215).

This means that such deconstruction simultaneously requires the construction that it forces open, that in the dissolution of its constitutive elements both returns to *as well as* distances itself from these elements. Nancy characterizes this relationship as ambiguous (see *D* 141/206), as a movement that is both a dialectical *Aufhebung* and one that breaks away from it (*D* 143/208; see also 157/226). Nevertheless, I am still left with the impression that Nancy, despite his analysis of such ambiguity, ultimately projects the meaning and orientation of such deconstruction into an openness beyond any horizon, into a nothing of the revelation:

What of the opening of Christianity or of Christianity as opening? What of—and this is at the bottom the real question—an *absolute transcendental of opening* such that it does not cease pushing back or dissolving all horizons?
This is our situation: no more horizons. (*D* 145/211)

For Nancy, infinite openness oriented to an alterity signifies an unlimited possibility and the necessity of "the very movement of deconstruction and dis-enclosure" (*D* 10/20), also—and in particular—in relation to itself. This is why the meta-critical dimension introduced by Christianity as a faith (in the sense of "faith" *and* "fidelity"; *D* 28/44) does not allow for a deconstruction of Christianity on the basis of an external, critical-philosophical dis-enclosure but rather forces Christianity to open up from within, causing it to transcend itself:

> Christianity is by itself and in itself a deconstruction and self-deconstruction. (*D* 35/55)

> In a sense . . . Christianity is in itself essentially the movement of its own distension. . . . Obviously, then, we must say that deconstruction, which is only possible by means of that distension, is in itself Christian. (*D* 149/217)

> Christianity itself, Christianity *as such*, is surpassed, because it is itself, and by itself, in a state of being surpassed. The state of self-surpassing [*autodépassement*] may be very profoundly proper to it. . . . It is this transcendence [*dépassement*], this going-beyond-itself that therefore must be examined. (*D* 141/206)

According to Nancy, such self-transcendence will, in a certain way, reach its own end. It is the fate of sense to move in the direction of the end of sense, which also means "the end of the self-surpassing of Christianity" (*D* 142/207):

> Thus Christianity is *in* the element of sense, in both senses, significative and directional, of the word. Christianity is par excellence the conjunction of both senses: it is sense as tension or direction toward the advent of sense as content. Consequently the question is less that of the sense of Christianity than that of Christianity as a dimension of sense, a dimension of sense that—and this is the point to be analyzed—is at once the opening of sense and sense as opening. . . . [*Sense is*] *complete sense in which there is no longer any sense.* (*D* 147/213–14)

The Opening as a Limitless and (De)Limited Movement: Boucle

But is such a limitless opening not self-destructive? Should it not simultaneously, and always again and again, obtain a limited *figuration*, a "sense" or "truth" that would not immediately drown in its own infinite openness? What name or notion, what figuration can be indicated and delineated by such opening if the name of God no longer suffices, and cult and prayer have become empty? These are the questions that Nancy poses at the end of a chapter entitled "The Deconstruction of Christianity": "But the question is thus posed: What is an opening that would not sink into its own openness? What is an infinite sense that nonetheless makes sense, an empty truth that yet has the weight of truth? How can one take on afresh the task of delineating a *delimited* opening, a figure, therefore, that still would not be a figurative capturing of sense (that would not be God)?" (*D* 157/226).

The marking of such openness should act as a limit in order to prevent it from becoming self-destructive and thereby devoid of sense. Yet such delimitation or demarcation should never become a "capturing of sense." Nancy characterizes this figuration of openness as "a matter of thinking the limit . . . the singular line that 'fastens' an existence, but that fastens it according to the complex graph of an opening, not returning to itself ('self' being this very non-return)" (*D* 157/226).

The French word that Nancy uses here—*boucle/boucler*—does not just mean "fastening" but also refers to the movement of a loop or looping. This is the movement of forming a circle, bending a line—or a belt or a piece of rope—so that it assumes the shape of a circle, whereby one end of the line bends toward the other end, almost touching it. This circle is not a closed circle but resembles the vertical, circular looping motion made by a plane in the air, a movement that never returns to its exact starting point. This could also be applied to language, to words (figures) that create a figuration of meaning with no intention of fastening sense, but merely of pointing toward the direction of the opening. In accordance with the dynamics of *boucle*, meaning cannot be grasped seamlessly. Rather, it shows the "nervation" of a meaning in the fastening or settling of "sense," as indicated in the above quotation (*D* 143/208; *boucler* in French). Sense is not homogeneous, which is why it cannot be deconstructed into its constitutive parts: in this way, sense is brought to its limits. As a result, sense appears as an *absolutum*: it has been dis-connected (in Latin, *absolvere*) from that which precedes it and has reached its limit. Ultimately, the presence of sense is similar to the infinite and always possible "pass" (in French, *pas*; see below) that may occur at its own limits. Sense is always fastened and simultaneously *in a loop*. Sense searches for its end, departs from itself in order to return to its point of departure, but without ever completely reaching this point of departure:

> The West itself, Occidentality, is what is carried out by laying bare a particular nervation of sense: a nervation in some way empty or exposed, that of sense as a settled affair, carried to the limits of sense. . . . Thus to deconstruct Christianity is to accompany the West to that limit, to that *pass at which* the West cannot do otherwise than let go of itself in order to continue being the West. (*D* 143/208)

In this essay, I would like to address the following key questions.First, if deconstruction simultaneously raises the question of the conditions of possibility for, as well as the open perspective of, monotheism and Christianity, then are the figure of such a specific religion and the nothing of its dis-enclosure not infinitely intertwined? Is a radical critique of transcendence and religion not linked to the given figure and the complex historical whole—the *assemblage* (D 149/216)—of religion? Does a certain return to such a given religion and its history—despite Nancy's resistance in this regard—not also form an unavoidable part of deconstruction as its first and lasting condition of possibility?

Second, are the modern transgression and exceeding of the self by the self as a self-critique and rational critique (Kant) and the self-deconstruction of monotheism not an excess of the same movement within the perspective of the absolute, of the nothing? Is it not a question here of dealing with the same excess, one that is typically modern? Within Christianity, is this not a possible excess of its own logic? And conversely: Can modernity itself be understood as the excess of a deconstruction of Christianity?

Third, could this perhaps be a reason, that is to say, due to the excess of modernity inherent in Christianity *and* modernity, for an intrinsic connection between the contemporary return of religion in its fundamentalist form and the deconstruction of religion?

Transcendence Without Return?

Through the unclosed circle of the loop, the transcending movement of a deconstruction that attaches itself to a given meaning in order simultaneously to disconnect itself from such sense and to exceed it ultimately refers to the openness of the direction and sense of all meaning. At this point, one could speculate whether this does not already involve a specifically modern sense of modernity, which would, in a certain way, introduce a particular kind of return to Christianity. This specifically modern form of a return to Christianity could in turn perhaps even be understood *on the basis of* Christianity seen as an excess of its own inherent sense of openness. This would be the movement that "destines us to the revelation of the revealable, or yet again to sense as pure, absolute, and infinite" (D 148/215). In this section, I would like to show the specific displacement that occurs with modernity in relation to the meaning of transcendence that precedes modernity and leaves it behind. This displacement is the pregiven condition of possibility of its deconstruction, as well as Nancy's project. In this way, I would argue, Nancy returns to this particular form of Christianity.

First of all, as the title of Chapter 3 of *Dis-enclosure* suggests, a deconstruction of Christianity is a "deconstruction of monotheism." After this chapter, the book predominantly turns into a deconstruction of a Christian variety of monotheism. Nancy correctly remarks that the essential difference between monotheism and polytheism does not lie in the number of gods but rather in how such gods operate and are present among humans (*D* 35/55). A plurality of gods would imply a multiple actual presence of gods, who make their powers, influences, and threats known in the world or who would otherwise like to help people. If the God of Israel is called the Only and Almighty One, then this is done in the sense that all power is his and his alone (*D* 36/55). Only he is divine. In this way, he distances himself from all earthly immanent, natural power. This is why Jan Assmann characterizes the monotheistic God as anti-cosmotheistic.[6] As a result, the monotheistic God is a God who utterly transcends this world and is absent from it. To believe in the monotheistic God is a "faithfulness" (*D* 36/56) to an absent God, and in this sense the monotheistic faith is atheistic (*D* 35/55).

   Nevertheless, the figure of God in Christianity is both present and absent, both immanent and transcendent: "The god withdrawn, the god 'emptied out,' in Paul's words, is not a hidden god in the depths of the withdrawal or the void (a *deus absconditus*)" (*D* 36/56). This already indicates that "transcendence" is an extremely ambiguous notion within the history of Christianity. In addition, the meaning of the term shifts completely with the development from a premodern, Christian philosophy to a modern, secularizing philosophy.

Transcendence in Modernity

Contrary to such Christian philosophy, modern philosophy interprets transcendence exclusively as nonimmanent, as something external to all inner-worldly reality. Transcendence is now thought of—and experienced as—absolute, that is to say, disconnected from all that is. Nancy's interpretation of *sense* at the limit of all sense as the direction of sense that in itself contains no sense and as a self-transgression that does not complete itself at the end of such excess grafts itself onto this modern notion of transcendence. In other words, this is a transcendence, or rather, a transcending, of premodern transcendence. What matters is "to think sense as the absolute opening of sense and to sense, but in a sense that is in a way empty, empty of all content, all figure, all determination." (D 148, 215) What matters is an "*absolute transcendental of opening*" (D 145/211).

Why this reversal? Generally speaking, one could refer in this context to the emancipation of modern culture on the basis of its Christian world view, as well as the marginalization of religion in modern societies. More specifically speaking, however, it was the rise of modern, positive, objectifying science that broke with Christianity and particularly with the medieval concept of science as informed and structured by Christianity. In this regard, our main focus should be on the crisis of the analogy between transcendence and immanence as it was conceptualized in premodern philosophy.

Modern science decided to utilize only nonambivalent terms, which were used in a disjunctive manner: that is to say, conceptual categories applied to various aspects of reality should be mutually exclusive. Analogy was rejected as being unscientific. Everything that was to be understood quantitatively, for example, should no longer become muddled with references to any qualitative notions. Modern science believed that phenomena such as weight, color intensity, and temperature had been erroneously interpreted on a qualitative basis, whereas they should be exclusively understood in terms of quantitative categories. Stones do not fall because they have an innate quality of coming to a halt when they hit the ground, thereby reaching their destined position in accordance with an intrinsic teleology. On the contrary, they are caught within a causally determined and quantitatively calculable force field of masses. Not only did this undermine classical teleological physics and its accompanying worldview, but it also problematized its metaphysical conditions of possibility. All in all, the break with analogous science leads to a mechanistic, self-absorbed worldview, as well as an inward-looking absolute concept of transcendence: one that no longer can have any meaning in reality.

Parallel to this modern reversal in the portrayal of science is a change in the way human beings are portrayed. It becomes difficult to salvage the humanity of human beings if they are merely viewed in terms of a reality similar to that of all other entities. What remains of the human soul, the *anima*? Within the perspective of reality as a whole consisting of analogous parts, the soul was viewed as a form of matter in which this whole was somehow formally invested, thereby allowing the soul to be "everything" in an analogous manner (*anima quodammodo omnia*).[7] Premodern humanity found its intrinsic teleological destiny, and thereby its *humanitas*, in grasping all that is. How can modern human beings formulate their humanity if they themselves are included as formal entities in the chain of universal causal determinisms and their quantitative reductions? How are we to conceive of a nonanalogical, nonteleological portrayal of human beings? On the one hand, modern human beings must withdraw and disconnect (*absolvere*) themselves from all transcendence; on the other hand, they still need to attach themselves to an elusive alterity, an *absolutum*, that is to say, a new, radical external transcendence and indefinable openness that can guarantee their humanity.

Without further elaboration, Nancy names Fénelon as representative of a Christianity that "dis-encloses in its essential gesture the closure that it had constructed" (*D* 10/21). Such a structure of a *dis-enclosing closure* does indeed appear in Fénelon's work, as in his doctrine of the will. Making the will absolute, disconnected from natural desire and its pregiven teleology, allows for a transgression of the will into an *absolutum* that can no longer relate, nor should it be related, to natural desires. The absolute character of this will must be protected by holding onto an absolute openness.[8]

Such a will, which, in line with the natural ontology of desire, must be understood as wanting or desiring nothing, can easily revert into a positive desire for nothing as an ultimate transgression and dis-enclosure of the dynamic of the will.[9] Does Nancy mold his analysis in a similar vein when he points out that we must understand our Christian heritage in relation "to sense as pure, absolute, and infinite"? Do we indeed have "to think sense as the absolute opening of sense and to sense, but in a sense that is in a way empty, empty of all content, all figure, all determination" (*D* 148/215)?

In Nancy's view, such a new humanism is a transgression, a "decomposition" (*D* 2/10) of classical humanism—an opening oriented toward an infinity at the limits of modern finitude. In other words, it is an opening that remains only so long as it manages to persist infinitely: modern human beings are "infinitely finite":[10]

> After all, "modern" signifies a world always awaiting its truth of, and as, world, a world whose proper sense is not given, is not available. (*D* 34–35/54)

> the most salient features of the modern apprehension of the world, and sometimes its most visible atheist, atheistic, or atheological traits, can and must be analyzed in their strictly and fundamentally monotheist provenance. (*D* 31–32/50)

> Deconstruction belongs to a tradition, to *our* modern tradition . . . [and modernity] is itself shot through and through with Christianity. (*D* 148/215)

All of this means that premodern monotheism and premodern Christianity actually do support such modern dis-enclosure as an "assemblage" (*D* 149/216). Monotheism has always included that to which it opens itself—and which forces it to open—as an assemblage that it also continuously transcends. This structure is typical of premodern medieval Christianity, which persists in conceiving radical transcendence and the absolute in a manner analogous to an immanent reality. However, this also means that its sense always runs the risk of being closed off prematurely. This applies not only to Christianity itself but also to modern atheism and humanism. A premature closure of Christianity could also consist in a particular modern closure thereof, one that is not unfamiliar to Nancy's project. Perhaps the modern closure of religion, as in its reduction to the morality of autonomous practical reason in Kant, supports Nancy's project of breaking open this horizon once again in the direction of a sense that can no longer be defined, just as modernity was able to point to such sense as the sense of religion. Interpreted in this way, the opening for the excess of such sense is still a return to the condition of possibility that precedes it. How could this ambiguity of the absolute within the religion of modernity and the modernity of religion be further explored?

The Absolute: An Excess of Christianity *and* Modernity—Nancy and Kant

If modern transcendence, understood as the absolute infinite that endlessly manifests itself at the limits of finitude, is a feature of Christianity and monotheism in general, then Christianity has always been modern. In this regard, Assmann points out that monotheism has always been a contra-religion,[11] a religion that resists the immanentism of the divine and cosmotheism. This lends it a certain instability. It is a religion that provokes within religion effects similar to those caused by science, generating a question of true or false and thereby an excluded third, a *tertium non datur*. In this respect, it turns itself into an absolute as the negation of its opposite, perpetually unable to rest within itself. As a monotheism, Christianity provides an ongoing resistance to superstition, to the continuous threat of the becoming absolute of what is not absolute. In the first instance, it is therefore always intolerant of itself, performing an incessant inquisition into what constitutes true doctrine and condemning all that is false.[12]

From its very beginning, monotheism has always contained this absolute *difference*, which is ultimately nothing more than the advancing *falsification* itself. This means that the nihilism and pure nothing of the revelation of sense are from their very beginning merely that which a deconstruction of Christianity reveals as the condition of possibility of Christianity *and* its self-deconstruction. Nancy provides several topoi as privileged witnesses testifying to this self-deconstruction: monotheism; demythologization; the composite nature of Christianity, which is Jewish, Greek, and Roman; the singularity of the Christian act of faith and the subject of faith; the Trinity; sin; reincarnation; prayer; the resurrection.

The Absolute in Kant

As mentioned previously, the ambiguity that accompanies absolute difference can be identified as the excess of both monotheism and the self-understanding of modernity. This ambiguity relates to an opening oriented toward an absolute alterity that always appears as at once disruptive and fundamental in monotheism *and* modernity. Monotheism and modernity both entail the excess of themselves at the center of their assemblage: they *are* this excess of themselves. This is expressed in a perpetual preoccupation with the limit and finitude, which are thought in their (de)limiting (founding) and unlimiting (unsettling) act in one and the same movement. Whoever thinks of himself as an excess of himself will continuously oscillate between being and nothing. In Nancy's view, Kant's philosophy is a key example and symptom of this.

Nancy points out that Kant's work can be read both as a denial and suppression of a Christian heritage, and as an integral continuation of it. This is why to characterize modernity as a break with Christianity proves to be unproductive (*D* 144/209). The complex relationship between knowing and believing, as formulated by Kant in his *Critique of Pure Reason*, points to this inherent ambiguity in Christianity.[13] In this context, the excess is mutual. Faith wants to be rational, and reason leads to a faith and an attitude of having faith in itself. Kant writes about defining the limits of both reason and religion. In doing so, he touches upon both a faith or reason in itself and on what he calls a faith *within* the limits of reason. Moreover, since reason does not encounter any limits posed on it from without, it is up to reason itself to define its limits. As a result, transcendentalism obtains an entirely novel meaning in Kant's work—several pluriform and related meanings, in fact—which has everything to do with the multifaceted self-definition of the limits of reason. This is not just a matter of defining the limits between that which is sensible and that which is understandable, between empirical and rational, but also of defining the limits between a priori and a posteriori. At the same time, such a demarcation implies a delineation of the validity of the transcendental movement of thinking itself, as well as the demarcation of its domain in relation both to a metaphysics of the transcendent and to empirically conditioned knowledge, including historically revealed religion. All pure a priori knowledge, in which no experience is given, is transcendental.[14] Transcendental and transcendent are no longer related in a positive manner but are removed from one another through a demarcation. In order to avoid any transcendental appearance, the fundamental principles whose application transgresses the limits of possible experience are referred to as transcendent fundamental principles, which are to be distinguished from the immanent ones, whose application remains entirely within the limits of possible experience.[15] Whereas premodern philosophy was based on the distinction *and* continuum between *transcendentalia*[16] and the predicates of an immanent reality, Kant instead invests everything in the distinction between transcendent and immanent.[17] Transcendental philosophy then becomes the self-reflective movement of thought that defines that limit. It is a reconstruction of a priori concepts that precede all possible experience and make such experience possible in the first place. The concepts of reason, or ideas, which appear in what Kant calls the transcendental dialectic and which can neither be affirmed nor negated by experience, define transcendental philosophy as transcendent in relation to all phenomena.[18]

Nevertheless, Kant is concerned here not just with this faith of reason in itself and its own ideas, but also with the rationality of—and within—(Christian) faith that reason reflects upon as a pregiven historical facticity. This struggle at the limits of reason is a matter for both reason and faith. One reason for this is that faith manifests itself as faith only where the limits of practical reason and the credibility of morality have been defined by reason itself, as well as where faith has subsequently secured itself beyond the logic of reason.

In this regard, faith is therefore already and always a transgressing opening and a preeminent articulation of the modern concept of transcendence: it is a relationship with the absolute, understood as that which exceeds every horizon. In the final analysis, this absolute will become nothing.

In the preface to *Religion within the Boundaries of Mere Reason*, Kant uses the model of two concentric circles. The inside circle of religion interpreted in philosophical terms (rational religion or *Vernunftreligion*), contained within the larger circle of statutory Christian religion, actually includes both circles. According to Kant, this inner circle is ultimately the domain and praxis of ethics. Insofar as religion can be indicated in accordance with practical reason, religion and ethics will have the same subject matter. The ethical-religious dimension of the wider outer circle, a circle in which various historical texts, rituals, and practices are constitutive, can only be indicated from inside this inner circle. Nevertheless, this does not prevent an examination of a religiosity defined a priori on the basis of revealed historical religion—the outside circle. This is what Kant does in relation to Christianity in *Religion Within the Boundaries of Mere Reason*.

Nonetheless, the boundary of the rational inner circle contained within the wider circle of religion is strongly delineated as an enclosure (or *closure*, to use Nancy's term). In Kant's view, both variants—ethical and religious—of the inner circle are completely identical. In doing so, Kant manages to keep outside the ethically irrelevant, or even misleading, content of religion, leaving it—without any possible mediation by reason—as something that has "passed" (or in Nancy's language: *surpassed*). Nevertheless, it remains to be seen whether or not such content, as an unmediated outside, could still return in the shape of a fundamentalist variant.

From the opening chapter of *Dis-Enclosure* onward, Nancy describes the ambiguity of reason and faith, of immanence and transcendence, of the self and an absolute alterity, as an attempt "to open rationality to the dimension appropriate to the absolute." In this way, Nancy forces open once again the clear, self-contained identification of both reason and a pregiven sense: "The closure invariably dis-encloses itself: such is the precise sense of the demand for the unconditioned that structures Kantian reason" (*D* 7/17). The identity of the two circles is nothing more than the "graph of an opening" of both the "self, being this very non-return to itself," and an "inscription of a sense that no religion, no belief, no knowledge can saturate or assure" (*D* 157/226).

Nancy interprets this similarity in the following way: "What thinking must then hold together [*receuillir*] is the void of this opening constituted by an absence of inheritors [*le vide de l'ouverture en déshérence*]" (*D* 2/10). Here, once again, the excess can be observed as this "holding together" of monotheism and modernity. The suture of both is the opening, and their relatedness to one another is that which is opened and dis-connected—an *absolutum*. As a consequence, Nancy believes—and in his eyes Kant does as well—that modernity could be described as follows: "a world always awaiting its truth of, and as, world, a world whose proper sense is not given, is not available, is, rather, in project or in promise, and perhaps beyond: a sense that consists in not being given, but only in being promised" (*D* 34–35/54).

This sense of modernity and monotheism is "absented in its very presence" (D 35, 54), or in a formulation quoted and commented above: "What of—and this is at bottom the real question—an *absolute transcendental of opening* such that it does not cease pushing back or dissolving all horizons?" (D 145, 211).

Deconstruction, Disintegration, Fundamentalism

For Kant, as we have seen, reason's return to religion as a given tradition is ultimately a folding back of reason upon itself. In the demarcation of its power, reason decides what is external to rational religion, as well as what must subsequently be left outside as external. Nevertheless, such—always possible—premature closure is not safe from a possible deconstruction. In Nancy's work, the demarcation of reason by reason in relation to faith is forced open once again, since reason encounters within itself the religious dimension of its own rationality and rational self-demarcation. Even the enclosed sense of religion is forced open once again in the direction of sense. However, the religion demarcated and left behind by reason as its outside also seems to return in another manner: as the operation and coming into force of that which was rationally excluded at the limits of reason. The operation of this excluded is fundamentalism. This is also why fundamentalism is a fully fledged modern return of religion. Nancy's phrase "Not a question of repainting the skies" (*D* 1/9) could be interpreted as a premature closure of the relationship with religion.[19] This desire to repaint the skies remains within a deconstruction of religion by Nancy both because of the ever-possible deconstruction of the demarcation of religion and through the return of the excluded in the closure of openness. The movement of deconstruction is an infinite movement. It is a deconstruction of deconstruction, that is to say, a deconstruction *of* deconstruction (*genetivus objectivus*) and a deconstruction *by* deconstruction (*genetivus subjectivus*). Unlike in Derrida's work, nothing is undeconstructable, not even deconstruction itself. The only exception would be the infinity of this movement of deconstruction, which oscillates between *decomposition* and *disassembling*, on the one hand, and *assemblage*, on the other, to use two key concepts introduced by Nancy in *Dis-enclosure*: oscillating between the opening and the surrender to an absolute nothing ("no repainting") and the desire for a new closure ("repainting").[20] In discussion with Derrida, Nancy refers to this undeconstructability of the ambiguous movement of deconstruction as the undeconstructability of "the active infinite: thus, the act, the actual and active presence of the *nothing* qua thing (*res*) of the opening itself" (*D* 176n12/20n2). The "nothing" of the opening means that it can—and must—close itself again at any time.

To Affirm Religion, to Deny Religion: Derrida, Heidegger, Patočka

In *The Gift of Death*, Derrida examines the relationship between deconstructive and phenomenological approaches to religion. He does so by comparing how Heidegger and the Prague phenomenologist Jan Patočka relate to Christianity. Derrida observes that:

> the Heideggerian thinking often consists, notably in *Sein und Zeit*, in repeating on an ontological level Christian themes and texts that have been "de-Christianized." Such themes and texts are then presented as ontic, anthropological, or contrived attempts that come to a sudden halt on the way to an ontological recovery of their own originary possibility. . . . Patočka makes an inverse yet symmetrical gesture, which therefore amounts to the same thing. He reontologizes the historical themes of Christianity and attributes to revelation . . . the ontological content that Heidegger attempts to remove from it.[21]

Whereas Heidegger, in Derrida's view, deconstructs Christianity by redirecting it to its "originary possibility" and thus attempts to disconnect it from its historical reality, as well as to open it in the direction of its *absolutum*, Patočka reinserts the absolute possibility of Christianity into its revelation, which refers to historical events in—immanent—time and reality.

Derrida repeatedly affirms this movement as a necessary one. There is no such thing as a "pure" deconstruction, since each deconstruction entails its own betrayal: a betrayal that in its turn must be deconstructed and that therefore, perhaps, could actually no longer be called a betrayal as such. But what about Nancy? For him, historical Christianity, as a figure and *assemblage*, has been "surpassed" as such (*D* 141/206). However, Nancy still appears to have an acute awareness of the double bind between Heidegger and Patočka that Derrida examines. After all, in Nancy's view Christianity itself is this very movement of surpassing: "That state of self-surpassing may be very profoundly proper to it" (*D* 141/206). Further on in the same sentence, Nancy remarks that this is not devoid of any ambiguity.

If there is any surpassing, then one must acknowledge the ontic supportive capacity of a specific historical religion, as well as the ontological dis-enclosure that forms part of the movement of opening and *self-surpassing*—and which, as the *religious*, could perhaps be distinguished from *religion*.[22] In such self-surpassing, the return to itself—as in the metaphor of the loop—must be maintained.[23] Nancy also points out why Christianity will therefore also always be the denial of its own self-deconstruction: "But, as we well know, in another sense Christianity is the exact opposite—denial, foreclosure of a deconstruction and of its own deconstruction" (*D* 149/217). Is the inevitable movement of a deconstruction of deconstruction not itself ultimately destined simultaneously to affirm and deny religion?

The Fundamentalist Return

"Indeed, within Christianity a specific type of conflict occurs, which is probably the conflict between an *integrality* and its disintegration" (*D* 144/210). One could ask whether the radical disintegration of deconstruction does not also evoke the equally radical integral *re*integration of modern fundamentalism. Assmann refers to the incessant reoccurrence of a counter-movement to the pure transcendence within monotheism as "contra-religion." As a consequence, monotheism is characterized by a specific instability and ambiguity. The monotheistic position is never definitely conquered and therefore continuously gives rise to purificatory counter-movements, which are themselves contested in turn. Such tension is typical both of certain forms of religious fundamentalism and of atheistic movements.

Nancy views the fate of Christianity as the fate of sense as such. He seems to identify this fate with what is referred to as "the end of ideology," which also signifies that the transgression of sense and the self-surpassing of Christianity have come to an end, or rather, have reached their end ("the end of the self-surpassing of Christianity"; *D* 142/207). The end of ideology then becomes the end of the big story about the promised end, the *eschaton* and completion. The fate of Christianity—the ideology of such completion of a promised sense—would then itself be surpassed. However, it also turns out to be a fate that, even nowadays, turns against itself once more, yet—as a *boucle* (in a loop)—has also reversed into its opposite. The premature closure of the Christian religion may be forced open in a dis-enclosure of its rational demarcation. That which has been excluded as irrational returns as the opposite of such enclosure.

According to Nancy, it is now no longer a matter of "either attacking or defending Christianity, that is, either damning or saving it" (*D* 141/206).

Instead, we must be concerned with "a future for the world that would no longer be either Christian or anti-Christian, either monotheist or atheist" (*D* 34/54). None of the double negations should turn into an affirmation: "For that, there remains for us neither cult nor prayer, but the exercise—strict and severe, sober and yet joyous—of what is called thought" (*D* 157/226). The Kantian project of an autonomous reason founded within itself is forced open just like the objectively given sense of a revealed religion. Neither the subject nor pregiven sense remain within themselves. However, their mutual relationship remains only a similar opening toward nothing, a comparison between two unknown variables. What remains is neither a humanism nor a kind of Christianity, neither religion nor atheism. This is where Blanchot sees an impasse: "A non-religious repetition."[24] He continues: "We carry on about atheism, which has always been a privileged way of talking about God. Conversely, the infinite extricates itself from the finite only as the latter's incapacity to finish finishing, as its endless pursuit of itself along the ambiguous detour of repetition."[25]

Blanchot suggests the possibility that such a "disaster" (that is, "the incapacity to finish finishing") could be a deconstruction and a way out of the absoluteness of modernity: "I will not say that the disaster is absolute; on the contrary, it disorients the absolute. It comes and goes, errant disarray."[26] But should such arriving and departing, such a manner of thinking—as a reflection upon and return to itself—not necessarily include and keep open memory as a form of repetition? "A non religious repetition"—is such a thing possible? In this regard, the final line of the introduction of Maurice Merleau-Ponty's *Signs* is worth considering: "History never confesses, not even her lost illusions, but neither does she dream of them again."[27] This could also be read as a return of history to itself in the form of a *boucle*. History never merely confesses, not even as a lost illusion, that which it never repeats.

Coda

Dis-enclosure ends with an evocation of the myth of Theseus. Theseus sought to free Athens from the levy it had to pay to Crete. He would announce his victory over the Minotaur by raising white sails at the moment he triumphantly sailed into harbor. However, he failed to replace the black sails—the sign of defeat—with the white ones for victory. He failed to do so because he had forgotten Ariadne—who helped him escape from the Labyrinth—and therefore memory itself. Forgetting Ariadne leads to disorientation, since she "is" the memory of his way out of the

Labyrinth. To forget Ariadne is to forget the pattern of the construction, the way passed and deconstruction—*dis-enclosure* and *closure*—as a way out; a forgetting of the opening and a missing of the goal. Because he forgot to raise the white sails, Theseus made it seem as if nothing had happened. It was as if no victory had taken place. *Dis-enclosure* aptly ends, so to speak, with an open ending, by pointing to the "infinitely repeated indecision of the myth"—the undecidability between "solitary languor" and "the unanticipated arrival of Dionysos": "But in reopening space, Theseus also rekindles the ambivalence inherent in separation and distinction. He abandons Ariadne on an island, brief punctual expanse—less place than midpoint of a churning liquid labyrinth. In the infinitely repeated indecision of the myth, Ariadne pines away, exposed to both solitary languor and the unanticipated arrival of Dionysos" (*D* 161/231).

—*Translated by Ron Peek*

PART III

Creation, Myth, Sense, *Poiēsis*

Intermezzo

As Parts I and II have demonstrated, Nancy conceives Christianity—or more generally, monotheism—as a religion that is marked from the outset by a secular structure. This secular structure consists not in the proposition of a unique God but in the way this God is present in the world. What is most important in the shift from polytheism to monotheism is thus not a reduction in the number of gods but a rearticulation of the relation between God and the world. Whereas polytheism affirms the immediate presence of gods and believes them to inhabit and organize the world, monotheism understands God as in retreat from the world and in principle out of reach. As Part III will show, one way of formulating this thesis is that monotheism implies a dissolution of *mythology*, that is, of "the paradigm of the given, structured, and animate universe" (*D* 15/28). The secularization monotheism and Christianity are engaged in can, in other words, be seen as a form of demythologization.

Being an originary tale of foundation, myth structures and animates the universe and in so doing serves as the assurance of a specific constellation of sense. By posing a God who is inaccessible in principle, monotheism is deprived of, or at least complicates, such a foundational and structuring value. The demythologization of religion has far-reaching implications, not only for the sense of the world and God's relation to it but, in consequence, also for the way God can be named, evoked, and represented. Since the monotheistic God resists immediate, full presence, the way he presents himself and is represented must be conceived, according to Nancy, as *literary* or *poetic* rather than mythological. Unlike the gods of polytheism, the God of monotheism can only be present indirectly, insufficiently, and momentarily. There can, in other words, never be a univocal, true, or final description of God or, for the same reason, of the world. Monotheism and secularism thus co-emerge when the universe is no longer given, structured, and animated, but, on the contrary, needs to be constructed, invented, and created.

Sense is therefore not primordially given but something that emerges *between* beings, as is, according to Nancy, wonderfully shown by Pontormo's *Visitation*. The retreat of the Christian God implies the absence of an absolute sense lying beyond the world and leads to a world in which sense exists in a relational rather than a transcendent manner. Referring to Blanchot's notion of an *"absent sense,"* being a sense "that makes sense in and by its very absenting" (*D* 86/130), Nancy characterizes Christianity as a form of "absentheism." Sense is thus not simply absent, as it is in nihilism, but rather fleeing, desired, retreating. By referring to Blanchot's notion, Nancy not only explains his view of sense but once more draws a connection between Christian doctrine and literature or poetry. A literary expression, as Nancy defines it, may be at once the most religious and the most secular gesture possible, since it is the exposition to this absent sense.

The connection Nancy draws between Christianity and literature is not surprising, considering that in his earlier works, especially *The Inoperative Community*, he already indicated that literature would displace mythology, or rather, that this displacement itself is literature. Literature and poetry mark, in other words, the retreat of an original foundational sense; they echo the interruption of myth. More specifically, literature and poetry do not provide a fixed and accomplished sense, a full presence, but are the expression of a creative and transgressive force, a force that resists presence. Following the early Romantics, Nancy thus proposes to understand literature or poetry not as a specific artistic genre but as the expression of the very act of creating: as *poiēsis*.

This view of *poiēsis* sheds light on Nancy's analysis of the idea of creation. One consequence of religion's demythologization is that God is no longer understood as a God-creator or a God-demiurge. By retreating the unique God from presence, Christianity has fundamentally if perhaps unintentionally revised the concept of creation. The idea that creation is an accomplished state of affairs produced by an independent producer is rejected and gives way to an active notion of creation as a momentary emergence, an opening—or dis-enclosure—of the world, resulting from the impossibility of its completion. Rather than presupposing a creator prior to creation, Christian monotheism advocates a certain idea of creation ex nihilo, of a creation from nothing and of nothing, a creation whose creator is itself *nihil*, absent. It is in this absence of an absolute sense-giver that Christianity and monotheism in general coincide with secular modernity.

The notion of *poiēsis*, finally, provides Nancy with a specific view not only of creation but also of community, of our being together in the world. According to Nancy, our idea of being together has always been characterized by a mythological search for a common figure or narrative with which we can identify. By contrast, Nancy tries to understand our being together as an act, a *praxis*, rather than as a fulfilled work or a closed figure. In this process, beings are conceived as simply living side by side, without sharing a common origin or destiny. Being nothing but the daily praxis of living together, community must be understood at an ontological level. This original co-existence of beings does not correspond to a common figure but is in itself figurative, or poetic. Our co-existence, in other words, can be conceived of as a form of co-*poiēsis*.

In the first contribution to this part, Aukje van Rooden discusses religion's retreat from myth and explores why Christian prayer can be seen as a practice that implies a demythologized, poetic way of evoking of God. She draws attention to the fact that prayer, being an addressing without the guarantee of being heard, at once evokes God and affirms his absence. Moreover, she demonstrates how prayer shows that the Christian self-deconstructive gesture is a linguistic one, thereby highlighting the performative nature of language.

In the second contribution, Michel Lisse addresses the revision of the concept of creation as a result of religion's retreat from myth, thereby exploring to what extent the Christian concept of creation bases itself on the model of literary creation. Tracking down the preparations of this revision in Nancy's earlier works, such as *Being Singular Plural* and *The Creation of the World, or Globalization*, Lisse shows why literary writing allows us to understand creation as a creation ex nihilo, that is, as a creation that is first and foremost an *ex-position*.

Further elaborating on this poetic way of creating, the third contribution in this Part—that of Anne O'Byrne—investigates the ontological implications of our being together, which, she suggests, must be conceived as co-poetic. Comparing Nancy's thinking with that of Arendt and the Romantics, O'Byrne emphasizes that God's withdrawal urges us to conceive of our being in the world as a *relational* being, which can best be understood in terms of birth and procreation.

In the fourth and final contribution to this part, Daniela Calabrò explores Nancy's revision of the notion of sense as that which emerges, and is born, within this co-poetic being. She elucidates this notion of sense by means of an analysis of Pontormo's painting *The Visitation*—discussed by Nancy in his essay "Visitation: Of Christian Painting"—considering it as one of the "places" where the dis-enclosure of Christian sense takes place, or, as Calabrò states, as one of the places where it has always already taken place—as in an immemorial past.

—Aukje van Rooden

"My God, my God, why hast Thou forsaken me?"

Demythologized Prayer; or, the Poetic Invocation of God

AUKJE VAN ROODEN

> "Prayer demythologized" [is] one of the most acute formulations of what is brought into play, in my view at least, by a "deconstruction of Christianity."
>
> —*D* 134 /195

A thesis only marginally stressed in *Dis-enclosure: The Deconstruction of Christianity*, though revealing one of its essential structures, is that a deconstruction of Christianity should be understood as a form of demythologization. Or, as Nancy has it, Christianity "understands itself in a way that is less and less religious in the sense in which religion implies a mythology (a narrative, a representation of divine actions and persons)" (*D* 37/57). The seemingly strange statement that the Christian religion increasingly understands itself "in a way that is less and less religious," is a reformulation of Nancy's central thesis that Christianity is a religion retreating from religion.[1] Insofar as religion is mythological in nature, Christianity distances itself not only from the religious but also from the mythological.

In the previous Parts of this volume, we have seen that this distancing should not be understood as an overcoming of religion. Instead, Nancy points out that Christianity, by its very structure, deconstructs its own religiosity. In this essay, I shall focus on a key moment in this self-deconstructive movement of Christianity: that of prayer, or more generally, of addressing God. According to Nancy, prayer—as one of the central elements of the Christian religion—reveals how Christianity contains in its heart, or rather *as* its heart, the absence of its God in principle and therefore the germ of its own secularization. If Nancy is right, then the basic structure of Christian prayer is revealed in the exclamation "My God, my God, why hast Thou forsaken me?"

One of the rare religious practices studied by Nancy, prayer plays a particular role within his treatment of a deconstruction of Christianity. It allows us to follow a line of thought that would otherwise remain rather abstract and therefore difficult to grasp. The text in which Nancy most extensively analyses the phenomenon of prayer is "'Prayer Demythified.'"[2] This text is significant not only because of its more concrete level of analysis but also because of how it tries to make sense of the question of Christianity's self-deconstruction as a question of *language*. As we shall see, Nancy not only introduces Christianity's distancing from the religious as a movement of demythologization, he explains this movement as a *poetic* movement, a movement that is proper to poetic practice. Contrary to myth, poetry does not provide a "representation of divine actions or persons," but, in a way, *presents* them.

I shall first examine why the Christian religion is a form of demythologization, as well as why Christian prayer is an example of that. Second, I shall investigate why and in what sense demythologized prayer can be understood as a poetic practice. Then I shall explain why this poetic practice places Christianity under the heading of the "sacred" and "faith" rather than that of the "religious" and of "belief." In the final section, I shall return to the question of demythologization and suggest that prayer's demythologization may perhaps also imply a mythologization.

The Absent God

So, why would the Christian religion imply a distancing from mythology? According to Nancy, the starting point of this distancing coincides with the shift from polytheism to monotheism. As developed in the more programmatic texts of *Dis-enclosure* ("The Deconstruction of Christianity," "A Deconstruction of Monotheism," and "Atheism and Monotheism"), Christian monotheism is, in Nancy's view, characterized not by a single God, as opposed to the multiple gods of polytheism, but rather by the way this God is present and, consequently, by the way in which he is represented. Polytheistic religions not only affirm the plurality of gods but claim the "effective presence" of these gods. They are believed to inhabit nature, a certain image, or someone's mind, and in doing so to influence the world (*D* 35/55). Another way of putting this is to say that the divine, within the polytheistic worldview, is always located in specific places that bear concrete and more or less stable features and are connected in a network charged with meaning. Polytheistic religion weaves this network "through the entirety of its myths and its rites" (*D* 35–36/55).

With the rise of monotheism, however, God is no longer conceived as present in the world but instead is believed to have retreated from the world by virtue of the very act of creating it. His divine power is thus no longer understood as locally embedded, but as abstract and transcendent.[3] The divinity of the monotheistic God, in other words, lies precisely in his absence: "He is a god whose absence in itself creates divinity" (*D* 36/56). It is this structural impossibility for the Christian God to present himself and to be represented that implies Christianity's retreat from mythology. Since this retreat from mythology is equally a retreat from religion as such, it has cleared the way not only for monotheism but also for atheism. In a way, Christian prayer is a direct result of the absenting of God. Addressed to that which is most hidden, without the guarantee of being heard, and often even pronounced in silence, prayer is simultaneously the *evocation* of God and the *affirmation of his absence*. It is no surprise, then, that an analysis of demythologized prayer is one of the ways in which Nancy examines the coincidence of religion and its deconstruction.

As Nancy indicates at the beginning of his text, the phrase "demythologized prayer" was originally used by Adorno as a definition of "the language of *music*," that is, "*demythologized prayer*, rid of efficacious magic. It is the human attempt, doomed as ever, to name the Name, not to communicate meanings."[4] In his commentary on Adorno's phrase, Nancy endows these words with a much broader meaning, indicating that they form an answer to the insistent and ultimately modern problem of "how to give sense, or more simply direction [*cours*]—refraining from making sense—not to a painfully revived religion but to the 'relics' . . . that an extinguished religion leaves in its wake—such as prayer, faith, the name *God* itself, and a few other attestations to an irreducibility of language" (*D* 187n1/190n1; trans. modified). In this commentary, Nancy parenthetically advances several very important theses concerning his view of religion. First of all, he dismisses the so-called "revival of religion" as the central question of modernity. As we have seen, Nancy's deconstruction of Christianity neither advocates a return to religion nor argues for its overcoming. Instead it tries to show how the Christian religion is, at its very heart, already secular, an overcoming of its own religiosity. Second, Nancy characterizes some of the most essential elements of the Christian religion (prayer, the name *God*, and even faith itself) as "relics." Although doing so may seem a cliché, it provides a very accurate description of

Nancy's understanding of Christianity's auto-deconstructive nature. According to him, Christianity is involved in a process of exhaustion and self-emptying of its significant content, leaving no more than a purified belief in an absent divinity. In a sense, Christianity thus becomes its own relic: it becomes that which remains when the divine is absent, extinguished.

Third, Nancy relates the reliclike, deconstructive nature of religion to language or, to be more precise, to an "irreducibility," an obstinacy of language. We could say that, due to the absenting of God, language itself has also become a relic. After the flight of the gods, holy names are lacking, as Hölderlin noticed, yet they linger on and offer a certain resistance. The retreat of God has left us with nothing but his name, a name deprived of meaning, whose referent is absent in principle. If we want to make sense of the irreducibility of language involved in the Christian religion, we must therefore start with an analysis of the concepts of "sense" and "meaning" within this religion. Indeed, Nancy has such an analysis in mind when he proposes characterizing Christian religion as a form of *absentheism* (e.g., *D* 18/32).

With this notion, Nancy points out that the monotheistic worldview does not posit a given and accessible divine sense, but sees the fact that sense has been withdrawn as itself divine. In taking this position, Nancy refers explicitly to Blanchot's notion of "absent sense," as sense that "makes sense in and by its very absenting," by its very irreducibility (*D* 86/130). By referring to Blanchot's notion, Nancy makes an interesting connection between Christianity and literature. What Blanchot calls "absentheism" is above all related to literature or writing and indicates exposure to a sense that withdraws from signification, or rather, the experience of this withdrawal. Basing himself on Blanchot's text "Atheism and Writing: Humanism and the Cry" (in *The Infinite Conversation*), Nancy points out that literature effectuates an emptying of sense similar to the emptying of sense effectuated by Christian monotheism. Although Blanchot's work is "devoid of any interest in religion," as Nancy formulates it, his notion of "absent sense" can thus be charged with a theological dimension.

For Nancy, absent sense serves as a key notion for understanding the consequences of the absenting of God in monotheism, whose scope can hardly be underestimated. In its affirmation of a world whose organizing principle has been withdrawn, Christianity presupposes a world that is nevertheless opened toward this beyond, while being itself deprived of absolute sense. According to Nancy, this is why Christianity confronts us with a task that is *the* task of modernity and to which he dedicates his entire oeuvre: the task of affirming that the world is *all there is*, that there *is nothing but the world* and, in consequence, that this alone makes sense. This does not mean, however, that the world closes down on itself, as we shall see.[5] Only when the world's creator is given and stands in effective relation to it does the world have a point of reference from which it can be determined that its totality *has* sense. As soon as this point of reference has been withdrawn, sense is no longer something given by a creator (or by us as his supposed substitutes), but is what simply is already there. The world as such is sensible, *is* sense (*SW* 8/19).

Thus, God's absenting does not mean that there is no sense, as nihilism advocates, because that would equally presuppose an absolute point of reference. Rather, there is always already sense, albeit a fleeting, momentary one that is never fully given. The retreat of God from the world, in other words, has given rise to an uncertainty regarding absolute signification or signifiability, and therefore also regarding the existence of God himself (*D* 86/130). As a result:

> there is, then, in this respect, no "question of God" that is to be asked as the ritualistic question of the existence or the nonexistence of a supreme being. . . . God is not within the jurisdiction of a question. . . . It is not that there is or is not a God. It is, quite differently, that there is the name *God*, or rather the name *God* is spoken. . . . If all questions intend a "what," a something, the name *God* corresponds to the order, the register, or the modality of what is not, or has not, any thing. (*D* 87/131–32)[6]

When Nancy points out that Christian monotheism is a form of "absentheism," he thereby states, to use our earlier vocabulary, that the God posited is not an "effective presence" within the world about which one could ask "What is it?" and "Does it exist?" With the rise of monotheism, the question "What is God?" became unanswerable in principle.[7] The only thing one can say is that its name endures in language, albeit deprived of full meaning.

The practice of praying plays a significant role in understanding this structure because it *performs* this deprivation of meaning. Or, as Nancy writes, it forms "neither a category nor a particular linguistic operation intended for a specific goal of signification or transmission, but indicates, on the contrary, a gesture, a posture, and a postulation according to which language is tensed to its limits, at its limit, which it exceeds while maintaining itself there" (*D* 131–32/192). In other words, prayer is a practice—a gesture—that defies and renounces the aspiration of providing sense.

This being said, the notion of "demythologized prayer" turns out to be tautological, since what is "demythologized" cannot but present itself by means of the kind of emptied linguistic gesture that is prayer. Prayer is, by its very structure, a use of language that already does away with myth in the sense that it defies "a narrative, a representation of divine actions and persons." Or, as Nancy states rather enigmatically at the beginning of his text: "'prayer demythologized' would only remain a paradox so long as 'prayer' has not been stripped of its character of—well, prayer" (D 130/190). Just as Christianity can be conceived as a religion retreating from religion, Christian prayer would be a prayer deprived of its character as prayer or, perhaps more accurately, prayer that deprives *itself* of its own character as prayer.[8]

Prayer as a Poetic Gesture

Rather than a means of communication, demythologized prayer should thus be understood as a *gesture* of and with language. The gesture of prayer aims to break through the representational function of language. With good reason, Nancy, like Michel Deguy before him, refers to Adorno's fragment on music. Music has always been considered a form of art that, on the one hand, is close to language yet, on the other hand, is at a distant remove from the regime of communication and representation. Although, as Nancy hastens to say, the music Adorno has in mind is opera (music that is *sung*), what is significant is that it is a use of language, whose meaning has been subordinated to the gesture, sound, and ritual of the utterance.

Such an interruption of the representational function of language became possible at the moment *logos* was freed of *muthos*. Whereas within the polytheistic worldview the world is believed to be structured by *muthos*, the very source of modernity lies in the separation of *logos* and *muthos*, that is, in the alleged freeing of the *logos* from a divine structuring power. Prayer, then, is the attempt to address, by means of *logos*, the divine that used to present itself in *muthos*. It is a gesture, a posture, that, as Nancy points out in "'Prayer Demythified,'" is that of a *"logos* without *muthos"* (D 132/194).[9] That is, in prayer the divine is not present or represented, it does not *inhabit* prayer as it inhabits temples or idols within polytheistic religions.

However, Nancy does not want simply to oppose *logos* and *muthos*. Instead, he seeks to destabilize this opposition. He therefore continues, somewhat hastily, to claim that, strictly speaking, this *"logos* without *muthos"* of prayer is also a *"muthos* without *muthos,"* taking into account the original meaning of the word *muthos*, which merely signifies "the spoken word" (*D* 132/194). Although one may wonder whether Nancy's explanation of *muthos* is as obvious as he considers it to be, it is clear that he discerns a kind of self-deconstructive movement within *muthos* itself. In other words, rather than *logos* substituting for *muthos after* the rise of monotheism, *muthos* ("effective presence") has retreated from *muthos* ("the spoken word"). To be more precise, *logos* and *muthos* seem to be mutually constitutive in the sense that *logos* is nothing but the name of *muthos'* retreat from itself.[10]

Far from playing a linguistic game, Nancy is looking for the incontestable core of prayer, since he is of the opinion that its consistency is not necessarily tributary to its religious use. This core is a linguistic gesture that pushes the communicative function of language to its limits, being not only a gesture addressed to an unknown addressee who may or may not perceive it, but also to an addressee who is in principle outside of language. This linguistic gesture is not a complete silencing of language, nor is it haphazardly saying no matter what. It is, rather, a form of language that is "almost suffocated—hoarse in any case, withdrawn from the full sonority of meaning, and from the possibility of a naming . . .; this language is not at all attached to a silence or some form of aphonic ecstasy, but rather to something like poetry" (*D* 133/194; trans. modified). The ultimate conclusion Nancy is heading for is that God can only be addressed in a *poetic* manner.

The little remark "something like poetry" is scarcely more than a hint, a gesture, that, at least in " 'Prayer Demythified,' " is not further elaborated. Nevertheless, I shall take this hint as a point of departure. Prayer must be viewed as an emptied language lacking a clear meaning, as suspense of communication in the form of an addressing without addressee. "God" is named, but this name is nothing more than that of a relic of religion attesting to the obstinacy of language. In other words, prayer is a hoarse, not to say idle, way of speaking into the void, addressed to an addressee who cannot be addressed as such.

Yet this speaking into the void appears to create an opening, an opening of language to what is beyond language. One could therefore say that the linguistic operation of prayer—like the lyrical apostrophe "O"— functions as a portal, providing access to the domain of language, but an access that is blocked at the threshold, only momentarily bringing to presence what is in principle out of reach. In this respect, the exclamation "My God, my God, why hast Thou forsaken me?" signifies not only Christian prayer but also the lyrical form par excellence, of which Shelley's "O wild west wind, thou breath of autumn's being" ("Ode to the

West Wind") and Baudelaire's "Ô toi qui, comme une ombre à la trace éphémère!" ("Je te donne ces vers") are merely derivatives.

What this opening in and of language consists in becomes clear when the function of prayer is deprived of its religious connotations and is examined in its daily, "profane" use. This daily use is above all a French one, though indirectly recognizable in other languages. Nancy offers as examples such expressions as *je vous prie* or *prière de répondre*, usually translated as "Please," but which would literally translate as "I pray you" and "I pray you to respond." These polite formulas, which implicitly accompany every linguistic exchange, are, in a sense, the condition of possibility for communication, an empty saying that is in fact nothing more than a movement of turning toward the other, a "letting be" of the addressee. As Nancy states, these profane formulas can therefore be seen as a "relic" of their religious use in addressing God (*D* 134/196).

Echoing Heidegger's view of *Dichtung*, Nancy points out that the remnants of prayer in language reveal a kind of *Ursprache*, an original opening that "let things be": "Essentially, the saying [the original saying, like that of prayer] exerts itself in letting the real—*res*, the thing—realize itself, that is, be what it is, and above all be *that it* is. This 'letting be' is its task" (*D* 135/197). In other words, if Nancy relates prayer to "something like poetry," he does so because the poetic character of language denotes that prayer is a saying that does not refer to a preexisting being. Nothing—no thing—is referred to but instead, the thing is realized in its naming.

In linguistic theory, this kind of saying would be called a *performative* saying, that is, an utterance that creates a state of affairs by the simple fact of being uttered. One could say that praying is nothing more than performing God by calling his name. It is nevertheless important to note that what is performed or realized remains in accordance with what Nancy referred to as "absentheism," that is, a realization of God not as an absolute sense but as an "absent sense." In other words, one must save this name from becoming "too imposing," in the sense that it would "impose, and impose itself, as the keystone of an entire system of sense" (*D* 88/132). What Christian monotheism—and prayer in particular— challenges us to think is that the assurance of such a system has absented itself and that therefore our world is sensible in itself, even before the imposition of any system whatsoever.

Nancy's project of a deconstruction of Christianity therefore aspires to show, by meticulously analyzing Christianity's presuppositions, that the name *God* simply *cannot* be significant, as Nancy states in "The Name *God* in Blanchot":

it [the name *God*] is majestic and awesome to the degree that it reveals the nonsignification of names. In [this] case, this name names
a sovereign power of the name that beckons—which is very different
from signifying—toward that absenting of sense such that no absence can come to supply a supposedly lost or rejected presence. . . .
God would be the name of that which—or of he or of she who—in
the name escapes nomination to the degree that nomination can
always border on sense. In this hypothesis, this name would de-
name names in general, while persisting in naming, that is, in *calling*. (D 88 / 132)

What is more, the name *God* is thus not only nonsignificant but also de-
names all other names, that is, excludes the possibility of naming the
Name—to use Adorno's words—of providing the very last word.

Within this impossibility lies the core of the entwinement of theistic
and atheistic presuppositions accompanying Christian monotheism. Calling the name *God* is thus, as Nancy states, following Adorno, a naming
of the Name that is doomed to fail, but, we might add, that precisely
because of its failure reveals our human condition, mourned in a desperate
"My God, my God, why hast Thou forsaken me?"

Adoration: The Bond and the Cut

This inherent failure of naming the Name presupposes a crucial conceptual distinction Nancy makes on several occasions, namely, the distinction
between the religious and the sacred. As we might expect, Nancy's treatment of notions like these leads to a deliberate displacement of their usual
meaning. Whereas over the years the critical rejection of religion has generally been formulated in terms of a desacralization, thereby equating the
religious and the sacred, Nancy uses the notion of the sacred to refer to
the *secular* aspect of religion. In Nancy's view, the sacred is thus not equal
to the religious but rather one of the indications that religion necessarily
surpasses itself. It is true that the notion of the sacred is relatively absent
in *Dis-enclosure*, but it is of major importance in some of Nancy's earlier
texts, which can retrospectively be considered preliminary explorations of
a deconstruction of Christianity.

One of the places Nancy underlines this distinction is in "The
Image—the Distinct" (in *The Ground of the Image*), a text that appeared
two years before *Dis-enclosure*. As Nancy states, religion—which literally
means "binding"—refers to realizing and maintaining a bond or connection with the divine or the supernatural. Such a bond can be established,

for instance, in sacrificial rituals or practices of exorcism. The sacred, by contrast, indicates the impossibility of such a bond, since what one wants to relate to retreats from presence. Whereas the religious implies some sort of homogeneity and continuity, the sacred is by definition unattainable and incommensurable. Religion and the sacred are therefore opposed "as the bond is opposed to the cut" (*GI* 1/11). As a result, the sacred is, essentially, nonreligious.

Although Nancy has always remained faithful to the conceptual structure of this distinction, the opposition between the religious and the sacred must not be maintained too strictly, primarily because Nancy uses other sets of terms in other contexts. At times, as in " 'Prayer Demythified,' " he also places the distinction at the heart of a single term—the religious—thereby emphasizing the *self*-deconstructive character of religion. In this case, "religion" is explained via both its possible etymological sources, namely, "binding" (*religare*) and "observing," "addressing," or "adoring" (*religio*).[11] The latter implies the dimension of the sacred, as Nancy explains:

> Ad-oration is literally the addressing of speech. . . . And if the adoration of idols . . . constitutes, throughout our entire tradition, even beyond religion, the touchstone or the *shibboleth* whose charge it is to distinguish "true" religion from the others . . . , it is clearly because . . . the "true" addressee of adoration is the real, whose presence is not to be confused with the given present [*le present-donné*]; it is the real whose presence gives or presents itself when it is "addressed." (*D* 136/197)

Once religion is interpreted as "adoration," "true" religion is thus distinguished from "untrue" ones. A religion is characterized as "untrue" when it adores idols, that is to say, particular objects that are believed to be the full—mythological—presentation of God, the *naming of the Name*, whereas "true" religion affirms that such a thing is impossible. According to Nancy, Christian prayer is a perfect example of Christianity's "trueness," since it is not an adoration of God's presence but a tentative, furtive, failing evocation of God—in the "possibility of never believing our prayers to have been granted, the possibility of never believing, therefore, that we have prayed enough, or never believing absolutely" (*D* 138/201).

The distinction that Nancy makes between the religious and the sacred, or between religion as binding and religion as addressing what is not given, can be broadened to include another distinction he makes with respect to Christianity's self-deconstruction, namely, the distinction between faith (*foi*) and belief (*croyance*; see *D* 12, 25, 51, 152ff/24, 40, 76,

220ff). In this context, "belief" belongs to the category of what has been called the religious, as opposed to the sacred (*GI* 1/11). It refers to those aspects of religion that present the divine, thereby allowing a bond to be established with it. "Faith," by contrast, belongs to the category of what has been called the sacred, which is required in a situation where the divine has retreated. Since the Christian God is absent in principle, Christianity is a *faith*, a faith in this absence, a faith in nothing, or, as Nancy formulates it in *Dis-enclosure*, a *"faithfulness to faithfulness* itself" (*D* 154/223): "Christian faith is distinguished precisely and absolutely from all belief. It is a category *sui generis*, which is not, like belief, a lack of . . ., a dearth of . . ., not a state of waiting for . . ., but faithfulness in its own right, confidence, and openness to the possibility of what it is confidence in" (*D* 153/221). Instead of something that can be confirmed or supported, faith is thus above all a *loyalty*, a loyalty in the absence of a guarantee.

Once more it becomes clear why Christian prayer can never be a question of presentation but at best only an evocation or an address—or rather, an evocation *by means of* an address. By placing Christianity under the heading of the sacred rather than the religious and, in consequence, under that of faith rather than that of belief, Nancy nevertheless stresses that one should not conceive of God as an absolute, transcendent alterity. In his analyses of Christianity, as in those of art, Nancy clearly distances himself from such a view. He stresses instead that, in placing the incarnation at the heart of its doctrine, Christian faith "open[s] the world in itself to its *own outside* (and not to some world-behind-the-world, to some heaven or hell)" (*D* 2/10; my emphasis). That is, the retreat of the Christian God has shown that our world is characterized by an inner outside or inner openness that prevents it from closing down on itself, of delivering its sense once and for all. In one word, it has *dis-enclosed* the world.

This dis-enclosure has, as we have seen, the result that sense is never either fully given or totally absent, but fleeting, momentary. If we want to affirm that we live in a dis-enclosed world, we should not cover up this openness by mythological narratives or representations but instead affirm it in the kind of poetic saying that prayer is or can be. If poetic saying is an exemplary form of addressing God, it is so because it attests, or rather, *performs* this opening. In pressing language to its limit, emptying its meaning, poetic saying exposes us to a beyond that is not some sort of *Hinterwelt*, or heaven, to be retrieved at the end of time, but is proper to and constitutive of the world as it is.

With this view, Nancy supports—although without naming him—Walter Benjamin's view of the "sacredness" of Hölderlin's poetry. Contrary to Heidegger's well-known and influential "mythologization" of

Hölderlin's poems, Benjamin tries to show that Hölderlin's later poems in particular are essentially *de*mythologizing. That is so because they do not represent God, gods, or divinity, as did his earlier poems, but, as Benjamin tries to demonstrate, they are themselves sacred in performing what it means to present something. Hölderlin's poems, in other words, do not represent or host the divine; they stand, in their own right, "beyond all sublimity in the sublime [*jenseits aller Erhebung im Erhabnen*]."[12] That is why they are not mythological utterances but attest to what Hölderlin calls a "sacred sobriety" (*heilige Nüchternheit*). This formula articulates the apparently contradictory logic Nancy lays bare in demythologized prayer—*apparently* contradictory because, like demythologized prayer, Hölderlin's sacred sobriety is not a contradiction in terms but a tautology. After all, what makes it sacred is precisely the fact that it is sober, beyond all elevation.

The Relic of Myth

Hölderlin's poetry—but he is just an example—is thus sacred because it is always *also*, and maybe foremost, a presentation of the act of presenting, a presentation of presentation, as Nancy would say.[13] But how is one to present without presentation; how is one to pray without prayer? What can one say if words are deprived of content? First of all, one does not manage by saying just anything. As Nancy points out in "'Prayer Demythified,'" poetry and prayer are alike in this respect: "One answer would be that it [prayer] will say whatever [*n'importe quoi*], as long as it says, but says at the very least according to the requirement or the desire of the saying: the desire to say the thing. On this point the worst confusion is possible: the essence of saying can turn into a 'saying for the sake of saying [*dire pour dire*]'" (*D* 134/196). Just as poetry can relapse into art for art's sake, prayer can relapse into a mere saying for the sake of saying. Nancy, once again referring to Adorno, states that the internal structure of art is not a monadic constitution that has its goal in itself but "points beyond it" (*M1* 35/63). It is a presentation that is always under way, a passage. That is why the sense of an artwork can never be grasped, pinpointed, but has to be sensed each time anew.

Clearly, Nancy understands demythologized prayer as "something like poetry" because—following Heidegger's *Dichtung* and Hölderlin's sacred sober poetry—he believes that poetry lays bare the logic of the *ontos*, of being, that is ours after the withdrawal of God. "Ontology," as Nancy paraphrases it in *Corpus*, "is affirmed as writing" (*C* 17). If our task today is to measure the true scope of this poetic ontology,[14] we should "empty and let be emptied out all prayers that negotiate a sense, an issue, or a repatriation of the real within the narrow confines of our faded humanisms and clenched religiosities," in order to "open speech once again to its most proper possibility of address, which also makes up all its sense and all its truth" (D 138/201). Nancy goes so far as to call this an imperative.

But would such an "emptied out" prayer—if we were ever to succeed in achieving it—distinguish itself from other linguistic practices, such as poetry? How—and here I repeat one of the main questions posed by Nancy in "'Prayer Demythified'"—"can a demythologized prayer be a *prayer?*" (D 130/190; my emphasis). In his text, Nancy focuses on explaining, first, why prayer is an example of religion's own demythologization and, second, why such prayer is an exemplary way of addressing the Christian God. This explanation, however, serves only as an answer to a second question that, in Nancy's view, is a "more demanding" reformulation of the first one, namely: "How can a demythologized prayer *pray?*" (D 130/190; my emphasis). A crucial but largely unanswered question is in what sense prayer can be distinguished from other forms of poetic saying. Considering that praying is something like poetry, how can one still affirm that one is praying instead of citing a poem? Put differently, why does praying still have a *religious* dimension?

Although Nancy's goal is to show that prayer and poetry are one and the same praxis, that is, making a gesture of ex-position to the world's "inner outside," he nevertheless points out the difference between the two at the end of his text: "prayer (*and in this it differs from the poem* as well as from discourse, even though the poem also tends in this direction) is chiefly characterized as speech *accompanying an act.* One prays with acts of worship, a prayer ritual (hands joined, kneeling), and one always prays with a prayerful gesture, however lightly sketched out" (D 138/190; my emphasis). For Nancy, prayer is distinguished from poetry in that it accompanies certain actions, rituals, and movements. In other words, prayer is a linguistic gesture that accompanies other, nonlinguistic gestures. But what does it mean that the poetic saying of prayer apparently cannot do without a certain ritual accompaniment in order to be prayer? In short, what is the function of this accompaniment?

The answer to this question demands a reconsideration of Nancy's analysis of the relationship between myth, religion, and poetry proposed in "'Prayer Demythified.'" As we have seen, according to Nancy the delicate and paradoxical address to the Christian God can be preserved only within a saying that is emptied of all representational and thus mythological content. Nevertheless, this emptied saying turns out to take place within the fixed and meaningful context of a specific place, a specific position of the body, a closing or lifting of the eyes. Given this ritual accompaniment, shouldn't we say that the opening toward an inner outside that exemplifies demythologized praying can only take place after being affirmed and recognized as such? Moreover, is this recognition in general not the condition of a performative act? In other words, could it be that the poetic saying of prayer, a saying that is an opening toward and *of* being, necessarily takes place within a realm that, though it may be deprived of referential meaning, is still *mythological* in the Aristotelian sense that it is a structuring, an emplotment of actions?

Although I must leave aside the question to what extent art or poetry demands a ritual accompaniment as well,[15] I would argue that the opening of speech that "makes up its truth" can be affirmed as such only because of this accompaniment. No matter how emptied its sense may be, in order to be affirmed as "absent sense," poetic saying can only take place under certain conditions. Maybe the poetic making or opening in which prayer consists needs first to be made itself. One could therefore ask whether prayer—or, more generally, the infinite suspension of meaning—can do without this relic of myth.

Literary Creation, Creation ex Nihilo

MICHEL LISSE

In *Dis-enclosure*, Jean-Luc Nancy suggests that in Western culture "God's act of creation" has provided "the least bad analogical recourse" for designating the "void-artist-body [*corps-vide-artiste*]" (*D* 69/99; first trans. modified). Working backward, from this we can posit, still speaking analogically, that God's act of creation generated the myth or concept of creation that is involved in the process and results of literary writing. Such a myth of creation should be understood in at least two senses: first, myth as an originary tale (*récit*) of foundation that has come down to us via the Judeo-Christian tradition (Genesis), and second, myth in Roland Barthes's sense as a semiotic message that aims to render innocent, to "naturalize" an ideological content (the myth of the author-creator, master of his text, the author as genius). This concept of creation in the more literary sense of the word should be understood as replacing or reinforcing the myth of creation in the first sense, then becoming myth in the second sense in its ordinary version. One might say that the concepts of the author and of creation undergo a similar fate in theories of literature: despite their acknowledged limitations and their notorious metaphysical grounding, they are still in use, and even being revived. To give a single potent example, I would point to the formation of programs of study in creation and in the theory of creation in universities in North America.[1]

In this essay, I hope to demonstrate, first, how Nancy, via a paleonymic analysis of the notion of "creation," prepares a thinking of the self-deconstruction of Christianity and, second, that this notion, as Nancy understands it, is related to literary creation. Paleonymy is a strategy that consists in using a metaphysical concept under erasure (e.g., the concept of Being in Heidegger, the concept of writing in Derrida), putting this old term to work in a new way. While Nancy does not lay claim to this logic, he seems to make use of it in discussing the concept of creation in several recent texts, including *Dis-enclosure* and *The Creation of the World, or Globalization*. Nancy's holds that the influence of Christianity upon the Western philosophical tradition has been decisive, and he sees Christianity as a process undergoing its own deconstruction, its self-deconstruction. That process then affects Western metaphysical concepts. In his strongest and most provocative formulation, Nancy sums up his hypothesis by affirming that the entirety of our thought is thoroughly Christian, even and especially if the reference to Christianity, while all-pervasive, "has been obfuscated *qua explicit reference* in and by philosophy" (*D* 139/204). Christianity, "and with it all monotheisms," Nancy writes, "can and must be considered as a powerful confirmation of metaphysics" (*D* 7/16). Christianity therefore will have been less the "*maladie honteuse*" (*D* 9/19) rejected by the Enlightenment than "the strongest *imaginary* resource" (*D* 7/21; my emphasis) of the metaphysics of presence.[2]

Being Singular Plural contains a paragraph about "the creation of the world and curiosity." There, Nancy, citing Augustine, Thomas Aquinas, Descartes, Malebranche, Spinoza, and Leibniz, asserts that the concept of creation somehow destabilizes the concept of production and the concept of the world as having an author. That is to say, in the attempt to think creation, one must renounce the concept of God as author of the world, of God as creator. Why? Because, for Nancy, the "defining characteristic" of the concept of creation does not lead one to posit a creator outside of creation but rather a "'creator' indistinct from its 'creation'" (*BSP* 15/34). That is quite different from mythological tales in which a god or a demiurge fashions a universe "starting from a situation that is already there" (*BSP* 16/34). A thinking of creation is based on the withdrawal (*retrait*) from or the deduction of what is already there, of the "given," Nancy states in *The Creation of the World, or Globalization*. More specifically, opposing any mythological cosmogony, which always presupposes something primordially given, he writes: "The world of myth, and of polytheism, is the world of given presupposition. Onto-theology—the suspension of myth—is, on the contrary, the order of posited presupposition: actively posited as the affirmation of the unique God and/or as thesis of Being" (*CW* 71/94).

One can see the parallels between monotheism, the religion of the one God, and metaphysics, the philosophy of Being. They both perform the same gesture: the suspension of myth. This is why ontotheology deconstructs itself: if the presupposition is posited and not already given, it "also contains the principle of its own deposition, since it cannot presuppose anything like a cause (nor, therefore, like an end) or like a production, without also extending, correlatively, the limits of the world" (*CW* 71/94).[3]

Where mythical cosmogony sees a god or a demiurge-artisan, the Western ontotheological tradition, as reinterpreted by Nancy, does not "see" anything or, more precisely, "sees" nothing. The concept of creation is thus radically opposed to the concept of production, understood as "fabrication that supposes a given, a project, and a producer" (*CW* 51/55). This necessarily implies a thinking of creation as creation ex nihilo. According to Nancy, it is important to reject the interpretation that creation ex nihilo refers to the œuvre of a creator who creates out of nothing, since this would still remain in the logic of the world as fashioned, admittedly out of nothing, but fashioned all the same. That is what Nancy calls "the fable of a producer supposed to produce without material (but certainly subject and substrate of his work)" (*D* 69/100)[4]—it is important to reject this interpretation in favor of a second interpretation elaborated by "a rich and complex tradition" (*BSP* 16/35). This second interpretation posits that " 'the creator' itself is the *nihil*" (*BSP* 16/35) and that therefore "this *nihil* is not, logically speaking, something whence what is created would come [*provenir*], but the very provenance, and destination, of something in general and of everything" (*BSP* 16/35; trans. modified). This leads Nancy to reject any notion of creation having any prerequisite or preexistence whatsoever: "the *nihil* is nothing prior" and "there is also no longer a 'nothing' that pre-exists creation" (*BSP* 16/35). Creation must now be thought as an "act of appearing [*surgissement*]," as an "arrival [*venue*] in nothing" (*BSP* 16/35). In this way, Nancy seems to adopt the theological or mystical hypothesis according to which "God empties himself of himself in the opening of the world," rejecting the hypothesis that holds that "God sustains himself as being, by himself, subject and substance of the world" (*D* 70/100). In *The Creation of the World*, this hypothesis of God as withdrawal, void, and opening of this void is set out:

> God annihilates itself [*s'anéantit*] as a "self" or as a distinct being in order to "withdraw" in his act—which makes the opening of the world. . . . The unique God, whose unicity is the correlate of the creating act, cannot precede its creation any more than he can subsist above it or apart from it . . . He merges with [creation]: merging

with it, he withdraws into it, and withdrawing into it he empties himself into it, by emptying himself into it he is nothing other than the opening of this void. Only opening is divine, but the divine is nothing more the opening. (*CW* 70/93; trans. modified)

Why does Nancy privilege this hypothesis over the one that takes God to be the "supreme being"? To answer this question, one would have to summarize the history of ontotheology, as Nancy has rewritten it in his books. Though that task is beyond the scope of this essay, a rough answer can be drawn from some of Nancy's remarks on Kant. Kant, he says, "opens implicitly and outside of theology a new question of 'creation'" (*CW* 66/84), and "Kant . . . was the first to explicitly confront the world as such" (*CW* 41/32–33). And yet, if Kant was the first, today his attitude seems to be outdated: "time has passed since one was able to represent the figure of a *cosmotheoros*, an observer of the world" (*CW* 43/37).[5] It is worth recalling that Nancy had projected a book called *Kosmotheoros*, which would have followed on from *Logodædalus*, the first volume of *The Discourse of the Syncope*. What caused this hiatus? If Kant was the first to think the world differently, not as having been created by a God/supreme being, he participated in a logic that subordinated world to worldview (*Weltanschauung*). In doing so, Kant participated in the tradition that he was deconstructing: "a world 'viewed,' a represented world, is a world dependent on the gaze of a subject of the world. A subject of the-world . . . cannot itself be within the world. Even without a religious representation, such a subject, implicit or explicit, perpetuates the position of the creating, organizing, and addressing God (if not the addressee) of the world" (*CW* 40/31–32).

However, it is implicit in Kant, thanks to him and from him onward, that a double, simultaneous movement takes place within ontotheological thought: in it, *the creator disappears into the very heart of his act and being is no longer presupposed*; we are talking about a *being without anything already given* (*être sans donné*): not as a substance, or a substratum, or a product, or a property, but as an act, equivalent to a doing.[6] With Kant and beginning with Kant, the thinking of creation abandons a certain theological vision, which associated creation and production or fashioning, in order to reach a creation-in-act, which "is through and through the mobilization of an act, and this act is that of a relation between two actors or agents, God and his creature, consequently each of them singular" (*CW* 70/92). With the move toward creation as act, we also abandon a conception of creation as what took place once only in a space and time that were already there in favor of an approach stating that creation "takes place everywhere and always": "Creation takes place everywhere and always—but it is this unique event, or advent, only on the condition of being each time what it is, or being what it is only 'at each time,' each time appearing singularly" (*BSP* 16/35). Creation is therefore the appearance of space-time, the appearance of all singularities and of their disposition (*partage*)—or, in other words, *ex*-istence:

> The *ex nihilo* contains nothing more, but nothing less, than the ex- of ex-istence that is neither produced nor constructed but only *existing* [étante] (or if one prefers, *étée*, "made" from the making of constituted by the transitivity of being) . . .
>
> . . . *ex nihilo* means that it is the *nihil* that opens and disposes itself as the space of all presence. (*CW* 71/95)

In order to prepare the ground for my reflections on the "literary" side of creation, I hope to invoke the echo of this crossing of creation and the act, of being and doing. I start with a Mallarmé citation from Blanchot's *The Book to Come*: "Impersonified, the book, as long as one separates oneself from it as author, does not demand the approach of a reader. As such, now, among human accessories, it takes place all alone: something made, being [*fait, étant*]."[7]

Blanchot holds this affirmation to be "one of Mallarmé's most glorious" because, in a few words, it states "the essential demand of the work." There is solitude: the volume takes place on its own; what's more, its accomplishment comes from a place: *it takes place* by itself; there is also, and above all, a double, aporetic affirmation: *fait, étant*, if I understand Blanchot correctly. He writes:

> This last assertion is one of Mallarmé's most glorious. It expresses, in a form that bears the mark of decision, the essential demand of the work. Its solitude, its accomplishment starting from itself as if from a place, the double assertion juxtaposed in it, separated by a logical and temporal hiatus, of what makes it and of the being in which it belongs, indifferent to "making"; its simultaneity, then, of instantaneous presence, and of the process of its realization: as soon as it is done, finished with being made, and saying no more than this: that it is.[8]

I began this essay by taking the concept of creation understood as God's act of creation to be the least bad analogy for the process of literary writing. In a fairly conventional way, one concedes that this process can be seen as creation in the "weak sense" (the same is true for artistic creation). Interestingly, Nancy does not consider artistic or poetic creation to be creation in the weak sense, but rather creation in the strongest sense. (Indeed, he seems to avoid the concept of literary creation altogether; I will return to this.) What takes place at the heart of the deconstruction of Christianity is a slippage of the concept of creation and of the associated theme of the image of God. This slippage is at work in Descartes and in Leibniz, where "the status of the real" flips over into the status of the possible," a possible that must be understood "as the unlimiting mode of openness and activity" (CW 65/81). Referring to Leibniz's famous phrase "the best of all possible worlds," Nancy argues that "the world is a possibility before being a reality" (CW 65/81) and, if the Cartesian theory of continuous creation in the third *Meditation* is taken into account, then creation is an incessant activity and an opening: "from creation as a result of an accomplished divine action, one shifts to creation as, in sum, an unceasing activity and actuality of this world in its singularity (singularity of singularities)" (CW 65/82). Or even a dis-enclosure: "the eclosure of the world must be thought in its radicalness: no longer an eclosure against the background of a given world, or even against that of a given creator, but the eclosure of eclosure itself and the spacing of the space itself" (D 160/230); a blossoming-hatching (*éclosion-explosion*), in which the world is constantly brought into the world, "a new departure for creation" (D 160/230). A change in the status of the creature follows from this: "the *creature* that was the finite image of its creator and consequently was bound to represent (interpret, figure) creation, itself, becomes a potential *creator* as subject of possibilities and subject of ends" (CW 65/82). This means thinking artistic or poetic creation no longer as representation but as the creation of meaning.

Being Singular Plural and *The Ground of the Image* (notably "Forbidden Representation") already touch on the theme of the image of God in terms of God himself. Recalling that creatures are a testimony to the love, goodness, and glory of God, "the very brilliance [*éclat*] of his coming into presence," Nancy advances a way of understanding "the theme of the 'image of God' and/or 'the trace of God' not according to the logic of a secondary imitation, but according to this other logic where 'God' is itself the singular appearance of the image or trace or the disposition of its *exposition*" (BSP 17/36). God and creatures are, in some sense, on the same footing, and, when Kant ruled out the theory of God as creator in the *Critique of Pure Reason*, a new question about creatures was formulated.

Let us now take a look at the title of Nancy's book *The Creation of the World, or Globalization*. It is banal to point out that the use of a genitive, which can be subjective or objective, permits an ambiguity, namely, whether the world creates or is created. This ambiguity is reinforced if we do not read this "or" as an exclusive one. In other words, it is possible that the world is at once creator and created, even that these two activities are really one, two sides of the same coin. Obviously, the question that arises is how Nancy defines the concept "world." He answers this question with a succinctness that will allow me to bypass an investigation of the many texts and books in which he discusses this concept. In *The Creation of the World*, the answer leaps out: "a world is a totality of sense" (*CW* 64/34; trans. modified). This answer obviously calls for further elucidation, especially on the point of sense. Again, I can keep things short: sense is "opening of the possibility of a referencing [*renvoi*]" (*PD* 172) or the "possibility of transmission from one place to another, from the one who sends to the one who receives, and from one element to another, a referencing that forms at the same time a direction, an address, a value, or a meaningful content" (*CW* 52/57). In this view, the world, issuing from nothing, ex nihilo, must have a value for itself, must leave behind its representation, and thereby be "without a God capable of being the subject of its own representation" (*CW* 43/38) or without any subject which "perpetuates the position of the creating . . . God" (*CW* 40/32). In this sense, the world is created ex nihilo, "configures itself, and exposes itself in itself, relates to itself without referring to any given principle or to any determined end" (*CW* 47/47).

But Nancy adds a clarification, even a limitation, to his answer about the world: "a world is only a world for those who inhabit it," that is, for whom it has a place, "its place, in the strong sense of the term, as that which allows something to properly take place" (*CW* 42/35). The world is only the world for singularities, for everyone, male and female, who shares in it. These "everyones" are only singular points in the dynamism of a sense that exceeds them, but these singular points are still necessary for the spacing, and therefore for the structure of referencing, and therefore also for the possibility of the extension of sense, for its resonances:

we are never, side by side, anything but singular points along a general dispatch [*envoi*] that sense makes of itself and to itself, and that begins and becomes lost long before and beyond us, in the indefinitely open totality of the world. But at the same time, these singular points . . . are themselves the necessarily discrete or discontinuous structure of the general spacing inside which a sense can resonate, that is, *answer itself* [se répondre]. (*PD* 172)

If these resonances, if the answer must necessarily be possible in order for there to be a referencing, and thereby any sense at all, then the world is not a world unless the singularities who share it "configure" it,[9] expose themselves, create it. In an almost phenomenological discourse, Nancy argues that "as soon as a world appears to me as a world, I already share something of it: I experience a part of its inner resonances" (*CW* 42/35; trans. modified).

These resonances reach us from other places, and I bounce them back by formulating them, thereby situating myself in a space made out of them. That is why I share the world as a plural singularity with others, who in turn share it with others and with me. In other words, I expose myself: "sharing singularity (always plural) means to configure a world, a quantity of possible worlds in the world. This configuration . . . allows the singularities to expose themselves" (*CW* 46/43–44).[10]

The world issues from nothing, ex nihilo. It is not a given, no more than sense is. Sense is not to be discovered (as something already there), once and for all, but is always to be invented (like what does not exist before its invention). This invention, which cannot be a hermeneutics (since this always supposes an "already there") is another name for creation. At this point in his argument, Nancy introduces the concept of enunciations as creators of sense:

> neither sense as direction [*sens*] nor sense as content is given. They must be invented each time: in other words, be created, that is, be created from nothing and be brought forth as the without-reason [*rien-de-raison*] that sustains, drives, and forms statements that are genuinely creative of meaning, as in science, poetry, politics, aesthetics, and ethics. (*CW* 52/57–58; trans. modified)

The absence of literature from the list of creative activities cannot be overlooked. Why is it not there? What might that mean? Might not literature be an activity that creates sense, too? I am, of course, aware of Nancy's work in collaboration with Philippe Lacoue-Labarthe, which sought to grasp the moment of the literary absolute, as well as how theoretical elaborations and desires to write obsessively return to this absolute. It is because of this awareness that I flag the absence of literature and ask where we would place the texts of, say, Proust, Kafka, Joyce, or Borges.

To be brief, let us focus, among the list of activities that create meaning, on the twin sisters poetry and philosophy. They seem to respond to what Nancy describes as our task: "creating a form or a symbolization of the world" (CW 53, 59) or even "*to create the world* . . .: immediately, without delay, reopening each possible struggle for a world" (*CW* 54/ 63)—given that this struggle takes place in the name of the ex nihilo, a thinking without model, as an invention of meaning. In philosophy, Nancy takes reflective judgments to be enunciations that create sense. A reflective judgment is one for which "the universal is not given." It is not possible to construct it via "the dependence of a concept on an intuition, which defines the conditions of a *possible* experience" (*CW* 60/70). In the absence of intuition, it is without criteria and faces "the inconstructable of an absence of intuition" (*CW* 60/70), which implies that this judgment will have to "let a void emerge" or "make with this void" (*CW* 60/70; not construct in the void). In short, as Nancy sums it up in a text first called "Dies illa," "not to construct, but to create" (*CW* 60/71).

Here we are dealing with a reprise of what Nancy discusses in "Dies iræ": when the particular alone is given, and when the faculty to judge must still find the universal, the judgment is said to be *reflective*. This is what Nancy highlights in reflective judgment:

> The reflective judgment *must discover* (*soll finden*). It must invent the law; it must produce by itself the universal. But it must produce it not as a phantom, a fiction of objects or objectivity that would cover up more or less well a lack in the theoretical possibilities of reason . . . it is not fiction in this sense that makes up the œuvre of reflective judgments. Rather, it is fiction in the strong sense, fabrication, the *poiēsis* of the universal. (DI 18–19)[11]

The verb *to create* is not used here, but if we substitute it for *to produce*, we obtain a statement that I believe could find a place in *The Creation of the World*: reflective judgment *must discover* (*soll finden*). It must invent the law; it must create *of itself* (ex nihilo) the universal. But it must not create it as, etcetera. One can also remark the exclusion of one fiction in favor of another, in favor of fiction in the strong sense, *poiēsis*, fashioning. Here the twin sister appears: "philosophy *versus* poetry does not constitute an opposition. Each of the two makes difficulties for the other. Together, they are difficulty itself: the difficulty of making sense" (*M2* 5/*R* 11).

These words of Nancy are taken from *Résistance de la poésie*, more precisely, from the first part of the book, entitled "Making, Poetry" ("Faire, la poésie"). For Nancy, poetry is defined by an access to sense: our only access to sense is by way of poetry, which means that poetry cannot be reduced to a literary genre but touches a whole series of discourses and activities that have poetic qualities: according to *Littré*, the word *poésie* touches on qualities such as richness, impact, color, and depth, which characterize good verse but can also be found elsewhere. This usage of the word in an absolute sense is doubled by a usage in a figurative sense: still according to *Littré*, whatever is elevated or touching in a work of art, a person, nature . . . is poetry. Nancy rightly notes that the figurative sense is only an extension of the absolute sense and that therefore poetry is always "properly identical with itself" and "at the same time always only a figure of that properness which cannot be assigned in any proper sense" (*M2* 3/9, trans. modified). The access to sense is therefore always displaced and reported, and the sense of this access, and with it the sense of "poetry," always remains to be made, as poetry is noncoincidence with itself. It is therefore also a negativity that keeps the elevated and the touching out of reach; in other words, access to sense is marked above all by refusal and flight from everything; access to sense is difficult. Nancy then compares the negativity of poetry and the "twin"[12] (his word) negativity of dialectical discourse, which sets out "the refusal of access as the truth of access" (*M2* 4/10). The difference between the two is that the latter promises a resolution whereas the former "persists with the difficulty" (*M2* 5/10; trans. modified). This difficulty implies that, when access to sense takes place, this access is perfect, but must always be remade due to this perfection: I would call this a conjunction of the best of (im)possibles and of (dis)continued creation, if I were to risk reformulating things in terms of creation. Poetry is therefore a *poiēin*, a fashioning (*un faire*), a "making an access be" (*M2* 8/14), which is at the same time an action, "the integral action of the disposition to sense" (*M2* 6/12) and an exacting, exigent of what is owed and of more than what is owed. It is sense as excess, an excess of saying, of meaning to say toward a saying more than saying, toward a beyond of saying.

But the half-sister, literature, seems to be excluded from the world where philosophy and poetry interact. Let us try to understand this exclusion. In his reading of an article in which Gérard Granel evokes "the poetry of the World" and the poet's ability to name "the reserve [*pudeur*] of the World" (*D* 165/107), thereby revenging himself on "philosophical impatience,"[13] Nancy argues that Granel hopes to position himself on the side of the poet and not on that of the philosopher when, for example, he writes: "what I just named descriptively (literarily? I hope not) 'a sort of hollow' is what Heidegger thematized as the 'there' (*le 'Da-'*) of Da-sein" (*D* 172/114)

Granel states that his naming is descriptive and hopes that it is not literary; we could also interpret this as hoping that this descriptive naming is not also literary, as if there were a certain relation between descriptive naming and literary naming, a risk of being inside literature as soon as one names or describes, or does both at once. This is how Nancy shifts the question toward poetry: "Granel wanted himself to be, sought himself, or hoped himself (promising? fearing to promise himself too much?) on the side of the poet (and not on that of the literary hack: he separates from the latter with an "I hope not," which proves his presentment of a possible mistake, a possible decorative heaviness, and the extreme fragility of an approach to the poetic by the philosophical" (*D* 71/101–2).

If I understand this correctly, the philosophical procedure can become poetic, the philosopher can be close to the poet, but this philosophical approach, in wishing to approach the poetic, also takes the risk of becoming a "mistake" or a "decorative heaviness": it risks becoming literary (or sliding into literature?). Despite my admiration for the work and the thinking of Nancy, in these lines he is too close to Granel's thinking for my liking in this association between the decorative obstacle and the literary, and between error and the literary. I fear that one can hear some Heideggerian echoes from *What Is Called Thinking?* in Granel's text, denouncing, after Socrates—the West's purest thinker because he does not write—the entry, which also seems to be a decline, of Thinking into Literature. Nancy could have distanced himself from Granel by recalling that some of his own books (notably *The Discourse of the Syncope* and *Ego sum*) seem to demonstrate that a thinker always needs to give writing its due. In order to be fair to Nancy, we should clarify two points. First, he distinguishes literature understood as a "literary genre" from literature as an undergoing of the "the cessation or dispersal of sense": " 'Literature,' here, does not mean the 'literary genre,' but any sort of saying, shouting, praying, laughing, or sobbing that holds—as one holds a note or a chord—that infinite suspension of meaning" (*D* 97/146). Second, Nancy also discusses the chasm (*antre*) between philosophy and literature. The flight of the gods, the withdrawal of divine bodies, has rendered impossible both their truth and the tale of this truth. Their bodies are lacking, are lacking as presence: "When the gods are withdrawn, their story can no longer be simply true, nor their truth simply narrated. There is absence of the presence which would testify to the existence of what is narrated, as well as to the veracity of the words that narrate" (*BT* 7/8; trans. modified). The withdrawal therefore caused the separation between truth and narration; around the now-empty tomb, a scene "simultaneously of mourning and of desire" is played out between philosophy and literature: "philosophy and literature, each in mourning and each in desire of the other, but each competing with the other in the accomplishment of the mourning and the desire" (*BT* 8). In this view, literature is no longer shunned, instead receiving a status that establishes it as a rival to philosophy.

Finally, let us be grateful to Nancy for having promoted writing. This leads me to turn to the last part of *Concealed Thinking* (*La pensée dérobée*) in order to venture some remarks on the magnificent lines dedicated to writing there. "Whoever writes answers [*répond*]": these are the opening words of "Answering for Sense." They immediately raise questions: To whom? To what? To what call? To what other voice? These questions apply both to the call and to the address. The words are "nothing other than sense" defined as "opening the possibility of an answer" (*PD* 172). Hence the new inflection a few paragraphs later: "whoever writes answers sense" (*PD* 173). If literature wants to say something, if whoever writes *wants* to say, then this has to do not with content but with the desire to say: whoever writes hears "saying desire itself as saying" (*PD* 171) and answers sense. This desire is defined as "the cut and the touch of a singular truth," which can only "come from the outside" (*PD* 175): from the ex where there is nothing (*nihil*), no god, no muse, no genius. This outside is "that of absolute sense" (*PD* 176), a stranger to articulate language, to the language of already-given significations, but an opening onto an unheard-of language, to come. To write is to expose oneself to the outside,[14] to a withdrawal of language, to a hither side of language, to a "nothing to say," to a "thing outside," to a "thing of the outside" (*PD* 176). One last inflection: "whoever writes answers this thing and answers for it" (*PD* 177) practices an incision "in language, made by the blade of an outside that is both one of nonlanguage and of a language to come or a desire for language" (*PD* 176). We can call that creation ex nihilo, poetic creation, literary creation.

—*Translated by John McKeane*

The God Between

ANNE O'BYRNE

God is not the limit of man but the limit of man is divine. In other words, man is divine in the experience of his limits.

 —**Georges Bataille, "The Divinity of Laughter"**

Jean-Luc Nancy is without doubt a post-Marxist, post-Heideggerian and—I would add—post-Arendtian thinker.[1] His ontology bears traces of all three, but this ontology flows, above all, from an attempt to think creation ex nihilo after the death of the creator God. Even now, so long after Nietzsche, and so very long after Descartes set the process of secularization in motion, it is a thinking that is only uneasily, hesitantly under way. We have gone beyond God, as Nancy puts it, but in a direction still too much determined by the thought of his death and by the necro-monotheist tradition when what is needed is an exploration of the direction—directions, rather—that are constantly newly opened by our rather than God's creative capacities. If we examine the movement of the deconstruction of Christianity insofar as it is the specific deconstruction of creation ex nihilo, Nancy's new ontology emerges as symbolic and poetic but also, as we will see, as a natal ontology.

Kristeva writes that "there is nothing more dismal than a dead God."[2] In "On a Divine *Wink*," Nancy argues that God has been exceeded, which "is not the same as the supreme being put to death" (*D* 119/176). What happens, then, to a deconstructed creator? He passes, not in the sense of passing away but of passing into the world. He passes first into

215

the specifically worldly problem of facticity. "Facticity" (that we are) forms a pair with "intelligibility" (what that means), and the problem springs from the gap that separates the two, a gap that did not exist for a being for whom knowing and being were one. Kant described this mode of knowing on the part of the creator God as *intuitus originarius*, a knowing that requires no object beyond itself and therefore allows for no gap between what is thought and what is. But, as Kant also made clear, our mode of knowing as finite beings is *intuitus derivatus*; our knowledge is always knowledge of something. At this point a gap opens between fact and meaning, leaving us with the question of how it can be possible to understand or grasp or speak about facticity at all. This is a worldly problem for Nancy, given that he, like Arendt, grasps from the start that to be natal is to be plural.[3] Because he thinks in terms of plurality ("that we are" rather than "that I am" or "that Dasein is"), the question of intelligibility becomes the question of the creation of the world. Whatever is or has been created is in principle meaningful. To create is to mean, and if the world is a created whole, then we and all its parts can have meaning in relation to that whole. After all, what the creator God gave us, beyond salvation or eternal life or security or absolute morality, was meaning, and in *intuitus originarius* we have a model for the resolution of the problem of facticity. If we can get access to a thought of creation *after* the creator, we are on our own way to meaning or, using Nancy's preferred term, we are on our way to not having but *being* sense (*SW* 8/19).

Our thinking runs up against the fact *that* we are, materially; our thought is confounded by the fact *that* the world is. Wittgenstein testifies to this experience of running up against in the *Lecture on Ethics* when he gives the example of the expression "I wonder at the existence of the world."[4] It is another way of framing the first question of metaphysics— "Why is there something rather than nothing?"—and what for medieval Christianity was the enigma of creation ex nihilo. According to the Christian model, when the creator created creation, he separated the world from himself. He brought it into being as distinct from his own being and brought us into being in his image. Thus we too were at a remove from him, and our being was separated from his, not least by the fact of our ignorance and wonder, glaring indicators of the separation in us of knowing and being. In this way the gap opens between facticity and intelligibility, between fact and sense. Nancy writes: "The world is the infinite resolution of sense into fact and fact into sense: the infinite resolution of the finite. Resolution signifies at once dissolution, transformation, harmonization, and firm decision. The world is the finite opening of an infinite decision" (*SW* 155/235). The world is not a space or place but the movement of fact and sense toward and into one another. Neither is exempt from the condition of finitude, but their resolution must happen infinitely, without limit and specifically without end.

As Nancy writes in *The Creation of the World, or Globalization*, if the creation of the world is understood as the result of an act that produced all of Creation out of an inert nothing (as though the nothing were its material cause), it is the story of a mysterious and now completed act of creativity. This understanding came under pressure early on from Descartes, Spinoza, Malebranche, and Leibniz, whose work began to turn us toward an understanding of Creation as a never-ending activity (*CW* 65/ 82), yet only with Kant was the possibility of God as creator and *ens summum*, the efficient cause of the world, eliminated, and only then could philosophy begin to work out the death, or the exceeding or passing, of God. One sense of the word *creatio* slowly gives way to another: the thought of creation as a given state of affairs cedes to an active sense where it is a matter of bringing into the world a world.

Yet, by replacing the thought of a completed act with that of ongoing activity, do we not make the need for an actor more pressing than ever? What sort of activity is creating? Who is capable of bringing into the world a world? Since it is mothers who are responsible for bringing each of us into the world, does this mean that He, the Creator God, becomes She? In a certain regard it does; He has become She to the extent that the world is not made but born.[5] Nancy ascribes to the "the world itself in its fact" an innateness, "whose structure is throughout the structure of birth and surprising arrival" (*SW* 155/234). Creation is not now a matter of production but rather of pro-creation or generation. But if this is so, it must put into question our understanding of birth, which has thus far meant being brought into a world already here, already old, and already constituted as world. This has been a crucial and by no means incidental element of what we understand by "birth"; it is what makes our mode of being historical. Yet even though we all know—or have an idea of—what it means to bring a baby, a being, into the world, it remains unclear what it can mean to bring a world into the world. If the world is a totality (at least a totality of sense), then how can one totality emerge into another (*CW* 64/79)?

The conundrum springs from the mistake of thinking in terms of *a* world, or a world among possible worlds, or, indeed, of world as distinct from some other unworldly realm. This is the Christian, Platonic mistake. There is no other, no place, no-thing, nothing out of which world, babies, beings, meaning, or sense emerge. There is no form according to which we were made, no Idea of which we are the shadow, no source of meaning other than the world itself. Coming to terms with this is the central work of the deconstruction of Christianity. Creation is the bringing (in)to world of world as such, the opening up of world. While it is true that there is no thing that is the source of creation, creation ex nihilo also turns out to be something that does not exactly happen ex nihilo because it does not exactly happen *ex* at all. Nancy writes: "The most famous mystical version of the creation, the *zimzum* of the Lurianic Kabbalah, states that the 'nothing' of creation is what opens up in God when God retreats into himself (in his entirety) in the act of creating. God annihilates himself as 'self' or as distinct being in order to retreat into his act—which is the opening of the world" (*CW* 70/93). The Lurianic God does not historically displace the Christian God, only to be displaced by godless modernity. Rather, the single God whose singularity coincides with the unique act of creation cannot survive above and beyond his creation. He folds himself into it, empties himself into it in the emanation and contraction that is the movement of creation: "This emptying is the opening of the void. Only the opening is divine, but the divine is nothing other than the opening" (*CW* 70/93; trans. modified). The question "Who creates?" folds into itself.

This is certainly no dead God. God has passed into the world, and now we have the altogether more interesting story of an ongoing, never-finished, natal activity of emerging despite being posited by nothing (*SW* 155/234). The *nihil* is mobilized as the opening of the world; the *ex* becomes the *ex-* of existence, which is neither produced nor constructed but *is*, transitively. Understanding the verb *to be* transitively and in an active sense means understanding that creation is plural and that we are together, with, and toward other beings. That is to say, what creation creates is relation. Letting God pass—that is, becoming an atheist—means opening the sense of the world (*SW* 158/238–39).

Put another way, creation happens according to the movement of Derridean *différance*. According to Nancy, *différance* is too often thought as the self-deferral of presence, "a sort of permanent flight from the asymptotic and unattainable 'self,'" whereas it should be understood as the generative structure of the ex nihilo (*CW* 72/97). Creation as active—more accurately, as both passive and active, not only reflexive but indeed middle-voiced—does have the temporal structure of deferral; as plural, it has the spatializing structure of differing. The self is quite displaced, and what comes to the fore is the world as constituted by the unending activity of differing and deferring among and between. It is not a matter of selves denied or refusing presence. As Jacques Derrida puts it in "Différance":

"One is but the other different and deferred, one differing and deferring the other."[6] Indeed, his essay is itself an attempt to think "being" as the "ex-" of existence, where the "ex-" is also the "ex-" of *ek-stasis*, of being ex-posed, of being in the world with others.

Derrida sets out to demonstrate the emptiness of Heidegger's ontological difference, and Nancy's work takes up the same project of inheriting and overturning Heideggerian ontology. Not only is being always an *instance* of being for Nancy; it is also always an instance of being *with*. Whatever exists co-exists. The world is the coexistence that puts existences together, and the question of the meaning of Being has become the question of being with and being together in the world, or *as* the world. When he argues that we are singular plural beings, it is not a matter of individuation, that is, of our having been individuated out of a primal unity, since being itself is singular plural, never merely present to itself. Being is as co-being. Since this co- is not subject to a logic of presentation, the with, or co-presence, "is . . . not pure *presence to*, to *itself*, to *others* or to the *world*. In fact, none of these modes of presence can take place, insofar as presence takes place, unless co-presence first takes place" (*BSP* 40/60). He insists on this a little later. The with as such is not presentable; it is "a mark drawn out over the void . . . constituting the drawing apart [*traction*] and drawing together [*tension*] of the void" (*BSP* 62/84). Presence is not so much displaced under these conditions of singular plurality as it is dismantled. "Meaning begins where presence is not pure presence but where presence comes apart [*se disjoint*] in order to be itself *as* such" (*BSP* 2/20).[7]

Symbolic Being

The space that thus opens means that Nancy's ontology is an ontology of symbolic being. In a footnote to *Being Singular Plural*, he writes: "the Greek *sumbolon* was a piece of pottery broken in two pieces when friends, or a host and his guest, parted. Its joining would later be a sign of recognition" (*BSP* 100n51/79n1). The Greek *sum* is the equivalent of the Latin *cum* (and of the English *con*); symbolism is, properly speaking, a matter not of representation but of relation, and not relation between idea and instance, object and representation, reality and image. It goes behind and beyond theories that take such relations as their starting point, since each such theory already presupposes being social or social being. Habermas's rationalist theory of communication, for example, relies on the thought of a subject capable of articulating her thoughts and desires to her fellows.[8] Marxist analyses of commodity and commodification, use and exchange value, depend finally not on a category of absolute value but on the existence of a plurality of singulars who engage in the activity of valu-ing.[9] Even Jean Baudrillard's hyperreality, composed of simulacra, relies for its coherence on the thought of a lost social reality of which the specta-cle is a representation.[10] The *sum* of *sumbolon* addresses this; it refers not to the specific relation of reality to the image but to the relation between beings. Nancy writes: "'spectacle,' 'communication,' 'commodity,' and 'technology' are no more than figures (albeit perverse figures) . . . of social reality—the *real* of social being [*l'être-social*]—laid bare in, through, and as the symbolicity that constitutes it" (*BSP* 57/79; trans. modified).[11] The relevant distinction here is between the concept of the real as such on the one hand, a concept that lurks behind the assumption of meaningful, lost symbolic orders as much as behind the assumption of otherworldly mean-ing, and a concept of reality as social, on the other. Social reality is always already symbolic; symbols form the texture of social reality. The symbol *is* the relation. Nancy writes:

> it is the job of the symbolic to create a *symbol*, that is, link, connec-tion, and to provide a figure for this linking or to make an *image* in this sense. The symbolic is the real of relation as it represents itself, because relation as such is, in fact, nothing other than its own representation. . . . The relation is the real of a representation, its effectiveness and its efficacity. (The paradigm is "I love you," or per-haps more originally still, "I'm talking to you.") (*BSP* 57–58/79; trans. modified)

The word *sumbolon* means "to put with." The friend puts her shard of pottery with her friend's shard. Doing so symbolizes their relationship. It is not something distinct from their relationship; it *is* their relationship. Furthermore, bringing home the critique of the hyperrealists, it is not a question of this being a symbol *rather than* an image. Symbolization does not require the banishment of the (mere) image; it only requires that the image/symbol be in play with connectedness and distance, in the space *between*. As he puts it: "The 'symbolic' is not an aspect of social being: on the one hand, it is this being itself and, on the other, the symbolic does not take place without (re)presentation: it is (re)presentation to one an-other according to which they are with one another" (*BSP* 58/80; trans. modified).

In addition, the *sumbolon* has a material existence; specifically, it has a surface and edges that will be set alongside and touch the edge of its com-panion piece. It functions through touch as much as by sight, allowing Nancy to make a shift away not from the ocular metaphor as such but from the assumption that what is primary is the singular seeing eye/I, seeing an object that is understood as not itself seeing. Instead, one edge touches the other, just as we touch one another. He writes: "We touch each other insofar as we exist. Touching each other is what makes us 'us,' and there is no other secret to be discovered or hidden behind this touch itself, behind the 'with' of co-existence" (*BSP* 13/32; trans. modified).

Yet this would seem to introduce another problem. If the emphasis is shifted to or shared with touch, does this not return us to the matter of skin touching skin or, if the set of beings regarded as relevant is appropriately increased, of surface touching surface? That is to say, does it not demand an understanding of the world and specifically the others who populate it in terms of accessible exteriors hiding inscrutable interiors? Does it not return us to the most troublesome aspect of modern subjectivity? In Nancy's hands, it is relations, trajectories, touches, glances, movements across a space that constitute the I. Interiority and exteriority are always in play, whether we mean the interiority and exteriority of the I or of the community, the we. For instance, in *The Experience of Freedom*, freedom is characterized as the "interior exteriority of the community" (*EF* 75/100). The fragments remain fragmentary. In *The Sense of the World* he writes: "*Symbola* are the potsherds of recognition, fragments of pottery broken in the promise of assistance and hospitality. The fragment carries the promise that its fractal line will not disappear into a gathered whole but, rather, will rediscover itself elsewhere, lip against lip of the other piece" (*SW* 136/208). The surfaces where the pottery was broken are external to the pieces, but internal to the reassembled pot.[12] Claiming its surfaces as exterior, the shard remains a fragment, a part of something lost; its incorporation into the reassembled pot, the transformation of those surfaces into internal surfaces, does not keep it from continuing to be a fragment. According to another quite beautiful image, the world is "a constellation whose compossibility is identical with its fragmentation, the compactness of a powder of absolute fragments" (*SW* 155/234). This compactness is our being with as fragments for whom being a fragment is neither an accidental or temporary state of affairs nor a question of having fallen away from an intact whole or of waiting to be gathered up (again) into a healed or mended unity.

In this way, we make a world. Nancy writes: "One could say that worldhood is the *symbolization* of the world, the way in which the world symbolizes in itself with itself, in which it articulates itself by making a circulation of meaning possible without reference to another world" (*CW* 53/59). Here, for all their richness and beauty, the images of pots and powder falter; they give us the shape and the ontological structure of the space of meaning without being able to account for the *movement* of circulation and the *innovation* essential to creativity. For this we need touch—skin to skin, lip to lip, surface to surface—and then some. After all, natality refers us to the fact that our very skin, itself the gift of our parents, was formed under the skin of our mothers and that our birth is our emergence from our mother's bodies. The loss of the maternal body may have to be mourned, but it alone is not determinative. The possibilities of our new, fragmentary being with others are essentially undetermined. The constitutive immemorial at the root of our natal being is a loss but also the opening for creativity. Our fragmented way of being demands not that we long for an original wholeness but that we reach for the power of creative newness. We have seen that birth sets us into an old world and orients us to the past by giving us the task of making the past our past; it also turns us to the future by having us make the world our world. We are engaged in a work of inheritance that is also a work of creation.

Being Poetically

While a symbolic ontology preserves a space for the God who folds himself into creation, it does not go far in helping us think about what becomes of the creative capacity or what the activity of creating or the movement of creation looks like now that God has passed. For this we need a poetic ontology: not a Platonic or Aristotelian ontology of *poiēsis* but a (post-)Romantic understanding of what it is to be, poetically. It is an ontology that grasps the relationship between godly creation, artistic creativity, and procreation. In Nancy's opus, what is at stake here is a movement from *The Literary Absolute* (written with Lacoue-Labarthe in 1978) to "Urbi et Orbi" (2001) in *The Creation of the World, or Globalization*. These texts are not endpoints delimiting an epoch before which there is no thought of poetic ontology and after which it becomes a moot point thanks to resolution or irrelevance. These are, rather, two attempts among many to think poetic being in a way that avoids the constraints imposed by separating *poiēsis* and *praxis* and that complements the play of interiority and exteriority is vital to symbolic ontology.[13] Nancy initially uses the language of production but turns later to a thought of creation that "is the exact opposite of any form of production in the sense of a fabrication" (*CW* 51/55). In the same way, what begins as a dialectic between artificial production and natural production (*LA* 49/70) develops into an understanding of the intimate link between creation and growth (*CW* 51/55). However, the neglected element—which is by no means absent from Nancy's work but which nevertheless does not find its properly generative place in this train of thought—is natality.

Already in Plato, *poiēsis* is understood as production and most often as an activity devoted to copying an ideal model. Thus, when the demiurge sets about creating the cosmos in *Timaeus*, he shapes matter after the Idea.[14] In the *Republic*, *poiēsis* is the activity by which the artisan produces an artifact in the material world by copying the Idea;[15] poetry, in turn, produces a copy of the copy. Yet in the *Symposium*, poetry in the true sense of the word is "calling something into existence that was not there before."[16] In each case, the thought of birth and reproduction is not far off; indeed, it could be argued (though this is not the place to do so thoroughly) that the context for each case is formed by the question of reproduction. For example, in *Timaeus* the *khōra* is both the *space* in which the cosmos comes to be and the unformed *matter* that will be shaped by the demiurge, just as the womb is the space for the formation of the new being and, in Plato's world, the maternal body provided the matter that would take the form determined by the paternal contribution.[17] In the *Republic*, the anxiety that motivates the construction of the ideal city is anxiety over the unpredictability of reproduction. After all, it can only be founded by a generation that is convinced it has no human parents; it falls when the marriage festivals fail and its citizens begin to reproduce in natural and unregulated ways. When Plato writes that "mimetic art, then, is an inferior thing cohabiting with an inferior and engendering inferior offspring,"[18] that is, a copy of a copy mingling with the lowest part of the soul and engendering unruly passions, he is relying on his own myth that like married with like will generally produce like.[19] This is the myth that informs all thought of *re*production. Yet that thought is efficiently displaced in the *Symposium* by Diotima's story of Eros and his parents, Resourcefulness and Need, whose very point is that mingling difference generates the new and that birth is the paradigm for calling into existence what was not there before. In all these cases, however, *poiēsis* maintains the sense of an activity undertaken for the sake of an end external to itself. This persists through Aristotle's inheritance of the term. Plato avoids separating *poiēsis* and *praxis*, instead thinking of *praxis* as a variety of *poiēsis* and an activity that is judged, like it, according to criteria of usefulness.[20] But for Aristotle the distinction is significant, with *poiēsis* understood as action or production that is judged in terms of an external object (*ergon*), while *praxis* is its own end.

However, as Nancy and Lacoue-Labarthe argue in *The Literary Absolute*, the Romantics make their appeal to *poiēsis*—translated into German as *Poesie*—in the course of a maneuver away from the product toward production. This gives every indication of being a move toward *praxis*, in this case a romantic poetic practice. For Romanticism, the art object produced by creative labor is less interesting than the activity of artistic creation itself; indeed, the Romantic artist's essential—perhaps his only—product is himself, a self that is neither an object nor quite a subject, neither finished nor ever completeable. Nancy and Lacoue-Labarthe describe Romanticism as "a poetics in which the subject confounds itself with its own production" (*LA* xxii), and thus the creator God finds itself transformed into the figure of the poet and creation becomes ongoing autopoiesis. This is not just a work for the poet-genius; rather, in this regard, "all cultivated people should be capable of being poets" since "man is by nature a poet."[21]

If the Kabbalah gives us the figure of God disappearing into his creation, becoming what is between his creatures, Romanticism famously reconfigures thought in terms of creativity as the province of the self-creating individual. Nancy and Lacoue-Labarthe's contribution is to show that the Romantics had a sophisticated understanding of the formation of this individual within a generative system and thus could envision creativity as happening between. They write:

> The poetic is not so much the work as that which works, not so much the organon as that which organizes. This is where romanticism aims at the heart and inmost depths . . . of the individual and the System: always *poiēsis* or, to give at least an equivalent, always *production*. What makes an individual, what makes an individual's holding-together, is the "systasis" [association, arrangement, standing together] that produces it. What makes its individuality is its capacity to produce, and to produce itself, first of all, by means of its internal "formative force"—the *bildende Kraft* inherited from the organism of Kant, which romanticism transcribes into a *vis poetica*—by means of which "in the Self all things are formed organically." (*LA* 48–49/69–70, quoting Friedrich. Schlegel, "Athenaeum Fragments," 338)

What makes God's creatures creative is the nothing of and in creation. As the space between, it is the indetermination that makes way for what is new. At the same time, the fact of this space gives rise to the question of these finite creature between whom space opens up; how is such a finite creature held together? How can it resist the vacuum pull of nothing? The Romantics' answer comes in the form of the *vis poetica*, which is neither a universal force that surges through us all nor the manifestation of a sentimental interiority but rather the production of individuality by systasis and by the individual. These are neither two different things nor even two moments in a dialectic. The *vis poetica* consists in the individual creating itself in association with others; it is our being together generating us as instances of being with. For us autopoiesis is always also co-poiesis, and this will always mark our separation from the creator God and separate our mode of creativity from his. Poietic praxis is our self-creation with others.

Although Nancy and Lacoue-Labarthe point out that it is necessary to grasp the dialectical unity of artificial production and natural production—that is, procreation, germination, and birth—and although they direct us to Schiller's use of *naïve* to refer to nativity as well as naïve innocence and indicate Novalis's treatment of the fragment as the seed that must germinate, they do not turn their attention to the richly relevant thought that co-poiesis is the essential form of our procreation. Novalis's image is vital and apt to a degree; the seed is indeed incomplete and will complete itself only through growth and maturity. Whether or not it will in fact germinate remains in doubt—"there may be many sterile grains among them"[22]—yet the form its maturity will take is already determined. That is to say, the image of the germinating seed gives us no hint of the radical indeterminacy that sent a tremor through Plato. The uncertainty and anxiety occasioned by the fact of sexual reproduction are only hinted at in Novalis's thought not of the seed but of the grain of pollen, the gamete that will grow and become only provided that it meets, fertilizes, and *grows with* the ovum into something other than either of them. Without sexual difference, reproduction really is only the production of the same; given sexual difference, we are obliged to abandon *reproduction* as an inadequate term in favor, in Nancy's case, of *creation* and *procreation*.

In fact, *creation* is precisely the term in which to uncover both growth and generation; the word is the etymological descendant of *cresco*, "to be born, to grow," via *creo*, "to make something emerge [*faire naître*], to cultivate a growth." Yet when Nancy draws our attention to this history, he picks up only one of these threads, describing the creation of the world as "the *nothing* growing [*croissant*] as *something*. . . . In creation, a growth grows from nothing and this nothing takes care of itself, cultivates its growth" (*CW* 51/55). On the one hand, this helps ensure that, in the aftermath of the Romantic shift to the activity of production, we do not lose sight of the fact that production produces products and creation creates creatures. In each case, something comes to be that was not there before, and this is what warrants calling the activity production or creation. (The language of things will eventually run aground, but we are forced to use the least specific formulation—*something*—at least provisionally, given the difficulty of even forming sentences without it.) On the other hand, to think of creation only in terms of growth is to ignore the differentiation that makes possible co-poeisis and indeed being with at all. As we have seen, the generative structure of the ex nihilo is *differance*; being with is the ontological condition of beings who share difference that is more than numerical or vegetative.

While thinking creation in terms of growth has the great advantage of letting it emerge as radically material (*CW* 51/55), only when we also pick up the other thread—creation as birth—does the origin of poetic being emerge. Arendt is right to claim that, when we each appeared, the world had never seen anyone quite like us before. Our natality is our plurality, the origin of the co- of co-presence and co-poeisis. Natality is also our singularity and singular newness, and the fact that no one has ever seen my like means that my birth brought into the world a being that was essentially unknown; unknown to the world, to those most intimately involved in bringing me to be and to myself. We have seen that the separation between being and knowing sets us apart from the creator God. Now it becomes clear that, under conditions of plurality, this separation happens in more ways than one. I begin to know myself only at a point when I have already long been surrounded by others who can claim already to know me. I *am* in the third person ("We're having a baby") and the second person ("You're a good child") before I come to be in the first person. I embark on the process of self-creation in a context created by those who have come before me, and I create myself in the face of a self already formed in that context and on my behalf. Much as our adolescent selves revolted against the thought, the people who raised us can rightly say that they have known us longer—if not better—than we know ourselves. Thus, insofar as I was anticipated, expected and had a place prepared for me in the life and the world of my family, I was known before I was. My co-creation was already under way before I was capable of taking it up as self-creation. And yet the truth of that adolescent resistance lies in the fact that we never are wholly known and the gap between knowing—on the part of whomever—and being, between being and knowing is where *poiēisis* happens.

Conclusion

This gap is the syncope to which Nancy guides us as early as *The Discourse of the Syncope* and as recently as "Verbum caro factum" in *Dis-enclosure*.

The term gestures in at least three directions, all relevant to Nancy's project: toward syncope as a fainting fit, a spell of unknowing; toward syncopation as the variation in a piece of music when a shift in rhythm puts a weak note at the beginning of a bar; and toward the Greek root *syncope*, which includes the verb "to cut" and the word "with." We are subject to syncopation in the sense that, when we come to self-consciousness, we already are and have already been for some time *with others*. From the start we are trying to catch up. If Hegelian dialectic works according to a three-part rhythm, this is the offbeat on which we each begin, the modulation that the dialectic absolutely requires in order to stay in motion and that it recognizes but cannot think.[23] Instead, it finds itself constantly interrupted, stalled, thrown off-kilter by new arrivals; a shudder runs through it just as the self is trembled through (*durch-zittiert*) by the self of the other individual (*BP* 30/40) but also by its difference from itself.

We stumble after ourselves; the dialectic shudders; identity trembles. In each case, Nancy generates a way of thinking about what separates and unifies at once. He writes in *The Discourse of the Syncope*:

> The syncope *simultaneously* attaches and detaches (in Greek, for example, the suppression of a letter in a word; in music, a strong beat over silence). Of course, these two operations do not add up to anything, but neither do they cancel each other out. There remains the syncope itself, the same syncopated, that is to say, cut to pieces (its first meaning) *and* somehow rejoined through amputation. *The same is erected here through its resection*: the undecidable figure called "castration" derives from this. (*DS* 10/14)

The sentence gives the word *resection*—which normally refers to the surgical removal of part of an organ—a double function: the same comes to be by being removed or removing itself from the (m)other; simultaneously, it comes to be by having part of itself removed. The loss is both that of being part of a whole, which we know from Dilthey is the structure of meaning, and the loss of part of oneself. We are born the same, syncopated, in the sense that we are neither part nor whole, neither imbued with meaning granted by that of which we are part nor already meaning ourselves. Meaning is the symbolic, poetic task conferred by birth.

This is what is at stake in the Greek *syncope* and the thought of cutting with. We are severed from ourselves and from our origin in another, but this cut both opens the space across which relation happens and establishes us as plural beings. As Nancy develops the Arendtian thought of natality and plurality, our being singular plural emerges as what gives meaning to us, jointly, but as a task or vocation. This is the *meaning* of finitude. He writes:

> The identity of the soul is finite identity, the finitude of difference that comes to it as actual difference, from another that is infinitely other. The finitude of the soul stems from this constitutive alterity of its *self*—whose vocation as subject requires an infinite completion and closure. Beyond birth, the subject will complete itself infinitely, it will be the sublation of its infinite determinations. It will be what originarily divides itself, *sich ur-teilt*, engendering from itself its difference and its identity. (*BP* 31/41)

When we let the creator pass, we open the space where we generate a meaningful world. It is a symbolic endeavor in that it is a work we undertake with others, a work in which I and we and our world are all at stake. It is a poietic endeavor in which "production" is no more (and no less) than the name for our engagement in the creation of our world. It is our natal endeavor because both the demand that we inherit and create and the power to create both unfold from our natal being. The difference between the creativity of the creator God and this creaturely capacity is, finally, the difference between an innatal being who never was not and a creative being who comes to the world with and out of others and undergoes a life of growth and transformation.

The Immemorial

The Deconstruction of Christianity, Starting from "Visitation: Of Christian Painting"

DANIELA CALABRÒ

A short but unusually charged essay by Jean-Luc Nancy, "Visitation: Of Christian Painting," will help us align his mediations on art with his deconstruction of Christianity. Let us begin with its opening words:

> Art never commemorates. It is not made to preserve a memory, and whenever it is set to work in a monument, it does not belong to the memorializing aspect of the work. . . . If art in general has any relation to memory, it is to that strange memory that has never been deposited in a remembrance, which is therefore susceptible neither to forgetting nor to memory—for we have never lived it or known it—but which never leaves us. . . . Art is what always exceeds itself in the direction of that which precedes it or succeeds it, and, consequently, also in the direction of its own birth and its own death. (V 108/9–10)

According to Nancy, Pontormo's painting *Visitation* can be understood as the immemorial place where the "dis-enclosure" of Christian religion in particular, and monotheistic and polytheistic religions in general, begins.

How can art without memory dis-enclose the chronological framework of religions? How can this immemorial place of art become birth and therefore dis-enclosure? What is it that art exposes? What does it make visible? What does it dis-enclose? And how, exactly, does *Visitation* represent the moment in which all of this is "set to work"?

About the Absence of Sense

Nancy focuses on art that "exceeds" itself, belonging neither to a past nor to a future. It does not reside in memory, nor does it disappear into oblivion; it withdraws from all sacrificial logic and does not follow Nietzsche's "death of God." Nancy therefore draws a clear distinction between mythological and Christian art. As Blanchot indicates, art can be seen as that which discloses "that profound immemorial memory that originates in times of the 'fabulous,' at the epoch when, before history, man seems to recall what he has never known."[1] The immemorial does not imply transcendence, a metaphysical sense, or a "beyond" but is the removal or the shattering deconstruction of given meanings: the meaning of monotheism, of Christianity, of the sacred, of sacrifice. According to Nancy, these meanings have lost their initial references and fall into *tautegoricity*, that is to say, into the closing off of reference to something "other." The metaphysical "has been lost with the destruction of sense, that is, with the completion and buckling of the West's resources of signification and meaning (God, History, Man, Subject, Sense itself . . .)" (*FT* 4/12–13).

Such a completion, in the double meaning of what has reached its goal and what has exhausted its own possibilities, gives rise to the absence of a goal to achieve and the absence of an end, of death. In a nutshell, this completion depicts, in the pictorial sense of the word, the *absence of sense*. The absence of sense is the explicit, visible retraction of sense—given that what retracts sense in the same movement "makes" it appear, causes (*poiēin*) it. In Nancy's words, "we are neither before nor after a Sense that would have been non-finite. Rather, we find ourselves at the inflection of an *end* whose very finitude is the opening, the possible—the only— welcome extended to another future, to another demand for sense" (*FT* 15/30). History gave us a way destined to extreme finiteness. Thinking of this finiteness without filling it or soothing it, without following any theology or negative ontology, means we find ourselves in a space that creates and undoes itself simultaneously and without mediation: "A finite thinking is one that *rests* on this im-mediation" (*FT* 14/29).

Somewhere, somehow, a horizon has been lost and the consolation of a limit annihilated. What remains is affirmation of the finiteness or the de-finiteness, so to speak, to which the absolute outburst, the *débordement*, leaves us all exposed and at the limit, like liminal figures of being. The loss of established and stable founding contours is a matter both of being at the limit and of the limit of being. These considerations are not mere wordplay but encapsulate the authentic challenge to thinking—or rather, they form the true condition and urgency of new thinking. The loss of horizon thus becomes philosophy's horizon. And this loss is found in the founding place par excellence: the passage from mythical thinking (the place of divinity's presence) to monotheistic religious thinking (the place of God's absence).

Nancy's position is clear: if, on the one hand, the end of metaphysics removes every link with traditional philosophy, and if, on the other hand, the deconstructive process inaugurates the place "to come" of the end of sense as death or as "awaiting (one another) at the limits of truth,"[2] the place of the im-mediation of sense can no longer present itself in an archetypal or archaeological manner. Therefore, there is no return to the origin but rather ex-position of/to a necessarily finite sense, in which resides the "the very *absolute* of existence" (*FT* 11/23):

> in our time, it's pointless to seek to appropriate our origins: we are neither Greek, nor Jewish, nor Roman, nor Christian, nor a settled combination of any of these—words whose sense, in any case, is never simply given. We are neither the "accomplishment" nor the "overcoming" of "metaphysics," neither process nor errancy. But we do exist and we "understand" that this existence (ourselves) is not the senselessness of a reabsorbed and annulled signification. In distress and necessity we "understand" that this "we," here, now, is still and once more responsible for a singular sense. (*FT* 15/31)

This formulation, which refuses to recoup any possible infinity and takes leave of all universality, is the crux of Nancy's thinking and its innovative force—the real bet he introduces into contemporary reflection and debate. In fact, it is here that a forum opens for talking about a "we" or a plurality without transforming this "we" into a substantial and exclusive identity and therefore falling back into a renewed self-position of *cogito* (meditation). In other words, this is what creates the conditions for talking about a "we." This is what it is left to us to think, after modernity.

In this context, Nancy begins his distinctive movement, the only possible movement that might still be called "philosophy." Far from considering this general retreat of sense as a disaster or a loss, "I—writes the philosopher—want to think of it as the event of sense in our time, for our time. It is a question of thinking sense in the absencing of sense. . . . It is a question of thinking what 'sense' can be when one has come to the end of sense understood in that fashion" (Y 109). Philosophy can no longer, finally, supply its own needs, nor can it, following Kant, continue to be "the philosophy that does not want to give sense but [wants] to analyze the conditions for delivering a coherent sense" (Y 109). Yet if philosophy today can neither provide meaning nor explain the conditions that would make it possible, what can it do? The answer the philosopher gives is both brilliantly simple and arduously complex. Following Nietzsche, he affirms that the end of sense "is revolution itself: the destitution of the authority of sense or of sense as authority" (Y 109), and, consequently, it is precisely "the entry into the unheard-of" (Y 109).

The absence of sense is thus really, as Nancy himself emphasizes, the purest assumption and prosecution of what had already been understood—at the transition of one epoch into another—by such authors and artists as Rimbaud.[3] Therefore "today this is where there is some sense: in saying sense is absent, in saying that this absence is what we are exposed to, and that this exposition constitutes what I will call not only our present history but, along with Rimbaud, our refound eternity" (Y 110). The "unheard-of" (Y 109) finds its explanation here, as well as its simple, hard, and difficult meaning. Making sense of this unheard of is a question of grafting philosophy onto a different "operation" (Y 109), onto a different *poiēin*, consisting in a sure modality of describing from the outside, which establishes the opposite movement of a double philosophical operating. On the one hand, it consists in the concrete act of speaking about the end of philosophical thinking as the internal limit of its own meaning. On the other hand, however, it is a question—finishing with the *description* from inside philosophy, of universal meanings and assumptions—of exposing philosophy itself to its "outside," that is to say, to the *inscription* on its skin, so to speak, on the events of the world in a universal singularity that no longer exists. However, given that this exercise of *ex-scription* (description of the outside from the outside) does not simply define a new horizon of philosophy, the result is not a simple dialectical change renewing the possibility of philosophy. Finiteness is not a negativity that is taken away and reconciled. It is instead an event that focuses attention on its own limit from within it. The lost horizon of meaning becomes the space in which its absence is exposed.

How can we *do* philosophy in the absence of a horizon of sense? How can we ready our ears for the unheard of? Nancy names this task *poiēin*, understood as an "operating" of thought that is exposed at its limits, that has no comforting horizon, a thought that is only the eternal exscription of meaning in retreat. This means that thought must dwell in the "no-place" that belongs to literature—as Blanchot indicates in his dialogue with Nancy—in the place where "there is nothing to hold, nothing secret." What operates is only the inoperative that permeates writing itself and, together with it, thinking.[4] Writing is, therefore, the place of the neuter (*le neutre*), of the impersonal. It is, as Roberto Esposito explains, referring to Blanchot:

> the form of expression that, unlike spoken language, finds its sense not in a "making work" but rather in an unactivating or an "unworking" that exposes it to an irremediable loss of control [*padronanza*]. Is it not always the case that writing "is the liberating passage from the first to the third person," that is to say, the "unlighted event that occurs when one tells a story"?[5]

The neutral to which writing alludes is the absence of purpose, the absence of an end, its emptying, its indefinite withdrawal from sense.

At this precise point, the thinking of Blanchot and Nancy interconnect. For both, the neutral creates the necessity for an impersonal, erasing, disappearing, and inoperative language. This is why the neuter has neither direction nor meaning. It is, rather, what is in between, what is always at a distance and what is therefore *immemorial*. Neutral language is language "when it pronounces without taking into account either itself or the one who pronounces it."[6] Because the neuter is an indefinite withdrawal from sense, finiteness should not be understood as something that implodes in the plane of immanence (Deleuze) or as what a transcendence reserves for us but as a permanent finishing with all meaning: "in finitude, there is no question of an 'end,' whether as a goal or as an accomplishment, and . . . it is merely a question of the suspension of sense, in-finite, each time re-played, re-opened, exposed with a novelty so radical that it immediately fails" (*FT* 10/21). In this permanent absence, in this incessant disappearing that is finiteness itself, the movement of existence is inscribed: "Birth has already turned us toward it. But how can we simply open our eyes? Death has already closed them" (*FT* 11/22–23).

We must think the finite movement of existence not according to an immanence of sense as opposed to an infinite transcendence but rather as a simple finiteness that has no immanence because it displaces, it moves, it refers again to an outside of the sense of every established immanence. The task of finite thinking is therefore to think that there is not an "'ounce' of sense that could be either received or transmitted: the finitude of thinking is indissociable from the singularity of 'understanding' what is, each time, a singular existence" (*FT* 11/23). This is where every birth and every death take place. But this "here" is an inappropriable place, like the finite sense of every existence that does not return to itself. In the end, Nancy writes that finite thinking must "*expose itself* to what is finite about sense" (*FT* 30/53). In fact, birth and death are the evidence that there is no ultimate sense, only a finite sense, finite senses, a multiplication of singular bursts of sense resting on no unity or substance. And the fact, too, that there is no established sense, no establishment, institution, or foundation of sense, only a coming, and comings-to-be of sense.

This thinking demands a new "transcendental aesthetic": that of space-time in the finite here and now, which is never *present*, without, however, being time pressed up against its continuum or its ecstasis. (*FT* 27/49)

Such is the divesting of thinking, the kenosis in which purpose and origin are emptied out.[7] It is a matter not of renouncing sense but rather of looking at sense in the opening and incompleteness of the present, in its lack of relation to anything, in its never coinciding with what we can look at or know about. This is not a question of going beyond, because the beyond is already *here*; it lies in the midst of the instability and opacity of the present, in its inexhaustibility. The dualisms, the oppositions with which we are used to thinking, no longer work. The divesting of thinking is also its "atheization": the withdrawal of gods, that is to say, of every perfection, of every reason, of every foundation that fills the opening of the here and now and also our references to this fullness as to something that is lost. In the moment when thinking divests itself of knowledge, evades itself as an intellectual act, it becomes not mystical but rather ethical: it becomes relationship, a relationship with the other, an opening of sense and not a matter of sense being fixed.

To understand this, it is necessary to revisit Christian themes and to question them from within. Nancy begins this operation in *The Inoperative Community* and continues it in *The Ground of the Image* (including "Visitation"), *Dis-enclosure*, and *Noli me tangere*.

Of an "Unheard-of" Visitation

What does *Visitation* "operate" (*poiēin*)? It operates the true act of creation, and in his analysis of it Nancy sets his notion of dis-enclosure at the heart of Christian painting. It is 1530. Pontormo paints one of his many *Visitations*. In it the immemorial and the unheard of take place. The Visitation is "absent from all remembrance but toward which an infinite memory endlessly rises, a hypermemory, or rather, an *immemory*" (V 108/10). After the Annunciation and before the Nativity, beyond the word and before anything visible, the Visitation's truth, its *shape*, consists in being without any shape, without any accomplished shape, without figure. The event does not provide any assurance; the painting simply reveals. It is the immemorial: that of which we have no memory because it is not the past but rather "to come."

The unheard of is all there in the scene of the Visitation: "the essential is hidden from sight and passes by way of the voices, by a touch of voice that makes the intimate and the unborn leap in their invisibility. What happens is a flash of spirit between two absent presences, two lives in a state of withdrawal from existence, as immemorial as they are unexpected and improbable, in the closed womb of a sterile woman and a virgin" (V 109–10/13). In fact, as soon as Mary presents herself to Elizabeth, the latter, overcome with joy by an act of grace, makes the Virgin's greeting resound inside her womb, the place where John the Baptist is waiting to be born: "as soon as I heard the sound of your greeting, the child in my womb leaped for joy" (V 109/12, quoting Luke 1:44).

Painting makes visible that which is held in the "not yet." Such visibility resounds and echoes like a voice and hearing that "must leap out at us" (V 110/13). Everything appears as though it has been interrupted; the wombs of the two women "touch without touching" (V 111/15). The shapes of their clothes are filled with the spirit; they are traversed by a gust that unfolds them, allowing the vision, promising their ex-position, the laying bare, the arrival, the birth. Portraits often seem to be waiting to receive the look of a spectator, a visitor, and something similar takes place between the four women who make up *Visitation* (Mary, Elizabeth, and the two servants) and us, between their gazes and our ability to see them. An immemorial presence lies hidden in Mary's womb, not visible to the eye. Nevertheless, it resounds and becomes the audible presence of a visible absence.[8]

Pontormo's painting gives us still more pictorial matter to consider: two men can be seen at the obscure edge of the scene. One holds a loaf of bread and a knife, the other, a bottle of wine. Another resonance, another rebound appears: the act of breaking bread and sharing wine, an act that today still marks the memory of Christian incarnation, though it sinks roots into Dionysian sacrality and is therefore mythical. The bread and wine constitute the highest mystery of Christianity because they are tangible signs of an absence of the divine. Pontormo's painting sinks such signs in the darkness at the edge of the scene and achieves—according Nancy's reading—a "remarkable gesture of turning away from the religious" (V 116/29). The painting sets forth the immemorial truth of a scene presenting an absence that is always already here and that deconstructs Christianity—as can clearly be seen—from inside.

The immemorial of *Visitation* is in fact "that site and moment of provenance and presence to which one does not return but which is *always-already-there* . . . therefore always to come again like the return of a past more ancient than any past, its *visitation* always reprised in a movement in which the surface itself rises up, billowing and leaping out" (V 118/ 35–36). Painting discloses the margins of every mythic or transcendent time: it opens a presence that, far from defining contours, shapes, figures, and spaces, absents itself, retreats, and in this movement is exposed to us. In Pontormo's *Visitation*, Nancy singles out the divine that stays secret and ciphered, but there precisely such retreat and absence constitutes visible presence. Painting is able to "utter" this presentation of an image that retains its exposition and, in so doing, it paradoxically exposes, presents, and offers itself. In this place lie the hidden truth of Christianity and the parameters of atheism, which is born not as its opposite but as its deepest correlation:

> The truth of monotheism is the atheism of this withdrawal [of the gods]. "Real presence" becomes the presence that is par excellence not present: the one that is not *there*. The one whose being-there is a being [*être*] . . . exposed to the elsewhere of this very place, in this place itself though without any visible or invisible elsewhere of this very place, selfsame with the canvas, here as in its swollen womb of painting. This painting proffers a *this is my body*: this is the exposure of the skin or the veil beneath which no presence is hidden and no god is waiting except the place itself, here, and the singular touch of our exposure: *jouissance* and suffering of being in the world, precisely there and nowhere else. (V 123/45–46)

Real presence is anything but present. It is the evident withdrawal to which every monotheism is bound: the Christian God, the Hebraic God, the Muslim God. It is their common alliance, revealed by the painting of the *Visitation*: an infinite exchange between representation and nonrepresentation, between the visible and the invisible.

The image is not given. The image of the *Visitation* is not operative; it immediately disembowels the thought of the here in an effigy of a beyond. At the same time, it dissimulates the disclosure of the promise or the awaiting. Painting, according to Blanchot, like poetry or literature in general, is inoperative. This inoperativity is inextricably bound up with what he calls the absence of the work, that is to say, that which "operates" from nowhere. In other words, the inoperative image is a nonspatial and nontemporal dimension that emerges from an *il y a* without name (Levinas) and can be seen as a necessary exposition (or *ex-peausition*, as Nancy says) to sense without being impossible to signify. This is why the *ex-peausition* described by Nancy and borrowed from Blanchot must be understood as a means of access to the world, access that is a preliminary opening containing all "books to come" and, for that reason, does not take place in a specific book. It is, rather, the mise en abyme of all literature or philosophy of presence. There is no rest, no "supplement of the soul" or *Hinterwelt*, but only an exposition of itself by the poetical image or poetic language freed from every representational function. As such, it concerns a painting or writing of the invisible, inaudible, which opens up the visible and audible space of the world. In other words, ex-position gives images and words to what is not visible or legible: every work of art is an attempt to open what remains closed in every opening of an essence, an attempt to visit it. The *Visitation* is therefore a touch of "pro-fération."

The inoperative image of the *Visitation* is thus "this opening of the place that gives rise to what has no place" (V 125/51). As Nancy observes:

> Nietzsche knew, first, the agitation that takes hold when presence comes to tremble as the premise withdraws. . . . Presence no longer breaks free from its ground; it does not disappear into it either; presence stands, vacillating, at the edge of appearing in a world where there is no longer a rupture or opening between being and appearing. It has itself become presence, this rupture. . . . Presence torn, wrenching presence. Presence is to the world in not being in that world. It stands before and in withdrawal from itself. (*D* 76/118)

This is the unthinkable of nihilism. It concerns the impotence of nothing; its last, extreme truth consists in its impossibility. That is why, for Blanchot—to whom Nancy dedicates two chapters in his *Dis-enclosure*—sense is not a matter of departing from the negation of God's existence but rather of thinking in such a way that one is "at the extremity and the extenuation of sense" (*D* 87/132). In this way, the painting of the *Visitation* is like a womb: it reveals an absent presence. In an atmosphere of suspension, it reveals a possibility of the impossible, of a mute waiting, of flesh that is spirit.

"Touching Without Touching"

Flesh that is spirit, the raising of the body (*levée du corps*), is the other place in which—according to Nancy—Christianity marks its deconstruction.[9] The Resurrection of the flesh constitutes the correlative of the Visitation. The raising of the body reveals a paradox that cannot be eliminated: the presence of a body—that of Christ—that is human and divine at the same time, or rather, the presence of a tangibility that is no longer within the scope of sensitivity. *Noli me tangere* is, in fact, impossibility in action, an interdiction, a lack *of*, a discarding *of*—that of Christ as a missing body, a body that withdraws from the human but that nevertheless, exactly *as* a body, enters the divine.

Noli me tangere contains an impasse revealing an expropriation in the body of Christ. This is summarised in two main Evangelical propositions: on one hand, *hoc est enim corpus meum*, and, on the other, *noli me tangere*. Nancy gets straight to the point by analyzing the *noli me tangere* episode in the Gospel of John. The risen Christ appears to the Magdalene, who, having recognized him, prostrates herself before him, seeking to touch him. Christ withdraws from that touch, however, saying, "*Noli me tangere*; do not touch me." This request is the opposite of that of the Last Supper, where Christ invites the apostles, his table companions, to eat and drink his body—*hoc est enim corpus meum*, from which will be derived the rite of the Eucharist—as a token of eternal life.

On the one hand, the body of Christ is transformed into bread and wine (and therefore becomes humanly tangible); on the other hand, at the moment of resurrection, the body of Christ becomes inviolable and untouchable. The tangible presence must dissolve, must slip away into absence, into the nontangible. "This point is precisely the point where touching does not touch and where it must not touch in order to carry out its touch. . . . We could just as well understand that it must not be touched because it cannot be: it is not to be touched" (*NT* 25 and 28/13 and 14–15). The resurrected body, according to Nancy, is neither the symbol of victory over death nor access to eternal life. Death has not been overcome, as religion assures us. Death spreads excessively. Christ dies indefinitely, and *noli me tangere* represents the sense of this missing death at the limit of his decease; or rather, it is the presence of an absence or of a disappearance infinitely renewed or extended.

What resurrection reveals is the impossibility of deceiving death. The truth of Christ is therefore in his disappearance, in his going away in order to reach the Father—as he says himself. The Father is nothing other than *absence*. Resurrection is not, therefore, a return to life but rather glory in the bosom of death. It reveals the truth of death: "The resurrection is not a resuscitation: it is the infinite prolongation of death that displaces and unsettles all the values of presence and absence, of animate and inanimate, of body and soul" (*NT* 44/73–74; trans. modified). Thus, in the Resurrection the infinite *otherness* of the body is revealed, its withdrawal from itself of itself. A body instead opens up this presence, presenting itself, putting itself outside, separating from itself, dispossessing itself of itself.

The body is all in its "being put in evidence," all in the surface of the ex-position, as in a painting.[10]

Thus, Nietzsche's saying "God is dead" in Nancy's opinion means that "God *no longer has a body*. The world is neither the spacing of God nor the spacing in God: it becomes the world of bodies. . . . It may be that all entries into all bodies, all ideas, images, truths, and interpretations of the body, have disappeared with the body of God—and perhaps we're left only with the *corpus* of anatomy, biology, and mechanics" (*C* 59–61). Nancy indicates in death the exposition of which everything is consti-tuted—not a final event, to which every thing should be delivered up by destiny or by Christianity, but rather an absolute exposition of all things, over which time stretches out or extends itself, "cracks without having begun, compresses and breaks open a mass of present [*une masse de pres-ent*] without past, opens wide an instant without precedent, bursts out of nothing [*crevasse de rien*]" (*PD* 187).[11] The time of death, mortal death, spaces existence as cracks space a wall: of nothing. This is because there is nothing in that space but exposition to irreducible finiteness. Thinking death is thinking such essential, absolute finiteness: absolutely detached from every accomplishment, from every infinite and senseless circularity. Therefore:

> Not a thinking of limitation, which implies the unlimitedness of a beyond, but a thinking of the limit as that on which, infinitely fi-nite, existence arises, and to which it is exposed.
>
> Not a thinking of the abyss and of nothingness, but a thinking of the un-grounding of being: of this "being," the only one, whose *existence* exhausts all its substance and its possibility. (*FT* 27/48)

Death is not the time to come of the end or the accomplishment of a final sense, as we are used to thinking in Christian optics, founded on the archaeological and teleological circle of a final eschaton. Death is the exposition of itself, of each self to what is always already here, like a fis-sure, like a crack, like the blade of a knife.

Death understood in this way goes beyond the sense of the universal end, of the cosmic nothing by which we will be swallowed up, according to an eschatological image of time. It is an infinitely finite death that has already arrived or, more appropriately expressed, that is joined to things, like a syncope, a stop, a *partition*. That is what thinking should tend toward, that from which it cannot constitutively withdraw: the exposition of the self to another than the self cannot be understood in isolation; it is like the blade of a knife that slices through skin and opens it. In this open-ing is the inside and the outside of our existence. Without secrets, as is the exposition and the nakedness of dis-enclosure.

PART $\boxed{\text{IV}}$

Body, Image, Incarnation, Art

Intermezzo

Whereas Part III deals with how the self-deconstruction of monotheism and Christianity entails a poetic mode of language and sense, this part examines how this self-deconstructive moment plays out in art and the image. Nancy suggests that art does not merely illustrate religion. Instead, the two are involved in the same self-deconstructive movement or in a process of a mutual dis-enclosure. Whereas art provides the sensible articulation of the internal destabilization of the religious mode, the unstable core in religion—an origin in its displacement—forms an integral part of the condition of art.

Nancy proposes that monotheism cannot be considered to be an evolutionary outcome of polytheism; instead, it is a rearticulation of the religious mode, equal to its gradual abandonment. The mythical mode of polytheism is associated with the effective presence of gods in a world structured according to the relationships between them, as set out in a myth that has the foundational value of an origin. For Nancy, the "mono" of monotheism signifies not only the fact that there is a transcendent God who is inaccessible yet still determines the state of being of the world but also the destabilization or the displacement of such an originary point.

This movement of demythologization implies a fundamental change in the status of representation—not only of religious representation or the religious image but, as Nancy argues, representation in a more general

sense. While polytheism is associated with mythological representation—in other words, with the visibility of the gods—and its art "provides
a vision of the gods" (*M2* 240/66), in monotheism myth, or the positive
representation of the actions of gods, transforms into negative formulas
signifying the absent presence of God. In a monotheistic context, the religious representation or the image must figure the displacement of the origin or the effacement of the model, and its proper subject matter becomes
the invisibility of the unique God.

Within the complex texture of monotheism, especially in its Jewish and
Christian form, the idea of creation ex nihilo provides, according to
Nancy, a figure of the simultaneous invention and displacement or even
erasure of the agency of God as an origin or model. Creation ex nihilo
does not mean that the world is created or miraculously appears out of
nothing. Rather, it is the opposite of fabrication or production according
to a preexisting model. Nancy insists that the *nihil* in this motif signifies
the absence of origin or, for that matter, of an agent-creator. Through this
motif, monotheism maintains a possible interpretation that the world is
without a model, but also without a producer. The kenotic aspect of creation ex nihilo, the fact that God is considered to empty himself into creation, signifies that God and the world are indistinguishable and are,
finally, the being of the world as such, without reason and without model.

According to Nancy, the idea of the incarnation forms a central self-
deconstructive aspect of Christian monotheism. As he points out, the
term *incarnation* cannot be understood as "representation" (*D* 81/125),
where the body is defined as a sensible manifestation of an invisible spirit.
By contrast, incarnation—in the theological sense of the term—refers to
the idea that God *becomes* flesh (*D* 81/126). This kenotic aspect of the
incarnation defines the Christian body not as a material exteriority enveloping a soul but as the taking place of the withdrawal of God (*D* 83/
127). In other words, incarnation is not a representation or imitation that
supposes resemblance and a model. The body is the place of the alienation
of God from himself; it is the material presentation of this alienation.

This displacement of the model or origin in the motifs of creation ex
nihilo and incarnation can be traced in the condition of art and the status
of the image. Nancy maintains that religious art, and specifically Christian
art, is not an illustration of the biblical story (*V* 122/44) and, in a more
general sense, even within the context of religion art is not religious (*M1*
99/157). In other words, religion does not provide a model, a truth, a
story that the artistic image illustrates or represents. Instead, the image is
itself without a model and shares the moment of the withdrawal of origin
that characterizes monotheism. Art, then, does not have representational

value; it is a presentation of an open absence. The illustrative mode becomes a presentational one: the image does not illustrate an invisible truth; it does not preach a univocal message. On the contrary, it is a presentation of the thing that appears, a presentation of itself, in other words, an address or a visitation. Art is engaged in a self-deconstructive movement like that of Christianity.

The first contribution, by Ian James, explores the initial ambiguity of the theological motif of the incarnation and emphasizes that, in Nancy's interpretation, it should be understood not as affirming a metaphysics of presence but as a presentation of an open sense. Boyan Manchev demonstrates that the body, viewed in the context of such a deconstructive reading of the incarnation, becomes the site of a constant creation or modalization and, as such, the central element in the discussion of Nancy's onto-aesthetic. In her contribution, Alena Alexandrova further discusses how art and the image exceed the illustrative mode with regard to religion and become places of presentation of the absence of model or origin. Finally, Federico Ferrari demonstrates how contemporary art echoes the dis-enclosure of religion to the extent that it identifies itself as a practice founded on nothing and constantly revives the absence of origin.

—*Alena Alexandrova*

Incarnation and Infinity

IAN JAMES

What happens with the body and with the world in general, when the world of the gods has been left behind, is an alteration of the world. Where there used to be one same world for gods, men, and nature, there is henceforth an alterity that passes through, and throughout, the world, an infinite separation of the finite—a separation of the finite by the infinite.

—*NT* 47/77–78

finiteness does not limit infinity; on the contrary, finiteness should give it its expansion and its truth.

—*D* 18/32

Closure

To a degree, Christianity can and must be considered a powerful confirmation of metaphysics. Jean-Luc Nancy clearly affirms this inevitable complicity of Christianity with a metaphysics of presence, and therefore with a certain trajectory of metaphysical thinking within Western and European philosophy, at the beginning of *Dis-enclosure* (*D* 6–7/15–17). It recalls the analysis of the Eucharist in his earlier work *Corpus*, according to which the phrase *Hoc est enim corpus meum* is seen as an assertion, tirelessly repeated, of the immediate presence of God, an affirmation that "God's *body* is *there*" (*C* 3). Such an affirmation of presence, Nancy suggests, reassures the believer about the solidity and reliability of the world of appearances; it calms and soothes "all our doubts about appearances, conferring, on the real, the true final touch of its pure Idea: its reality, its existence" (*C* 5). This affirmation of presence lies at the heart of the Christian doctrine of incarnation, which is encapsulated in the doctrine of "*homoousia*, consubstantiality, the identity or community of being and substance between the Father and the Son" (*D* 151/219). Here, then, is a religion whose supreme being is the efficient cause, foundation, and guarantee of the presence of beings, a religion in which incarnation is thought doctrinally as the presencing of divine spirit in fleshy matter, and in which this union is tirelessly reaffirmed in the ritual of the Eucharist. Christianity might well appear as nothing other than a religion obsessed with presence, with the presence of spirit within matter, with the enclosure of the infinite within the finite—a religion that installs a metaphysics of presence as its first and final gesture.

It is hardly surprising, then, that Jacques Derrida in *Le toucher—Jean-Luc Nancy* should have described his friend's "deconstruction of Christianity" as "such a difficult, paradoxical, almost impossible task, always exposed to being nothing more than Christian hyperbole."[1] If Christianity is a religion in which the excess of divine or infinite spirit is persistently and insistently recuperated as presence within the bounds of the finite, then any attempt to affirm that excess as a deconstructive resource for the constitutive self-overcoming of Christianity might well always inevitably emerge as a further instance of recuperation, as a further moment in which Christianity affirms itself and maintains itself as a totalizing installation of presence. The autodeconstruction of Christianity would then appear only as its hyperbolic reassertion: "Thus the deconstruction of Christianity would have its work cut out for it, to infinity."[2]

Derrida describes his troubled questioning of Nancy's deconstruction of Christianity as that of a spoilsport, who, like an incorrigible choirboy ("and Jewish, no less"), raises a dissenting murmur at the moment when a candle is lit in all the Catholic churches of the world.[3] The distance he takes from Nancy in *Le toucher*, a distance Nancy refers to subsequently as "a skeptical or rabbinical distance" (*NT* 110n19/25n4), marks or opens up a decisive difference between the two thinkers. This difference relates to the question of the inevitable "belonging" of Christianity to the metaphysics of presence and to the trajectory of philosophical thinking that marks the history of that metaphysics. Put rather schematically, the belonging of Christianity to metaphysics, for Derrida, makes its deconstruction an infinitely paradoxical if not impossible task. This belonging, for Nancy, makes the deconstruction of Christianity both necessary and inevitable.

Opening

In the opening chapter of *Dis-enclosure*, Nancy defines the sense he gives to the term *dis-enclosing*. How he relates this to the history and inner structure of metaphysics is decisive in two closely interconnected ways.[4] First, the term *dis-enclosure* could be understood in relation to Derrida's troubled questioning of the deconstruction of Christianity in *Le toucher*. If such a deconstruction, according to Derrida, is difficult, paradoxical, and quasi-impossible, then, Nancy would reply, the history of the transvaluation, destruction, and deconstruction of metaphysics has shown that it is no less unavoidable and inevitable insofar as the closure of metaphysics always and necessarily entails its own self-overcoming or dis-enclosure. First, the impossibility of Christianity's deconstruction will necessarily appear as the inscription of the impossible within the very structure of Christianity. This means that, second, and whether one likes it or not, the necessity of Christianity's deconstruction will be discernible within the sense, structure, and articulation of Christian thought and doctrine; it will unfold within the very becoming of the Christian tradition and the historical culture of which it forms a part.

The meaning ascribed to "dis-enclosure" in the opening chapter of *Dis-enclosure* clearly marks both a proximity and a distance between Derrida and Nancy. For the former, the resources for a deconstruction of the metaphysics of presence will certainly always be found already at work within the tradition. This is, after all, a very Derridean point and affirms a classic deconstructive gesture. However, these resources cannot, for Derrida, be harnessed from within the more restrictive limits of Christian theological doctrines themselves.[5] For Nancy, by contrast, the skepticism, ambivalence, and equivocation Derrida shows toward Christianity will already be found "structurally" at work within Christianity. Such ambivalence and equivocation articulate the inevitable dis-enclosure of the very movement of closure with which Christianity can and must be associated.

If the sense given to "dis-enclosure" can be understood as a repetition of a classic deconstructive gesture, then what, exactly, is at stake in the distance or difference between Derrida and Nancy? How and why do the two differ so markedly on the question of Christianity's "belonging" to the tradition of metaphysics? Derrida remarks in *Le toucher* that the deconstruction of Christianity, always in danger of being nothing more than Christian hyperbole, would have "its work cut out for it, infinitely." Not only a difficult, almost impossible task, it would also be an infinite or never-ending task. Yet for Nancy, the deconstruction of Christianity is concerned with infinity less in the impossibility or limitlessness of its task than in its grappling with how the body of Christian thought and doctrine engages the notion of "infinity."

At stake here are both a thinking of the body and the different ways in which Derrida and Nancy think about the inner structure of Christian incarnation. The distance or a difference between Nancy and Derrida can perhaps be located in their very different understandings of the Christic body and of the relation of the infinite to the finite that this body articulates. This is a difference over the (im)possible or inevitable dis-enclosure of Christianity and over the (im)possible or inevitable delimitation of its finite limits. Ultimately, it might be a difference over the status and nature of the "infinity" that Christian incarnation will always already have engaged.

Incarnation

Throughout *Le toucher*, Derrida persistently associates his troubled questioning of the deconstruction of Christianity with what he calls a "deconstruction of the *body*, of *corpus*, and therefore of Christian 'touching.' "[6] At stake here is a complex interrelation between a specific trajectory within Western and European philosophy and the history and inner structure of Christian theology. Within this shared philosophical and historical trajectory, the figure of touch, Derrida argues, organizes a manifold tradition of thinking that incorporates, among others, such diverse names as Maine de Biran, Ravaisson, Kant, Husserl, Merleau-Ponty, and Deleuze. This tradition has given rise to what Derrida calls "an *affair*, a sort of plot, a philosophical intrigue of touch" that has been played out along the cultural boundaries separating France, Germany, and England.[7] Derrida also poses the hypothesis that this tradition is continued, complicated, and interrupted in twentieth-century thought, most prominently in the development of phenomenology from Husserl on and then, specifically, in the work of Nancy as it developed from the 1970s to the 1990s. Touch, then, provides a figure that allows Derrida to reread the philosophical corpus of his friend, and specifically it provides a figure that allows him to situate and problematize his friend's "deconstruction of Christianity." Moreover, it offers Derrida a "way of rereading everything in consequence," all of Nancy, and "the whole philosophical tradition as well."[8]

Across the interlinking and meticulous analyses of *Le toucher*, the doctrine of incarnation emerges as a decisive moment in the " 'tactilist' or 'haptocentric' tradition" that, Derrida argues, joins European philosophy and Christian theology together in their shared belonging to the metaphysics of presence.[9] In particular, Derrida highlights a specific relation of phenomenological thought to the doctrine of incarnation as he pursues his troubled questioning of Nancy's deconstruction of Christianity. Christianity is, Derrida suggests, above all a religion of touch, or of the haptic:

> all the Gospels present the Christic body not only as a body of light and revelation but, in a hardly less essential way, as a body *touching* as much as *touched*, as flesh that is touched-touching. Between life and death. . . . One can take the Gospels to be a *general haptics*. Salvation [*Le salut*] saves by touching, and the savior, that is to say, he who touches, is also touched: he is saved, safe, unscathed. Touched by grace.[10]

If this is so, that is because of the very fact of incarnation. Jesus Christ, as divine spirit made flesh, is a presence who touches the world with divinity and who allows divinity to be touched, or, as Derrida puts it: "Not only is Jesus touching, the One Who Is Touching, he is also the One Who Is Touched. . . . he is *to be touched*, capable of and needing to be touched. This is the condition for salvation. To be safe and sound, to attain immunity, *touch*, to ouch him, Him."[11] Touch, presence, and the presence of a divine or infinite spirit to touch lie at the very heart of the Christian narrative, as Derrida shows by highlighting a whole series of episodes from the Gospels in which Christ touches or is touched.[12]

This analysis of the Christic body, the doctrine of incarnation, and of "*general haptics*" that the incarnate body of Christ inaugurates is developed further in the fifth "Tangent" of *Le toucher*. Here Derrida again emphasizes that the deconstruction of Christianity has, both for Nancy and throughout own his discussion, been associated with the deconstruction of the body and of Christian "touch." The "Tangent" is devoted to a close reading of Jean-Louis Chrétien's *The Call and the Response*,[13] a work that brings together elements of Aristotelian and Thomist philosophy with twentieth-century phenomenology (specifically Husserl and Merleau-Ponty). In so doing, Chrétien develops a philosophy of incarnation and touch that integrates theological and phenomenological perspectives, modernizing Aristotelian and Thomist thought, on the one hand, and explicitly theologizing phenomenology, on the other. There is a sense in which, for Derrida, Chrétien's thinking is paradigmatic of what is at stake in the Christian doctrine of incarnation and in the "*general haptics*" that it installs more broadly within theology and philosophy: "I do not know," he writes, "any thinking that is more forceful and coherent, more prepared to give to the concept of *flesh*—to flesh touching and touched—the Christian vocation to which I have frequently alluded."[14]

Specifically, Derrida discerns in Chrétien's system the operation of a "spiritual touch." In Chrétien, spiritual touch emerges as a key principle that organizes and articulates his conjoining of Aristotelian and Thomist, theological and phenomenological thinking. Chrétien invokes Aristotle's account of intellectual contact (in which the intelligible is "touched" by human intellect) and Saint Thomas's affirmation (after Aristotle) of the immediacy of intellectual touch and of the primacy of the intelligible over the sensible.[15] This, Derrida argues, allows Chrétien to assert a primary and radical "transitivity" of spiritual touch, which underpins the intelligibility of phenomenal appearances, and to oppose this to the "reflexive" touch of embodied auto-affection within phenomenology.[16] Where, within the affections or finite embodied perceptions described by phenomenology, touch is subject to a reflexivity (it is a mode of self-touch), for Chrétien, this touch is always the touch of something radically other that modifies it, namely, the pure intelligible, infinite spirit, the divine. It is this transitive contact with a primary order of the intelligible, this "spiritual touch," that, for Chrétien, underpins and guarantees all finite perception and that differentiates his thinking so markedly from, say, Merleau-Ponty's phenomenology.[17]

What is at stake here, of course, is the Christian thinking of incarnation. Chrétien offers a Christianization of Aristotle via Saint Thomas and a phenomenologization of both in a thinking of the "transitivity" of a "spiritual touch" that underpins and guarantees finite sense perception. Derrida highlights the importance of the doctrine of incarnation here, and, in particular, he highlights the specific relation of the finite to the infinite in what he calls Chrétien's "hapto-onto-theo-teleology of Christian flesh."[18] In Chrétien's spiritual touch, Derrida suggests, "infinite touching, *mutuus contactus* with God is at issue. . . . And it is this spiritual touch, *immediate*, infinite, that, in essence and par excellence, would teach us, would call us to *think* what touching truly means."[19] If the Christic body is "the One Who Is Touching" and also the "One Who Is Touched," in which the divine or infinite spirit touches the finite world and is touched by it, then this structure can also be discerned at work more generally in Chrétien's theologico-phenomenological account of perception and of the intelligibility of appearances. The immediate presence of the divine in the body of Christ is also a guarantor of the immediacy and presence of phenomenal appearance, of its solidity and intelligibility: "Immediacy is the absolute truth of divine touching, of the 'the hand of God,' of his Incarnation in the Logos or the flesh of the Son—and therefore of *creation*."[20] What is at stake here is a transcendence of the infinite, its alterity and discontinuity in relation to the finite, but also at the same time its immediate presence within and its contact with the finite. What is at stake is presence itself, the structure of a metaphysics of presence in which "the Incarnate Word or the Infinite Logos" are touched in a way that grounds and guarantees the being of beings in their self-identity and presence.[21]

Derrida's analysis of Chrétien brings out the way in which the Christian doctrine of incarnation is paradigmatic for a philosophy of touch (thought as originary intuition) and for a metaphysics of presence more generally. It also suggests the way in which the phenomenological account of presence may always be intimately and inescapably bound up with Christianity and its "*general haptics.*" Despite the manner in which Chrétien differentiates his "spiritual touch" from the sensible, auto-affective touch of, say, Merleau-Ponty, his reworking of the doctrine of incarnation nevertheless shows us "what touching truly means."[22] It is, Derrida suggests elsewhere, "up to others to demonstrate, if they can offer proof of it, that they have nothing to see in, to do with, or to touch on in the history and story of this truth."[23] This would apply, then, to all philosophies of touch, to the phenomenologies of Husserl, and Merleau-Ponty, to the array of thinkers Derrida invokes across the pages of *Le toucher*, and most importantly, of course, to Nancy himself.

At the end of the fifth "Tangent," Derrida nevertheless differentiates Nancy's thought from that of Chrétien. In Chrétien's writing, there is no thinking, he reminds us, of the spacing of bodies, ecotechnics, and the originary prostheticity of technics.[24] Yet despite the clear differences between the two thinkers and their apparent incompatibility, Derrida is clearly troubled by the way in which elements of Nancy's discourse appear exchangeable with elements of Chrétien's. He describes their thinking as "Two thinkings of substitution, then, but two tangential thinkings— though no doubt incompatible. A troubling, even dizzying, duality, through which one might be tempted—Temptation itself—to substitute one for the other."[25] This possibility of substitution, the exchangeability of the terms of Nancy's deconstruction of Christianity with the most coherent philosophical rendering of a "Christian touch" concerns Derrida. If Nancy concedes that the very heart of Christology and of the Christological tradition is grounded in the doctrine of *homoousia*, the identity and consubstantiality of Father and Son, infinite and finite, then, Derrida might ask, why does he not simply steer clear of Christological language, the language of touch, and all the dangerous metaphysical baggage they carry with them?

The answer, of course, for Nancy is that this baggage can and must be unpacked differently. Nancy readily concedes that the Christian doctrine of incarnation has had an immeasurable impact upon the development of European thought and culture. He does nothing to lessen the weight of the "the philosophic gigantomachy surrounding intuition and intuitionism" that, according to Derrida, a "Christian touch" has installed within the tradition of haptocentric metaphysics.[26] In the chapter of *Dis-enclosure* "*Verbum caro factum*," Nancy affirms this: "*verbum caro factum est. . . .* That is the formula of the 'incarnation' by which God makes himself man, and that humanity of God is indeed the decisive trait of Christianity, and through it a determinative trait for the whole of Western culture—including the heart of its 'humanism,' which it marks indelibly" (*D* 81/125). Clearly Nancy, like Derrida, is aware of the stakes that are in play in any philosophical deployment of the thought of incarnation and of touch. Yet the account Nancy gives of the "word made flesh" in this and other essays of *Dis-enclosure* is quite different from that given by Derrida in his analysis of Chrétien's "spiritual touch." The tempting substitutability that troubles Derrida at the end of the fifth "Tangent" may well be tempting and perhaps even inevitable, given that both Chrétien and Nancy are thinking from within a Christological framework. Yet within that framework, Nancy argues, another thinking can and must be discerned.

At the beginning of "*Verbum caro factum*," Nancy suggests that the term *incarnation* is usually understood as the incorporation into a body of an "incorporeal entity," or as a mode of "transposition and representation" by which a material body as exteriority encloses an unrepresentable "soul or spirit given in interiority" (*D* 81/125). This common understanding is, however, not what a literal and more precise reading of the "word made flesh" would imply: "If the word *was made* flesh, or if (in Greek) it became flesh, or if it *was engendered* or *engendered itself* as flesh, it was surely the case that it had no need to penetrate the inside of that flesh that was initially given outside it: it became flesh itself" (*D* 81–82/ 126). The Greek *logos sarx egeneto* allows Nancy to specify a more literal reading for the doctrine of incarnation, whereby the "word" is not incorporated into or enclosed by flesh but is, rather, produced or presented *as* flesh. This literal reading lies at the heart of Nancy's "other" thinking of Christian incarnation and, arguably, at the heart of the entire project of the deconstruction of Christianity. What it suggests, crucially and decisively, is that incarnation is not a matter of representation, or of the presence of spirit within flesh (its re-presentation as it touches or comes into contact with flesh). Rather, it is a matter of *presentation* and of a specific logic of presentation. Within this logic of presentation, it is not substance, ground, identity, and presence that are engaged and affirmed. Presentation, here, enacts an emptying of substance, an ungrounding of ground, a voiding of identity, and a withdrawal of presence. This literal reading of *verbum caro factum est* as a logic of presentation underpins Nancy's understanding of monotheistic creation and the key emphasis he places on the Pauline doctrine of kenosis.

This doctrine has a rather marginal and disputed status within Christology and Christian theology more generally. Far more orthodox is the doctrine of hypostatic union, according to which divine spirit and mortal flesh are conjoined in the body of Christ in a manner that affirms their shared essence (*homoousia*), or consubstantiality. According to Nancy's interpretation, kenosis is the movement by which God is thought to empty or void himself of his divinity in the event of incarnation. It is the movement by which " 'god' made himself 'body' in emptying himself of himself," or "the emptying out of 'God,' . . . his 'emptying-himself-out-of-himself' " (*D* 83/127).[27] The doctrine of kenosis is decisive for Nancy's understanding of Christian (and more generally monotheistic) creation and decisive also for his understanding of the auto-deconstruction of Christianity. It underpins his view that the Christian God is a God who alienates, atheizes, or atheologizes himself in the act of creation: in "emptying" himself out into matter. God as a principle is emptied of substance, presence, and auto-sufficiency. He becomes nothing, and the "something" that becomes is devoid of all foundation or guarantee of presence. As Nancy puts it: "The 'body' of incarnation is therefore the place, or rather the 'taking-place,' the event, of that disappearance" (*D* 83/127).

According to Nancy's reading of kenosis, then, the withdrawal of presence and the "emptying out" or vanishing of substance articulate the real inner structure of Christology, of Christian creation and incarnation. The doctrine of the supremely powerful God who exists as substance and who then creates the substance of the world from nothing would therefore be an illusion of a metaphysical appropriation of Christianity. This would also be true of the doctrine of incarnation thought as hypostatic union and as the shared essence of spirit and matter. Within Christianity, therefore, the doctrine of creation as the production of something from nothing (by a supreme creator God) always conceals or is internally inhabited by a "nothing of creation." That is to say, creation as the production of substance is haunted by the event of the world's appearance as an emptying of substance. Ultimately, the creation of the world is the "void" or "nothing" of the event of presentation. By the same token, the doctrine of hypostatic union is always inhabited or haunted by that of kenosis, and every *hoc est enim corpus meum* is haunted by a *noli me tangere*.

Nancy's more literal reading of *verbum caro factum est* places the apparently marginal doctrine of kenosis at the heart of Christology and therefore makes Christianity in its most inner logic an atheology of presentation in the withdrawal of presence, substance, foundation, and ground. If this is so, then it is easy to see why he affirms that Christianity's belonging to the totalizing closure of the metaphysics of presence will always, and always already, be accompanied by its dis-enclosure, by its opening out onto an irrecuperable excess of metaphysics. Derrida's troubled concern that the terms of a deconstructed Christianity could be substituted for those of Chrétien's phenomenologized theology is misplaced. His worry that Chrétien's "spiritual touch" might always be in some way at work within, or implied by, a deconstructive or deconstructed thinking of (Christian) touch could be countered with the thought that an (auto-) deconstructed Christianity will always already have inhabited its more orthodox counterpart.

Perhaps what is really at stake here is whether the "God who empties himself" of kenosis can ultimately be substituted for, or recuperated by, the "supreme God" who creates the world and maintains it as substance and grounded presence.

Infinity

It is here that the chapter "A Faith That Is Nothing at All" in *Disenclosure*, on the motif of "ontological kenosis" in the work of Gérard Granel, can be seen to be of key significance.[28] Nancy introduces Granel as a singular thinker who succeeds in combining broadly Heideggerian and Marxist philosophical affiliations with a clearly affirmed adherence to the Catholic Church and a Christian profession of faith. Commenting on Granel's late essay "Far from Substance: Whither and to What Point?" (*D* 163–74), Nancy highlights the way in which Granel separates the doctrine of kenosis from its theological origin in the writings of Saint Paul in order to give it an ontological status: Granel's essay traces a trajectory in modern philosophy from Kant to Heidegger (via Husserl) in which the presentation or manifestation of phenomenal appearances is thought, in various ways, as an emptying of the being of beings or as a voiding of their substantiality (*D* 64/92–93). In tracing this trajectory, Nancy argues, Granel combines three registers: a philosophical register with a theological register, and both of these with a register that allows him to pursue the thought of "ontological kenosis" further than does Kant, Husserl, or Heidegger. This third register Nancy identifies as a thinking of the body as a site of world disclosure, or more precisely, of embodied perception as a mode of spacing through which phenomenal appearances manifest themselves.

What is perhaps most interesting here is the way in which Nancy's presentation of Granel resembles or resonates with his own thinking. Crucially, Granel's discourse, like Nancy's deconstruction of Christianity, combines "an extremity that is proper to thought and the apparently allegorical resource of the theological," both of which have "in the midst of the philosophical propos, an alliance as unassuming, or secret as necessary" (D 65/94). At the same time, Nancy's philosophy, like Granel's, moves beyond Heidegger by placing the body as a pluralizing site of the event of phenomenal appearance. In the thought of both, the body is, as Nancy says of Granel, "nothing other than the diverse aspects of the open" (D 68/98) and "the ontological void, vacuity as a diversifying opening of appearing" (D 68/98).[29] To a certain extent, perhaps, Nancy's essay on Granel implicitly or tacitly acknowledges a philosophical debt to his former teacher and philosophical mentor. At the same time, however, although the essay marks a proximity of his thinking to that of his former teacher, it makes certain qualifications or indicates aspects that Granel himself does not develop. To this extent, the essay on Granel can be seen as a means by which Nancy reads himself, by which he reflects on the mutual imbrication of the philosophical and the theological in his own thinking and on the meaning of his own appropriation of the doctrine of kenosis.

If Granel's thought differs from or moves beyond that of Heidegger in that it places a key emphasis on the body as "the diversity of the open," this is because, Nancy indicates, it is concerned with the elaboration of the event of world disclosure as a "poietics of the world." Where the author of *Being and Time* gives an account of "being in the world" as a pragmatics of concerned circumspection, Granel offers an account of embodied perception as a creative "poetry of the world" (D 66/96). Much of Nancy's analysis in his essay on Granel is oriented to an elaboration of this embodied, perceptual "poietics" (D 66/96) of world disclosure and its relation to the concept of ontological kenosis.

At a key point in his discussion, Nancy draws attention to the way in which Granel affirms the event of bodily world disclosure as that which cannot itself be disclosed, grasped, or known (hence it is a "ontological void" or an emptying of substance; D 68/ 98). He also draws attention to the way in which Granel compares the "ontological void" of world disclosure to a "creative act of God" in its very unknowability (D 68/98). Here Nancy identifies an ambivalence or ambiguity in the rather sudden shift from a philosophical to a theological register. The ambivalence or ambiguity turns on Granel's use of the word *creative*. Such a term, Nancy argues, necessarily entails a switching between two distinct concepts of creation (*D* 69/99–100). On the one hand, the undisclosable, ungraspable "nothing" of creation could be seen as "*nihil* opening as world" (*D* 69/100; that implied by the doctrine of kenosis and a logic of presentation as emptying or withdrawal). On the other hand, the "nothing" of creation could be that from which the supremely powerful creator God of Christianity produces "something." Nancy has clearly detected within Granel's discourse a slippage between the registers of a Christianity that affirms a voiding of substance and a withdrawal of being (that of kenosis) and the Christianity appropriated by a metaphysics that would affirm nothing other than the substantiality of being and grounded presence.

Nancy concedes that, in this slippage between one conception of creation ex nihilo and another, Granel is clearly attempting to call into question the ontotheological fable of the supreme creator being by means of the atheological divinity of kenosis (in much the same way as Nancy himself does in "*Verbum caro factum*"; *D* 69–70/99–101). Yet he is concerned by the mode Granel's invocation of "creative act of God" and by the possibility of a confusion between the two "nothings of creation" or a substitutability of one for the other. Nancy writes:

> In both of these cases, confusion would come down to identifying that which, in Christianity, proceeds from an outside of the world (God coming into the world, God remaining inaccessible to the world), along with what must be understood of the world as the "formality" of its "opening": the latter is not outside the world, although it is not inside it either; it is not an other world, nor is it a beyond-the-world, since it opens this world to itself. (*D* 71/102; trans. modified)

These two conceptions of a "nothing" of creation can and must, Nancy asserts, remain distinct: that which is of the world (albeit not "in the world") is very different from an outside of the world. And yet, he concludes: "If confusion threatens, then this is because there is resemblance here, and if there is resemblance, then this is perhaps not without witness to some filiation leading from Christianity to the thought of the ontological void, or even from a paradoxical fulfillment of Christianity in its own exhaustion" (*D* 71/102). Such a conclusion, Nancy adds, is not permitted by Granel's line of thinking and is not to be pursued in this essay. It could be added further, however, that it is, of course, just this conclusion that Nancy pursues in his deconstruction of Christianity more generally and his thinking of incarnation in particular.

What is at stake in this possible "confusion" between two conceptions of the "nothing" of creation is, precisely, the question of infinity. More specifically, it is a question of how the infinity that is implied in the Christian concepts of creation, incarnation, and touch is to be thought. It might be worth recalling at this point that Nancy clearly distinguishes between "good" and "bad" conceptions of infinity as they are thought by Hegel. In *Hegel: The Restlessness of the Negative*, Nancy invokes this distinction in explicit terms: "An infinite process does not go on 'to infinity,' as if to the always postponed term of a progression (Hegel calls this 'bad infinity'): it is the instability of every finite determination, the bearing away of presence and of the given in the movement of presentation and the gift" (*H* 12/19). "Bad" infinity, then, would imply the infinity of a progression or unending expansion: it would be a continuation of finite space into infinity without limit or end. "Good" infinity is actual and, as it were, already traversing or folded into the finite.[30] In a note toward the beginning of *Dis-enclosure*, for instance, Nancy explicitly invokes Hegel's "good" infinity and aligns it with the "nothing" of the event of world disclosure or the "*nihil* opening as world" (*D* 69/100): "the actual infinite [*l'infini actuel*]: thus, the act, the actual and active presence of the *nothing* qua thing (*res*) of the opening itself" (*D* 176n12/20n2; trans. modified). The emptying out of substance in Christian creation and in kenosis, the "nothing" of the presentation of world and flesh is, for Nancy, always an actual infinity: it is the indetermination, ungraspability, and withdrawal of the event of presentation itself. The infinite is not a continuation of the finite without limit; rather, it is inscribed within the finite as the delimitation, dis-enclosure, or internal "infinitization" of finitude itself.

Significantly, this invocation of "actual" infinity appears in the context of a reference to Derrida: Christianity, Nancy proposes, is a voiding of substance, a presentation in withdrawal, and as such it opens within the world "an alterity or an unconditional alienation" (*D* 10/20). Yet, he goes on to specify, this "unconditional alterity" that Christianity opens within the world needs to be differentiated from the motif of the "indeconstructible" in Derrida. It needs to be distinguished, he adds in the footnote, precisely to the extent that it is a question of actual infinity thought as the "nothing of creation," as the opening or presentation of world-disclosure itself.[31]

We can, on the weight of this short footnote, take a certain measure of the distance or difference between Derrida and Nancy on the question of Christianity. Derrida discerns in Chrétien's thinking a "spiritual touch" where the finite comes into contact with the infinite in the Christic body of incarnation. The infinite in this case is the divine, and touch is a *"mutuus contactus* with God."[32] Derrida's concern about the substitutability of the terms of Chrétien's phenomenologized thinking of incarnation is countered by Nancy's insistence that in each case a different mode of infinity is at stake. Chrétien's infinite, in its transcendence and alterity, would appear here as a "bad" Hegelian infinity, an infinity thought from the perspective of metaphysics as an infinite continuation of substance above and beyond the limits of the finite. Nancy's infinity would always be actual, the nothing of the event of opening or presentation itself, which withdraws all presence or substance.

In this context, Nancy's essay on Granel could be read as a response to Derrida. He aligns himself not with Chrétien, the synthesizer of Aristotle, Saint Thomas, and phenomenology, and the thinker of incarnation as hypostatic union. Rather, he aligns himself with Granel, the synthesizer of Marx and Heidegger, and the thinker of incarnation as kenosis. If there is a possible substitutability of terms, it could be inferred, it is not between Nancy and Chrétien but rather between Nancy and Granel. However, Nancy, unlike Granel, takes great pains to insist that the "nothing" of creation implied by "ontological" kenosis is always an "actual" infinity, "the actual infinite." If "good" and "bad" infinity can be confused or substituted for one another, it is because they are both at work in different moments of the Christological tradition. Yet the "bad" infinity of a metaphysical Christianity will always already be inhabited by an "actual" infinity of a Christianity that opens the world as an unconditional alterity (*D* 10/20). Thus Christianity itself will always, and necessarily, be an unfolding of its own auto-deconstruction.

༄

In *Being and Event*, Alain Badiou writes: "The thesis of the infinity of being is necessarily post-Christian."[33] Citing Aristotle, he describes the manner in which an ancient Greek thinking of being as finite is entirely compatible with the orthodox thinking of the "infinite" Christian creator God.[34] Indeed, he suggests that the latter is an unbroken continuation of the former,[35] or, as he puts it: "The infinite God of medieval Christianity *is*, as a being, essentially finite."[36] To this extent, he would agree with both Nancy and Derrida that the orthodox understanding of the Christian creator God is deeply complicit with a metaphysics of presence and, as a continuation of the finite into infinity, is a "bad" infinity, as described by Hegel.

Both Badiou and Nancy see the inscription of "good" infinity within being, or the thought of infinity *as* being, as the means by which thinking might begin to extricate itself from its entanglement with the metaphysics of presence. Both, of course, think the infinity of being in very different ways: for Badiou, infinity can only be thought mathematically, according to post-Cantorian set theory and according to a rigorous set of protocols.[37] For Nancy, as I have shown, infinity is the nothing of a presentation in the withdrawal or emptying of substance. Badiou would no doubt view Nancy's infinity as inescapably "bad," given the filiation, albeit complex, of Nancy's "presentation" to the Heideggerian "giving" of being.[38] And yet, despite the crucial differences, infinity for both is the "other of the void" (*l'autre du vide*), it is immanent to finite being; it is irreducible alterity, and the "irrepresentable."[39]

In this sense, both Nancy and Badiou agree that "the thesis of the infinity of being is necessarily post-Christian." It is just that, for Nancy, the post-Christian is lies at the heart of the incarnate body of Christianity itself as the internal motor of its constitutive self-overcoming. This alignment of Nancy with Badiou—a convergence, as it were, of very divergent lines of thought—shows the extent to which the question of infinity in its "good" and "bad" guises informs two of the most significant new developments in "postmetaphysical" French thought over the past twenty years. Nancy's project of a deconstruction of Christianity needs to take its place within, and be interpreted according to, this broader attempt to think beyond the metaphysics of presence by way of a thinking of being as "actual" infinity. Arguably, this thinking of infinity has a central place within Nancy's thought from the mid 1990s on.[40]

Viewed in this light, Derrida's concerns about Nancy's deconstruction of Christianity need to be reframed or resituated. The most pressing question may not be whether Nancy's thinking of incarnation and touch can be substituted for Chrétien's "infinite touch" understood as a "*mutuus contactus* with God."[41] More pressing may be the question of how thought can best "cure" itself of "bad" infinity through a rigorous thinking of being as "actual" infinity. In this context, Nancy's deconstruction of Christianity stands, alongside the rival mathematical ontology of Badiou, as one of the most important contributions to recent French philosophy.

Ontology of Creation

The Onto-aisthetics of Jean-Luc Nancy

BOYAN MANCHEV

The idea of creation lies at the core of the four domains in which Jean-Luc Nancy's thinking is most influential today: thinking about the world (one would traditionally refer to this as ontology); thinking about art and, in particular, the image (i.e., "aesthetics"); thinking about the sacred and religion; and thinking about politics. In this essay, I will explore the common dynamic that draws them together, since I believe a grasp of this dynamic is crucial for understanding Nancy's thinking and the radical challenges it poses.

Nancy's entire "aesthetic" thinking is governed by the notion of creation. At the same time, creation is obviously an ontological (or, more precisely, ontotheological) notion—it has to do with the coming into being of the world. Indeed, after Heidegger and Deleuze, and alongside Negri and Badiou, Nancy is perhaps today the philosopher who most emphasizes the question of the world. Creation is Nancy's ontological concept par excellence: to think about the world, as he conceives this task, is to think about it *as* creation. We should therefore approach Nancy's concept of creation from an ontological perspective, one that turns out to be a matter not of ontologizing aesthetics but of aestheticizing ontology—of making it *onto-aisthetic*.[1] Given that the creation of the world evidently starts out as a theological idea, Nancy's insistence on creation could reductively be viewed as a return to the ontotheological tradition. This would be a hasty and simplistic conclusion, however. We can understand the centrality of creation to Nancy's project of deconstructing Christianity and, more generally, monotheism only by tackling the idea of creation in all its complexity and on the proper level. Why should we perceive the world through its creation?

Should creation in Nancy be understood in a doctrinal sense, as a positive positing of the world in the void? No, it should not. The two radical views of creation that can be identified in Nancy's work promote a radical critique of any idea of creation as positive positioning, that is to say, as *pro-duction*. In this essay, I shall be contrasting these two "views"—a *radically negative ontology* (or *ex-nihilistic ontology*) and a *modal ontology*.[2]

The Creation ex Nihilo of the World: An Ex-Nihilistic Ontology

Radically negative ontology involves radicalizing, even exceeding, any view of a fundamental negativity that would be a "pure" negativity, a "negativity without function," according to Georges Bataille: a *basic nothing*, a *very simple nothing*. Nancy formulates his idea of nothing in *Being Singular Plural*: "The nothing (in order to keep this dried-up word and to make it incisive for every 'abyss' and all their various depths), which is 'at bottom' [*au fond*] nothing and no more than the nothing of a leap into nothing, is the negativity that is not a resource but the affirmation of ek-sistent tension: its intensity or surprising tone of existence" (*BSP* 173–74/ 199–200). The basic thesis of Nancy's radically negative ontology is that the world is created ex nihilo. We know, however, that it is God who creates the world ex nihilo. How, therefore, can we avoid a somewhat regressive return to the theological register? First, for Nancy God the creator is a void. This supposition may seem similar to the tradition of negative theology—of Meister Eckhart, for example. Is this, therefore, a new version of negative theology? Before we can answer this question, another one arises: Is Nancy's God, this God-void, still a *creator*? "He [God] didn't do anything," Nancy affirms in his short lecture for children "In Heaven and on Earth" (*NT* 95/61). Is this, then, an inoperative god (*un dieu désoeuvré*)? In *The Space of Literature*, Blanchot has already put forward a radical affirmation according to which creation is God's "least divine" function.[3] That affirmation is based on an alignment of creation with activity. It falls under Blanchot's radical critique of the work—the *opus*—and inherits a function, an activity (*ergon, energeia*) whose main concept is that of *désoeuvrement*, "unworking." This critique goes hand in hand with Bataille's critique of Hegel and therefore of dialectic negativity, and it likewise ends in an apologia for a pure, radical, empty negativity, a negativity that is not active, but *effective*.

Nancy's God, who has not done anything, has indeed done nothing: he has done the nothing. Yes, he is a void, but he is an effective void: "By hollowing himself out, god opens the void in which the world can take its place" (*NT* 92/55); "He didn't do anything. . . . At that moment, god did not open the void to the earth; rather, god is the void that is opening up" (*NT* 95/61). Thus the image of the God-void automatically contributes to the radical critique of negativity; it is an integral, even central part. Of what does the void empty itself? Of substance. The void empties itself of a substantial void: of negativity. Creation is an emptying of substance. This affirmation merely confirms the hypothesis to which Nancy subscribes, following Bataille, Blanchot, and Merleau-Ponty (in *The Visible and the Invisible*), in the tradition of the major ontotheological and dialectical critiques of negativity. The thesis of the creation ex nihilo of the world—the *ex-nihilistic* thesis, if I may venture a coinage, is different from a *nihilistic* thesis. Nancy's first solution can therefore be designated a radically negative ontology in that it is a critical radicalization of the concept of negativity.

Therefore, the first radical transformation in Nancy is that God does not create the world ex nihilo; it is the *nihil* that creates. How does it create? By emptying itself.[4] *The Creation of the World, or Globalization* supports the affirmation in "In Heaven and on Earth": "In creation, a growth emerges from nothing and this nothing takes care of itself, cultivates its growth" (*CW* 51/55). This void, however, in emptying itself, growing, is the world itself. God is converted into world (*CW* 44/39). Therefore, God is the world. This is not a pantheistic identification; it is no longer an apophatic affirmation. On the contrary, insisting on the question of God stands for a more radical philosophical insistence: an insistence on—and for—the world. Therefore, a second radical transformation occurs. This is the transformation of God—the nothing that creates—into world, the immanentization of everything outside the world as world: "In so doing, it [God as subject of the world] suppressed itself as God-Supreme-Being and transformed itself, losing itself therein, in the existence for-itself of the world without an outside" (*CW* 44/39); "At the end of monotheism, there is world without God" (*CW* 50/54). A "world-becoming" (*mundanization*) is thus presented as the first moment of globalization, that is to say, the *creation of the world* (*CW* 44/40). Thus, rather than returning to atheological problematic, the image of the God-void is necessary only to affirm an ontological view by means of the radicalization of the concept of creation ex nihilo. This is the core of *The Creation of the World*.

The Displacement of the Origin and the Failure of
Messianic Logic

The idea of an auto-beginning, of an immanent, autopoietic force in the world—an idea that is theological in substance—does seem to persist in Nancy. Structurally, radically negative ontology no doubt risks being converted into negative theology, even though Nancy himself firmly asserts that negative theology is finished: "this is the end of negative theology as well as the end of a phenomenology in general, albeit that of the inapparent" (*CW* 72/98). If not just negative theology but even "negative phenomenology" is finished, are what one may call the "negative ontologies," whose history ranges from Hegel (at least) to Heidegger (at least), also finished?[5] The heritage of negativity is no doubt here a theological heritage, but one that is far from being a direct, "substantial" heritage; it is a structural heritage. It is the heritage of what I call "messianic logic." The term *messianic logic* conveys a hypothesis according to which postcritical ontological regimes are organized around a common structural core, notably, the idea of an event that deposes the ontological regime in its entirety, that puts an end to the order of the order. From Hegel's *Absolute* or Heidegger's *Ereignis* to the event in Badiou's ontological project, this event is the heir, legitimate or otherwise, of the messianic event, whether of redemption and salvation or the end and conclusion of a being.

Indeed, Nancy needs the theological thread only to affirm the radical nature, hollowed out, of the question of the world. Instead of rejecting the theological heritage of the idea of the creation of the world, Nancy faces up to it in order to go beyond any silent or unconscious overdetermination risked by negative ontologies. It comes as no surprise, then, that Nancy's radically negative ontology is decisively separated from any messianic logic: it does not end in an absolute event. At this point Nancy is undoubtedly close to Bataille, who had given up "all hope" and any promise of salvation (according to Blanchot's requirement, which the author of *Inner Experience* [orig. 1943] evokes in his work): his tortured thinking, contaminated by the irreducible, agonizing presence of the "vacuum" of the *outside*, is immune to the immunizing force of the messianic promise and of its modern figures.

The problematic of the messianic explicitly manifests itself in Nancy's text heralding the problematic of the "deconstruction of Christianity," "Of Divine Places." It precedes the return of the messianic figure in Derrida's "Faith and Knowledge: The Two Sources of 'Religion' at the Limits of Reason Alone" and Agamben's *Homo Sacer.*[6] The messianic problematic of the *Wink*, the signal, is also central in *Dis-enclosure*, outlined in the crucial text "On a Divine *Wink*." However, despite the fact that the project of deconstructing Christianity comprises many categories that imply a messianic horizon (the event to come or the empty signal announcing it), Nancy is explicitly opposed to messianic rhetoric. Thus, in the opening to *Concealed Thinking*, he writes: "for my part, I remain reticent about this vocabulary of the messianic" (*PD* 14n1). Indeed, Nancy presents himself as one of the major critics of messianic logic and therefore of negative ontologies.

At a profound, structural level, Nancy's radical criticism of messianic logic consists in what may be described as a *displacement of origin*. A careful reading of *Corpus* reveals an important conceptual displacement, a substitution: the image of an "original" creation—therefore of an origin of the world—is replaced by the idea of a constant creation, of creation as the becoming-world of the world. "As for creation, it is eternal," Nancy affirms (*C* 111). The idea of origin is deposed by the idea of creation—deposed, or, more precisely, deconstructed, in the strictly conceptual sense. But, going beyond the understanding of deconstruction as an undoing of conceptual oppositions, one reaches a radical analogy postulated by Nancy and accentuated by Derrida: the analogy between the concepts of deconstruction and creation. Nancy asserts: "The creator's strength comes from the original deconstruction of any recognizable image" (*C* 63).[7] The power (*pouvoir*) of the creator (and not the act of creation—a symptomatic conceptual displacement) is therefore far from being conceived as a positive *dunamis* that, in a founding act, inserts the world into the void.

Nancy goes beyond messianic logic by displacing the idea of absolute origin, thus exhausting his resource—the idea of an absolute moment of beginning or of an absolute starting moment that necessarily determines an absolute moment of completion. By displacing the origin, Nancy transforms it into becoming, that is, into creation. It is possible to see this conceptual operation as transforming the ontological regime into *catastrophe* in the sense of René Thom, not as an eschatological event through which the ontological order is ended but as a modal change in regime. The chain of conceptual equivalence that organizes the conceptual scheme of Nancy's thesis can therefore be presented as follows: the vacuum hollowed out = the void opens up = the void cultivates its growth. There is nothing at the beginning, or rather, there is nothingness at the beginning: "The withdrawal of the beginning belongs to the self-beginning. The beginning remains ungrounded" (*CW* 80/113). Whether the vacuum is hollowed out or cultivates its growth, the beginning is concealed. Since God is the world, the result is a self-beginning by self-annihilation, by the annihilation of the origin—the concealment of the beginning, in a both nihilistic and anarchic ontology. One can venture to use the term *ex-nihilist* because the *nihil* is apparently nothing other than the intensity of the *ex-*, of the growing movement of spacing out: the *very simple nothing*, that is to say "the affirmation of ek-sistent tension: its intensity" (*BSP* 173–74/200).

Let us hold on to this *tensive* and therefore effective moment. It is the central moment in the radically negative solution of Nancy's ex-nihilism. The unfounded *nihil*, for Nancy, is far from the risk of self-exhaustion in a *Bodenlos*, a "bottomless." It is a tension, not a substance; one might even say a "pure force." Thus, the ex-nihilistic thesis opens up a crucial perspective for thinking about the world, an intrinsically political perspective that no longer consists in the issue of activity (linked by its Aristotelian provenance to a concept of substance), but in the issue of effectivity (which is very different from effectiveness).

The Modal Ontology of Creation

Has the world, therefore, been created? The world is creating itself. The creation of the world is not a founding act: it is a permanent creation. To be more precise: creation does not stop; it is itself the world. The name that this continual creation receives in *Corpus* is *modalization*. It may therefore be postulated that the two structural moments of *mondialisation*—which, in opposition to *globalization*, is for Nancy the name of the world's becoming world, that is, of its creation—are *mundanization* and *modalization*. Are these structural moments also successive, or are they instead alternative?

In "modal ontology" we have a possibility that has never, to my knowledge, been examined in detail, and I will take this possibility as the starting point of my reflections on metamorphosis as an ontological concept.[8] The concept of modal ontology is outlined in the sections "Corpus: Another Departure" and "Glorious Body" of *Corpus* (*C* 51–55 and 61–65). The term *modal* is introduced as a possible attribute of an ontology within the context of reflection about the body: "*Here*, in an essential, all-embracing and exclusive way, ontology is *modal*—or modifiable, or modifying" (*C* 53). Later, in the section "Glorious Body," the modal moment is linked to a new view of creation:

That God created *limon*, and that he made the *body* out of *limon*, means that God modalized or modified himself, but that his *self* in itself is only the extension and indefinite expansion of modes. This means that "creation" isn't the production of a world from some unknown matter of nothingness but consists in the fact that *the* matter (only that which there is) essentially *modifies itself*: it's not a substance, it's the extension and expansion of "modes," or, to put it more precisely, the exposition of what there is. (*C* 61)

According to the modal ontology that postulates at its very core a movement of metamorphosis, God creates *by altering* (*himself*). No doubt, then: modification is God. In the first instance, God is transformed into the world; in the second, God is the metamorphosis of the world. Creation is therefore *modalization* or *metamorphosis*. This equivalence becomes explicit further on, in relation to *technē*: "*Technē*: 'technique,' 'art,' 'modalization,' 'creation'" (*C* 65). There is no origin of the world, nor any self-beginning. The world is only self-modalization. Even though in *Corpus* this principle of self-modalization receives the grandest name of all—*God*—this name signifies nothing but that power, or rather, that immanent, self-modalizing force in the world, the force of an absolutely immanent world.

This is the logical sequence of this argument, comprising a series of semantic equivalences, in whose succession radical semantic transpositions take place: the exposure of what *there is* = exposure of God = God is what *there is*. There is only exposure of the exposure, which is actually creation. This complex line of argument, which seems to approach a tautological affirmation, resonates with the structure of the ex-nihilist transformation (or rather, the reverse, since the ex-nihilist thesis is developed later): the creation of the world ex nihilo is a creation of the *nihil* by the *nihil*, and this nihil-god, who is annihilated while ex-nihilating himself, is the world. The equivalence, even identification, of God as self-modalizing power of the world and of what *there is* takes place through a complex operation, through which a third term emerges: matter. Indeed, this term is at the center of the chain of equivalence, which suggests the underlying presence of a radical and crypto-Spinozist operation, namely, the identification of God and matter. God who creates by modalizing (himself) (as world) is nothing other than matter. We witness the following semantic displacement in the formulation quoted earlier: "[that] means that God modalized or modified himself, but that his *self* in itself is only the extension and indefinite expansion of modes. . . . *the* matter (only that which there is) essentially *modifies itself*: it's not a substance, it's the extension and expansion of 'modes'" (*C* 61). God *is* "the extension and indefinite expansion of 'modes'"; matter is "the extension and expansion of 'modes.'" God and matter are the same thing. God *is* matter or matter *is* God.

The Creation of the Body

> The ontological body has yet to be thought.
>
> —*C* 15

The created world is body. The created world is *the* body. "And if the *body* is par excellence the thing *created*, if 'created body' is a tautology—or, rather, 'created bodies,' for *the* body is always in the plural—then *the body is the plastic material of spacing*, without form or Idea" (*C* 63). The issue of creation is therefore an affair of body. If the body is only "*the plastic material of spacing*," then it is the movement of creation itself. The fact that "the *body* is par excellence the thing *created*" does not in any way mean that the body is the result of the creative act, that it is *produced*, even that it is *one* product: creation is what goes radically beyond the logic of production. If the body is unproducible, however, this does not mean that it is a substance, either in the Aristotelian sense or in the Spinozist one. The body, the created par excellence, is not a substance, and yet it has no origin, no beginning or self-beginning: it *begins* in the midst of the modes, it is the direct beginning through the modes, without the principle of a unique substance, as is required by Deleuze.[9] The body is, therefore, the plastic matter of spacing; it is itself "always bound for," with no possibility of hypostasis as the moment-point of beginning. It is where the body in Nancy encounters Blanchot's radical ontological critique, translated by the notion of *beginning again*. We must therefore think of the transformation of the "*limon*" (*C* 61) as a transformation of the body, or of bodies, as Nancy insists. The *aestheticization of ontology* therefore necessarily postulates a radical thinking, not only of matter, but of the body, of *bodies*, and therefore of finitude.

In order to understand Nancy's "aesthetic thinking," we therefore need to go beyond phenomenology. In particular, we tend to associate Nancy's concept of image too quickly with an aesthetic regime, without understanding that it initially operates as an element of Nancy's ontological—onto-aisthetic—critique. Until we do so, we cannot understand Nancy's thinking about the arts. Whereas Deleuze's and Derrida's radical critiques of Platonic-Christian filiation released the ontological power of the image, Nancy attacks its immunization in the aesthetic regime by re-opening its "demonic," that is to say, *material* power. In affirming that the only original dimension of the act of creation is the "original deconstruction of any recognizable image" (*C* 63), Nancy attacks any onto-mimetology and any iconology of the image. Creation is an affair of the body: not of the body-image of Platonizing Christianity but of the image-body. "The body is an image—insofar as the body is the visibility of the invisible, the bright plasticity of spacing" (*C* 63). The image is, therefore, very different from an element in a system of representation or a tool of expression. It is nothing other than the mode of creation-modalization.

Nancy continues: "The very *idea* of 'creation' is the idea, or thought, of an originary absence of Idea, form, model, or preliminary tracing. . . . It's the very plasticity of expansion, extension—where existences *take place*. The *image* (that it thus is) has no link to either the idea, or, in general, to the visible (and/or intelligible) "presentation" *of* anything at all. The body's not an image-*of*" (*C* 63). Therefore, *the idea of "creation" is the idea of an inherent absence of idea*. However, this idea of the inherent absence of idea has had a name since Plato, and that name is phantasm, the protean creation of the *Sophist*.[10] Therefore, the creator, Nancy's "inverted god." the god deconstructing any recognizable image, would be a sophist god. Once again, however, this sophist god has already been named by Plato: it is Hades, that is, the god of death, designated in the *Cratylus* "an accomplished sophist." The *philosopher* Hades

> will have nothing to do with men while they are in the body, but only when the soul is liberated from the desires and evils of the body. Now there is a great deal of philosophy and reflection in that, for in their liberated state he can bind them with the desire of virtue, but while they are flustered and maddened by the body, not even father Cronus himself would suffice to keep them with him in his own far-famed chains.[11]

From then on, however, the Platonic soul led nowhere save to the space of complete disincarnation, to the kingdom of the dead. Indeed, is Hades not the authentic prototype of the philosopher and his kingdom—Plato's City?

Nancy's sophist god, the ex-nihilist god, is, by contrast, a god of bodies, the plastic spacing of the sacred power in the surge of matter. No more body of god. In its place: *divine places* = body/god(s).

Thus, with Nancy we face the possibility of juxtaposing the "monotheistic" ex-nihilist regime of creation and the modal regime of Greek thought, where creation is always presented as a form of metamorphosis. The link would be made through Plato, who undoubtedly opens up the *conceptual* conditions of possibility, of monotheistic thought. For him, as for Nancy, all things considered, the phantasm—the inherent absence of idea—is synonymous with metamorphic power. A scrupulous analysis of the *Sophist* would demonstrate this. The conceptual leap taken by Nancy in *Corpus* affirms it in one fell swoop: the formula *the idea of "creation" is the idea of an inherent absence of idea* amounts to this: *the body is the plastic matter of spacing.* The act of ex-nihilist creation is a modal act.

The Finished Body of Creation

Modal thinking, thinking about the modalization of the body or the modal body, modifiable and modalized, goes so far as to empty the divine body itself of substance by "reducing" it—by spacing it, by opening it up—to a pure modalization, to an altering movement. In a monotheistic, even Christian mode—from the perspective of the project of deconstructing Christianity—modal thinking about creation, thinking about the *ontological body*, would have totally new and radical consequences.

In *Noli me tangere*—a book that takes up the central themes in Nancy's work of the 1990s: the *body* and *touch*, rewording them from the perspective of deconstructing Christianity—an emphasis on the finite body paradoxically goes hand in hand with the image of the raising up of the dead body, which Nancy prefers as the literal translation of the Greek *anastasis*, resurrection: "Onto the *horizon* of finite life (the 'horizon' is the limit) is superimposed, without being opposed, an infinite raising up [*levée*]" (*NT* 112n33/n2; trans. modified). It is not necessary to say at what point the figure of the resurrection may seem problematic in the context of thinking that is meant to be *radically* finite (because, evidently, the verticality of the resurrection, in being superimposed on the horizontality of the dead body, makes a figural pact with it, and the figure that springs forth is nothing other than that of the cross . . .).

However, a fundamental link between the infinity of the raising up and finitude can at least be inferred. We should not lose sight of this daring relationship, especially since it is effectively inscribed (ex-cribed?) in Nancy's philosophical texts. First, the raising up is postulated in *Noli me tangere* as that which cannot be sublated (*ce qui ne se relève pas*): "This *rising up* is not a sublation [*cette levée n'est pas une relève*]. . . . It makes the truth of a life rise in it, the truth of all life insofar as it is mortal and of every life insofar as it is singular" (*NT* 18/33–34; trans. modified). That which cannot be sublated is finitude—that is to say, *différance*. Derrida's phrase in *Speech and Phenomena*, "*The infinite* différance *is finite*,"[12] could not be more apt in this context. Nancy, in his important lecture "The Free Voice of Man," presented twenty-five years ago at the symposium in Cérisy-La-Salle entitled "The Ends of Man—on the Work of Jacques Derrida," tackles Derrida's affirmation as follows:

> *Speech and Phenomena* shows that *différance* (of writing, or as writing) is finite: "Infinite *différance* is itself finite." . . . And that is to

say, the infinity of the deferring of presence *ipso facto* constitutes (if this word applies here) finitude; that is to say, it excludes the dialectical recourse of finity (which is not finitude) to infinity, and opens the without-recourse of an *end* bereft of the *telos* of presence. Difference, which *is* nothing, *is* therefore finitude, which in its turn *is* nothing (this "nothing," this thing, *res*, would have to be analyzed; but perhaps what would be at issue in any such analysis would be duty).[13]

Nevertheless, could a thinking of the resurrection be reconciled with a radical thinking of finitude? The paradoxical response is "yes." The *raising up* in Nancy's radical reading is not governed by anything other than the movement of a difference or alteration. This movement is transposed into a progression, or rather, a totally new conceptual alteration, which is presented in the form of an alteration of the alteration. First, the alterity that governs the raising up is that of the father's transcendence, the *very other*, "reduced" to, or transformed into, an "other":

> The difference, though (a slight difference, difficult to discern), has to do with what *anastasis* is not or does not bring about from the self, from the subject proper, but from the other. *Anastasis* comes to the self from the other or arises from the other within the self—or again, it is the raising of the other in the self. It is the other that rises and resurrects [*qui se lève et qui ressuscite*] within the dead self. (*NT* 18–19/35)

Second, however, the raising up is linked to the presence of a woman, a sinner: Mary Magdalene. In the movement of the alteration, Christ's risen body becomes *a* body, having risen from the tomb, infinitely differing in its finitude from the body of Mary Magdalene:

> *Noli me tangere* is the word and the instant of relation and of revelation between two bodies, that is, of a single body infinitely altered and exposed both in its fall [*tombée*] as well as in its raising.
>
> Why, then, a body? Because only a body can be cut down or raised up, because only a body can touch or not touch. A spirit can do nothing of the sort. A "pure spirit" gives only a formal and empty index of a presence entirely closed in on itself. A body opens this presence; it presents it; it puts presence outside of itself; it moves presence away from itself, and, by that very fact, it brings others along with it: Mary Magdalene thus becomes the true body of the departed. (*NT* 48/79)

This raising is therefore a raising up of the dead body as a dead body, in its infinite alteration. It is a difficult, daring thinking, which is close to that of Bataille: not experiencing the decay, the corpse, as the dead body of god, as the corpse of God, but death itself as body, finitude as an infinitely transformable body, with no salutary power, and yet free, savagely free, without principle.

Thus *modal ontology*—conceived according to the idea of creation as metamorphosis—necessarily leads to the rejection of messianic or salutary logic. In attempting to go beyond the obvious, one could ask a more complex, somewhat heretical question, notably, whether the emphasis placed on *anastasis*, the resurrection or raising up, is not charged with the task of opposing messianic thinking. If the Messiah has *passed* once and for all, then what would be to come is the infinity (present) of his raising up (rebirth/re-surrection): the infinite coming of presence. Thus, paradoxically, for Nancy *anastasis*, the resurrection, is conceived not as a return to the regime of the infinity but always as a modalization of the body. It is therefore thought from the perspective of a radical finitude, as *onto-aisthetic*.

The infinity of the raising up is therefore the infinity of finitude. The deconstruction of Christianity, to come to its appointed end, should be the affirmation of radical finitude. While it shows, first, that infinity opens up alongside finitude (in the infinity of the "raising up"), this infinity is subsequently affirmed as the infinity of finitude itself. The project of deconstructing Christianity is therefore entirely governed by the requirement of an *infinitely finite* thinking.

The Matter of the World: Politics of Creation

The path from the figure of the resurrection to a radical materialism is a difficult, paradoxical one. It is a path that requires courage and bold thinking, and yet it is very different from the way of the cross. It is onto this path, it seems to me, that Nancy has ventured.

Leaving aside for a moment the question of the "compatibility" of ex-nihilist and modal themes—Is the idea of permanent modalization compatible with that of a permanent creation ex nihilo?—let us assume that *The Creation of the World* is an extension of the route taken by *Corpus*. This would mean that the modes to which *Corpus* refers are also the modes of the emptying of substance—the *hollowing out*—that is another name for the act of creation. What modifies (itself), according to *Corpus*, is matter; what empties out substance is the void. However, a seemingly absurd conclusion will then be reached: matter is the void. Nancy is undoubtedly aware of this risk. In *The Creation of the World*, he tackles this paradox head-on by affirming that "The *ex nihilo* is the genuine formulation of a radical materialism, that is to say, precisely, without roots" (*CW* 51/55). In a more tangible mode, the question could be reworded as follows: Is a groundless materialism not in danger of becoming a materialism without matter?

The question of the link between modal ontology and Spinozism becomes imperative here. Is not the affirmation outlined in "Glorious Body" witness to an unconfessed Spinozism?[14] Nancy himself remains reticent about Spinoza's ontology (*CW* 112n10/81n1). Does this reticence represent a backing down from the radical propositions of "Glorious Body"? I believe it does not, indeed, that this reticence, expressed ten years later, is in keeping with the radicalness of the affirmation of *Corpus*. Although the thesis developed in *Corpus* indicates a Spinozist tendency, that is a radical, paradoxical Spinozism: a Spinozism with no substance. Modal ontology involves thinking of metamorphosis as the ontological regime in itself: "God had made himself body, he had been extended and molded *ex limon terrae*: out of the fat, smooth, deformable extension of clay, the *raw* matter, consisting entirely of modalizing, or modification, rather than substance" (*C* 61). Matter is not a substance; it is a "pure," not substantial, modalization. Nancy's paragraph opens a radical critique not only of the Aristotelian notion of matter as substance but also of the Spinozist notion of substance. This paragraph actually displaces the main issue. For him, the issue of the creation of the world is henceforth worded as follows: *What* matter of the world?

While ex-nihilist ontology is extended through the modal perspective of *Corpus*, the apparent paradox it concerns (a groundless or rootless materialism could prove to be materialism without matter) can be understood as follows: the materialism of the ex nihilo is radical because it opposes a substantialist notion of matter. Radical materialism is the materialism of a modal and modalizing matter. Modalization is actually the only matter: therefore, matter is itself creation. It is, as Negri in turn postulates, revolutionary: matter is an immanent transformation in the world.[15]

This is why the issue of the creation of the world is inevitably also a political issue in the wider as well as stronger sense of the term. It comes as no surprise, therefore, if this question is inevitably raised as a question of a *struggle for a world*. The penultimate paragraph of the first chapter of *The Creation of the World*, "Urbi et orbi," opens up the question of action, thus establishing a direct relationship between the notion of the creation of the world and political action—the struggle: "*To create the world* means: . . . reopening each possible struggle for a world" (*CW* 54/63).

This question, the question of the struggle for a world, is the most urgent, decisive question we are facing today, at a moment when each day the forces of the new reaction are absorbing further any potential for transformation in order to submit it to the imperatives of (economic) growth, which has resulted in the alteration of "our" world. To hold the question of the world demands courage—and Nancy's thought of the world holds it at the highest pitch of its demand, while daring to venture in the direction of answers still to be imagined.

—Translated by Christine Blackmore

Distinct Art

ALENA ALEXANDROVA

art has been homogeneous with religions. But within religion itself, art is not religious.

—*M1* 99/157

Art has always maintained a special relationship with the divine—struggling to figure it, to present it, or to negate it. As Jean-Luc Nancy might formulate it, art bears witness to the opening of the divine, or to the divine as opening: in other words, to the world as it is. It is "homogeneous with religions," but even within religion, it is never religious (*M1* 99/157; trans. modified). Art, specifically the image, occupies an aporetic place with regard to religion insofar as by virtue of its impossible task—to figure the invisible—it deconstructs religion from within.

Themes pertaining to the project of a deconstruction of monotheism and Christianity persistently appear in a number of Nancy's essays on art, most of them not included in *Dis-enclosure*. Throughout these earlier texts, Nancy indicates that art, specifically the image, is at the heart of such a deconstruction.[1] In order to show how this is so, I will address two sets of issues: on the one hand, the way in which Nancy conceives the notions of image, representation and painting, showing the intricate relationship with their monotheist provenance and, on the other hand, the way in which he interprets theological themes such as creation ex nihilo and incarnation.

Invisibility, Indivisibility

The role of art in the self-deconstruction of monotheism can be understood better if it is considered in the context of the difference between polytheism and monotheism.[2] In a number of texts, Nancy insists that the difference between poly- and monotheism is a matter not of numerical reduction, but of displacing the plurality of gods present in the world with the unicity of a god who is withdrawn and absent from it (*D* 22/36). According to him, the word *God*, in its monotheist articulation, ceases to belong to a particular being "but names the divine as such, the divine as a unity or a single thing" (*NT* 78/26). As such, it signifies the withdrawal of God from presence in the world, or the transformation of the divine into a name. This name can be said to be a proper one to the extent that it names one being, and at the same time it exceeds the modality of being proper insofar as it names "being" or the "divine" as such. In polytheism, by contrast, the gods are distinct beings, each one with a proper name (e.g., in Greek religion Zeus, Athena, Dionysus). Nancy points out that this implies they are present *in* the world and interact with each other according "to relations of power, of threat, or of assistance" (*D* 35/55). Thus they organize the world, or give meaning to it. Their actions are represented in mythical narratives and in a plethora of images. Polytheism, in other words, is a religious mode that is associated with the *visibility* of the gods and its art "provides a *vision* of the gods" (*M2* 240/66). Insofar as myth provides a narrative that gives meaning to the world, it postulates an origin, something pregiven or primordial that explains the world in terms of precedence and provenance (*CW* 69/91).

Monotheism, Nancy claims, "is in truth atheism" (*D* 35/55). It is engaged in a self-deconstruction insofar as it understands itself in an increasingly less religious manner, in the sense that it no longer holds onto a mythology, or representation, of divinities and their actions (*D* 37/57). Central to this movement of demythologization, or *atheization*, is the rejection of the presence of gods *in* this world.[3] By contrast to the effective presence of a plurality of gods, the monotheist god, whose unicity implies his withdrawal from presence, can no longer be conceived as being an origin or a primordial narrative that prescribes how the world should be. In monotheism, myth, or the positive representation of the actions of gods, transforms itself into negative formulas that signify the absent presence of God.

Nancy suggests in *The Creation of the World, or Globalization* that the movement of the atheization of monotheism or the withdrawal of God from the world implies, in fact, that there is a "world without God, that is to say *without another world*" (*CW* 50/54; my emphasis), an "*absent-heistic*" world (*CW* 51/54). In other words, according to Nancy, the name *God* does not stand for a being *outside* the world, a *cosmotheoros*, "an ob-server of a world" (*CW* 43/37) that is itself invisible. "The divine" in its monotheist articulation does not signify a relationship with another world but *another* relationship to the world, which no longer fits "the paradigm of the given, structured, and animate universe" (*D* 15/28). The history of the monotheist God, as a history of the attempts to define what that name stands for, is a history, according to Nancy, of "atheism itself, in its most rigorous proceedings" (*D* 21/35). This name, he concludes, therefore des-ignates "an ontological tautology" or "the premise or principle of a pre-supposed totality founded in unity and in necessity" (*D* 21/35). However, this totality in its unicity is nothing but the world itself, that is, things as they are.[4] One of Nancy's central claims is that, with the invention of monotheism, the world is no longer dependent on gods who give sense and direction to it but gives itself as itself; there is no longer a giver of sense.[5] As he puts it: "the tautology of the world is simply displaced there into the tautology of God" (*D* 20/34). Consequently, the meaning of such a formula is both absolutely specific and absolutely open. In other words, it renders the fact of the world's existence as it is.

In the context of Nancy's analysis, the invention of monotheism is as-sociated with a fundamental change in the notion of representation and the visual image. Traditionally, the invisibility of the monotheistic God is associated with the ban on the graven image, whose most formal expres-sion is to be found in Exodus.[6] The universal God is "a jealous God" who withdraws into invisibility and thus makes himself absolutely distinguish-able from the false gods of the idols.[7] Whereas the plurality of gods, as Nancy writes, "constitutes their visibility, whether potential or actual, as well as their presence" (LP 240/66), monotheism is characterized by the "*indivisibility* of God withdrawn into His unity" (LP 240–41/66; my emphasis). He insistently points out in different texts that what is central to monotheism is not the unity of God, as that unity is not a result of a simple reduction of the number of gods, but his *indivisibility* as a central property of this unity.[8] Nancy's emphasis on God's indivisibility rather than his invisibility is a result of the strategy he uses in his analysis of the self-deconstructive aspects of monotheism. In his view, monotheism deconstructs itself precisely because it is engaged in a relationship with itself. The presence of God in himself and for himself amounts to his inaccessibility, and the immediate consequence of this movement of *self*-determination is his unity or indivisibility. As a result, the *mono-* of the one God, if we accept Nancy's line of thinking, is the outcome not of his uniqueness and universality but of his relationship with himself. Indivisibility, then, signifies that this being is invisible, not because it is in another, transcendent world but because it *coincides* with the world as it is. Therefore, the *mono-*, according to Nancy, signifies precisely this coincidence, the tautologies of God and the world displacing each other. The world, its being, becomes a tautology precisely because it is not determined by anything beyond it; it is as it is without any external guarantee. Consequently, I can conclude that the atheist moment of monotheism, or the surpassing of the mythical mode (what Nancy calls "demythologization"), is co-original with the invention of invisibility as a proper representational modality of God. In order to substantiate that claim and reveal the finer details of such a thesis, I will examine the way Nancy interprets the motif of creation ex nihilo, which forms, according to him, "a nodal point in a 'deconstruction of monotheism'" (*CW* 70/93).

Creation ex Nihilo

Nancy points out that the motif of creation ex nihilo has a double status—it is both "overused by monotheism" and at the same time it indicates "the wearing out [*usure*] of monotheism itself" (*CW* 67/86). In the traditional interpretation of this motif, "nothing" is "used as a material cause" and supposes an agent or a subject, which produces out of that "nothing." Understood in this way, according to the "theological *doxa*," it becomes "the most disastrous of concepts," according to Nancy (*CW* 67/87), because it signifies causal production that presupposes subject, will, and intention. In this interpretation, the creator has the power to determine what is created and to assign an end to it. Moreover, the creature is considered to be a representation, "an image of" its creator.

According to Nancy, however, the three monotheisms, especially in their mystical traditions, have maintained the openness of the meaning of creation and, in fact, have developed this motif quite differently. Creation, especially creation ex nihilo, is the opposite of production or fabrication, which presupposes a producer and a project. It does not mean that the world is "fabricated *with* nothing," nor does it mean that it comes "*out* of nothing (like a miraculous apparition)" (*CW* 51/55). "Nothing" is obviously not "a pure and simple nothingness" (*CW* 51/56). On the contrary, it signifies the double fact that creation occurs without anything pregiven or presupposed (i.e., it is without a model), as it is ultimately "the without-reason [*rien de raison*] of the world" (*CW* 51/56). The *nihil* in this motif stands for the fact that the world is as *it is*, without a model and without a reason. In this sense, the motif of creation ex nihilo becomes the point at which monotheism understands and, in fact, invents itself as atheism. God creates without a model, and by emptying himself into that creation, he *coincides with the world*: "The unique God, whose unicity is the correlate of the creating act cannot precede its creation any more than it can subsist above it or apart from it in some way. It merges with it: merging with it, it withdraws in it, and withdrawing there it empties itself there, emptying itself it is nothing other than the opening of this void" (*CW* 70/93). If we follow Nancy's line of thought, the theme of the indivisibility of the monotheistic God, therefore, is to not be understood only as a reduction in number—there is only one god. More importantly, the *mono-* is to be understood in the sense that god is indivisible not only in and for himself (the traditional theological interpretation) but in the sense that God is *indivisible from the world*. In the act of creation, "God annihilates itself [*s'annéantit*] as a 'self' or as a *distinct being* in order to 'withdraw' in its act—which makes the opening of the world" (*CW* 70/93; my emphasis). Nancy adds that theology has, in fact, gradually "stripped itself of a God distinct from the world" (*CW* 50/54) and calls the moment of the coincidence or the indivisibility between God and the world *absentheism*.

In this way, the indivisibility of the monotheist God is related to his invisibility, but not in the sense that he is not accessible to seeing. I can conclude, following Nancy, that invisibility is a result of the very *coincidence* of God with the world, of the *nihil* and the without-reason of creation. Nancy points out that an important implication of the motif of creation ex nihilo is that any presupposed position is questioned and rendered unstable, in contrast to the mythological mode, which supposes an origin and understands the world as an animate universe: "Being falls completely outside of any presupposed position. . . . Being is not the basis of the existent, or its cause, but it 'is' it or it 'exists' it" (*CW* 68/88–89).

The collapse of the distinction between creator and creature has larger implications for the articulation of the notion of representation within a monotheist context and for the way art understands itself, its potential, and its failures: "Hence, even the *creature* that was the finite image of its creator and consequently was bound to represent (interpret, figure) creation, itself becomes a potential creator as subject of possibilities and subject of ends" (*CW* 65/82). Nancy would insist that creation is not a representation—the creator does not create a creature that represents him—nor does it simply signify the state of affairs as a static state of the world. Instead, creation is "the bringing forth of a world" (*CW* 65/82), continuously and at every moment, as an act that is dissociated from model or origin. Then the image and (religious) art, in their relationship with the divine, would not figure a transcendent invisible, an inaccessible beyond, but would signify the coincidence of the invisible with the world. The most religious of images cannot represent anything that is out of this world; instead, it presents the *nihil* of creation by representing the world as it is.

For this reason, art cannot be placed in a position of figuring, illustrating, or representing the divine. If it claims to be religious, art is exposed to an impossible task, or at least a paradox. It must either function in the mythological mode, which affirms a pregiven origin to be imitated, or it must invent the visibility of the divine (and the divine with it) every time it claims that it makes an image of it. Instead, as Nancy points out: "the work of art is always also a meaning at work beyond the work [*à l'oeuvre au-delà de l'oeuvre*], as well as a work working and opening beyond any meaning that is given or to be given" (*CW* 54/63). Art is, or rather has, the potential of being, the activity of creating the world, as Nancy insists, "immediately, without delay" (*CW* 54/63), because art is the sphere that understands itself (perhaps also because of a certain articulation of creation in monotheism) as work without any pregiven sense, independent of any "goal of mastery (domination, usefulness, appropriation)" (*CW* 54/63).[9] However, this independence of the work of art (here I would maintain the double sense of the expression—as the "piece of art" and the "work," the "labor" of art, which is precisely art's worklessness, its *désoeuvrement*, does not signify or echo a religious beyond or transcendence, insofar as they are also pregiven meaning and independent of the world, nor does it repeat the monotheistic definition of "the absolute" understood as absolute autonomy. Nancy shows that what is at work in art and in monotheism is not the tautology of self-postulation but the logic of creation, the world as coming out of nothing, where "nothing" signifies the modellessness, the without-reason and without-end of the world (*CW* 54/63).

Representation

In his text "Forbidden Representation," published in *The Ground of the Image*, Nancy argues that the forbidding of representation central to some versions of monotheism is not to be understood as belonging to the regime of iconoclasm, nor does it belong to an abstention from images (*GI* 30–31/62–66). Instead, this issue is related to idolatry, not to the image as such. The idol, which is not an image of God but a fabricated god, is valued not for what it represents but for itself insofar as it is considered to be a divine presence (*GI* 30/63–65). By contrast, as Nancy indicates, the monotheistic Jewish God has "no form at all" and therefore "has no image either. He has no resemblance other than that of a man, but this is neither a resemblance of form nor one of content (man is therefore made in the image of that which has no image)" (*GI* 30/64). Therefore, what is forbidden in the Jewish tradition is not the image as being an "image of" but rather the idol, which is attacked not for being an imitation but because it asserts its "full and heavy presence" closed upon itself "where nothing opens (eye, ear, or mouth) and from which nothing departs or withdraws" (*GI* 31/65).

If we follow Nancy, the monotheistic forbidding of representation should not be understood as the result of God's jealousy of other false and fabricated gods, as is stated in the Old Testament, but rather as determined by a crucial element of the monotheist articulation of the notion of god, in particular, as I would suggest following Nancy, by the notion of creation (*CW* 51/55). The suspicion attached to the graven image should be understood as related to its *fabricated* nature, which implies that it is an imitation of something pregiven, a preexisting original. It is precisely this, according to Nancy, that belongs to the mythological mode, to the regime of foundational myth characteristic of polytheism (*CW* 69/91–92). In this sense, the idol viewed from a monotheistic perspective is a result of an invention of a god as the model for the image. In other words, the production of idols is a *fabrication* of gods by man. By contrast, in Nancy's interpretation, within monotheism creation does not have any model: it is the world itself. Seen in this light, the ban on graven images, on the production of idols, is not the result of the visual inaccessibility of God (it would be impossible to have a sensible representation of something that cannot be seen; therefore, all images that are made by human hand will necessarily be false) but of the very structure of creation, which is not carried out by a producer and is without a model.[10] This ban can be interpreted as a moment in which monotheism forbids not the image as such but the fabrication of gods, or production in the mythological mode, according to a foundational myth. In this sense, the forbidding of representation is a decisive moment in the separation of polytheism from monotheism. Monotheist iconoclasm involves a condemnation of images because it presupposes "a certain interpretation of the image as a closed presence . . . opened onto nothing" (*GI* 31/66). Thus the forbidding of the representation of the divine is a result of the rejection of the mythological mode; it can be interpreted as an affirmation of the modellessness of creation.

This condemnation of images in a monotheist context, which is also present, though in a different way, in the Platonic motif of the image as "weak" and "deceitful" because it is a simulation of an absent original (*GI* 31/66), according to Nancy forms an important aspect of our contemporary understanding of art. As he puts it:

> within what has since the Renaissance gradually come to be named "art," what will always have been at stake is the production of images that are exactly the opposite of making idols and exactly the opposite of an impoverishment of the sensory: not a thick and tautological presence before which one prostrates oneself but rather the presentation of an open absence within the given itself . . . of the so-called work of "art." This presentation is called *représentation* in French. Representation is not a simulacrum; it is not the replacement of the original thing—in fact it has nothing to do with a *thing*. It is the presentation of what does not amount to a presence, given and completed. (*GI* 32–33/68)

Representation has absence at its heart. It is opposed to the immediacy of the "being-posed-there" of the idol, and it never simply reproduces a preexisting original. Instead, "it presents what is absent from presence pure and simple" (*GI* 36/74). In order to flesh out this idea, Nancy differentiates between the "absence *of* the thing," which is related to "the problematic of its *re*production" and the "*absense within* the thing," which is related to "the problematic of its (re)presentation" (*GI* 37/75). Representation understood as conditioned by an "absense within" gives way to a notion of an open image, an image that does not represent in a univocal manner.[11] I would call this a self-deconstructive image, an image whose only model is the absence of a model. Such an absence can be understood as a trace of the monotheistic articulation of God, who, according to Nancy's interpretation, is not a model of his creation. On the contrary, he empties himself into his creation (which is "his image," as theology has it) and thus annihilates or deconstructs the difference between creator and creature, or, finally, the very operation of mimesis, the existence of a presupposed model and even the very couple model-representation. In the "Opening" to *Dis-enclosure*, discussing the issue of reason, Nancy emphasizes the need to pose not only the question of the *alter* (the relational other within a couple), but also that of the *allos*, the entirely other (*D* 6/15). Correspondingly, we could affirm the need to discuss a similar issue with regard to the image, to think of it not only in terms of the *alter* as a member of a couple (that of model-image, which is related to the couple creator-creature) but also in terms of an *allos*, as something exceeding that couple. The image, then, is not a result of a mimetic operation, or rather, it is a result of the paradoxical operation of a mimesis of the *allos*, "everyone's other" (*D* 6/15), of an operation of *allo-mimesis*. Art, then, inherits an understanding of the image that is opposed to the mythological mode (it is no longer a reproduction of a pregiven original) and keeps in itself the motif of the without-reason of creation.

Nancy's statement that God, in monotheism, becomes nothing other than "places" (*CW* 69/91) implies that the image, and specifically religious art, is one of the material places that point to his withdrawal.[12] This is a theme that appears in "The Look of the Portrait," where Nancy discusses the effects of the monotheist articulation of God on the image. The art of the icon becomes an art of a negative theology, in other words, an art that presents the absenting of God:

> The icon exposes the invisible; not by rendering it properly visible but by exposing the presence of the invisible, calling thereby for a vision other than that of sight. The invisible God is not simply situated away from our eyes; rather, He is invisible in and for Himself. . . . In truth, the one God is less invisible (in the sense of being hidden) than nonappearing; far from being a matter of making this nonappearance appear (this nonappearance considered as the very act of God, his *modus operandi*, so to speak), it has to be a matter of presenting its presence, which is itself absence. Equally, the iconic figure is not a visage but a face; it exposes the nonappearing face of the whole of the visible. (*M2* 241/67–68)

In Nancy's interpretation, religious art is necessarily defined by a negative moment—its proper subject is the inaccessibility of God and its task, the figuration of that inaccessibility. However, when seen in the light of what I described above, this impossible task is not a result of the invisibility of God; it is determined by his *indivisibility* from the world. If the image claims to represent the divine, it must negate itself or its representational value, according to the traditional understanding of the invisibility of God. However, insofar as it is part of the world, it also presents itself in its *materiality*. In this sense, Nancy will argue that religious art is not religious; the paradox of the representation of the invisible God transforms itself into the self-presentation of the image. This image does not illustrate a sacred subject but is itself sacred, or, as Nancy prefers to name it, "the distinct."

In the context of Nancy's deconstructive project, art and monotheism must be thought as co-original. On the one hand, art—or the image—

gives invisibility to monotheism as a negative and yet, paradoxically, sensible modality of the withdrawal of God. In turn, monotheism gives to art the internal opening toward indefinite sense that results from such a withdrawal. Thus the self-deconstructive, open image is one of the places where religion retreats from religion, and the image itself becomes the material index or mark of that retreat. The singularity of each image (and not only of religious images) or each artistic gesture, or the uniqueness of the work of art, echoes the ex nihilo of creation because it deconstructs the creator-creature and model-image couples. This would be one way of understanding Nancy's thesis that art is at the heart of the self-deconstruction of Christianity (*GI* 139–40n4/15n1). The subsequent development of this idea in Nancy's writings on visual art is closely related to his radical rethinking of the Christian idea of incarnation.

Incarnation

In his essay entitled "*Verbum caro factum*," included in *Dis-enclosure*, Nancy identifies the Christian idea of incarnation, or the formula "by which God makes himself man" (*D* 81/125), as a decisive aspect of the movement of Christianity toward its own deconstruction. As he points out, the term *incarnation* can be understood in two ways. Generally, it can refer to the entering of an incorporeal entity into a body and implies that the body is defined as a place occupied by an invisible soul or spirit. Understood in this way, its meaning can be extended to that of "representation," where the body is defined as a sensible manifestation of a spirit that cannot be represented (*D* 81/125). By contrast, incarnation in the theological sense of the term refers to the idea that God *became*, or rather was *engendered*, as flesh (*D* 81–82/126), resulting in one person with two heterogeneous natures. In this second sense, the Christian body, Nancy argues, is not a material exteriority enveloping a soul but a spirit moving out of itself, out of its "pure identity," in order to "identify itself not even *with* man but *as* man (and woman and matter)" (*D* 82/126). According to Nancy's interpretation, the incarnate God is not a visible representation of an invisible entity but a God whose gesture consists in the alienation of himself or "the emptying out of God" (*D* 83/127). The body then becomes the name of "*a-theos*" (non-God), precisely the opposite of an immediate and self-sufficient presence (like that of the idol; *D* 83/127). As Nancy concludes, "The 'body' of the 'incarnation" is . . . the taking place" of the withdrawal of God (*D* 83/127), in other words, not a representation or imitation that suppose resemblance but a place of the alienation of God from himself: a material presentation of that alteration.

In the context of Nancy's thesis that monotheism is atheism, incarnation can be interpreted as the idea of the final dissolution of God into the world, his "renunciation of divine power and presence" (*D* 36/56). Incarnation, then, places God and humans in a relationship that exceeds the "drama of resemblance" between creator and creature, as set out in Genesis.[13] In this sense, it also exceeds the drama of representation—the creature is not an "image" or a representation of its creator. The creature *is* the model; God *is* human. The body of the incarnation, if Nancy's interpretation can be extended further, is not created *in the image of* God, but in the image of the *absence of a model*. As Nancy points out in *Corpus*, the creator cannot be thought as reproducing his image. Instead, his power resides in the initial deconstruction of any recognizable image, since the created world does not imitate anything but the inimitable. As Nancy phrases it, the body is plastic matter, which spaces out without form and without idea. It is motion, modalization, a coming into presence. The humanity of God, which, according to Nancy, is both "the decisive trait of Christianity" and "a determinative trait for the whole of Western culture" (*D* 81/125), in fact deconstructs the idea of an all-powerful creator that precedes his creation; it indexes the very modellessness of creation.

Within the context of Nancy's project of a deconstruction of Christianity, the body becomes a place of what I can call the operation of *allo-auto*-mimesis. The incarnation can be understood as the *auto*-mimesis of man, who creates God in his own image; but that auto-mimesis implies that God is a man, an *a-theos*. By contrast, incarnation signifies the complete alienation of God from himself. In this sense, it can be understood as a moment of *allo*-mimesis, the paradoxical imitation of something entirely other or inaccessible—as a mimesis of the absence of a model or origin. This should not be understood as a theme coming from negative theology—as a mimesis of the absence *as* origin (or as absent God)—but in a more radical way, to use Nancy's phrase, as a mimesis of "the empty heart of the void itself" (*D* 3/11). The idea of the incarnation, therefore, if we follow Nancy, constitutes a double moment within the self-deconstruction of monotheism. On the one hand, it gives way to the sensible representation of the divine, and, on the other, it makes the image atheistic—the image of God is an image of *a-theos*, or an image of man.

Such a line of thinking resonates strongly with the interpretation of the incarnation and its significance to art given by Georges Didi-Huberman in *Confronting Images: Questioning the Ends of a Certain History of Art*. He argues that, although Christian art can generally be envisaged in the context of mimetic representation, an "imitation inherited from the Greco-Roman world," such notions tend to "ignore their own limitations by blocking access to their own crises."[14] Instead, it is important to consider Christian art within the power of the complex and open sense of incarnation, which implies *alteration* rather than imitation. For Didi-Huberman, incarnation altered the sameness of the transcendent God in order to be able to think the drama of the archiresemblance between God and man, which is a drama that turns around the death of the god-image required by his very incarnation.[15] In his view, incarnational images are *desire-images*, since they constitute a paradigm, a matrix of relationships in which man tries to think himself in the image of his God. In the interpretation of Nancy and Didi-Huberman, there is an overlap between the *allo-* of the monotheist God and the *auto-* of the relationship of humans with themselves. In the case of incarnation, the auto- is the moment of the auto-mimesis (which is in fact allo-mimesis—imitation of the absence of a model) of man, who creates God in his image. And conversely, as Didi-Huberman puts it, incarnation is the moment when man thinks of himself in God's image.

Giving God a body gives way to the visible image by making it possible to represent the divine in the body of a man. However, it also introduces a complication that does not allow the image to be a mere imitation of the God-man, for the representation of God would, in fact, be a representation of a man. As Didi-Huberman points out in *Fra Angelico: Dissemblance and Figuration*, this is the issue of how to distinguish sacred from profane bodies in the image and—in a broader sense—sacred from nonsacred images.[16] The necessity of making such a distinction makes it impossible for the image to remain within the illustrative or figurative mode. In the paintings of Fra Angelico, for instance, the sacred image is distinguished through what Didi-Huberman calls a "zone of relative disfiguration"—a part of the painting that has a referential function but does not represent univocally, always referring to something other than its immediate referent.[17] In *Noli me tangere* (1438–50, fresco, convent of San Marco, Florence), for example, the nearly formless red blotches of paint that represent the stigmata on the feet of Christ are spread over the surface of the meadow, where they represent flowers. Consequently, such a zone consists in a constellation of blotches of paint, which do not have representational value and highlight the materiality of the painting, its presence. With the notion of "the distinct," developed in the opening chapter of *The Ground of the Image*, "The Image—the Distinct," Nancy articulates a similar issue related to how images convey the sacred. By contrast to Didi-Huberman, however, he claims that "the distinct" is an aspect of every image that exceeds representation; it is simultaneously the demonstration of the sacred and the abandonment of the religious mode in the image.

Several aspects of a notion of a self-deconstructive image can be identified in Nancy's essays on the image and visual art. This notion depends upon, or is at the very least developed in parallel with, the project of a deconstruction of monotheism and Christianity. The first of those aspects is the absence posited at the heart of representation. This absence "within the thing," as Nancy puts it, is an effect of the withdrawal of the monotheistic God and of the motif of creation ex nihilo. However, he goes a step further by explicitly arguing that the image exceeds representation, in the sense that the image becomes the very intensity of the material place, the mark, the stigma (*GI* 4/16). If representation is to be understood as a presentation of an open absence that is informed by the motif of the withdrawal of God, then the image, or "the distinct," as he calls it, is related to the Christian motif of a God who withdraws from all religion, a God whose incarnation, becoming a body, in fact marks the disappearance of God, giving way to images. Then the "religious" image figures not a transcendent invisibility but the body of a man and the world as it is. In so doing, it delivers itself in the material intensity of its address, insofar as it is the world itself, without model or origin.

Visitation—Christianity as Painting

Nancy addresses the issue of religious art, and specifically Christian painting, in "Visitation: Of Christian Painting," which appears in *The Ground of the Image*. A central thesis in this essay, which focuses on *Visitation* (1528–29), by Jacopo Pontormo, is that Christian images cannot be reduced to being illustrations of biblical stories and that art cannot be placed in a position of being the medium of a memory: "Art never commemorates. It is not made to preserve a memory" (V 108/9). The painting depicts the scene of Mary visiting her cousin Elizabeth. After receiving the angel of Annunciation, Mary hears that her cousin has become pregnant at an advanced age and goes to visit her. Upon their greeting, Elizabeth's child (John the Baptist) leaps in her womb. From the numerous paintings representing this scene, Nancy chose the second interpretation by Pontormo (in San Michele, Carmignano, Florence). The affectionate embrace between Elizabeth and Mary is staged in bright colors and draped cloth. The two protagonists are duplicated in the figures of two other women, probably their servants, who, by contrast, stare frontally at something outside the scene in a rather melancholic way. This essay is not an art-historical analysis of Pontormo's painting but rather an attempt to conceive the *event* of the painting, which exceeds its narrative aspect (i.e., being a painting about the story of the Visitation of Elizabeth by Mary). Nancy argues that Christian painting is not a representation of a Christian subject. Any image can successfully convey a story, but that does not make it a true instance of Christian art. On the contrary, the more it identifies with the illustrative mode, or the more "pious" it is, the more it is crushed by its subject matter (*GI* 6/20). Instead, Christian painting *is itself* Christianity, "or something of Christianity *in* painting or *as* painting" (V 122/44; my emphasis).

Didi-Huberman makes a similar observation about the paintings of Fra Angelico. His paintings do not claim to be visual translations of Christian stories: that is, they are neither narrative nor illustrative. The painter employs this nonrepresentational strategy to translate in pictorial terms the mystery of the incarnation, which determines the figurative aspect of Christian images—they are almost always corporeal representations. According to Didi-Huberman, Fra Angelico found a way to render the mystery, to locate the properly sacred aspect of his paintings in a network of dissemblances, in the "pictorial poetics of blotches and traces."[18] Precisely this indexical, material, in other words, presentational (and specifically not representational) aspect of his paintings, the "visual and colored intensity" that "sought presence before representation,"[19] is the location of sacred meaning. The enigma of the material presence of the blotch of paint renders the mystery of the incarnation.

As Nancy would add, the enigma of a colored blotch does not stand for anything transcendent; it is the presentation of its own materiality. By breaking out of the representational economy of the painting, it highlights the fact that it has no model and hides no invisibility other than the intensity of its presence. Thus, the religiosity of Fra Angelico's paintings is to be found not in its representational or narrative aspect (in fact, there is no such thing as a religious image for Nancy) but in the way it highlights the materiality of its own presence, presents itself to its beholder, addresses itself by intensifying his or her presence. According to Nancy, "presence is not a form or a consistency of being; it is access" (*M1* 66/114; trans. modified). In other words, an address—an invitation to see, to see the invisible—is "the ordinary demand of painting," but to see it "not beyond the visible, nor inside, nor outside, but right at it, on the threshold, like its very oil, its weave and its pigment" (*M1* 59/106). Painting is thus not reducible to illustration or representation. In fact, Nancy points out that the prefix "*re-* of the word *representation* is not repetitive but intensive" (*GI* 35/73) and that representation is not, in fact, a copy or an illustration but a "presence that is presented, exposed, or exhibited" (*GI* 36/74).

Nancy concludes in "Visitation" that Christian painting indicates what is at stake in Christianity. Insofar as it is a representation of the divine, it actually abandons the religious mode. It announces the withdrawal of the gods, and it is "the atheism of that withdrawal" because it exposes the material place "selfsame with the canvas" (V 123/46), beneath which there is nothing hidden and "no god is waiting except the place itself" (V 123/46). By figuring the imageless god, Christian painting figures the metamorphosis of the invisible divine into the intensity of a place that opens itself to presence; a place that presents itself. The image is, in fact: "the *there* of a *beyond*. It is not at all its 'representation': it is a thinking-there, thinking as the effectivity of a *place opening itself to presence*" (V 125/51). To summarize, Nancy does not give painting a role in something that would *mediate* Christian self-deconstruction. Instead, it is the place, or rather, the event, the taking place of this self-deconstruction. Such a line of analysis is informed by a radical rethinking of the incarnational formula and displaces the properly religious element in what is generally referred to as Christian art. Nancy concludes that "every mode of painting," being incessantly exposed to the withdrawal of God and to "real presence" that "is *par excellence* not present," actually embodies, or shares, the becoming body of God and its aporias (V 123/46). As a result, every image exposes such atheism and incessantly reflects upon the limits of representation and the representation of those limits. By perpetually presenting its *body* to us, it exposes the modelless formula of creation.

The Dis-enclosure of Contemporary Art

An Underpinning Work

FEDERICO FERRARI

But at the same time each thing, in the distance in which its self-coincidence is separated in order to coincide with itself, leaves behind its status as a thing

I would like to let his thoughts run freely on the surface, incoercible, self-evident, without delays. I can only work on the margins, on those points that do not appear, that remain hidden in the cellar, where the pillars of the foundations start. There is nothing else to do but leave everything as is, to take up everything, once again and endlessly, but underpinning (*en sous-oeuvre*). In these few sentences that I will allow to rise on the surface, on my skin, on the outside and at the edge of my thoughts, there where everything seems clear and complete, the sense that Jean-Luc Nancy attributes to the image and to (contemporary) art, in their relation to a self-deconstruction of Christianity, will become manifest, condensed in a kind of living architecture. In more general terms, one could find a key to interpret Nancy's entire work where the double movement between presence and absence (with all its corollaries: inside/outside, intimacy/exposure, sense/meaning, body/soul, death/resurrection, etc.) is happily resolved. What is exposed is the very method of Nancy's thinking, a singular dialectical movement that appears disorienting because of the apodictic power of the reasoning that seems to break into splinters rather than to lead toward a concrete definition of Hegel's philosophy, the great school of thought in which Nancy was schooled.

and becomes an intimacy. It is no longer manipulable. It is neither body, nor tool, nor god. It is outside the world, since in itself it is the intensity of a

The movement of Nancy's philosophy is all in the distance or, better yet, in the distancing of the distance that, in this specific case, the distinct of the image preserves in its essence. Nancy's world resides in this distancing of the thing from itself, this becoming other in order to become what it is. To put it otherwise, it is the movement that every presence performs to become real, to access its own reality or, to put it still another way, to access the sense of its own being here. This movement, however, is never definitively completed, or better yet, its completion is its resumption to infinity: the aim of existence is this ending in an outburst of the infinite (*éclat d'infini*) that does not conclude and cannot be concluded but finds in this impossibility, in this suspension or exemption of sense, in this event that cannot be explained and does not require explanation, its true conclusion.

Nancy's thought is a dizzy movement and yet very real and truly exposed to the dimension of an experience of sense that goes beyond any system of codified meanings that would be ready to use. His way of proceeding is manual, preindustrial. It is a thought that moves by stops and starts (attempts and corrections), by *tâtonnements*. It is closer to the craftsman, with all the ramblings and inaccuracies that this entails, than to the technician intent on finding a repeatable formula applicable to the widest possible cases. It would be impossible to derive a software program to implement it. At best, one can observe how he works, but even then there is nothing to do but watch and then continue on one's way. The only thing that happens, if something does happen, is a kind of passion of the senses in the most complete exemption of meanings. (This disposition of openness toward the other, which comes when we least expect it, is perhaps the furthest thing from *caritas*. This attitude of openness to what comes from outside, from the alterity of absent sense that is the divine in its manifold forms, comes to disturb the empty stronghold of the ego gloating over its own certainties. Expectations of love that gives *a* sense to the loneliness of existence.)

Let's begin to work down there, at the basal underpinning (*en sous-oeuvre*), in the cellars of thought. In fact, it is a question of getting ready to penetrate what is apparently impenetrable: the surface, the skin of images. In order to try to understand Nancy's thinking about images, one must investigate how it is possible that the most profound intimacy shows on the very surface of the image. This is a difficult knot to untangle, since, *concentration of world. It is also outside language, since in itself it is the assembling of a sense without signification. The image suspends the course of*

in some ways, the image is precisely the place where intimacy is right at (*à même*) the skin. The place where sense seems no longer to refer to anything but to expose itself in its utter nudity. It is as if the thing in the image, in taking its distance, finally becomes visible. In the everyday, that very thing that would remain hidden from its use function. It is by exposing itself as inoperative (*désoeuvrée*) on the surface of the image that the thing can capture its own intimacy. The inactive character of the image, its not taking part in what has an immediate function or possibility of use, is what renders the image closer to the sacred object, to what is deprived of its worldly qualities in order to be offered to the glance in the empty space that surrounds it. Here overlap all the themes of the sacred, the inoperative (*désoeuvrement*), and the offering (*offrande*), from Bataille, Blanchot, and Nancy, in a series of deferrals and distortions. What is fundamental for us is that this phenomenology of the sacred finds in the image, as Christianity conceived it, a point of contact that informs the entire Western tradition as we now know it. Yet one must still think through what happens to the image when it becomes a new object of use in a society of mass communication. Here let us move on to the issue of the end of the self-deconstruction of Christianity, when not only would the divine become world but the whole world become a commodity. Let us proceed one step at a time.

In the image is concentrated the sense of the real, but not in the sense that in the image there is *more* reality. In fact, in a certain sense the image lacks the real, since the real always breaks the image, as it breaks any imagination (as Lacan would say). But the image is a resemblance (*ressemblement*) of sense. The image opens up the possibility of a sense of the world that is "outside" the world. This formula, apparently senseless or aporetic, is the heart of the theme of the image and its relation to a self-deconstruction of Christianity. In fact, this is what remains to be thought: a totally worldly sense that, however, is and must remain at the same time outside the world, just as Christ is God become man who, even though part of the world, does not belong to it. The image, like Christ, opens a distance between the world and itself. So, just as the image withdraws (*s'écarte*) from the world, creating a distance between itself and the world, in this way allowing the unseen of the world to be seen, so Christ designates the possibility of an existence and a sense that are not in another world but in a space and a time, in the rhythm of a

the world and of meaning—of meaning as a course or current of sense
(meaning in discourse, meaning that is current and valid): but it affirms all

space-time that is different and differs from the world of things. The image is the sign of a coming apart or of an always possible opening in the real. It is as if it indicated from always and for always that the world, the thing, is never completely present to itself but has within itself a gap or a distance consigning it to an excess that is neither visible nor traceable. The work of art is the index of this impossibility, this impossibility of closing the sense of the thing, of the world, in its representation, whatever that may be. There is no absolute glance capable of attributing an identity to the thing. There is only a glance capable of rendering to the thing its internal distance, its constitutive side, or, to put it another way, its difference. In this, every image is not only of the order of the sacred, that is, something distinct from the real, as Nancy writes, but an index of the intimate and essential distance that every thing has in itself, that is, an index of God, an icon. This does not mean that every image is religious or, even less, pious, but that it is the tangible sign of an unbridgeable excess, an opening of sense without end, beyond any signifying system and identification; and that in the Western tradition this opening has acquired the name of God. In the ground of the image there is nothing to see except the groundless opening of sight that every time is astonished anew by the infinite coming of the world (of God) to itself.

The image, like Christianity, creates a suspension of the world and in so doing gives the world a sense that cannot be reduced to any meaning. No image finds a definitive meaning, and none can say the meaning of the world. There is no name for the image, just as there is no Name for God, after the coming of Christ. So, just as the image is the real that takes a distance from itself, the Christian God is nothing other than the world, which distances itself from itself to become that which it is. But just as there is nothing beyond the surface of the image (there is no reality truer or more profound), so there is no divine world beyond the surface of God. In a certain way, one could say that God is the skin of the world, whereas the world shows itself and allows itself to be touched by preserving the sense of things. God is the world or, better, the becoming world of God coincides with the becoming world of the world. God is, after all, the guarantor without guarantee that the world will never coincide with itself in any possible *Weltanschauung*. God is the guarantor without guarantee *the more a sense (therefore an "insensible") that is* selfsame *with what it gives to be sensed (that is, itself). In the image, which, however, is without an*

---

who announces to every man and every woman, whatever his or her condition, nature, or age, that this possibility of sense will be preserved intact for him or her until the end of time. Everyone will be called to account for the sense of the world, to give it a sense or to receive it from the world.

Faith in God is nothing other than faith in this miracle of sense, in this multiplication, even when everything appears to be already said and decided. Whoever believes in God inhabits that unstable surface where the world seems to disappear in the distance which that opens within it. Whoever has faith does not care any longer for the things of the world, as if they were everything, because he is kept in the distance. It is in the void of the distance, in the nothing of world that it creates and from which it creates, that the world of whoever has faith appears. In this sense, the self-deconstruction of sense that Christianity acts out, with the resulting destruction of all given values, is also an attempt to escape a nihilism that it has itself brought into evidence. Nihilism is, after all, caused and "overcome" by Christianity, even though, obviously, it is a question of agreeing on the term *overcome*, since it would seem that Christianity is not really capable of overcoming nihilism—being based on a continuous subversion of meanings to the advantage of an opening of sense—but rather poses the problem of a "creative nihilism," that is, of a nihilism that, rather than just placing emphasis on the destructive phase of given values, concentrates on the mystery of a continuous creation ex nihilo, of the sense of the world (something that Nietzsche had understood, speaking of an active nihilism). The self-deconstruction of Christianity is the movement of an active deconstruction, toward which Nancy pushes the last phase of Derrida's deconstruction, for which many times—very often unfairly—he has been reproached, as if in the deconstructive movement the insistence on the de-privative were too strong and the movement of re-edification too weak.

The description of the self-deconstruction of Christianity performed by Nancy is, therefore, in the end, the most profound experience of a gesture of openness or, better, of disclosure, a gesture that opens and closes at the same time: dis-enclosure (*la déclosion*). This gesture coincides, in turn, with the theme of a radical experience of freedom. After all, in the speech of the Grand Inquisitor Dostoevsky already brilliantly characterizes how the essence of Christianity can be found in a new experience of freedom, completely severed from any principles of authority and *"inside," there is a sense that is nonsignifying but not insignificant, a sense that is as certain as its force (its form).*

therefore always in precarious balance, in a tense oscillation of choice between the good and the "anything goes" of an all-out nihilism. Christianity is the great destroyer of every given foundation, and it is therefore the sign of the end of a world and the opening of a space without boundaries, where the free choice of a possibility of life is enforced. Christianity is in itself the critical movement of its self-dissolution, where the dissolution, however, is its greatest fulfillment: "Who has found his life will lose it, and he who has lost his life because of me will find it" (Matthew 10:39).

Even in this brief summary of Nancy's work, it is clear how his entire discourse is obsessed with a kind of clarification of this self-deconstructive element of Christianity, which, spreading in every direction, leads toward a necessary "secularization" (perhaps it would be best to say "mundanization," understood as a becoming world) of all theological and religious foundations. In short, it is as if Nancy were trying to prove that the West, even in its nihilistic results, is essentially Christian. There is no opposition, therefore, between a Christian West based on values (the current discourse of the neo-religious Vulgate) and a nihilist West that has lost these values by entering into an age beyond or outside of value. The root of the historical movement of the West, of its phenomenology, would be the same; in fact, it is the same inevitable movement that from the appearance of the man-god and his death leads to an all- out nihilism. So nihilism *is* still Christianity, provided that it is clear that Christianity has always been the dissolution of itself, that is, that Christianity *is* nihilism, the experience of nothing as the source of creation, that is, no longer the search for a creator outside the real but the vision of the real itself as a creative act starting from nothing. If this is the case, then one can and should say that Nancy has always remained a Christian thinker, that is, a nihilist. Therefore, he is not a critic of Christianity but a Christian thinker tout court. Starting from this consideration, we can return to the issue of the image with the knowledge that, from whatever side one approaches it, the work of Nancy speaks of only one thing: the self-deconstruction of Christianity.

༄

What has always struck me in the way Nancy confronts the subject of the image, and of art more generally, is the lucidity with which he grasps its

One could say that the image—neither world nor language—is a "real
presence," if we recall the Christian use of this expression: the "real presence"

shift from tradition to the present, whose results are so difficult to interpret when one tries to avoid a simple or historicist reading of the phenomenon of contemporary art. Nancy's inquiry is particularly useful in
providing an instrument to interpret the temporal movement of art, its
shifting in time starting from a certain immobility in space. If, in fact, the
theme of the "thing," of "real presence," to which the work of art refers,
in its minimal shift between sacred space and profane space, from which
derives its necessity to stand at a distance, to create a distance and a distinction between these two spaces, is central to Nancy's interpretation of
art and its relation to the deconstruction of Christianity, equally important, even if less investigated, is the question of the temporality of art,
which opens up the entire question of the complex relation between art's
"ambition for eternity" and its always-renewed contemporaneity, con-
signed to the finitude of any existence. What strikes one in the deconstructive gesture that Nancy applies to art is its capacity to open up a
different temporal dimension of artistic practice, while remaining firmly
anchored to the temporality of today. Nancy thinks and makes one think
the *cum* that unites all time, as if, as in his singular plural ontology, simultaneity and contemporaneity of time were somehow co-originary with the
singularity of an age. There is art today because the time of art is always
contemporary with any age.

But in order to discover Nancy at the bottom of contemporaneity, to
somehow take up his gesture, let us start with some simple questions.
What does art refer to today? Of which time does art speak today? With
which time contemporary art is in tune? In relation to what time would
or should artistic practice be contemporary? In relation to the time of the
tradition of its own discipline or to the time of the world, to the contingency of today? And what relation is established between the time of the
Western Christian tradition of art and its nihilistic ending, present *in nuce*
in the historical avant-gardes and today completely disclosed? What marks
the temporal dis-enclosure of contemporary art?

These questions cannot be answered without a long digression concerning the reality of what today we call contemporary art, its supposed
closure, agony, and death, and its equally imaginary origin, gestation, and
rebirth. Let us try, therefore, to sketch a temporal topography of the dis-
enclosure of contemporary art, one in which we can maneuver, remaining
well aware that, to forge a good map, we should view the territory from

is precisely not the ordinary presence of the real referred to here: it is not the
god present in the world as finding himself there. This presence is a sacred

on high, should position ourselves outside it, as if from an airplane or a satellite. But unfortunately, as we know, we humans cannot step outside of time. We can only steer a course very close to what we observe.

A first map would show a contemporaneity characterized by a phenomenon of decadence. The world of art is said to be experiencing a relentless decadence; the whole system is said by now to be devoured by the market or by a more tenuous, and for this reason dangerous, reproduction of the always-identical in a multiplication of clichés dictated by the hyper-simplified rules of fashion and by a globalization that lowers the level of (the practice of) taste. Of course, it would not be hard to demonstrate these hypotheses. Everyone can observe how the "world of art" is reproduced to infinity on a single matrix, in which are indissolubly interwoven market, jet set, worldliness, and critical flimsiness. This is the world of exhibitions of new artists "sponsored" by collectors and galleries (in the sense that collectors and galleries pay museums for the shows and they, in turn, build their programs on the bases of market "funding"). It is the world of curators who act as critics and critics who act as curators, in an absurd short circuit where those who should account for the quality of exhibitions are called upon to mount them, in a sort of double blackmail or consortionalism between programmers and critics: "I call you to mount a show, so you will write well of what I will program in the future; I write well of what you program, so you will call me to mount a show." It is also the way of mega-exhibitions, of the great anthological exhibitions identical in every part of the globe, where changes resemble the restyling of big-brand automobiles. It is the glamorous and superficial world of an international elite that no longer feels the need to discover, to understand, and therefore either *to be* in the excitement of artistic creation or *to have* the means to understand it, but simply itches to appear in vogue (*à la page*). The contemporary, therefore, would be the place of this decadence, of this loss of the vital tension of art, of its anarchic experimentation, deprived of any ties. And as a result, ours is also a time of critical inaction, of the relentless decline of a real and strong critical dimension, and of its imminent death. Ours is an age, therefore, not very different from the end of Antiquity, a late empire that spins on itself, blind to its own destiny.

Within this devastated and devastating scenery there are, at the margins, some pockets of resistance, some survivors of an almost disappearing tradition who preserve tenaciously and almost in a concealed and esoteric *intimacy that a fragment of matter gives to be taken in and absorbed. It is a real presence because it is a contagious presence, participating and participated,*

way the light of a possible future resurrection or rebirth of art. Some artists and some critics—*certains*, as Huysmans wrote in 1889 with respect to his own contemporary art—are lying in wait at the edge of time (some steeped in resentment, some indifferent to everything), waiting for new times or, in a messianic spirit, for the time to come. For the time being, it would only be a matter of resisting the garbage and nonsense that rules the present, and of providing, at the same time, evidence of another art, the tradition of art, the true art, one that goes beyond the temporal threshold and reconnects to a unique time, motionless but changing, an immutable substance in the mutability of forms.

In a hypothetical second map, we would instead see the profile of a time that would allow the emergence of something new, an art finally free of the obsession with a transcendental or social mission in the widest and strongest sense. Art, by making the experience of non-sense its own, as already indicated by the historical avant-gardes (Dada above all), and by reelaborating it to infinity, would plunge into the midst of our time, taking on and representing all possible contradictions. Thus we would have before us an art in which the playful, the ironic, the technological, the alternate, and the engaged were merged, without any possibility of continuity—an art, therefore, that tried in every way to get rid of a tradition that is too burdensome and by now completely inadequate to interpret the time to come. To be sure, there would still persist citadels of latecomers nostalgic for an art that is anachronistic, if not pompous, but soon all this—all the ideological, aesthetic, and generational resistance that prevent a full affirmation of the "art of today"—would be swept away by a new that advances, relentless, in the direction of history. Without any regrets for "high" art, which looks either backward to tradition or forward to eternity, the art of today, "accomplice of the contemporary" (as Saul Steinberg has remarked), tied to the reality of facts, would be an art of contingency, of the ephemeral and the impermanent, because this would be the time in which it lived.

Unlike the avant-gardes, today's art would seek not to move forward but to jog in place: it would make use of today's fragmented and quantum time in order to be totally present, totally glued and, in its view, adequate to what is happening. An art, therefore, that does not want to be "pure" but is in fact bastard and hybrid, not afraid of being confused with the

communicating and communicated in the distinction of its intimacy.
That is in fact why the Christian God, and particularly the Catholic God,

---

market, with the post-pop, with pornography, or with a spectacular ideology. Within what the great market of the globalized world, nihilist and relativist, has to offer, its boundaries are unstable, its forms changing and elusive. In short, on closer examination, this second map is equivalent to the first one: it would suffice merely to turn it upside down for us immediately to realize this. The high and the low would have changed places, but, in a play of mirrors, each would lay claim to the center and to the superiority of its point of view.

But there exists a third way. In our time, two different practices coexist that, by a strange irony of history, share the same name: that of *art*. These two practices appear to be similar, or at least assimilable to one another, because they share the same social and cultural space. But they are in fact radically different. If they were not, all dichotomies between decadence and the persistence of a true tradition or between senescence and irruption of the new would fail. Two different entities are not comparable: a pear is not the decadence of an apple, and an apple is not the new with respect to the inadequacy of the pear. So, one can only speak of a system of homonyms, in which coexist an art that follows the dictates and the ideal drives of an ancient tradition and an art (which we would rather define with an *X*) that would be structured according to rules and demands completely unprecedented in the history of humanity, such as communication, marketing, the globalized marked, the dissolution of taste, and the fragmentation of cultures. The end and the new beginning would not coincide, but they would express two different worlds, world that are by now irreconcilable, divided by a deep hiatus, by a genetic gap inevitable and revolutionary.

Contemporaneity, therefore, would be an age entirely unprecedented in the history of art, an age in which two similar but different modalities of dealing with the field of representation co-exist, more or less pacifically: on the one hand, art; on the other, one of its genetic modifications whose boundaries and evolutionary limits still remain to be investigated. None can foresee yet whether the two organisms will be able to live together for long, even if, as often happens, it is legitimate to suspect that the mutating structure will crush the original one, taking over the entire scene, unless the finalities of the two organisms reveal and manifest themselves to be radically different.

Obviously these are only some of the possible scenarios through which we can view the controversial phenomenon of the contemporary. What remains alive in every one of us is the impression of an artistic and theoretical unrest of great wealth and variety, where the contemporary seems characterized not by temporal continuity but by a series of fractures and short circuits from which burst forth heterogeneous if not conflictual temporalities. Our age would seem to emerge, indeed, as one in which time explodes in all directions. In a certain sense, therefore, it would be—as Nancy has made clear here and there—an age of the world whose resonances with the Rome of the fifth century are not entirely nonsensical. In fact, we live in a time similar to when the "pagans" were slowly acquiring an awareness of change, of an obscure change in everything that up until then had supported their civilization, but, at the same time, an age in which the "Christians" still had no idea of the history that Christianity would have opened up, well beyond any imminent apocalypse.

Both were living at the crest of an age: for the pagans it was the end; for the Christians, the beginning. The maps that we have outlined point exactly to this situation of uncertainty, always in a precarious balance between beginning and end, epilogue and origin of something totally unprecedented. Basically, now as then, we are living a dizzy experience of time, but our time travels at a speed incommensurably faster, and for this reason our time is not completely comparable to the temporal fluctuations of the past. In fact, it would suffice to increase the unit of measure of time, for instance, from years to centuries, and we would see that the acceleration taking place is without precedent in history.

But then, going back to our initial questions, to which time does contemporary art point? Of what is it indicative, in a still mysterious way?

Perhaps we can find a possible answer, once again, in terminology that Heidegger employed to indicate the coming of the last god: art is a *Wink*, a sign that has no fixed interpretative code, a sign that must be interpreted anew every time. But above all, it must be recognized as a sign. Like contemporary art, the last god (who, after all, is nothing other what remains of the divine at the end of its process of self-deconstruction) asks to be recognized beyond any model or pattern, ritual or preestablished symbol, just as in the age of unfolding secularization, of the deafening silence of God, a sign appears that points to the last god, so contemporary art emerges as an incessant and exhausting attempt at a practice that tries to

own absence, since he is no longer anything but the passion of the intimate and
*the intimacy of suffering [*du pâtir*] or of feeling and sensation: what every*

---

define itself as such, especially when the very sense of the word *art* seems swallowed up by the prevailing nothing and its deafening communication. To put it another way, the sign of art refers to a bottom without bottom where the gesture of creation is to fish by casting a line into nothing. Art is the sign of an origin founded on nothing and seems destined to disappear and to be regenerated in this nothing forever. It is a practice without foundation, save for its original nothing and its obstinate will to create its sense out of that nothing. Once again, at the end of the self-deconstruction of all Western categories emerges, brought to an extreme, the original theme of all monotheisms: creation ex nihilo. Art today points to this creation of world sunk in the most absolute nihilism, in a total loss of celestial bodies and in the void of a mute heaven. It is an art of disaster and of an opening without end, but also an art of an original time that endlessly regenerates itself, in the impossibility of grasping its own beginning and end.

Thus, when Francis Picabia in 1920 dropped the famous spot of ink on a white page and gave it the title *The Holy Virgin*, he somehow performed a radical experience of disaster and opening, of the dis-enclosure of the system of representation of the Christian West and its self-deconstruction, which has lasted two thousand years. That is, he did not perform a blasphemous or provocative act but showed the nihilistic outcome of the Western (i.e., Christian) representational system. Representation has no longer any possible meaning, failing, in an apparently definitive way, any (divine) design, any rule and preestablished canon. What is left is the risk of a formless ink spot that makes any "virginity" of the sheet, any semantic purity, impossible. There is no longer a pattern, that is, a coded structure of available meanings, and not even the possibility of pure absence. But something is there: a spot that is exactly what it is in its distance from itself. For Picabia, post-Dada and a nihilist, this "something" points in the direction of chance—we shift from the non-sense of representation (after the emergence, always more unavoidable, of the nihilistic character of the Platonic-Christian West) to the representation of non-sense. Today, Nancy's work similarly leaves us to think (and to show) the sense of non-sense, that is, the sense of a world that seems no longer to have any sense or direction but that in this non-sense finds the deepest experience of sense: the sense of nihilism, the creation of an unjustifiable sense starting from nothing.

thing gives to be sensed insofar as it is what it is, the thing itself distinguished in its sameness.

Contemporary time, this fragile and unstable time that is left at the end of the self-deconstruction of Christianity and the West, takes shape not as a place of certainties in which to become rooted but as an enormous lab, in which forms of life and unprecedented temporal forms appear and disappear at a speed never before experienced by art and, more generally, by mankind. The acceleration of time and its duration seem to modify qualitatively the very notion of the contemporary. Contemporaneity is so fast and ephemeral that it undermines the very concept of time. In this situation of uncertainty, in this space where time seems to have acquired an infinitesimal unit of measure, where all the present seems to be concentrated in the moment, the diaphanous light of another and immobile temporality can appear, like lightning. No longer an elsewhere, a lost past or a future utopia, but a *hic et nunc* so punctual it smashes, in a dazzling short circuit, all temporal dimensions. This lightning, this excess of light liberated, concentrated in an infinitesimal point, on the changing surface of a work of art, unstable and perishable, is perhaps not yet discernible by our glance, accustomed to different chiaroscuros and different speeds. It will be necessary, perhaps, for another glance and another perceptual dimension to really be able to grasp the diaphanous light that is dawning. Perhaps then, in a somersault of the instant in on itself, art will appear sub specie aeternitatis, thus taking on its own untransferable heredity and regaining possession of its own elusive destiny. Or, to put it another way, art will be in the end—in the time of the end that is also the end of time—the sign of nothing or the exposed intimacy of "what every thing gives to be sensed insofar as it is what it is, the thing itself distinguished in its sameness."

—Translated by Massimo Verdicchio

On Dis-enclosure and Its Gesture, Adoration

A Concluding Dialogue with Jean-Luc Nancy

JEAN-LUC NANCY AND THE EDITORS

After reading the manuscript of *Re-treating Religion*, Jean-Luc Nancy proposed responding in the form of a dialogue about the central issues, problems, and perspectives of a deconstruction of Christianity and monotheism more generally. This conversation took place at his house in Strasbourg on June 27, 2009. At that time, Nancy was working on *Adoration*, the second volume of his *Deconstruction of Christianity*, which appeared in spring 2010. As a result, this dialogue not only deals with the general topics of Nancy's project but also creates a bridge from *Dis-enclosure* to the new book. On its back cover, Nancy expresses the development of thought between the two as follows: "If the word *dis-enclosure* [*déclosion*] indicates the necessity of opening reason up to a dimension that is not 'religious,' but that transcends reason itself . . ., *adoration* tries to name the gesture of this dis-enclosed reason."

On Religion: Its Retreat and Its Philosophical Re-treatment

THE EDITORS: Before we enter our dialogue concerning the basic issues and problems of a deconstruction of Christianity and of monotheism in general, may we concentrate for a moment on the word *religion* itself, as it appears in the title of this book, *Re-treating Religion*?

JEAN-LUC NANCY: Thank you. My first remark about that is a general one, concerning the very fact of discussing religion. If we "re-treat" religion [*la religion*], even in its retreat, what are we actually doing? What is "the" religion that is in retreat, and who is asking us to "re-treat" it? If by "religion" we mean a connection to certain observances, according to the etymology of *religio* as the strict observance of rites, as a link to the foundational myths upon which these rites are based, and as the experience that everything should be brought back to God or to the gods—then no, that is not what I am talking about. I am talking about prayer, but I am not suggesting that we pray. For me, it comes down to a question that is the flip side of deconstruction: Do we still need to retain the name of God? This is a recurring question, which many people ask in reaction to my publications on the deconstruction of Christianity, and it will come up in your questions today.

So, on the one hand, there is religion as reference to the gods, and on the other, there is a whole group of practices and observances that exist in society, even in a "dechristianized" society, or one in which religion has been lost. We must understand that there is a category of people in contemporary society who need the "reassurance" of religious practices such as baptism, marriage, or burial, for example.

When we speak of civil religion, as Régis Debray and many others in France do at the moment, we lament the fact that the Republic does not have its own celebrations and ceremonies, not even baptism. About twenty-five years ago, when Strasbourg was a socialist municipality, they devised a socialist baptism. I never saw one, but a ceremony was created, which took place at the town hall. It wasn't a resounding success; I don't think many people took their children . . . I'm not talking about civil religion in a practical sense, as a particular ritual organization.

In a general sense, I don't think that religions or rituals—civil or noncivil—can be invented. They are a product of mores and customs. They develop in the course of history, and they break down in the same way. The creation of rituals for reassurance, in order to forge a set of boundaries, is inevitably destined to fail.

AUKJE VAN ROODEN: In the introduction that we wrote for this book, we avoided placing too much emphasis on the religious, postreligious, or prereligious element of your work on the deconstruction of monotheistic religions, and we chose instead to underline its philosophical dimension. Your project is from the outset a philosophical venture that touches upon certain aspects of what we understand by "religion."

J-LN: OK, I agree. But at the same time my project is also—by contrast to a purely theoretical or speculative philosophical project—a project that has a certain practical element or impact. If I were to be asked, "You say much about God, about faith . . . about religion—does anything of religion itself remain for you, anything to be 're-treated'?" I don't know how I would reply. It's a question that I haven't tackled myself.

But I know that the question does arise. If my project is neither about rituals nor a speculative exercise for intellectuals, what is it? First of all, I seek to convey an attitude, a spiritual attitude: yes, we are open to the infinite. Let's say it, let's show it. It's palpable, it's not just "words."

LAURENS TEN KATE: Would you say that you prefer to speak about monotheism or Christianity rather than religion?

J-LN: Yes, yes.

LTK: But reopening monotheism is not the same as reopening religion.

J-LN: That's true. But when we call monotheism, and in particular Christianity, "the religion of departure from religion"[1] as Marcel Gauchet does, what kind of religion are we talking about? Is there a religion from which we have departed? Then there is the religion *of* departure, and what do we do with that? That's the problem with talking about religion: What concept of religion are we talking about?

LTK: So, to add an observation to what you suggest here, we could say, for example, that Christianity as the religion of departure from religion is exactly the religion that makes it possible for people in the twenty-first century to baptize their children without believing, which means that they can perform a ritual such as baptism in a way that is devoid of content, without a framework or without reference to any transcendence. And yet this gesture still has a certain, quite strong sense. You could say that Christianity is exactly that, that its "persistence" in our time implies that people can be very strongly attached to this religious fabric, which is, as you described it earlier, reassuring, while being 100 percent secular.

J-LN: Yes, that's true. But by that token we might wonder whether Christianity hasn't always been more or less removed from ritual. I often refer to Meister Eckhart, for example, and his definition of prayer as an act that unburdens us of God, even as we pray *to* God. But a whole, broad tradition showcases this distance from ritual, which is perhaps the self-deconstruction of religious ritual.

In my opinion, the observation of religious rituals is important because they provide a sort of security and assurance. Here, I think we are onto something very important: this is where monotheism comes in, that is, the religion that departs from the world of instrumental rituals allegedly leading to "something" good, instead opening a space for rituals that is abstract and "without content." In this scenario, we depart from the world of rites, which was characterized by assurance, by a certain security, by a number of advantages, as were the religions of antiquity. In that world, sacrifices were made to the gods, at their request, in order that the harvest be good, in order to win a war, and so on. Nowadays, we must look to ourselves for help. We look to ourselves and not to rituals, no more than we look to vague, exalted feelings, such as those exhibited by certain "new-born" or "charismatic" believers. No, we ourselves "are" the charisma, in our humanity, in our technics [*technique*], in our simple existence.

Today especially, the three monotheisms are exhibiting a notable rigidification of rites as abstract rites, in addition to a certain reduction to those rites. Muslim, Christian, and Jewish fundamentalists aren't necessarily the only examples of this; there is a whole varied tradition of piety, of observance, of spirituality, even of asceticism in which the ritual act becomes the center of the religion. It concerns people who, *in* or *beyond* this rigidification of ritual, have, at the same time—and perhaps only in exceptional moments—a thought, a reflection, a spiritual connection to what I call the opening in the world, which doesn't belong to the world. This is certainly an ambiguity: the violent reduction to empty rites sits alongside this dis-enclosure, this relationship that opens an outside the world in the world. This is a bit like the ambiguity that Kant explored: I can never say whether an action is performed out of duty; I can never say whether an action is ever performed truly in faith or from pure observance.

But in any case, I think that it touches upon a very important point in the rupture that monotheism represents with all that is called religion everywhere else, in all other cultures of the world. I think that Jan Assmann's recent book *Violence and Monotheism* points in this direction.[2] It is first and foremost a book attacking fundamentalists. However, at the heart of his analysis, Assmann says succinctly something that I really like, because it echoes exactly what I like to say about the fact that Christianity installs a separation between the two kingdoms: the City of God and the City of the World. Assmann writes that the whole monotheistic tradition rests upon this, upon the desire to shield men from the domination of men. Ultimately, this means that all monotheism is rooted in the separation between religion and politics. This is why, according to Assmann, monotheistic religions are religions that affect one's whole life, which is to say that, in monotheism, rituals are necessarily surpassed. There is a need to perform them, but there is also a need to lead, for example, a Christian life. This separation of the secular and temporal from the religious differs between and even *within* the three monotheisms. It shows itself in varying ways, to various degrees, and sometimes, as in some influential currents of contemporary Islam, this separation is less clear. I think that within monotheism, even in Catholicism, the spirit has never been limited to religious ritual but is the spirit of a life that "lives" this division.

The Deconstruction of Christianity: Its Philosophical Sense and Relevance

IGNAAS DEVISCH: We would now like to turn our attention to a question that has preoccupied us intensely: the "status" or, if you like, the sense of your project.

While reading *Dis-enclosure*, we thought a great deal about the necessity of this book. The stakes of the book, if we understand it correctly, are to show that Christianity has "prepared," if one can say that, the gesture of deconstruction. If Christianity means "living in this world as outside of it" (*D* 10/21), it has tilled the ground for deconstruction. Have these stakes not, in an analogous way, already been clarified by the act of deconstruction itself? Doesn't your entire oeuvre bear witness to this fact? Why, then, repeat this philosophical gesture with the deconstruction of Christianity if nothing new is at stake, if the outcome is more or less comparable—that is, clarifying the way in which the world does not have one meaning [*sens*], but that it *is* sense and thus that we are faced with existing [*nous avons à exister*] and that this means not being immanent. What does the deconstruction of Christianity allow us to understand that philosophy has not been able to show?

J-LN: That's an extremely fair question. It could be answered but . . . It's a point that demonstrates itself, as it were, via philosophy itself, which is self-dis-enclosing.

ID: Perhaps not less useful than all philosophy, of course . . .

J-LN: Yes, but one still has to remember why this motif is being introduced here. I must reply to that in several directions. The first is perhaps a somewhat retrospective or anamnestic direction, interior to philosophy: for example, concerning all that might surround the theme of sense. However, increasingly it seems to me that this very movement, which is interior to philosophy, proceeds from a certain impetus that comes from Christianity.

What is Christianity? According to Heidegger, it is an aggravating episode of metaphysics (of the "metaphysics of presence," that is, of beings [*l'étant*] without Being [*l'être*]). But Heidegger himself, as we know, began by working on the phenomenology of religion, by reading Saint Paul, and I think that there are many Christian and Jewish motifs to be found there, as Marlène Zarader shows in her books on Heidegger.[3] What is hidden behind all this?

If we go back to what lies behind the world of Heidegger, we find Nietzsche. A great debate with Christianity runs through the entirety of Nietzsche, but there is something complicated about his involvement in this debate: that is to say, in effect, Nietzsche treats Christianity for the most part precisely as metaphysical, as an institution of pure morals and of ressentiment. But there remains 1 percent of Nietzsche in which he shows himself to be the best Christian imaginable. He is the one who, in *The Antichrist*, says: "There was only one Christian, and he died on the Cross";[4] he presents Christ as a "Free Spirit," renouncing the dogmas that form his own doctrine.[5] With Nietzsche there is already a hint of your question, when at the end of the aphorism on the death of God, he says: "God is dead, we have killed him . . . but what sacred games shall we have to invent?" Nietzsche's big question has always been: What is coming next? And what's more, how are we to understand "sacred games" if not by the word *ritual*?

If we go back even further in the history of philosophy, we come to Hegel. The whole of the Hegelian dialectic system is a sort of secularization, if you like, of the Christian model, of Christianity itself already interpreted, but interpreted philosophically, because Christianity is what lent itself to philosophical interpretation. It also has a philosophical origin. The entirety of Hegel's work says this: the infinite is in the finite.

And if we go back further, before Hegel, there is Kant and his formula of a "religion within the boundaries of mere reason." This expression, the title of his famous book of 1793, is what arises when the ontological proof of God—the first death of the metaphysical God—is brought to light. But Kant's book opens something that has never really been taken up again by philosophy: the idea of a rational and modern religion. This brings us back to the discussion about our use of the word *religion*, where there is a great deal of hesitation between a usage denoting an ensemble of rituals and something more vague that is the very idea of a relationship with a God, a relationship that leaves ritual devoid of meaning and of concrete effectivity. In *Religion Within the Boundaries of Mere Reason*,

Kant expresses the idea that it is not enough to be a philosopher. There must also be a kind of religious institution [*culte*], a kind of modern religiosity. I hope to deal with a dimension of this in the second volume of *The Deconstruction of Christianity*, that of adoration. I am not proposing a "rational religion" but simply, as I have said, an attitude, a spiritual conduct.

ID: What does the deconstruction of Christianity add to this analysis, to this task with which Kant charges philosophy?

J-LN: What deconstruction adds, in this moment, is that, while being aware that it comes from within philosophy, deconstruction in some way works against philosophy, despite itself. In this, Derridean deconstruction is the inheritor of Heidegger's destruction. Perhaps it is the inheritor of all that has taken place since Kant.

Perhaps this brings us back to questions such as: How do we understand that this is not just a theoretical issue, or even that this question calls into question the very distinction between theory and practice? It's a question that we might ask along with Heidegger, an ethical question in the archi-originary sense of the word. Heidegger says that *ethos* precedes any division between logic, physics, morals, and metaphysics. This is something that Levinas brings out strongly, with the recurring problem that these works give the impression that the ethical represents a return toward God, or of God. But we can also understand that all that remains for Levinas is a question of sense, of relation, of tension. Sense *is* necessarily a relation; there is necessarily tension. It is a question of practice, or even of praxis, of praxis in the sense of an Aristotelian drama; it is a question of action that transforms the subject without producing any object. And it is also the question of something modern philosophy finds very difficult to discuss: feeling, the affect of the other and toward the other, or, in other words, the emergence of sense, which always also involves sensing, the sensual, the sentimental.

Living Together, Civil Religion, Adoration

ID: The notion of "civil religion," as Rousseau conceives it, brings together several questions concerning living together in a secularized world. It can be seen as the antinomy of a Kantian "unsocial sociability" (*ungesellige Geselligkeit*). These two concepts show that, when we are many—that is, when "we" *are*—we are absent from ourselves. Living together is the main question we face in modernity. It is, of course, also a question for the deconstruction of Christianity: How do we form social bonds, how do we form any sort of bond, without stifling the singularity of the individual and its relations with the other? If we begin (and end) with, let's say, "naked existence" [*l'existence nue*], as in your thought, the problem is perhaps not only the risk of stifling the singular but also the empty, exposed nature of this naked mode of existence. Naked existence is not nothing, but it's certainly not much. It could be true that living together is nothing more than that, but this truth itself perhaps does not form any bond.

J-LN: It's quite possible that that is the limit of philosophy, but the aim of deconstruction, to think living together as defined by an outside, also leads to a thinking of this idea of forming bonds and of civil religion. Fidelity, passion, sentiment, adoration: these are themes that I will address in a sequel to *Dis-enclosure*. In that sequel, *Adoration*, I begin with adoration and quote a passage from *Religion Within the Boundaries of Mere Reason* in which Kant says:

> Thus the consideration of the profound wisdom of divine creation in the smallest things and of its majesty in the great whole, such as was indeed already available to human beings in the past but in more recent times has widened into the highest admiration—this consideration not only has such a power as to transport the mind into that sinking, annihilating mood [*sinkende . . ., vernichtende Stimmung*], called *adoration*, in which the human being is as it were nothing in his own eyes, but is also, with respect to the human moral determination, such a soul-elevating power, that in comparison words, even if they were those of King David in prayer . . ., would have to vanish as empty sound, because the feeling arising from such a vision of the hand of God is inexpressible.[6]

Man feels himself to be annihilated by the feeling of adoration; it reduces him to nothing. To create a secular transcription of this passage from Kant, one would need only to remove the word *creation* and the name of God, because the passage ends with man's admiration of God's law [*droit*] in all things. For us, nowadays, the rejection of all teleology and all theology, and of course of all theo-teleology, does not alter the fact that we still, indeed increasingly, are confronted with (for example) the question of the origin of the world, of the Big Bang, and so on, confronted with the question of what we do to nature with our technics, even while we ourselves remain a product of nature.

I mean that Kant tries to think the feeling, the sentiment—I would call it a sentiment without ressentiment—of relating to a dimension of the world that, without needing to be finite, without requiring a creator or an end, is the very existence of the world; this bare existence of the world surpasses the capacity of thought to seize upon it and opens something up. What? Perhaps nothing, but it opens onto something in which we can feel annihilated, not in the sense of being destroyed but in the sense of being reduced to nothing very much, in the face of immensity.

This is perhaps the nucleus of something that appears in philosophy precisely in this text from Kant, although it is not absent from Hegel or Heidegger. I believe that in Heidegger this comes down to what he analyzes as "availability" [*Gelassenheit*]. But until now philosophy has had trouble moving in this direction, in opening up the feeling of the infinite, even though this was always present for philosophers . . .

To continue with the retrospective that I began a few minutes ago: if I go back beyond Kant, what do I find? I find the *Lumières*, and all the great classical metaphysicians from Leibniz to Descartes, via Malebranche, and even contemporaries of the great empiricisms. And we ought to go back even further, to the end of the Middle Ages: you could say that the whole era from the nominalists to Kant truly moves toward the "death of God," which is to say that God becomes the God of metaphysics. And so the "end" of classical metaphysics, the end that begins with Kant, is marked by a certain dimension, the dimension that Kant perceived: the dimension that he feels to be a religious, affective dimension. I think that we are grappling here with the same problems, which the *Lumières* set aside and which for us still go back to religion. These are the problems of feeling, not as "sentimental," as "ressentimental," or as "passionate" in the anxious, fitful sense of the word, but sensibility and sense, sense for Sense itself . . .

Rousseau's attempts to formulate a civil religion—which make him, in this sense, akin to Kant—like all subsequent attempts at civil religion, have regularly failed, except perhaps for something that wasn't really an attempt to create a civil religion: what happened in the United States. This was a very unusual situation, because that country began almost as a theocracy. What exists there is not even civil religion; it has truly retained something of theocracy, while remaining a state of law, a secular democracy. This means that something very specific exists in the United States, in which, ultimately, religiosity is constantly reconstituting an entirely moral God, a God who rewards and punishes and who leaves to one side any relationship with the world, with existence, whatever that might be, and whether that relationship be based on adoration or admiration. I think about this world as Wittgenstein describes it in his *Lecture on Ethics*. Wittgenstein is extremely perspicacious when it comes to religion. He has a sense of what religious spirit is, even as he explains that what we call "creation" is nothing but the existence of the world *as* a miracle. I think that's magnificent. The world is there. That's it.

Here, we fall into modern history, which goes back to, which is completely linked to, this history of philosophy. We stumble upon civil religion precisely as the need for an affective element: Rousseau says that the whole order of laws and contracts must be made perceptible [*sensible*] to the heart. This seems to be an affective element that should be integrated into politics, but modern politics is based on a city that is entirely human and that has no relationship to a divine city. What remains is a God who is only inside, in the manner of Rousseau's God, who is a God of conscience and who has no place in the order of the world, of society, or of the social contract. Presented in these terms, in the terms used by Rousseau, it has never worked.

ID: The big question then, is that of the city, of living together and being affected, a question you began to address in *The Inoperative Community* in 1982. This is also Rousseau's problem, that of civil religion. Society needs "more," a reason why we should want to live together and why all of this is related to passion, to feeling. Nevertheless, it's also a risk, if one thinks about totalitarianism. It's a necessity but, at the same time, it's a big risk to think it. Tackling the issues surrounding the ethics of passion and feeling is therefore crucial for our society. All the extreme-right movements now springing up in Europe, for example, reserve a central place for passion.

J-LN: It is as if feeling can only be envisaged in the public domain as dominant, identity-based passions, which are communitarian, nationalist, and so on. That is all we end up arousing, and, to a certain extent, deep down we have never known any other collective passions than these. In its worst manifestation, this is fascism, and in its less strict forms it is populist nationalism.

Personally, I think all this goes through a stage in which we clearly recognize that everything we are talking about here touches on politics but cannot be satisfied by politics. We recognize that one ought to begin by delineating the sphere of politics, which would certainly be very difficult. How should politics indicate and, above all, make possible an action based upon passion, upon affect, without seizing upon it for its own purposes?

ID: Perhaps that is exactly the danger, that politics thinks that it can satisfy these feelings . . .

J-LN: That's it, exactly. And that's the express thought process of the far right, which is in truth a little fascistic and at the same time completely cynical; it knows that it is exploiting emotion. To respond to this, we need to propose that passion and the affective order in general, just like the order of sense, *need not* be satisfied, sated, or fulfilled. However, they do need to be recognized, accepted, and exerted.

Through what we know about the experience of love, we know that there is an image of fulfilled love, of satisfied love, and we also know that this image very quickly becomes grotesque. At the same time, it's compli-cated, because necessarily this *must be* part of love. Love is not an exercise in taking the correct distance, either; it also needs the framework of pas-sion, indeed, of fusion. The truth of love depends upon this: fusion, com-munion, must be in sight, if I can say this, but not as a "goal"—simply as a dynamo, an impetus, not as an aim or as something that must be renounced for moral-Lacanian reasons (the acceptance of castration, of lack, of separation, etc.). The infinite of love ought neither to be attained nor renounced, but always brought into play; it is a fundamental but highly delicate condition.

Self-Deconstruction Between Self-Postulation and Self-Criticism

ALENA ALEXANDROVA: Our next question deals with the issue of the "auto-," of the "self-" in the expression "self-deconstruction": a tradition's engagement with itself. One of your central theses is that Christianity is undergoing a process of self-deconstruction. This could be interpreted as a tautological operation of self-postulation, of self-affirmation. In many cases, in religion, in art, in politics, such an operation is masked by notions of God, of transcendence, of a grand narrative that conceals that act of self-postulation. At the same time, these traditions contain the openness within the very same notion of God, of the open, of transcendence. In other words, on the one hand, the name of God functions as a screen concealing the groundlessness of the act of self-construction. On the other hand, this name signifies nothing, an opening or a void.

In order to illustrate my point, I will use the notions of immunity and auto-immunity, which are two different things. An organism or a tradi-tion can criticize itself in order to improve itself, but it can also criticize itself in order to appropriate any possible external criticism and therefore make itself stronger. What would then be the role of a philosopher who carries out deconstruction or a deconstructive reading? Where does the "self-" come into play, and doesn't the qualification "self-" in *self-deconstruction* diminish the role of the philosopher, of the reader, too much and give too much agency to the tradition itself? Would self-deconstruction mean just following the inherent ambiguity of the tradition? If yes, then fine, but isn't it true that every religious tradition has always engaged in self-interpretation, self-rereading?

J-LN: Any *monotheistic* tradition, at least, I would say. Indeed, in the three monotheisms, there has always been this question of engagement with oneself, with one's "self": self-criticism, the revision of foundational texts, and so on. The Bible is full of that. You could say that the Torah seems to be presented *as is*, without the possibility of self-criticism, but this is a very superficial view of the Torah as Law. Moreover, not all Judaism is to be found in the Torah. First of all, there's the tradition of the Talmud, then there are the prophets, who incessantly criticize at least part of the heritage of the Torah. With monotheism, one is immediately in the realm of interpretation. This becomes particularly striking with Christianity, because from the beginning Christianity has openly developed through a conflict of interpretations. At the center of this conflict of interpretations is what is called the *kērugma*, the religious message at whose center is the humanity of Christ. The humanity of Christ, the question of whether he is of a double nature (human and divine) or rather a single nature, was the locus of the ruptures, wars almost, of early Christianity. Later, it is precisely from here that the idea of deconstruction comes: that is to say, Christianity has continued to demand a "return to origins" that invokes a change in the interpretation of these origins. What was the sixteenth-century Reformation, which led to Protestantism, all about? First of all, the Reformation contended that the Scriptures had been forgotten. And later, in the twentieth century—I am speaking about the Christianity in which I was brought up, and perhaps you four too—was a demythologized Christianity, one "de-Churched," so to speak, unburdened of the Church—we spoke about this earlier. It has been the same with Islam up until now, specific to the history of Islam, where interpretation was brought to an end. But Islam also began, and continued for a long time, in the interpretation of its own world. In Hinduism or Shintoism, there are different schools, different currents; therefore we interpret differently the same body of texts and, shall we say, the same deities of reference, though on the whole it has remained self-identical. In the three monotheistic religions, the desire for reinterpretation via a return to origins has been more radical and more or less constant.

It is the movement of this *self* that seems remarkable to me. It means that each of these branches of monotheism somehow represents itself as a subject that must return to itself, that must find something more "pure." This has modern, "secular" parallels, which are not always sincere. Descartes too claims that the science of the ancients is a hidden science that needs to be rediscovered. But he doesn't believe it; in fact, he believes that he is inventing a modern science, and he is pretending that it used to be hidden because this is a framework that works well. The Jewish, Christian, or Muslim model is not one of hiding or of being hidden. Monotheism does not say that something has been hidden but rather that it has been lost, or perhaps that it has never been there: so we need a better understanding of the original message. It is in this loss of self and this desire to find one's "self" that monotheism differs from the great polytheistic religions, such as Hinduism or African and Oceanian religions. In these rich traditions, it is meaningless to speak of a return to something primal. Or even, one could say that in these traditions the return to the primal is always a return to tradition, to what is already well established—we must follow our ancestors' actions, and so on. In monotheism the return is an infinite return, without any "first," pure state.

Buddhism is more ambiguous, because it is instead made up of a great diversity of interpretations, of codes, and, from time to time, we also say that we need to return to and consider the life of the Buddha: the virtuous and simple nature of his life. But we do not see such a visibly subjective movement in Western monotheism. Nevertheless, Buddhism is ultimately a revision of Hinduism: a return to the inside and a surpassing of the inside of Hinduism. But it too is an infinite return.

There is therefore this kind of relation to the self in monotheism as a whole. And it is this reflexivity that Heidegger takes up in philosophy under the name of deconstruction or destruction, which is surely no coincidence. Destruction for Heidegger is the demolition of all ontology, of ontology itself, whether ancient, traditional, or modern. He tries to depart from ontology in order to find a moment when one can, like the first Greeks, keep vigil over being. However, I do think that Heidegger also gives an indication, from the moment he realizes that this has never happened before, but that this supposed "past" lies in front of us, that it *is* to be found. It is not therefore a return but an advance, an opening.

So, that's the first element of my answer. This first element means that what we call "deconstruction" is necessarily a self-deconstruction. In a certain way, it is tautological to say "self-deconstruction." You cannot deconstruct something that belongs to someone else. If I deconstruct something of someone else's, I simply break it.

But there is also a second element: it shows that there is only ever a "self" in the absence, almost in an originary loss, of this self, to which one allegedly returns. This is why I said that Heidegger ends up saying: No, that never happened, the pre-Socratics are not the dawn of thought, but its future. And in this sense, there is no "loss" at the origin. The origin cannot be lost—or gained. It is something to be neither given nor taken away. It is a dispatch [*envoi*], an impetus.

Let me make a brief parenthetical remark. It is interesting that philosophy never does this, that it never goes back to its own origins—at least not before Heidegger. Philosophy has a starting point, if you like. It's Plato, and then philosophy recognizes that Plato had his own predecessors: Parmenides, Heraclitus, and so on. All that is ordered around Plato: first of all, there is the relationship of Plato to Parmenides. More broadly speaking, there is also the relationship of Plato to Pythagoras; that is a starting point to which we can never return, as one would to a point of originary purity. You can choose to be a Platonist, for example, but you can never say that this is more pure, that after this point there would be a sort of loss or perversion. Alain Badiou would like to think of himself as a Platonist, in some way, but he would never say—I am sure—that Aristotle is a perversion of Plato: that would be nonsensical to him. He would reply that things change, that one thing merely follows another.

By the same token, this movement, this return to oneself in monotheism, gives rise to the demythologization of the world and, precisely, to "departure from religion." This means that this very movement calls the character of this "self," of this self-deconstructing "self," into question; one could then say that the "self" itself is deconstructed. This return is, it has to be said, more strongly marked in Christianity since it gives rise to the Reformation; and via the Reformation and beyond it, it gives rise to the demythologization of the world. At the end of all this, we come to Nietzsche and his description of the "only Christian, who died on the Cross," which we discussed earlier. This means that you cannot be Christian simply by belonging to something. That, I think, is related to this structure of the self, which means that the self is always in the self [*dans le soi*] that is constructed as relation to the self, that *is* a return to the self. All the self that returns to itself finds is yet further returns to the self. This "Christian" that Nietzsche speaks of is not a "self" who has an allegiance to a "God." He is in the divine in man, which is engaged in an infinite process of seeking and finding *itself*.

I really liked your question, because I said to myself, this requires me to take precautions that I had not considered. If I speak of "self-deconstruction," perhaps I am moving a little too fast, because it certainly must not come across as an autonomous or autarchic operation that would, in effect, become self-establishing or self-reestablishing. Precisely this operation, which needs deconstructing, is self-deconstructing itself. There could be a danger here that "the religion of departure from religion" is also the religion of the return to religion. For a long time, since I have been working with the (self)deconstruction of Christianity, I have often seen how keen priests and theologians are on this: in it they see a new possibility to return to pure sources. But according to my analysis, Christianity argues instead for the infinity of such a return and thus that a pure source is impossible.

Self-Deconstruction as Self-Betrayal: The Essence of Monotheism?

AVR: With regard to this act of self-deconstruction, in *Dis-enclosure* you firmly stress that we should be careful not to fall into a "Rousseauism of Christianity," that is, to postulate a "good primitive Christianity, and then to proceed to lament its betrayal." (*D* 150/218). It is not a question of saving Christianity, nor, for that matter, of overcoming it. At the same time, however, you are concerned for the future, concerned about what could "ignite" in the wasteland that we have "created or allowed to grow" by abandoning reason, entrusting ourselves to understanding. More precisely, according to you, there is the threat of a "(sur-)religious" resurrection (*D* 3/11). In order to ward off this threat, you incite us to ask ourselves what Christianity represents "essentially" (*D* 10/20), what is the core or the distinctive characteristic of Christianity. But couldn't it be said that this task is equally motivated to some degree by Rousseauism, because it presupposes that, over the course of the process of secularization, one has lost sight of the hidden truth of modern secularization, which is the truth of Christianity? Certainly, you underline the fact that, if there is "betrayal," it is Christianity or monotheism that "betrays" itself as a constitutive act. This is its self-deconstructing gesture. Moreover, you suggest that the betrayal of this betrayal—of the self-deconstruction—is inherent to the ambiguous condition of Christianity. But do you not suggest that the threats of our times come from the fact that we have forgotten this ambiguous and self-deconstructing condition, presented as an "essential," even "primitive," condition of Christianity? Or do we need to say that the avoidance of risk today is not really constituted by a return to a pure origin, as we find in Rousseauism, but rather by a return to the impurity of the origin? But, even then, I would say that there is still a return, or a sort of call for a revitalization of what Christianity was in its ambiguous act of self-deconstruction.

J-LN: Yes, it's certainly difficult, perhaps impossible, to do without a sort of model for the return. I can't do without it either, because I claim that the initial form of Christianity involves this or that, and so on. But therein lies the difficulty of Heideggerian destruction, of the step back that must be a step forward (which we spoke of earlier), and of the ambiguity that is in Rousseau himself, between the designation of a supposedly primal [*primitif*] and pure state, and the knowledge, also found in Rousseau, that there is no primal state. If this primal state exists, it's a representation we create for ourselves. However, that said, early Christianity is the birth of the West, so it is judeo-romano-greek. And in this respect, one could say that things are as at all births; by this I mean that one never comes back *to* a birth, even less back to *before* a birth. But one comes back into birth, especially if birth is an ongoing event that continues until death. So, in birth, one can always seize that which, precisely, cannot be reduced to an initial unit. It is completely absurd to come back *to* birth, as if one were completely within it and one could begin again from nothing. On the contrary, it still makes sense to adopt once again the view that there should be this heterogeneous totality, grouped around a single unit that cannot be grasped and that continues throughout life, and to work on this. Thus, if we speak in terms of a return, the return to Christianity is inseparable from the return to Hellenism. Hellenism is not a completely pure, *as is* entity, and we will never get to the end of its deconstruction. Deconstruction, of course, always means at once demolition and reconstruction.

AVR: We are still a bit perplexed by the mixture of two tonalities in your answer. On the one hand, there is the tonality of the deconstruction of Christianity, which seems to be a descriptive project, describing the self-deconstructing gestures of Christianity. By contrast, on the other hand, there is a tonality we can call normative. This normative tonality seems to us to lie in the description of the threat of our times. There is a threat, but what exactly is this threat, and why? What measures do we need to take to do away with it? I would say that the desire to do away with it obviously results in a normative consideration. That is what we have tried to grasp.

J-LN: The threat perhaps began under another form with fascism, and even before fascism, in certain aspects of religion, certain types of art—art for art's sake—and certain forms of spirituality or spiritualism surrounding art, as in Malevich, for example. And the threat is that we should have entered a period when, to put it bluntly, one seeks to compensate for the lack of the modern rationality of the *Lumières* with a hefty dose of irrationality, of all kinds of modes of identification, of the activation of passions. Today, Islamism and all other forms of integrism and communitarianism are striking examples of this. There is a danger that all this will be paid for by a reduction of rationality to nothing more than technics. In this case, technics is put beyond suspicion, but for the rest in this New Age, anything goes, right up to the *burqa*. This question is central to a difficulty experienced by many African students, particularly in France: How can traditional countries adapt to Western rationality without adopting it? How can you become scientific and still be an animist? I would say that this is a real issue: a number of fundamentalist movements react to the extension of Western techno-scientific rationality. But they react in an extremely ambiguous way, because they want both to resume a spiritual power and to do nothing to prevent the importation of technologies. I often wonder what will come of the fact that this universal use of all of our technologies creates completely different contexts: for example, at the moment there is a clash between the cultural development of Iran—a country with a very rich intellectual tradition, one that helps define Iran today—and its regressive forms of government. Now, our rationality is in our technics—that's for sure, but you cannot add to that a nonrationality, a "faith" or a "revelation" that comes from elsewhere . . . It is reason itself that must be dis-enclosed.

In effect, you're right, I am normative, which means that I say: one mustn't do that, one mustn't juxtapose technical reason and religious irrationality. What should one do? Perhaps one needs to open up once more the inside of rationality in general. One should be able to say how science is getting better and better at showing something that is neither outside of its knowledge nor opens onto a religious *super-knowledge* (as those who claim that the ultimate truth is in the Bible or the Koran wish it to be). Perhaps science is setting out another regime, just as technics opens up an indefinite multiplication of ends, of means that are in themselves ends, with the effect that we no longer know which side we are on in relation to the end. Even if you take a technical order that seems to have a clear end, such as the whole of medicine, for example, this order multiplies the possible ends—survival, people who avoid death for a significant period of time thanks to transplants or stem cells, or simply the prolongation of life for someone who is nonetheless in a very serious condition, and so on. Many lifestyles are presented as new ends, without our really knowing how to speak of them as ends, because there is no religion that presents them in this way. So doesn't this indefinite multiplication of the ends of technics require us to rethink our very understanding of ends or of teleology in general?

In *Dis-enclosure* I am perhaps at once threatening, normative, and a catastrophist because at that time I was thinking about fundamentalism a great deal, perhaps too much. But I would say that it still in some way comes down to the same thing. As long as God was not dead, we were able to think that there was some sort of Regulator who, in spite of everything, brought a certain sense of ultimate ends and supreme good. Now it's a question of bringing nihilism out of the interior of nihilism, as Nietzsche says.

I know it's always dangerous to speak like that, as if it were a sort of prophecy, where the doom-laden message is accompanied by a message announcing how this doom or catastrophe can be averted. In this book I wanted to emphasize that this is the first time that humanity has recognized its capacity for self-destruction—not for destroying mankind, one man at a time, but rather for the possibility that there could be a destruction, whether of nature or of natural equilibrium or of mankind by wars, such that everything would be eliminated. This raises a real question, based less on the fear that this might happen than on what it might that man is able to go to such lengths, and thus, how we might think of man. One option is thinking man from the perspective of his movement to his own limits: whether they be the limits of his destruction, or those of . . . adoration.

LTK: In *Dis-enclosure*, you suggest a way of thinking about man, or humanity, from the viewpoint of the ambiguous condition of Christianity, thus from this double bind of simultaneous self-constitution and self-deconstruction that you describe in the relationship to the self. As Aukje van Rooden notes, you present this double bind as the truth of Christianity, or at least the essence of Christianity, which we seem to have forgotten.

J-LN: Yes, certainly, though I would say that, while the notion of forgetting an essence inevitably attracts attention here, but I would stress as much as possible that it is not a question of something that has been forgotten but rather of something that could be invented now, beginning from what has already been opened up or outlined by Christianity. In *Adoration*, for example, I name one chapter "Mysteries and Virtues"; in it I talk about

Christian mysteries and theological virtues. Afterward I thought to myself: How can I propose a secular translation or transcription of two words so heavily infused with this Christian quality? On reflection, I thought, I mean "Illuminations and Drives" [*Éclairs et pulsions*]. I illuminate myself when I think that. *Mystery* means something that is self-illuminating, that shines in itself and that is therefore not at all hidden. This isn't my thought; it is one that comes from far in the past. That's why earlier I said that we need to relate to what has already been opened up or traced by Christianity. More precisely, this is not even a thought that I could say we need to *find once more* in the history of Christianity; it's rather something that we need to allow to invent itself, to allow to come before us.

As for "virtue" and its secular transformation "impulse," I wonder: What does virtue mean? In modern times, we have transformed virtue into a virtuous disposition, but even Spinoza was well aware of what virtue meant. It's an active force, a strong disposition to do something. On top of that, I read this in Freud: "The theory of the drives [*Triebe*] is, so to speak, our mythology. Drives are mythical entities, magnificent in their indefiniteness."[7] This passage from Freud is not often spoken of, but it indicates that Freud was aware that the drives are not physical realities. To qualify them as myths is really Freud's ultimate break with all mechanical, hydraulic, and economic models. At the same time, choosing to speak of drives means that Freud wholeheartedly rejects any talk of religion. To say that the drives are our myths means that today we do not have any other words to describe an originary or founding element that defines and gives meaning to the *impetus* [*poussée*]—a word that could be confused with instinct, at least in English. But the German *Trieb* is, of course, a drive. A drive is a sort of automatism. Now, there is perhaps no other word with which we can attempt to express that we are being driven [*poussé*] without finality or causality: on the one hand, humanity has the means to destroy itself, and, on the other, we can see that humanity is always driven to live and to survive. So, I'm not saying that from here we can move directly to virtue or that I'm going to establish a sort of religion of impulses, a church where we can worship the Holy Drive . . . but this serves to illustrate the fact that it is not entirely a question of removing ambiguity from the situation, but rather of understanding why there is this ambiguity. After all, ambiguity means that we cannot stay in the continuous, linear schema of rationality. How can we not wonder what it is in ambiguity, which is perhaps there necessarily, what is the element that could lead elsewhere?

That said, this ambiguity is precisely the ambiguity between religion as a system of securing and domination and the same religion as opening the sense of the infinite, and opening to the infinity of sense. These aspects are almost inseparable within Christianity, and this is why it is not that easy to separate everything out. People find it all too easy to cast the Roman Church as the villain and then to see in another camp a beautiful, pure spirituality . . . But that is too easy, precisely because our civilization is made up of this mixture, of the ambiguity of the two. For a long time I have refused to consider Christianity a Western disease. That's something I hear so much, and there's certainly an aspect of Nietzsche that tends toward this view. But I would say that it's absurd, because this disease is congenital to the West. This is something I have often debated with Philippe Lacoue-Labarthe, because he adored saying that Christianity was a disease. In the sense of a physical sickness, it's like a cancer; in that of a moral sickness, it's crooked, hateful. But then, how could he say that? The whole of civilization would then be sick . . . We could also say—indeed, it's often said—that the whole of the West is a sickness . . . But then, what or who is sick? What is the health that has been lost?

AVR: How can one *adore* saying that?

J-LN: You're right, that's exactly it—Christians have aroused a raging anti-Christian current, a current that we can understand perfectly well but of which we need to be wary, because it can become a type of Manicheism, preventing us from being able to analyze our own culture. And, as has been suggested, we cannot say that we are sick without knowing what sort of "health" we should have.

Deconstructing Christianity—What about Judaism and Islam?

LTK: In the preamble you wrote for the present book, you describe a certain privileged condition of Christianity. "Only Christianity produced itself as 'the West'; and it alone decomposed its confessional features and disintegrated its religious force." Does that mean that Islam, the religion that has received the least attention in your research, has not produced itself as the West? In spite of the fundamental distinction that you introduce between Christianity and the other monotheisms, your entire study of the deconstruction of monotheism in no way distinguishes between these three traditions; indeed, it attempts to present common characteristics. Can you apply what you are saying about the deconstruction of monotheism—notably, that it opens up a "world without God"—to Islam? Do the God of the Tenach, the God of the Scriptures, and the God of the Koran touch one another so intimately that you can say of these three, describing them according to their distinctive traits: "the unicity and the unity of this 'god' . . . consists precisely in that the One cannot be posited there, neither presented nor figured as united in itself. Whether it be in exile or in diaspora, whether it be in the becoming-man or in a threefold-being-in-itself, or whether it be in the infinite recoil of the one who has neither equal nor like . . . this 'god' . . . absolutely excludes its own presentation" (D 41/62–63)?

AA: Following on from this, one can focus this general issue by analyzing the complex status of the body in Christianity—between presentation and representation, or in a different context, between invisibility and visibility. Would this complexity of the body be the distinctive feature of Christianity, compared to the other monotheisms?

On the one hand, you remark that "monotheism will have represented nothing other than the theological confirmation of atheism" (D 20/34). This is because of the monotheistic articulation of the notion of God, which posits his withdrawal from the world and ultimately his coincidence with the world, as your interpretation of creation ex nihilo suggests. The unicity of God is signified in the monotheistic traditions through negative formulas—invisibility, absolute transcendence, irrepresentability. However, you point out that the idea of the incarnation is one of the central self-deconstructive features of Christianity: its "decisive trait" (D 81/125). In this case, by contrast to the other monotheisms, there is an emphasis on God having a body, being engendered as a body. Incarnation in the theological sense of the term cannot be understood as representation, as a spirit that inhabits or enters the body. On the contrary, it is the site of the alienation of God, "emptying-himself-out-of-himself" (D 83/127), and the material presentation of such alienation. Unlike the other monotheisms, Christianity is associated with the visibility of the divine, not as a representation but as a presentation. What about the other monotheisms: Do they enact similar events, moments, presentations without representation?

J-LN: I would say that there are two ways to deal with the division of the monotheisms into three; in my work up until now I have focused on one of these ways. The first way highlights the oppositions between the three; the second, which I favored, involves looking at emphases, taking each of these gods as a particular emphasis placed on the One God. So, I understand the *One* as the retreat of God as being behind these emphases, the One not in opposition to the multiple but rather as a suppression of itself, of the divine. But you could say that the God of Judaism is the God of alliance; therefore he is the God of relationship and address. Christianity recognizes the God of love, who at the same time embodies man's love for God who saves him. (Here we would need to look at salvation and man's love for the God he is called to love.) This love takes the unique form (in comparison with the other monotheisms) of the *body*, as you put it so well, which reveals the divine, making it visible and perceptible in its invisibility. This event (the coming of Christ) is repeated in Christian ritual. It is not a representation, and thus this event, which is the corporeal approach of the one who is at the same time the most distant, cannot be found in the other monotheisms. The God of Islam is he who is, in a certain way, the most properly, the most visibly the God of infinite retreat, yes. This God is most manifestly outside of all possible manifestation. In my opinion, it is important to show how the three go together, echo one another [*se renvoient l'un à l'autre*], and how there is, if you like, a certain proximity. I don't know if I would speak of an intimacy between the three traditions, as you do, but there is certainly a question of intimacy *within* the monotheisms: a closeness that we can treat in an Augustinian way by saying that God is *interior intimo meo*. That is to say, the intimacy of the three monotheistic gods, of the three characters together, would be what opens man up to what I call . . . ultimately, yes, the infinity of sense. So, it's an opening, by alliance and address, by love, by the infinite, incomparable distance of God.

But at the same time, obviously, we can't leave things there. The three are also mutually exclusive; they repel each other very strongly. There is a big difference, though, between the way in which Judaism and Christianity repel each other, on the one hand, and, on the other, the way in which Islam and this Judeo-Christian "bloc" repel each other.

LTK: Could you expand on the complex polarity that you posit between the monotheistic religions, while claiming that a continuity links Abraham and Moses to Jesus and to Allah? If it is true, as you say, that the gods of the three traditions intersect in a fundamental way [*se touchent*]—in the experience of God, in their theological makeup, in their representations in ritual and imagery—how are we to understand their opposition? As a historical development?

J-LN: Yes. I think that Islam is constructed in an entirely different context, and in a different politico-religious framework. Judeo-Christianity comes from an ancient world that is completely uncertain, unsettled, and dislocated, lacking the spiritual assurance that the philosophies of the third, second, and first centuries before Christ (the stoics and epicureans) display in abundance. This uncertainty is inside Judaism, in particular, and that is what has created movements such as the Essenes. But Islam is formed by a number of Arab peoples, not all part of one political unit, who lived at the time of the (beginning of) the decline of the Roman Empire and civilization. This was, at the same time, the beginning of a new political and cultural order. This new order, this new grouping of peoples, of nationalities, is surely perceived by Islam as one theologico-political unit. This creates a totally different starting point. The heterogeneity of the three monotheisms also applies to the difference between Judaism and Christianity. But I find this more difficult to enunciate, because it seems that we must wait a long time before we encounter in Western history a Judaism that is completely detached from Christianity, even hostile toward it. In the beginning, Christianity and Judaism overlapped a great deal. Christians were considered Jewish in the religious sense for a much longer period than you might imagine, in Asia Minor, for example. Starting in the fourth century, the hostile opposition between Christianity and Judaism was, deep down, concerned with the Roman Empire, the Church and its role in the Empire, the fact that Christianity had become the religion of the Empire. In my opinion, this opposition works in favor of the Jews, by this I mean those Jews who, without becoming Christians, understood that the Kingdom of Israel had come to an end and that all that there was left to do was to be Jewish without awaiting the Kingdom of God on earth. So, in fact, they became implicated in a logic, shall we say, of two kingdoms, while still awaiting the reconstruction of the Temple (and even that later became more complex). What's more, there is the theological opposition to the Christian dogma and narration of the incarnation. All that manifested itself late in history.

As for the aggressive opposition between Christianity and Judaism, that is to say, Christian anti-Semitism (something I develop in the Preamble to this volume)—I would say that I do not even want to talk about anti-Semitism as a hatred of the Jews as a race or as a people; Christianity's hatred of the Jews is a hatred solely directed at the Jews of the *diaspora*. It is not hatred of the Jews of Jerusalem or of the Temple: that ended with the first Christians. It's the diaspora that is the object of hatred. Why? I have come up with a hypothesis about this, which perhaps goes a little too far but which I think is interesting: the Jews of the diaspora bear witness precisely to that to which Christianity ought to bear witness, namely, *living in the world without being of the world.* Christians cannot bear this because it constitutes a denunciation of their political and imperial betrayal; therefore, it is a betrayal of Christianity itself. This is why we need to explore whether the currents of Christianity that have been most radical, spiritual, and pure have also been the least anti-Semitic. If there is something positive in the tradition of Christian Europe as far as the Jews are concerned, it is the idea that the Jews bear witness to this tension, which works between *and* within the two monotheisms of the Judeo-Christian "bloc": the relationship to this affair of inside/outside, of two kingdoms, of two powers.

So, to return to your questions, here is what I want to say now: in this affair of the separation between two worlds we discover the greatest difference between the three religions of the West. This is a historical difference but also a contemporary, even an urgent one. To begin with, Christianity is characterized internally by a spiritual vein that is initially marked out by Augustine, by Augustinianism, by the mystics, then by the Protestant reformers; this vein leads to something that we can define as the *self-deconstruction of Christianity*. This self-deconstruction leaves aside all the myths, norms, and politico-religious monuments of the Catholic and Protestant churches. Second, Judaism, for its part, has stuck to a radical separation of the state and the secular world; nevertheless, it is the religion *in* this world that has most exactly maintained its religious identity. Judaism is the religion that tends increasingly toward a repetition of its rites—except where Judaism has been an extraordinary source of inspiration for thought: from Spinoza to Freud. This inspiration gives rise to an internal deconstruction of Judaism, but one that does not appear as Jewish any longer, because it is the result of work by people who have departed from religion. So, in Judaism we have a religion that continues to affirm its status as a religion and does not get involved in the world through political domination. Third, and in a different direction, Islam echoes what I was saying earlier: it began and continues, I think, in a certain indistinction between the two worlds. On this point, I remain very pragmatic, as I do not have enough historical or theoretical knowledge to think this through fully. All I have done is to suggest a method for reanalyzing the monotheistic heritage. Islam presents itself—and many Muslim intellectuals are troubled by this—as a religion based on a dual principle: it is from the start both political and religious; you have the Caliph and the Imam. This dual principle has never been clear in the history of Islam.

LTK: Islam can also be considered as the religion that has best showcased the fundamental debate between faith and knowledge, between religious obedience and the freedom of human reason. From its beginnings, Islam has been engaged in an uncertainty—as is obvious, for example, in the work of Al-Farabi or Averroes, or in the spirituality of Sufism—regarding the status and the politico-religious power of "revelation," condensed in the Koran. How would you say that this uncertainty is connected to the indistinction of the two worlds that you described?

J-LN: Yes, certainly, but precisely this indistinction has, at a given moment within Islam, almost allowed faith to throttle faith. It is surprising to see how, over the course of Western history, this great civilization has stopped interpreting its own revelation . . .

LTK: From the triple configuration of the West, which we are in the process of exploring in this dialogue, come three relationships to the act of self-deconstruction, three attitudes toward the complicated structure of inside-outside, a structure that leads us to what you call the infinity of sense (and of the world). There are three relations, meaning that the three monotheisms have contributed to the formation of the West. The deconstruction of monotheism, which you pioneered, is the deconstruction of this triple configuration, isn't it? This would also mean the deconstruction of the three monotheistic gods. Until now, you have concentrated on the Christian God and on the difficult concept of his incarnation, his resurrection, and the dynamic of the Trinity. At the same time, you yourself speak of "God" in experimental and hesitant terms. It seems that the self-deconstruction of the monotheistic gods invites us to speak of God beyond monotheism. Of God, or of the divine beyond monotheism, because these are two words that you use, sometimes one, sometimes the other, as if you were hesitating . . .

J-LN: Yes, if one says "divine" one is still saying "God." I believe that "divine" has had a use for me in the past because, for example, in the title of the work "Of Divine Places" the adjective *divine* is nevertheless very human. I mean: we say "it's divine," we talk of a "divine surprise," we refer to "a diva." Thus, we can quite easily use the adjective *divine* as if it were detached from God. Of course, this is cheating, but it is perhaps a useful form of deception because it displaces, in language, the opposition between man and God.

But in his retreat God is a god precisely in relation to nomination; here, indeed, is perhaps one of the points at which the three monotheisms have most in common [*se touchent le plus*]. We know that the first of the gods, that of Judaism, has a name, but that it cannot be pronounced, that it is not to be pronounced, that it remains forbidden. The second, that of Christianity, does not have a name, but to him we apply the common noun [*nom*], of God which has become a proper name [*nom*] and thus, as there are three persons, there is the Son who becomes man/God with a proper name. He is called Jesus, but Jesus is just a displacement of the nomination "God." Perhaps this "Christ" is the only God of Christianity, but this is simply because he is distinct from the other God-person of the Trinity: the Father. The one we call God, before any other, is God the Father; he's the *good* God of Christianity, but also of the other two monotheisms. Christianity adds a name for the very relation, inside of "God," of his own "goodness" (or love, or desire)—this is the "Spirit," the "Holy Spirit."

The third God, that of Islam, has his name, but it is the name of the Distant One, of the Unknown in a very radical sense. The ninety-nine other names of God in Islam are all superlatives, names of excellence, of traits that are the highest, the most "everything," and so on. So this divine triplicity is affected by the question of nomination. And, interestingly, these are three ways of denying the simple possibility of nomination, of proper names. This means straightaway that there is an enormous difference from other religions in which the gods have proper names. Whether it be Osiris or Zeus, or the Aztec gods, or the gods of Shintoism, of which there are, I think, more than a million, they all have their own names . . . I cannot think of one who is "good" in the sense of the unnamable God, who precisely because of his distance is the generous, protecting, sometimes consoling, in short, "good" God. The question therefore, is one of nomination: "Good." The "name" is the name of "good."

On the Word *God* in a Deconstruction of Monotheism

LTK: But this nomination is linked to history, to the configuration of historical religions, not to an eternal being. Allow me to develop this problem in another direction, that of the consequences of the use of the word/name *God* in your writing.

In working on this book with the other contributors and in discussing your texts, in particular "On a Divine Wink" (*D* 104–20/155–77), we were struck by the fundamental ambiguity of the word *God* in your analyses. As Alena Alexandrova has already remarked, this ambiguity lies in the fact that God refers to a kenotic gap that deprives God of all content, of all identity, and at the same time refers to a "screen" covering this limitless concept with a new substance, in the form of an "I" or a "self" that posits itself. On the one hand, you show that the God of monotheism is nothing but a space, where "the absenting of presence" takes place (*CW* 69/91–92), a space that gives a "place" to something or someone who is not of the order of being. By contrast, in "Of Divine Places" we read that the question of God's being—as an identity, or as you put it, as a "being-one"—is the essence of monotheism: the essence of this gesture of the cover that fills the God-space by transforming it into a transcendent guarantee. This means that the God of monotheism "is" good, vengeful, powerful, merciful," and so on (*IC* 111–12/2–3).

Monotheism unsettles all talk of "God" and, as a result, unsettles all religion. In the history of monotheisms (their narrations, their theology, their art), which you have studied extensively, we can identify two configurations of this unsettling. First of all, there is the astonishing fact that monotheism is, in general, a type of atheism, that its God is nothing but someone absent [*un absent*], or, even better, a gesture of absenting. Second, there is in Christianity a radicalization of this God/absenting in the notion, the story, and later the dogma of his incarnation: God un-gods himself by becoming a man. Both configurations present God as a non-God.

Next, it is this unsettling that, according to you, opens modernity. Shouldn't a deconstruction of monotheism limit itself to researching this unsettling and its importance for the philosophical analysis of what "modernity" and the "modern world" are, and avoid engaging once again in talk of "God," however paradoxical and ambiguous this might be? Can the deconstruction of monotheism continue presenting God in this paradoxical way if it wishes to believe in the impossibility of such a presentation? Doesn't any usage of the word *God* "resuscitate" religion? Doesn't it "save" religion, doesn't it "re-paint" the heavens (*D* 1/9)?

J-LN: I quite agree that most of the philosophical systems that I try to follow or that have been passed down to me lead to abandoning any name for God. There is no supreme being, no type of subject, no individual, no entity. But then, what are we to speak of? The infinite, the open? Here, the problem of naming, of our language, is exacerbated. Isn't there always a danger of substituting for the singular proper name what precisely should not be a proper name, but a common noun? That is to say, we substitute a general quality for something that designates a person, who is not, in fact, a "quality." What I mean is that a proper name *designates* rather than *signifies*. So, the history of Judeo-Christianity offers an answer to the question "How can the proper name of a unique God at the same time be the Infinite, the Open, and so on?" This answer is that, through the incarnation and the life of the man-God Jesus, we can say that *any proper name* is the name of God. This approach can also be seen in Levinas's rethinking of the God of Judaism. All others present—and do not *re*present—God to me, and thus also present to me the proper name, insofar as it is proper, precisely insofar as this name does not refer to any determination, but remains purely deictic. Such a presentation takes place by designating God.

This would be one possibility. I would almost say that, for me, this begins to take us back into the dangerous territory that is the quest to know whether we can have rites, prayers, and myths that would all denote, address, exclaim, and even adore God. Perhaps, therefore, we should let go of the name of God altogether and only keep proper names. This would be a way of combining the two approaches, the one that avoids speaking of God and the other that keeps the name of God only as a modality of any proper name, yours or mine.

A third approach or hypothesis is that God is a common noun that has become a proper name. This assumption that the common noun *God* or *theos* is a proper name is a quite singular historical phenomenon: it was Plato who first wrote *theos* in the singular (and not in the plural, *theoi*) and nobody knew how to translate or to understand this passage from the *Theaetetus*. This exceptional rupture with the gods of *mythos* opens up the possibility of a proper name, *God*, a unique, singular name that signifies not a particular identity but a void. The monotheistic religions are a product of this rupture.

LTK: Indeed, the debate about the use of the word *God* is meaningless without a deconstruction of the history of the name of "God" as you are now describing it. But do you not go slightly further than this in outlining a certain modality of speaking in terms of "God" for our times, following Heidegger—that is to say, in presenting the last God as a passer-by, *im Vorbeigang*? Isn't this view of God as a passer-by a case of designating God in an ontological way—however experimental, because here being itself is thought as the open, and as the event of the opening of beings by *Dasein*?

J-LN: That's it, I think; the passer-by *is* not, but he opens and opens himself. We're not that far from Heidegger here. Except for the question of the name. The passer-by is not a concept or a hypostasis: it's a proper name that, once again, does not refer to any identity or property—an unknown proper name.

In his little book *Adieu*, of which I am very fond, Jean-Christophe Bailly suggests naming God *the open*.[8] Bailly has never had any religion in his life; however, he speaks of a world that is not at all closed. On the contrary, according to him, the world has a dimension of the open that is, at its most basic level, that of sense. Well, that's really quite close to what I have tried to say, isn't it? In this book, there is an expression that

I think is charming, and that I have remembered ever since I read it: "Atheism has not managed to irrigate its own desert." So, ultimately, I am responding to the call of this phrase: I am trying to irrigate and to bring water into the desert of atheism.

As Gérard Granel explains, in the text that I comment on in *Dis-enclosure* (D 61–74/89–104; see also D 163–74/105–16), *dius* is the day, or rather, the separation of day and night. In a way therefore, it is precisely the open; God is the open, or the opening, and that's what all the old cosmogonies of the Middle East are founded upon: separation, either of the earth and the heavens, or of the earth and the waters, or of the shadows and the light—but always separation. So, in one sense, saying "God" with a capital letter is nothing more than making a proper name out of a common noun that itself signifies opening, separation, dehiscence. But I am very aware of the fact that speaking of God in this way, as separation and as opening, is always threatened by two dangers: the danger that this *dius* might lose its character as a proper name and become a concept, and that it be reduced to the God of Christian history, which has been associated for centuries with an institution, with an ecclesiastical monumentality that places an enormous burden on "God."

I have just one thing to add. I want to point out that God in our culture—and this must also be the case in Arab culture; think of *Insha'-Allah*—seems to be a ubiquitous word in language. God is a word that is used a great deal as an exclamation: "My God," "Good God," God only knows!" The exclamation "God" is part of our communication, whether we are religious or atheist. Religion and atheism meet in this simple and trivial word.

Deconstruction, Demythologization, and the Performativity of Myth: On Adoration and Exclamation

AVR: Doesn't this phenomenon of exclamation as practice and as performance bring us back to the question of myth, which you were talking about earlier, that is, the question of the paradoxical persistence of mythical performativity in monotheism and modernity? This would call on us to think once again about what the "divine" and "God" mean.

One of the main arguments of *Dis-enclosure* is that the deconstruction of Christianity implies a demythologization. A mythological religion, in short, presupposes that the world is structured, governed, and animated by the effective presence of the divine, a structuring that is produced by a narrative of the origin: by myth. The Christian religion, on the contrary—and I quote you—"understands itself in a way that is less and less religious in the sense in which religion implies a mythology (a narrative, a representation of divine actions and persons)" (*D* 37/57). Put another way, because religion implies mythology, Christianity is not only the religion of departure from religion but also a religion of departure from mythology.

But could we not also say that the mythological element is inversely proportional to the religious element, in other words, that a religion that is increasingly less religious involves a greater amount of mythology? Myth, after all, is not the recognition or the representation of a divine order, but its performance. So, if the divinity is not present and localizable, but everywhere and nowhere, don't we need recourse to some such performative gesture to evoke it in its absence? To put it another way, isn't myth even more necessary as a component of atheism, even a condition of its possibility? And doesn't the almost obsessive importance attached by modern man—believer or nonbeliever, secular or religious—to rituals, to tales, to phrases to recite, to prayers, and to objects, not only in church but also in the privacy of one's own home or in practices that are not overtly religious, such as sport, hint at that?

J-LN: Yes, if you define myth as the performance of what nonetheless remains elusive rather than as the expression of a divine presence, then you are approaching an atheist religion. It is close, for example, to exclamation as a "practice" that says nothing, that performs nothing but a pure—I don't even know if you could say tautological—intensification of pleasure [*jouissance*], like sexual climax, through an exclamation that says nothing. This could be romantic or erotic, but it says nothing other than a sort of desire to recapture—or even to indicate, to evoke—on a linguistic level that which eludes language.

Insofar as the use of the name of God is concerned, you find that with exclamation in general. Then one finds a whole issue with regard to language, a language, in some way, of pure address, or rather, we ought to say that it is a limit not of language but of the voice; it is simply the voicing of something that is in itself silent, unvoiced. This means that it borders on being a cry of sexual exclamation; it is on the borderline between a cry and a groan or sigh. The same can be said of exclamations of love: when lovers exclaim "Oh, I love you!" they're not saying anything at all.

LTK: Is what you refer to as adoration always a kind of exclamation, as you describe it here?

J-LN: I don't really know. I take adoration in the context of art. Art is adoration; it is to address a prayer. Here I am thinking, among other things, of the practice of the Orthodox monks of Mount Athos, who say the name of Jesus Christ as they breathe; this exercise can last all day. This can be likened to examples in poetry, and to all types of address in literature through the centuries: the first line of the *Iliad*, for example ("Sing, goddess"). And then there's music, precisely relating to the name of God is Schoenberg's *Moses and Aaron*. These are the last words of the final act, when Moses, in his debate with Aaron, who had "capture[d] the infinite in a likeness" (Scene 4 of the second act), addresses God, exclaiming: "*Unrepresentable God*. Unspeakable, many-meaning *idea*."[9] Therefore Adorno, commenting on *Moses and Aaron*, was able to say that "all music attempts to pronounce the unpronounceable name."

In any case, music plays a considerable role in the monotheistic religions because it is a way of praying without words—that, too, I call adoration. But that can be found everywhere in the traditions of modern music, poetry, and art, and not only in the religious world. Their "adoration" consists in the fact that they are outside of words or—like poetry—in words, but precisely in the mode of apostrophe, by being able to remain suspended in relation to the development of meaning.

God and Address

AA: I would like to follow up briefly on the issue of address—of the name of "God" as a gesture of addressing. This concerns a category of words in language that function as the tools of address—deictic words such as *I* and *you*, which have no meaning outside the communicative situation. The proper name, too, has a very particular meaning—it signifies a singular person. This is the "place" in language of addressing oneself and of being addressed, also of presentation and precisely not representation—if you like, of the intensity of being there. So, in a sense, there is a logic or mechanism of address, of presentation not only in music, as you say, but also in visual art, in poetry. It has something to do with presence not as a static presence in the physical sense but as an intensity of presence. The word *God*, then, could be understood as a deictic word; it has meaning only in the situation of its use, as a tool of address that is in fact ultimately open.

J-LN: Yes, the visual arts, painting: if they are not a representation that can be used in a useful manner, they send a message, they speak in an apostrophe or exclamation. It happens in moments of intensity. Often I want to question how we distinguish between the methods of good and bad images, or how we distinguish between those images that count as art and those that do not. Well, we must still admit that it's a feeling; you can feel that there is something reaching out to you. By contrast, if you're looking at images in a magazine, obviously there is still something that calls you, but the call of advertising is not an intense one.

AVR: I still wonder about the status of works of art in your thought. You said earlier that there are certain areas of life, such as art and love, that are distanced from functional, that is, economico-political uses. But what element or aspect ensures that these remain at a safe distance?

J-LN: The work of art—but also the work of thought, or the work of love, the work of whatever it might be in life (encounters, thinking)—has a dual characteristic that is almost an antinomy: on the one hand, it opens up a space that is nothing but a promise; on the other, it is completely realized and complete. On the one hand, something can be fully accomplished, finished as Beethoven's Fifteenth String Quartet is finished, completed. This is not a promise. I once had a conversation with Jacques Rancière about this. I said that politics is obliged to promise, and then it is lambasted because it doesn't keep these promises. Rancière said to me, "Yes, but if you put it like that, everything, even literature, promises, but it doesn't keep its promises." *Remembrance of Things Past* is simply *there*. Just as the Fifteenth Quartet is there. And it's the same with love: love can be lost, it can betray or be betrayed, it can die, and so forth, but the fact remains that when it's love, it's love. Even if love seems to be linked to promises—I love you, I promise that I'll love you forever—this doesn't mean that it's not entirely different from political promises, which simply put things off until later. So, the paradox is that, on the one hand, this something is realized—it's done, it's finished—and yet, at the same time, it's infinite, because at that very moment what has been done opens itself, reopens itself to a number of possible encounters. This means that one can always return to the Fifteenth Quartet; one can always return to *Remembrance of Things Past*. You can always, to put it in terms of utility, make use once again of that which does not have utilitarian value; you can always use it again, precisely because it is not exchangeable. Even love, once it is over, once you have moved on, exists in a sort of eternity: you don't use it, but it has its own meaning there, in that eternity.

Dis-enclosure of Religion, Dis-enclosure of Art

AA: We could say that *art* is a name that does not have any referent (just like *God*), that it is ultimately open; it can be used as a proper name, as

Thierry de Duve remarks. My first question, then: Can we speak about a dis-enclosure of art in a way similar to a dis-enclosure of religion? And if we focus on art, is art simultaneously departure from art or, as you sometimes formulate it, art without art? Perhaps we would not even have an artwork that can be shown, written about and perceived, nor an artist who creates it, but a gesture, an intensity. Do we need the name *art*? My second question: You say that within religion itself art has never been religious, in the sense of being appropriated by religion. Of course, there is religious art in the proper sense of the term—art that treats religious subjects—but in its own terms, in the terms of our current discussion about presence and intensity, art has never been religious in any way. Can you comment on this entanglement between art and religion?

J-LN: First of all, I have never thought of that. But I think that we could speak of a dis-enclosure of art, provided we recognize that art is always in a state of dis-enclosure. Although there are closures in art, as in politics, the principle of art as a gesture in itself, if you like, in its own work, is that it is in dis-enclosure: it doesn't close, it opens. Can we say that the "open work" of Umberto Eco is a tautology?

Historians tell us that what remains of the most ancient works of humanity is not art but rather religion, magic, witchcraft, and so on. Yes, there has always been a difference between the religious gesture in the sense of conjuration, sacrifice, ritual, and the fact of giving birth to a visual, sonorous, dancing form. But it's my deep conviction that humans at Lascaux, at Altamira, at Chauvet performed religious and artistic gestures at the same time. The artistic or nonartistic nature of African works of art has been discussed at length, for example: they are deemed to be religious objects [*de culte*]. Nevertheless, there are religious gestures that seem to exemplify the creation of forms. But it is never merely that. There can be gestures that are purely ritualistic: for example, altars made of piles of earth, used for the sacrifice of chickens, simply because it has always been this way. The chickens' blood flows, and, in the end, you are left with heaps of very old, dried blood. To us, that might seem like a work of art. But it isn't that at all, for an African that is not art, nor is it for us. But a statue, that's different.

I would therefore identify two human gestures. There is the ritual gesture of representation, of the representation of God, of a divine force, and, well, that can go as far as veneration, as far as relating to the work as to the sacred. Here, monotheism is particularly interesting, because it states that such a relation would be idolatry. Here it also gets into a very complex relation with art. The other gesture is that of form for its own sake, the liberation of a form in its own right. There is no reciprocation of this second gesture; there are no rewards; it's not a case of "I say my prayers, and God will protect me." Rather, "I do a drawing, and it won't do anything; my drawing will not protect me." Quite the contrary, I would perhaps add . . .

AA: Perhaps the cultic aspect you mention is present in art right now: you go to a museum and you will be "rewarded." So it seems that art might always maintain this cultic aspect, which is precisely not religious in the monotheistic sense. Perhaps this aspect is always present in any image that is the object of a public gaze.

J-LN: That's true, but it's an ambiguity different from the ambiguity of art and religion. What you're saying is a bit different, that the work of art is, itself, taken to be a religious object. I agree about that. But it is not something that takes place entirely after the end of religion—that is, at the beginning of modern times, as an ensemble within which representation and behavior are duly organized. It's an essential aspect of monotheism itself; in monotheism, you can have idolatry of art.

The three monotheisms have an interesting relationship to art, because two of them have nonfigurative arts, which distinguishes them from Christianity. This means that art in Judaism and in Islam seems to be entirely devoted to divine service: we mustn't dwell on the figure itself or on any figure of this world. But, at the same time, the paradox is that, especially in Islamic art, architecture, and decoration, this provokes a liberation of form in its pure state, which means that there are certain periods, certain places in Islamic art that make an impression precisely through the purity of forms, through emptiness (the open space of mosques, etc.). Now, the question is to know whether art can itself become a sort of religion [culte]. This question is felt very strongly today, because religion's place sits empty.

This question also concerns another thing you said, that is, the problem of the necessity or otherwise of the word art. This is an unsettling question because when the word art is completely detached from the sense of an artistic activity it becomes tautological, doesn't it? Art is art, and thus it's also art for art's sake. At the same time, it both brings out something that is the internal truth of art and isolates a sort of a superior entity that is art, with which we ought never to get involved and which we should be able to forbid ourselves to talk about. We should speak only of the arts, and speak of them only by their given names: music, painting, cinema, poetry. However, we come across the word art on its own through the fine arts: the fine arts (*beaux-arts, schöne Künste*)—first and foremost this means technique, because *art* means technique, the techniques of beauty. And what is beauty?

Our whole tradition since Plato and Plotinus tells us that what is beautiful is a flash of *truth*. So beauty means being something extra, a supplement, a glimpse of truth: presence itself. Also, I often want to defend the word *art* and say, "Well, art is technique, that is, having *savoir-faire*." (The word *technique* can, at least in French, be linked back to *savoir-faire*. This is useful because "technique" immediately has a technological, mechanical feel to it; I prefer the term *savoir-faire*, but what does it relate to? To something, to whatever nature alone cannot do.) So, "art" as *savoir-faire* has a meaning in relation to what can be sensed, and even to what is sensual. "Religion," by contrast, can also signify *savoir-faire*, but this is not at all technical, because a technique has to be acquired, created according to a project; it is, shall we say, the quest to create a new form. *Religio* means observance—something is given and I must simply observe it. Obviously, there can be a certain *savoir-faire* in observance, but in my opinion there is no real technique to religion. There is an institution of religion, which defines practices [*cultes*], rites, and so on. The practices that you describe in relation to art are diffuse, ambiguous; they have an economic and socio-ideological character. But art is the *savoir-faire* of a palpable form.

Art Between Visibility and Invisibility: The Public and the Private

AA: We come across a crucial historical distinction when thinking about the relation between religion and art. The religious object has a social function precisely because it's hidden. It's not supposed to be seen; it has a supposedly divine origin; and it's displayed to the public on special occasions. In the Renaissance, the term *art* was invented to designate images created by artists and defined by a proper theory: the object of art becomes the object of private appreciation in its own terms. So it's a question of public visibility versus private appreciation. If now we have public hypervisibility—as exemplified in the huge exhibitions where millions of visitors "consume" art—couldn't we also say that we have the possibility of a private micro-appreciation, of invisible art or not publicly visible art?

J-LN: Yes, something has happened to art, a certain privatization of art, in particular of painting, which developed from murals and frescoes and has taken on a smaller format. But what now happens in museums and large exhibits is a return to a sort of public visibility, which is complicated and unwieldy. We find ourselves in a cult of consumption, but at the same time, a big exhibition of Cézanne or Monet or of the treasures of Tutank-hamen is like a deprivatization. We are given the ability to see, and from that something happens in the museum that is on the order of con-templation.

I put on an exhibition myself, on drawing, two years ago in Lyon. I didn't know whether the people I saw there (I mingled with the visitors . . .) were part of the practice [*culte*] or whether they loved art. They were attentive, intensely attentive . . .

AVR: In this particular case, doesn't the very word *art* or the use of the word art designate a technique that makes a particular few lines a work of art, something to be contemplated?

J-LN: Yes, drawing is perhaps something that exposes technique. The exhi-bition was centered on drawing as the birth of the line, rather than as the completed drawing or the world of regulating ideas. Matisse once said: "One must always search for the desire of the line,"[10] the desire of the line for itself, not his desire or mine, but the point at which it wishes to stop or die away. It's beautiful; I put it on the wall of the exhibition. This formulation by Matisse expresses very well what I wish to consider in the complex relationship between religion and art. Where is this sort of objec-tivity, this sort of reality in itself that Matisse addresses? The line does not exist, but all the same it is, and that too says a lot about the body of the artist, her hands, her arms, which she will move in such and such a way. And I would say that the line is obviously not religious because it is not a goddess who must be obeyed.

Literature and Art Between the Exceptional and the Ordinary

AVR: If I understand correctly, we would have to say, on the basis of your thinking, that, properly speaking, art is born at the moment when the divinity withdraws from the world, at the moment after which the sense of the world is no longer a *given*. This seems to imply that art, as an excep-tional representation of truth, is a thing of the past. It is no longer a ques-tion of the end of art as proclaimed by Hegel. Quite the contrary, whereas for Hegel art ends at the moment when it is no longer an idea in a percep-tible form, according to you, this is the very moment when art begins. It is a question of art or *poiēsis* when there is no longer a perceptible repre-sentation of a model, of a principle, of a preexisting idea, but where palpa-ble presence is itself a given, a gift. This is why the deconstruction of

Christianity takes place, so to speak, in art. But it also seems to follow that it does not happen only or exclusively in art, but potentially in every word, in every image. What happens or is expressed in Pontormo's *Visitation* or in a poem by Hölderlin is not something exceptional but something that is happening everywhere, at every moment: it's the "happening" [*se passer*] of the world from nothing, for nothing. That is why "literature" for you is—and I quote what you say in *Dis-enclosure*—"any sort of saying, shouting, praying, laughing or sobbing that holds . . . that infinite suspension of sense" (*D* 97/146), a suspension of sense that results in the retreat of the divine. So, it seems to me that you associate yourself, but for the opposite reason, with the Hegelian argument that art no longer has a "supreme destination," that it becomes something radically commonplace. But if art is no longer an exceptional, extraordinary practice and a supreme task, if it does not have any fundamental, general, even ontological exceptionality, then what form does the exceptional role of poetic works take in your thinking?

J-LN: First of all, I wouldn't say that art has become commonplace. To say that it does not have a supreme destination is for Hegel the same as saying that it is meant to represent truth, that there is some sort of truth in representation. In fact, for Hegel, art is completely caught up in religion because there is an aesthetic religion that proceeds from and in some way prepares the terrain for revealed religion. Therefore, when Hegel says that art no longer has this destination and that it is a thing of the past, he sees art simply as the representation of a truth that has a higher place in religion, and an even higher place in philosophy. After that, it is more complicated for Hegel, because in the *Aesthetics* we get the distinct feeling that he knows that there is something else at stake, but he does not really say so. In any case, I would say that, yes, art is indeed always exceptional, because it is precisely the exception by which something banal or commonplace can be not "said" but perhaps "presented" . . .

LTK: Performed?

J-LN: Yes, performed; I was going to say exclaimed, perhaps.

AVR: OK, I agree, but no longer performed as the expression of another world or in the name of any other world except that of the commonplace. That's why I said that art has become something radically commonplace. I meant that what art expresses is precisely the fact that there is no other world than this one.

J-LN: Yes, but there are two ways of saying that there is nothing but the world. And that is the problem of a large portion of contemporary art. There can be a huge ambiguity in many works of contemporary art, which is that when we say that there is only our world, we say this on the level of signification. And then we go and create works that are full of meaning. I'm thinking, for example, of the work of an artist who created a work on the rape of women in Bosnia. Well, when faced with this sort of thing, increasingly I say to myself: "Right, what is this? It's politics with pictures, in which art's proper moment has passed." But at the same time it's not that I, personally, claim to know what needs to be done. I don't know anything, and I also understand that artists are often compelled by all this. But at the same time, I think that we need to resist this tendency, too, because in art there is always something other than meaning. And art is not a cry or laughter or a sobbing of just any kind, either.

AVR: But what distinguishes a "nonliterary" cry from a "literary" cry, a "literary" exclamation from a "nonliterary" exclamation?

J-LN: Perhaps one only truly receives a cry, laughter, or tears if one can also link it to a literary cry that, in some way, through works of art, will give it and has already given it the power and value of its pure expression. In this way, it is detached from the thing that makes a particular person cry out at a particular moment. By the same token, it sends us back from literature to this cry or these tears. Perhaps ultimately we are never completely outside of religion in these gestures. What is the secret link between all the cries of the world, the cries of Christ on the cross and the cry of the Consul throwing himself into the volcano at the end of Malcolm Lowry's *Under the Volcano*? Obviously, on hearing a scream one is immediately struck by the information contained in this scream, which indicates pain or fear. But at the same time, we hear it as a cry, as a cry alone. In any case, I think it is interesting to think about this type of contact, almost a gathering in of the strangeness and heterogeneity between things like the cry, laughter, tears. And I would put prayer together with this, but in the more banal, secular sense of asking someone for something: "Je te prie de . . ." (I ask you to . . .); "Je vous en prie" (Don't mention it).

LTK: What I hear in your words now is a sense that you are problematizing the distinction between the exceptional and the commonplace, without wishing to identify them.

J-LN: Yes, but it's also because this is a complicated affair. When we speak of art, we don't just have to think about works like Manet's *Luncheon on the Grass* or Beethoven's Fifteenth String Quartet. Art doesn't end there. It is also made up of the transmission of the effects it produces. I'm not saying that it informs the whole of everyday life but that it has, nevertheless, an existence that may extend far beyond the place where the work alone is to be found. This can be seen, for example, in Proust's sentences, which remain in the realm of the exceptional, which are always surprising, but which start from everyday circumstances, ultimately, from circumstances of life and of culture that are transformed under the influence of Proust, among others.

Creation and the Image Without Model

AA: As a last brief theme in this conversation, I would like to take the term you just used, that of the *transmission* of what is exceptional in art, in another direction: that of your analysis of creation. In your view, creation cannot be understood as transmission of some pregiven genetic material or model. In this sense, it's not even a spontaneous creation and the ex nihilo is not a spontaneous appearance out of nothing. In Christianity, but also in other religious traditions, there is a distinction between an image that appears spontaneously without being made, for example, the face of Christ on the veil of Veronica, and images that are made or fabricated. However, the latter are still fabricated in the image of that spontaneously created image. Even in this case, it is a question of the transmission of a pregiven model. But often the question of spontaneous creation is actually a formula masking the fact that something has been fabricated. As I understand it, you detach the question of creation from that spontaneous moment. So, creation is not only one singular moment.

J-LN: No, not exactly. But first, I would say there is indeed a question about transmission, of course. So when we speak about the *self* as the absolute, or the *self* as a *punctum*, in that *punctum* there is perhaps no transmission. Of course, there is transmission, there is genetic material, and this is part of what connects us all to the rest of the world. But if we take creation as such, I would say that genetic material is a *nihil*. Perhaps we can say this: if we go back to the idea that God created the world, God created man in his image. But God does not have an image. So, the image of God is the image of nothing. It could be said that there is a transmission that is not exactly a genetic transmission, if we can speak in these terms.

In incarnation—in Christianity—this becomes more complicated: the son of God, who was engendered by him, does not have any of the genetic qualities of the father, and yet he becomes a man. In fact, the human generation of Jesus is a repetition of his divine generation. This is why we say that it is a generation that takes place in the body of a virgin. In fact, it is not a generation but rather an emanation or a "procession." Next, through Christ, man is reengendered by God, that is to say, he is brought into a new life: the new man. In fact, yes, a relationship of engendering runs through creation, which only confirms that this is not a relationship of fabrication. In heaven there is the generation of the son; on earth, the generation of the son is repeated—nowhere is there creation. We can therefore say that, because God has no face, there cannot be an image of God; what is transferred—the genetic material—is precisely without image.

—Translated by John McKeane

Notes

Preface

1. Published in *Bijdragen: International Journal in Philosophy and Theology* 69, no. 3 (2008).

Preamble: In the Midst of the World; or, Why Deconstruct Christianity?
Jean-Luc Nancy

EPIGRAPH: Paul Celan, "Mandorla," in *Poems of Paul Celan*, trans. Michael Hamburger (London: Anvil Press, 1995; orig. 1967), 192. As a technical term in art history, *mandorla* designates the elliptical, almondlike shape inside which Christ in Majesty is depicted.

1. That Christianity should be as Greek as it is Jewish—and as Jewish as it is Greek, Joyce would have said—is what we learn from historians such as Moses Finley or Arnaldo Momigliano. In general terms, the deployment of Christianity disguised the complexity of its provenance, when in fact this provenance allows us to understand how this deployment was a response to a profound movement in the Mediterranean world. On this topic, see Paul Veyne, *Quand notre monde est devenu chrétien (312–394)* (Paris: Albin Michel, 2007). A more provocative work was recently published by Bruno Delorme, *Le Christ grec: De la tragédie aux Évangiles* (Paris: Bayard, 2009).

2. It is not a question of merely contributing a certain representation: at issue is a mutation of affect and of existential dispositions. As Günther Anders states quite rightly, "each foundation of a religion [is] a veritable revolution in the emotional history of humanity, a veritable refoundation of sentiment." See his *L'obsolescence de l'homme* (Paris: Ivrea, 2002; orig. 1956), 347. This remark is important because it displaces the most common characterization of religions as

systems of representation (fantastical or not). Their representational schemes are in effect nothing other than the taking shape of a nascent sentiment as it attempts to express itself. When a civilization has defined itself as being outside or beyond religion, it calls in turn for a new sensibility, and that is indeed what Anders set out to do in this book from 1956. Without following in his footsteps, we can, like him, recognize that the "melancholy of the nihilist" is indeed the affect that arouses in us protest and the desire for revolution.

3. Ludwig Wittgenstein, *Tractatus Logico-Philosophicus* 6.41 and 6.432 (London: Routledge, 2001).

4. Peter Brown, *The Body and Society: Men, Women, and Sexual Renunciation in Early Christianity* (New York: Columbia University Press, 1988), 186–87.

5. See, e.g., his *Critique of Practical Reason* (1788), pt. 1, bk. 1, chap. 3: "Of the Motives [*Triebfedern*] of Pure Practical Reason."

6. In the period of Christianity's first growth, it also had strong recourse to the opposition between worlds or realms, which was expressed in the "gnoses" where Christianity and Manicheism mingled. The gnostic temptation, which reappears periodically in new forms and can be seen to innervate puritanisms and the religiosity of " 'sects,' bears witness to a double desire: at once to sharpen the opposition between one realm and the other, between light and darkness, and to appropriate a knowledge (the meaning of "gnosis") of and from this opposition. This temptation thus signals precisely what it is important to move away from.

7. See Jacques Derrida, *On Touching—Jean-Luc Nancy*, trans. Christine Irizarry (Stanford: Stanford University Press, 2005; orig. 2000). [In French *salut* can mean both "greeting or salutation" and "salvation."—Trans.]

8. The claim that Socrates and Christ can be identified with one another confronts head-on the opposition that is usually established between the two, most elaborately by Kierkegaard. Indeed, for him the truth discovered by recollection is incompatible with the truth for which a subject must break off and be reborn. I do not wish to oppose this thesis, no more than to subscribe to it: I wish to consider a structural similarity where the "right here" of the "outside" essentially passes to one side of the contrast underlined by Kierkegaard. But what is at stake is still the same "passion of the infinite" (Sören Kierkegaard, *Concluding Unscientific Postscript* [Princeton: Princeton University Press, 1968], 192).

9. [*Déposition* has several meanings: (1) deposing an authority figure; (2) an account given under oath, a submission; (3) the representation of the body of Jesus as it is being taken down from the cross; (4) to deposit something, such as a thesis in a library.—Trans.]

10. Claude Lévi-Strauss, *The Naked Man: Mythologiques 4* (Chicago: University of Chicago Press, 1990; orig. 1971), 694.

11. ["Christianity" is *christianisme* in French. *Chrétienté* has been translated as "Christendom" throughout.—Trans.]

12. Heidegger shows this in *The Principle of Reason* (Bloomington: Indiana University Press, 1991; orig. 1957).

13. For Jan Assmann, nothing less than "the original impulse of biblical monotheism" is to be found "in its capacity to trace a boundary between domination and salvation, between political power and divine power, and to dispossess the leaders of the world of salvation and religious leaders of violence" (*Violence et monothéisme* [Paris: Bayard, 2009], 10). I refer the reader to Assmann's text for the elaboration of his thesis, to which I think (Judeo-)Christianity and Islam give two different, even divergent developments, though both are indeed developments of this "tracing of boundaries," despite all the contrary indications to be found in the history of these religions. Among all the historical characteristics that one could collect to show that the distinction between the "powers" of this world and of Heaven plays a cardinal role throughout Christianity, I choose this one: the university, when it appeared in the high Middle Ages, was qualified as the "third power." This shows that it responded to the conception of autonomous knowledge as an activity independent of the two powers that were exercised as spiritual power and political power—both outside of knowledge, of the idea of free knowledge. See, for a further discussion of Assmann's work on monotheism, Laurens ten Kate's contribution to this volume and the Concluding Dialogue with Jean-Luc Nancy.

14. Dostoevsky's Prince Myshkin encapsulates this auto-apostasy: "In my opinion, Roman Catholicism is not even a faith, it's a continuation of the Western Roman Empire, and everything in it is subordinated to that idea, beginning with their faith. The pope seized the earth, an earthly throne, and took up the sword; since that time everything has gone the same way, except that to the sword they've added lies, intrigue, deceit, fanaticism, superstition, and evil-doing. They have trifled with the most sacred, truthful, innocent, and ardent emotions of the people and bartered them all, all of them, for money and paltry temporal power. Is not this the teaching of Antichrist? Atheism was bound to come from them! Atheism did come from them, from Roman Catholicism itself! Atheism first came into being through them: could they believe in themselves?" (Fyodor Dostoevsky, *The Idiot* [Oxford: Oxford University Press, 1992], 574). One must, of course, also consider the "continuation" of the Western Roman Empire; there is much to be said about the relations of the Orthodox Churches to "paltry temporal power." But this is not the place to do so, no more than it is to examine the role of the Reformation in the evolution of the relations between Churches and States. In one sense, and from the perspective adopted here, the Roman Church sets the tone for our consideration of the inner contradiction between the separation and the distinction of the "kingdoms." But there is no reason to be content with condemning this Church alone or more than others: it is rather a reason to ask oneself what, with the collapse of Rome and the possibility of a "civil religion," caused the West to enter into this contradiction, in which Islam was perhaps formed from the beginning, but which it was long able to resolve in its own way. *What dissociated men from their gods, what made it so that "myth," on the one hand, and "idol," on the other, became the names of illusion and dishonesty—that is the event in which we find our origin.* An irreversible, enduring event, of which we are not yet able to take our leave.

15. What's more, this hatred is deployed in the epoch when the Roman Church is engaged in the Crusades, which is to say, in the enterprise most obviously contradictory to the separation of the "kingdoms."

16. The Church's forging of the expression "deicidal people" (which it eventually abandoned) is theologically so incoherent that the hatred behind it becomes glaringly obvious: if God had to die for the salvation of mankind, then deicide or deicides clearly entered into the economy of this salvation. This is a point that has been commented upon, just as the role or sense of Judas in the history of Jesus' passion has been abundantly commented upon and discussed.

17. One would of course have to be much more precise with regard to this history. In the feudal era, even if feudalism is implicated both in the monarchies and in the first attempts at establishing a new Western Empire, there is something that can—or must—be distinguished from the simultaneity (conflictual or not) of the two realms or the two swords. There is a stronger mutual intrication between the religious order and the order of vassalage and suzerainty, where the values of the oath of allegiance and of fidelity—and thus of a sworn faith—play a major role. The particularity of this formation only brings out more clearly the difference between it and the modern or premodern state that succeeds it and makes the separation between the orders much more stark. The sovereignty of the state is not suzerainty. The latter operates, one could say, according to a religious politics [*politique*]; the former clears religion away. Eventually, sovereignty of the state tends toward a "civil religion," which it fails to institute because the state's essence is not religious and because at bottom it is entirely "of this world." One might think that today Islam is opening in Europe the possibility of an entirely new elaboration [*mise en oeuvre*] of this distinction.

18. At most I would mention, in accordance with what has been said by thinkers and historians who are competent in these matters, that the caliphate was instituted via modalities that did not truly originate in the sayings and writings of the Prophet, and to which the clashes between tribes after Mohammed's death were not unconnected. Nonetheless, the sentiment of the necessary distinction has not failed to appear in the history of Islam (e.g., when Ibn Arabi distinguishes prophets, sheiks, and sovereigns).

19. Here I intersect—albeit in a rather different spirit—with the thinking of Whitehead, who speaks of "the present immediacy of a kingdom not of this world"; see the chapter "God and the World" in *Process and Reality* (New York: Free Press, 1978; orig. 1929), 343.

20. Serge Margel, *Le silence des prophètes: La falsification des Écritures et le destin de la modernité* (Paris: Galilée, 2006), 265.

21. Not "indiscernible" in the sense that Leibniz gives it, that is, where two realities cannot be brought back to the same essence, of which they would simply be multiple realizations. That is to say, also in the sense in which an existence must be considered to be an "individual essence." There is certainly much to explore in examining the question of singularity within the order of technical objects and of existence insofar as it is caught up in technical relations. To find

and to open the order of the singular in the apparent indiscernibility of the technical order is one of our tasks.

22. In truth, philosophy and literature share this function, in a sharing that is extremely complex and always in transformation. But this is beyond the scope of the present essay.

23. J. M. Coetzee, *Elizabeth Costello* (London: Vintage, 2004), 150. [Nancy quotes from the French translation by Catherine Lauga du Plessis (Paris: Seuil, 2004), which uses *adoration* for "worship."—Trans.]

Re-opening the Question of Religion: Dis-Enclosure of Religion and Modernity in the Philosophy of Jean-Luc Nancy
Alena Alexandrova, Ignaas Devisch, Laurens ten Kate, and Aukje van Rooden

1. Gianni Vattimo, for example, in *Belief* (Cambridge: Polity Press, 1999) and *After Christianity* (New York: Columbia University Press, 2002), welcomes a certain return of religion in our "postmodern" time, that is, a post-Christian "belief" still strongly embedded in the "best" (pluralistic, nondogmatic) parts of the Christian traditions. From the opposite perspective, Daniel Dennett, in *Breaking the Spell: Religion as a Natural Phenomenon* (New York: Viking, 2006), and Richard Dawkins, in *The God Delusion* (Boston: Houghton Mifflin, 2006), resist any return of religion in favor of a rigid atheism that neutralizes religion as an illusion, albeit a "natural" one. See further: Peter Berger, *The Desecularization of the Modern World: Resurgent Religion and World Politics* (Grand Rapids, Mich.: Eerdmans, 1999); Paul Heelas, ed., *Religion, Modernity, Postmodernity* (Oxford: Blackwell, 1998); and Hent de Vries, ed. *Religion: Beyond a Concept* (New York: Fordham University Press, 2008).

2. "Une religion de la sortie de la religion." See M. Gauchet, *The Disenchantment of the World: A Political History of Religion* (Princeton: Princeton University Press, 1999; orig. 1985), esp. 101–15, where this formula is translated "A religion for departing religion," and 200–7, where the author speaks of "The Religious after Religion."

3. In its Judeo-Christian form, monotheism has always, paradoxically, involved a critique of religion by creating a distance between the divine and the human world, by stressing humans' responsibility for their lives, and by privileging the authentic individuality of the believer. In Augustine, the freedom and responsibility of humanity in the face of man's distance from God reaches an intense pitch in a radically individualistic understanding of religion and religious life. Charles Taylor, in *Sources of the Self: The Making of Modern Identity* (Cambridge: Harvard University Press, 1989), 127–42, traces modern individualism back to early Christianity and Augustine.

4. See "Of Divine Places," *IC* 110–51.

5. See, e.g., *IC*.

6. For analyses of art and literature, see: *M1*, "The Look of the Portrait" (*M2* 220–47), and *GI*. For politico-religious myths, see *IC* 43–81/107–74, and *NM*. Nancy shares and discusses the concept of *désoeuvrement* with Maurice

Blanchot, who responded to *IC* with his *The Unavowable Community*, trans. Pierre Joris (New York: Station Hill Press, 1988; orig. 1983). For *partage*, see, e.g., SV and *IC*. For the "with," see "Cum" (*PD* 115–21) and Jean-Luc Nancy and Laurens ten Kate, "'Cum' Revisited: Preliminaries to Thinking the Interval," in *Intermedialities: Philosophy, Arts, Politics*, ed. Henk Oosterling and Eva Ziarek (Lanham: Rowman & Littlefield, 2010), 37–43. On the in-between, see, e.g., "Between Us: First Philosophy" (*BSP* 21–28/40–48).

7. See esp. *SW* and *CW*.

8. *SW* 183n50/91n1; *BSP* 197n20/34 n1 and 200n52/81n1; *PD*, 155.

9. See Charles Taylor, *A Secular Age* (Cambridge: Harvard University Press, 2007).

10. This structure of inside-outside forms one of the central themes throughout the contributions to this volume. See esp. Nancy's Preamble.

11. See also, on the meaning of the concept of dis-enclosure—and on the difficult decisions involved in translating its French/German/Greek origins (*déclosion—Unverborgenheit—aletheia*), the "Translator's Foreword," *D* x.

12. *C*; see also *UJ*.

13. *PD* 159–88 and EG.

14. For Löwith's position, see, e.g., *Weltgeschichte und Heilsgeschehen: Die theologischen Voraussetzungen der Geschichtsphilosophie* (Stuttgart: Kohlhammer, 1953); *Permanence and Change: Lectures on the Philosophy of History* (Cape Town: Haum, 1969); *Christentum und Geschichte* (Düsseldorf: Pädogischer Verlag Schwann, 1955). For Blumenberg's position, see esp. his *The Legitimacy of the Modern Age* (Cambridge: MIT Press, 1983; orig. 1966).

15. Taylor's thesis that one of the driving forces behind the disenchantment of the world "has always been the Jewish and then the Christian religion" ("Ein Ort für die Transzendenz?" *Information Philosophie* 2 [June 2003]: 11) is supported by the detailed historical explorations of Michael Allen Gillespie, in *The Theological Origins of Modernity* (Chicago: University of Chicago Press, 2008). Manfred Frank, in *Der kommende Gott: Vorlesungen über der neue Mythologie* (Frankfurt a. M.: Suhrkamp, 1982), assesses the resurgence of "Mythos" in modern culture. Alister McGrath, adopting an apologetic outlook, defends the meaning of Christianity in a secular era by pinpointing the presumed shortcomings of atheism for dealing with the complexities of modern life—see his *The Twilight of Atheism: The Rise and Fall of Disbelief in the Modern World* (London: Random House, 2004). Although Nancy takes the problematization of the secularist paradigm in a direction quite different from these scholars, he shares the questions they raise.

16. E.g., in *D* 1/9 and more extensively in EG 79.

17. See Michel Foucault, *The History of Sexuality, Vol. I: An Introduction*, trans. Robert Hurley (New York: Random House, 1978; orig. 1976), and esp. his groundbreaking article on Bataille, "Préface à la transgression," in Michel Foucault, *Dits et écrits*, ed. D. Defert and F. Ewald (Paris: Gallimard 1963), 1:233–50, esp. 233–35.

18. See Creston Davis, John Milbank, and Slavoj Žižek, eds., *Theology and the Political: The New Debate* (Durham: Duke University Press, 2005). A survey of the field can be found in Hent de Vries and Lawrence E. Sullivan, eds., *Political Theologies: Public Religions in a Post-Secular World* (New York: Fordham University Press, 2006), a volume to which Nancy contributed his "Church, State, Resistance." In addition, from the domain of political science, one should mention Jacques Rollet, *Religion et politique: Le christianisme, l'islam, la démocratie* (Paris: Grasset, 2001).

19. See Gauchet, *The Disenchantment of the World*, e.g., 130–44.

20. Ibid., 104.

21. Ibid., 103. The debates provoked by Gauchet's book have induced the author to rephrase and revise his analysis: see his *La religion dans la démocratie: Parcours de laïcité* (Paris: Gallimard, 1998), *Un monde désenchanté?* (Paris: Éditions de l'Atelier, 2004), and his discussion with Luc Ferry, *Le religieux après la religion* (Paris: Grasset, 2004).

22. The term *dual history* is introduced by Gauchet; see *The Disenchantment of the World*, 104.

23. See Jürgen Habermas, "Faith and Knowledge," in *The Future of Human Nature* (Cambridge: Polity Press, 2003), 101–15; orig. 2001), one of the first publications in which the concept of the post-secular was introduced—issued only a few months after the attacks on the World Trade Center in New York on September 9, 2001; idem, *Between Naturalism and Religion: Philosophical Essays* (Cambridge: Polity Press, 2008; orig. 2005); and Habermas's dialogue with the present pope, Benedict XVI, in *The Dialectics of Secularization: On Reason and Religion* (Ft. Collins, Colo.: Ignatius Press, 2007), also Jürgen Habermas, "On the Relations Between the Secular Liberal State and Religion," and Pope Benedict XVI, "Prepolitical Moral Foundations of a Free Republic, both trans. Anh Nguyen, in *Political Theologies*, ed. de Vries and Sullivan, 251–68. On Habermas and the post-secular, see Rudolf Langthaler and Herta Nagl-Docekal, eds., *Glauben und Wissen: Ein Symposium mit Jürgen Habermas* (Berlin: Akademie, 2007), and Hans Joas, "Post-Secular Religion? On Jürgen Habermas," in his *Do We Need Religion? On the Experience of Self-Transcendence* (Boulder, Colo.: Paradigm Publishers, 2008), 105–11; Joas calls "Faith and Knowledge" "epoch-making."

24. Habermas, *Between Naturalism and Religion*, 242.

25. Habermas, "Faith and Knowledge," 105.

26. A similar critical view of Habermas's approach can be found in Thomas Schmidt, "Der Begriff der Postsäkularität," in *Politische Theologie—gegengelesen*, ed. Jürgen Manemann and Bernd Wacker, *Jahrbuch Politische Theologie*, vol. 5 (Münster: LIT, 2008), 248: the treatment of the post-secular continues to reduce "religion to secular reason as the legitimizing criterion for religion's public use." For further critical analyses of Habermas's notion of a post-secular society, see also Joas, "Post-Secular Religion?" 106–7.

Valuable reflections on and definitions of the post-secular can be found in de Vries and Sullivan, eds., *Political Theologies*, e.g., in Hent de Vries, "Introduction: Before, Around, and Beyond the Theologico-Political," 2–3: "one [should understand] the term *post-secular* not as an attempt at historical periodization (following on equally unfortunate designations such as the 'post-modern,' the 'post-historical,' or the 'post-human') but merely as a topical indicator for—well, a problem." This problem is, first of all, de Vries states, quoting Joas, "a change in the mindset of those who, previously, felt justified in considering religions to be moribund" (*Political Theologies* 2–3; "Post-Secular Religion?" 107). De Vries then shows that this shift pertains to a change in the "self-understanding" of secularism (whether the self-understanding of citizens, of the state, or of the body politic), but, again opposing Habermas, he claims that what is needed in thinking and criticizing the post-secular as a condition or concept is an approach starting from religion (with all its ambivalence), rather than from secularism. In elaborating this point, de Vries refers to Derrida's "Faith and Knowledge: The Two Sources of 'Religion' at the Limits of Reason Alone," trans. Samuel Weber, in Jacques Derrida and Gianni Vattimo, eds., *Religion* (Stanford: Stanford University Press, 1998), 1–78.

27. See Richard Rorty and Gianni Vattimo, *The Future of Religion*, ed. Santiago Zabala (New York: Columbia University Press, 2005).

28. See on Chrétien's work, Ian James's contribution to this volume, "Incarnation and Infinity."

29. See Dominique Janicaud et al., *Phenomenology and the "Theological Turn": The French Debate* (New York: Fordham University Press, 2000), 16–103, for Janicaud's essay, and 107–241 for responses by Courtine, Ricoeur, Chrétien, Marion and Henry. For a more detailed confrontation between Nancy's deconstruction of Christianity and the theological turn in phenomenology, Laurens ten Kate, " 'Intimate Distance': Rethinking the Unthought God in Christianity," *Sophia: International Journal for the Philosophy of Religion and Philosophical Theology* 47 (2008): 327–43.

30. The suggestion of a "phenomenology of the nonapparent" was introduced by Heidegger in 1973, in the Zähringen seminars. It was more or less adopted by Marion, Chrétien, and, in a different way, by Levinas—the latter's critical discussion with phenomenology and his claim that phenomenology would exclude the nonapparent as its "other" date from his *Totality and Infinity: An Essay on Exteriority*, trans. Alphonso Lingis (Pittsburgh: Duquesne University Press 2003; orig. 1961). See, on the history of this phenomenology of the nonapparent, Janicaud in *Phenomenology and the "Theological Turn*," 28–34.

31. Jean-Luc Marion, "Metaphysics and Phenomenology: A Relief for Theology," in de Vries, ed., *Religion*, 284; also in Jean-Luc Marion, *The Visible and the Revealed*, trans. Christina Gschwandtner and others (New York: Fordham University Press, 2008), 50.

32. Derrida's *On Touching—Jean-Luc Nancy*, trans. Christine Irizarry (Stanford: Stanford University Press, 2005; orig. 2000), esp. 165–200, and Francis

Guibal and Jean-Clet Martin, eds., *Sens en tous sens: Autour des travaux de Jean-Luc Nancy* (Paris: Galilée, 2004) have been platforms for this exchange. See Ian James, "Incarnation and Infinity," in the present volume for a comparison of Nancy's thought and Derrida's comments in *On Touching*.

33. See, for a discussion of this text, Marc De Kesel, "Deconstruction or Destruction? Comments on Jean-Luc Nancy's Theory of Christianity," in this volume.

34. Hent de Vries, *Philosophy and the Turn to Religion* (Baltimore: Johns Hopkins University Press, 1999), x.

35. Ibid., xiii. Such rethinking starting from Derrida can be found in contemporary theology as well as philosophy. See, for a place where both disciplines meet and intersect, John D. Caputo and Michael J. Scanlon, eds., *God, the Gift, and Postmodernism* (Bloomington: Indiana University Press, 1999); John D. Caputo and Mark Dooley, eds., *Questioning God* (Bloomington: Indiana University Press, 2001); John D. Caputo and Michael J. Scanlon, eds., *Augustine and Postmodernism: Confession and Circumfession* (Bloomington: Indiana University Press, 2005); and Merold Westphal, ed., *Postmodern Philosophy and Christian Thought* (Bloomington: Indiana University Press, 1999). For a treatment of the question of what "remains" of religion today by highlighting a specific theme (that of suffering and pain) from various interdisciplinary perspectives, see: Robert Gibbs and Elliot R. Wolfson, eds., *Suffering Religion* (London: Routledge, 2002). See also, from the field of theology: Mark C. Taylor, *Erring: A Postmodern A/theology* (Chicago: University of Chicago Press, 1984); idem, *After God* (Chicago: University of Chicago Press, 2007); Walter Lowe, *Theology and Difference: The Wound Of Reason* (Bloomington: Indiana University Press, 1993); Graham Ward, *Christ and Culture* (Oxford: Blackwell, 2005); and François Nault, *Derrida et la théologie: Dire Dieu après la déconstruction* (Paris: Cerf, 2000). From the field of philosophy, see: Kevin Hart, *The Trespass of the Sign: Deconstruction, Theology, and Philosophy* (Cambridge: Cambridge University Press, 1989; rpt. New York: Fordham University Press, 2000); John D. Caputo, *The Prayers and Tears of Jacques Derrida: Religion Without Religion* (Bloomington: Indiana University Press, 1997); Kevin Hart and Barbara Wall, eds., *The Experience of God: A Postmodern Response* (New York: Fordham University Press, 2005); and Yvonne Sherwood and Kevin Hart, eds., *Derrida and Religion: Other Testaments* (New York: Routledge, 2005), esp. part 7, "La/Le Toucher (Touching Her/Him)."

36. De Vries, *Philosophy and the Turn to Religion*, xiii.

37. Alain Badiou, *Saint Paul: The Foundation of Universalism* trans. Ray Brassier (Stanford: Stanford University Press, 2003; orig. 1997), 5. See, for a comparison of Badiou's and Nancy's work, Ian James, "Incarnation and Infinity," and Boyan Manchev, "Ontology of Creation: The Onto-aiesthetics of Jean-Luc Nancy," in the present volume.

38. See Giorgio Agamben, *The Time That Remains: A Commentary on the Letter to the Romans*, Trans. Patricia Daley (Stanford: Stanford University Press, 2005; orig. 2000), 23 and 51–53.

39. Giorgio Agamben, *The Kingdom and the Glory: For a Theological Genealogy of Economy and Government: Homo Sacer II* (Stanford, Calif.: Stanford University Press, 2011; orig. 2007), 4.

40. See Slavoj Žižek, *On Belief* (London: Routledge, 2001), 147; see also idem, *The Fragile Absolute—or, Why Is the Christian Legacy Worth Fighting For?* (London: Verso, 2000), and idem, *The Puppet and the Dwarf: Christianity's Perverse Core* (Cambridge: MIT Press, 2003), in which Žižek analyzes the "core" of Christianity as *between* perversion and subversion (as the original German title reads) and, like Nancy, defines Christianity as a form of atheism (e.g. 171).

41. Žižek, *The Puppet and the Dwarf*, 78.

42. Ibid., 91.

43. See, e.g., Ephesians 1:1.

44. Peter Sloterdijk, *Sphären*, vol. 1, *Blasen*, chap. 8 (Berlin: Suhrkamp 1998), and vol. 2, *Globen*, Introduction and chap. 5 (Berlin: Suhrkamp 1999). For a confrontation between Nancy and Sloterdijk, see Laurens ten Kate, "Zwischen Immunität und Infinität: Der Ort in Peter Sloterdijks Sphärologie, im Hinblick auf seine Durchdenkung der christlichen Erbe," in *Die Vermessung des Ungeheuren: Philosophie nach Peter Sloterdijk*, ed. Koenraad Hemelsoet and Sjoerd van Tuinen (Munich: Wilhelm Fink, 2009), 120–30.

The Self-Deconstruction of Christianity
François Raffoul

1. Jacques Derrida/Jean-Luc Nancy, "Responsabilité—du sens à venir," in *Sens en tous sens: Autour des travaux de Jean-Luc Nancy*, ed. Francis Guibal et Jean-Clet Martin (Paris: Galilée, 2004), 192.

2. In the chapter "Urbi et orbi," Nancy describes globalization as "the suppression of all world-forming of the world" and as "an unprecedented geopolitical, economic, and ecological catastrophe" (*CW* 50/53).

3. Slightly further on, Nancy states in a note that the term *globalization* could just as easily be referred to as "agglomerization" (*CW* 118n5/20n1), in reference to the *glomus*. As for the concept "bad infinite," which Nancy borrows from Hegel, it signifies in this context that the infinite "is indeed the one that cannot be *actual*" (*CW* 39/29), that is, the bad infinite "of a 'globalization' in a centrifugal spiral" (*CW* 47/46), which Nancy contrasts with the actual infinite of the finite being (see *CW* 71/95). For Nancy, the infinite in action signifies the world itself as "absolute value," that is to say, as the existence of the world put into play as "absolute existence" (*CW* 44/39) so much so that it is necessary "in the end, that the world has absolute value for itself" (*CW* 40/30).

4. Included in *GT*, 5–71.

5. Martin Heidegger, "Overcoming Metaphysics," in *The End of Philosophy*, trans. Joan Stambaugh (New York: Harper and Row, 1973).

6. Heidegger writes: "Overcoming is worthy of thought only when we think about appropriation [*Verwindung*]" (ibid., 92; trans. modified). Thus an originary reappropriation of metaphysics is for him ultimately the objective of the overcoming of metaphysics.

7. Martin Heidegger, "The Way Back into the Ground of Metaphysics," in *Existentialism from Dostoyevsky to Sartre*, ed. and trans. Walter Kaufmann (New York: New American Library, 1975), 267.

8. Martin Heidegger, *Nietzsche*, vols. 3 and 4, trans. David Farrell Krell (New York: HarperOne, 1991), 223.10.

9. Martin Heidegger, *On Time and Being*, trans. Joan Stambaugh (Chicago: University of Chicago Press, 2002), 24.

10. Martin Heidegger, *Basic Writings*, ed. and trans. David Farrell Krell (New York: Harper & Row, 1993), 231.

11. In *Dis-enclosure*, Nancy warns us not to "confuse" this nothing or this void with nihilism (*D* 3/11); he explains in *CW* that the nothing in the ex nihilo of creation "fractures the deepest core of nihilism from within" and that the motif of creation (which for Nancy lies in the ex nihilo) "constitutes the exact reverse of nihilism" (*CW* 71/95). Nihilism constitutes raising the nothing into a principle, whereas the ex nihilo signifies the absence of principle: The ex nihilo means the "undoing of any principle, including that of the nothing" (*D* 24–25/39).

12. Heidegger, "Overcoming Metaphysics," 85.

13. Ibid.

14. Martin Heidegger, *The Principle of Reason,* trans. Reginald Lilly (Bloomington: Indiana University Press, 1996).

15. "It is important, therefore, that we not take the assemblage of Christianity en bloc, to refute or confirm it, for that would be tantamount to placing ourselves outside or alongside it" (*D* 149/216).

16. On this concept of *chose-rien*, "no thing" or "the nothing as thing," where nothing can also mean "something," or *res*, see *CW* 69/90.

17. Gérard Granel, in his 1955 translation of *Zur Seinsfrage* (*On the Question of Being*), was probably the first to translate Heidegger's *Abbau* as *déconstruction*. In that text, Heidegger attempts to explain the senses of *Destruktion* by referring to those included in *Abbau*. Derrida explained in many interviews that he had used *déconstruction* to render *Destruktion* as Heidegger employs that word in *Being and Time*. This equivalence appears mainly in commentaries, articles, and books by French thinkers; *Being and Time* itself was not completely translated into French until François Vezin's version of 1985. In these earlier works, *déconstruction* may have been used to translate *Destruktion* because the more obvious translation, *destruction*, had been attacked as misleading, given its negative connotations. Some believe that Vezin proposed using *désobstruction* for *Destruktion* in his translation specifically to avoid *déconstruction*, which by then would have been evocative of Derrida.

18. Martin Heidegger, *Being and Time,* trans. Joan Stambaugh (New York: State University of New York Press, 1996), 288.

19. For more on this point, see Nancy's "Cum" (*PD* 115–21) and Jean-Luc Nancy and Laurens ten Kate, "'Cum' Revisited: Preliminaries to Thinking the Interval," in *Intermedialities: Philosophy, Arts, Politics*, ed. Henk Oosterling and Eva Ziarek (Lanham: Rowman & Littlefield, 2010), 37–43.

20. As Derrida explains in a 2004 interview: "A slogan, nonetheless, of deconstruction: being open to what comes, to the to-come, to the other" (Jacques Derrida, "Jacques Derrida, penseur de l'événement," interview with Jérôme-Alexandre Nielsberg, L'humanité, January 28, 2004, http://www.humanite.fr/2004-01-28_Tribune-libre_-Jacques-Derrida-penseur-de-levenement).

21. Jacques Derrida/Jean-Luc Nancy, "Responsabilité—du sens à venir," in Sens en tous sens, 191.

22. Derrida thus writes: "I will say, I will try to show later in what sense impossibility, a certain impossibility of saying the event or a certain impossible possibility of saying the event, obliges us to think otherwise . . . what possible means in the history of philosophy. In other words, I will try to explain why and how I hear the word *possible* in the statement where this 'possible' is not simply 'different from' or the 'contrary of' impossible, why here 'possible' and 'impossible' *mean the same*" (Jacques Derrida, Dire l'événement, est-ce possible? with Gad Soussana and Alexis Nouss [Paris: L'Harmattan, 2001], 86). This renewed thought of the possible and impossible allowed him at times to use the expression: "condition of possibility (or impossibility)," e.g., in Paper Machine, trans. Rachel Bowlby (Stanford, Calif.: Stanford University Press, 2005), 84. On this question, see my "Derrida and the Ethics of the Im-possible," Research in Phenomenology 38 (2008): 270–90.

23. "The idea of creation . . . is above all the idea of the ex nihilo" (CW 51/ 55).

24. See the discussion of Gérard Granel, "Far from Substance: Whither and to What Point? Essay on the Ontological Kenosis of Thought since Kant," in the chapter "A Faith That Is Nothing at All" (D 63–74/89–116).

25. In French, mettre au monde has the colloquial sense of "to give birth." However, a few pages further, Nancy states: " 'Coming to the world' means birth and death, emerging from nothing and going to nothing" (CW 74/101).

26. On such a poverty, see the edition and translation by Philippe Lacoue-Labarthe and Ana Samardzija of the Heidegger conference held on on June 27, 1945, La pauvreté (Die Armut) (Strasbourg: Presses Universitaires de Strasbourg, 2004).

Deconstruction or Destruction? Comments on Jean-Luc Nancy's Theory of Christianity
Marc De Kesel

1. Jacques Derrida, "Faith and Knowledge: The Two Sources of 'Religion' at the Limits of Reason Alone," in Religion, ed. Jacques Derrida and Gianni Vattimo (Cambridge: Polity Press, 1998), 1–78.

2. Ibid., 50. See also 50–51: "Life . . . is sacred, holy, infinitely respectable only in the name of what is worth more than it. . . . The price of human life, . . . the price of what ought to remain safe (heilig, sacred, safe and sound, unscathed, immune), as the absolute price, the price of what ought to inspire respect, modesty, reticence, this price is priceless."

3. Ibid., 44–45.

4. Ibid., 44: "Without the performative experience of this elementary act of faith, there would neither be 'social bond' nor address of the other, nor any performativity in general."

5. Derrida's term for this kind of double-bind logic, "auto-immune auto-indemnification," is borrowed from biological or, more precisely, medical science (ibid., 42–47).

6. This is why a touch has always already touched—and thus contaminated and subverted—the untouchable. When, in his comments on Nancy's deconstruction of Christianity, Derrida discusses some passages on touch in the Gospels (*On Touching—Jean-Luc Nancy*, trans. Christine Irizarry [Stanford: Stanford University Press, 2005], 100–3; orig. 2000), he emphasizes the fact that Christ indeed touches (to heal the blind and cripples), but never without being touched himself. This is why, according to Derrida's reasoning, John's Gospel (where "literal allusions to touching are rarer," 102; trans. modified), in particular the "Noli me tangere" passage, is an exception to the logic of deconstruction with regard to touch.

7. See, e.g., *D* 34/53, where Nancy claims that we must "cease all our efforts to 'cure' the 'ills' of the present-day world (in its privation of sense) by some return to Christianity in particular, or to religion in general, for it is a matter of grasping how we are already outside the religious."

8. See *NT* 15–16/29–30: "Only thus does the 'resurrection' find its nonreligious meaning. What for religion is the renewal of a presence that bears the phantasmagoric assurance of immortality is revealed here to be nothing other than the departing into which presence actually withdraws, bearing its sense in accordance with this parting. Just as it comes, so it goes: this is to say that it *is* not, in the sense of something being fixed within presence, immobile and identical to itself, available for a use or a concept. 'Resurrection' is the uprising [*surrection*], the sudden appearance of the unavailable, of the other and of the one disappearing *in the body itself and as the body*. This is not a magical trick. It is the very opposite: the dead body remains dead, and that is what creates the 'emptiness' of the tomb, but the body that theology will later call 'glorious' (that is, shining with the brilliance of the invisible) reveals that this emptying is really the emptying out of presence. No, nothing is available here: don't try to seize upon a meaning for this finite and finished life, don't try to touch or to hold back what essentially distances itself and, in distancing itself, touches you with its very distance. . . . It is as though it were touching you while permanently disappointing your expectations, touching you with what makes rise up before you, for you, even that which does not rise up. This uprising or insurrection is a glory that devotes itself to disappointing you and to pushing your outstretched hand away." See also *C* 61–65/54–57 on the theme of the "glorious body" and Boyan Manchev's article in this volume.

9. Derrida, "Faith and Knowledge," 48–49.

10. For the metaphor of the "ellipsis" used in this context, see ibid., 39. It is one of the basic motifs in Derrida's deconstructive theory, developed in his early

writings. See, e.g., "Ellipsis" in *Writing and Difference* (Chicago: University of Chicago Press, 1978; orig. 1967), 295–300.

11. A Derridean deconstruction lays bare how a supposed identity is based in an *"originary* repetition" (In "Ellipsis," the identity is that of the "book," which is the result of "writing" and "closes" itself off from "difference"; Derrida refers to the work of Edmond Jabès.) Difference and repetition form the basis of what is considered to be sameness and identity. See *Writing and Difference*, 295: "Repetition does not reissue the book but describes its origin from the vantage of a writing which does not yet belong to it, or no longer belongs to it, a writing which feigns, by repeating the book, inclusion in the book."

12. Jacques Derrida, *Of Grammatology* (Baltimore: John Hopkins University Press, 1997; orig. 1967), 158.

13. See, e.g., Jan Assmann, *Die Mosaische Unterscheidung oder Der Preis des Monotheismus* (Munich: Hanser, 2003); idem, *Monotheismus und die Sprache der Gewalt* (Vienna: Picus, 2006); Marc De Kesel, "Religion und/als Kritik," in *Wieder Religion: Christentum im zeitgenössischen kritischen Denken* (*Lacan, Žižek, Badiou u.a.*), ed. Marc De Kesel and Dominiek Hoens (Vienna: Turia & Kant, 2006), 15–39.

14. In "A Deconstruction of Monotheism," listing the characteristics of the "self-deconstructive character of Christianity," Nancy mentions that "monotheism is in truth atheism" (*D* 35/55). See also "Atheism and Monotheism" (*D* 14–28/27–45).

15. This is why the truly atheist position is more difficult than is commonly presumed. It is not a matter of believing there is no God but of fighting that "belief" as well—to prevent the certainty of God's nonexistence replacing the certainty of his existence. It is a matter of cultivating an uncertainty in order not to turn it into a new kind of certainty, a new kind of "God."

16. Nancy's work is a perfect illustration of this kind of twentieth-century criticism.

17. "Being with" is a major theme throughout Nancy's work, discussed especially in *BSP*. Nancy stresses again and again that *Dasein* is to be defined as "we," as plural, a nontotalizing plural or "singular plural."

18. In the New Testament, one finds the idea that Christians dwell in the world, yet are not of the world (see John 15:19; 17:14–16), but not the express formulation. The latter originates in the anonymous second-century *Letter to Diognetus* (6.3; see http://www.ccel.org/ccel/schaff/anf01.iii.ii.vi.html). For allusions to the idea in the New Testament, see also 1 Cor. 7:29–31: "the appointed time has grown very short. From now on, let those who have wives live as though they had none, and those who mourn as though they were not mourning, and those who rejoice as though they were not rejoicing, and those who buy as though they had no goods, and those who deal with the world as though they had no dealings with it. For the present form of this world is passing away." (I quote from the *English Standard Version* of the Bible.) According to Assmann, this subject position is typical not only of Christianity but also of monotheism

in general, insofar it defines man as subject to nonworldly Law. "He who observes the commandments, lives like a stranger on earth. As one reads in Psalm 119:19: 'I am a sojourner on earth; hide not your commandments from me.' Abiding by the Law means living as a stranger on earth, even when staying in the Promised Land. The Law describes a counterfactual order, which changes us into people living in this world without assimilating to it. Monotheism lays the basis for an existential unworldliness" (Assmann, *Die Mosaische Unterscheidung*, 137).

19. Martin Heidegger, *Being and Time*, trans. Joan Stambaugh (New York: State University of New York Press, 1996; orig. 1927), 31 and passim.

20. Hegel defines the condition of the modern bourgeois thus in "Die bürgerliche Gesellschaft," *Grundlinien der Philosophie des Rechts*, § 182–256.

21. In the final pages of *Limited Inc*, Derrida stresses the unconditional character of his deconstruction, even in the ethical sense of the word: "In the different texts I have written on (against) apartheid, I have on several occasions spoken of 'unconditional' affirmation or of 'unconditional' 'appeal'. This has also happened to me in other 'contexts' and each time that I speak of the link between deconstruction and the 'yes.' Now, the very least that can be said of unconditionality (*a word that I use not by accident to recall the character of the categorical imperative in its Kantian form*) is that it is independent of every determinate context, even of the determination of a context in general" ("Afterword," trans. Samuel Weber, Jacques Derrida, *Limited Inc* (Evanston, Ill.: Northwestern University Press, 1988; orig. 1977/1990), 152; my emphasis.

Sense, Existence, and Justice; or, How Are We to Live in a Secular World?
Ignaas Devisch and Kathleen Vandeputte
1. Ludwig Wittgenstein, *Tractatus Logico-Philosophicus* (London: Routledge, 2001), 6.41.

2. Aristotle, *The Complete Works of Aristotle* (Princeton: Princeton University Press. 1999), 1105b15–1109b25.

3. This text originally appeared in the journal *Epokhè*, no. 5 (1995); it was later included in *BSP* 177–183/203–211.

4. In the English translation of his text on compearance, Nancy explains in a note the semantic similarities between the French *comparution* and its English equivalent "compearance," both meaning "to appear in court": "*La comparution* refers to the act of appearing in court having been summoned. 'Summoning' carries a much stronger notion of agency than the more disembodied *comparution* and lacks the commonality implied in the prefix. The Scottish common-law term 'compearance'—although foreign to most English ears—conveys the meaning exactly" (Com 371n).

Between All and Nothing: The Affective Dimension of Political Bonds
Theo W. A. de Wit
1. E. H. Kantorowicz, "Pro Patria Mori in Medieval Political Thought," in idem, *Selected Studies*, ed. Michael Cherniavsky and Ralph E. Giesey (New York:

Augustin, 1965), 308–24. Kantorowicz is, of course, the great authority on medieval political theology; see his *The King's Two Bodies: A Study in Medieval Political Theology* (Princeton: Princeton University Press, 1957).

2. Mercier and Billot are quoted from Kantorowicz, "Pro Patria," 309; trans. modified.

3. See Christian Duquoc, *Dieu différent: Essai sur la symbolique trinitaire* (Paris: Cerf, 1977).

4. Marcel Gauchet, *La religion dans la démocratie: Parcours de la laïcité* (Paris: Gallimard, 1998), 8.

5. Kantorowicz, "Pro Patria," 308, 309.

6. Ibid., 315.

7. Ibid., 324.

8. Ibid.

9. Walter Benjamin, "Theorien des deutschen Faschismus," in idem, *Schriften III* (Frankfurt am Main: Suhrkamp, 1972), 238: "Any future war is at the same time a slave revolt of technology."

10. Eric Voegelin, *Die politischen Religionen* (Stockholm: Bermann-Fischer, 1939). See also John Gray's actualization of this in *Black Mass: Apocalyptic Religion and the Death of Utopia* (London: Penguin, 2007).

11. Thus Kantorowicz (in "Pro Patria," 324) remarks that a tendency to substitute the fatherland for God has become more and more obvious since 1914.

12. See "Politics II," in *SW* 103–17/163–82 (see also "Politics I," *SW* 88–93/139–47), and CSR.

13. See *SW* 90, 92, 109/142, 145–46, 170–71.

14. Kantorowicz gives an example of the last from premodern times in "Pro Patria." In Tolomeo of Lucca, he finds that willingness to fall for the fatherland is rooted in love: *amor patriae in radice charitatis fundatur.* Insofar as love means "not to put one's own things before those in common, but the common things before one's own," *amor patriae* deserves the highest honor, for all other virtues hinge upon love (321).

15. See EM 32: "If something such as 'race' exists, in the sense of racism, then nothing needs to ex-ist; all is already given in the essence of the races, in this implosion-into-the-self that the idea of race entails."

16. "War, Right, Sovereignty—Technē," in *BSP* 101–43/125–68. In the German version, which appeared in *Lettre International*, Nancy makes clear that he has Schmitt's version of the doctrine of sovereignty in mind. See "Der Preis des Friedens: Krieg, Recht, Souveränität—Technè," *Lettre International* 14 (1991), with a number of further references to the work of Schmitt.

17. Carl Schmitt, *The Concept of the Political*, trans. George Schwab (Chicago: University of Chicago Press, 1996), 45.

18. See Francis Guibal's excellent article "Le signe hégélien: Économie sacrificielle et relève dialectique," *Archives de Philosophie* 60 (1997): 265–97. Nancy refers to Hegel as a source, too, e.g., in "The Unsacrificeable," *FT* 51–77/ 65–106 passim.

19. A good example of this type of liberalism may be found in Richard Herzinger, *Die Tyrannei des Gemeinsinns: Ein Bekenntnis zur egoistischen Gesellschaft* (Berlin: Rowohlt, 1997).

20. Thomas Hobbes, *Leviathan*, ed. Crawford B. Macpherson (London: Pelican, 1968), 272.

21. Schmitt, *The Concept of the Political*, 65.

22. See the Preface to the 2nd ed. of *Political Theology* from 1934: "We have come to recognize that the political is the total, and as a result we know that any decision about whether something is *unpolitical* is always a *political* decision" (Carl Schmitt, *Political Theology: Four Chapters on the Concept of Sovereignty* [Chicago: University of Chicago Press, 2005; orig. 1934], 2). With regard to the question whether "everything" can be termed political, see also Jean-Luc Nancy and Philip M. Adamek, "Is Everything Political? (A Brief Remark)," in *The New Centennial Review* 2, no. 3 (Fall 2002): 15–22.

23. With regard to the need for a civil religion, see also *D* 3ff/11ff.

24. See: Jean Bauberot, *Laïcité 1905–2005, entre passion et raison* (Paris: Seuil, 2004), chap. 10, "La religion civile, impensé de la laïcité française," 163–87; and Marcel Gauchet, *La religion dans la démocratie*.

25. See J.-L. Nancy, "Conloquium," in Roberto Esposito, *Communitas: Origine et destin de la communauté* (Paris: Presses Universitaires de France, 2000), 3–10; republished in a reworked version entitled "Cum" in *PD* 115–121. Nancy distinguishes between "fascisms," which carry out their "labour of death [*oeuvre de mort*]" in the name of the community as a people or self-constituted race, and the equally deadly "communisms," which through political praxis aim to establish a community of a self-constituted humanity.

26. This is very explicitly so in Scruton's "In Defense of the Nation," in *The Philosopher on Dover Beach* (Manchester: Carcanet, 1990), 299–329. See also Scruton's *The West and the Rest: Globalisation and the Terrorist Threat* (London: Continuum, 2002). Scruton posits and defends a continuity between the political theology of premodern Europe and the modern nation state as its successor. In the "Conclusion" to the book (157–61), Scruton openly expresses his nostalgia for British autarchy.

27. The Dutch politician Geert Wilders and his Partij voor de Vrijheid (Party for Freedom) explicitly argue this. Wilders proposed banning the Qur'an in the Netherlands, as it would represent a "fascist book." Obviously this was meant as a provocation to Muslims (his suggestion received no support from any party but his own), in the hope that the inflammatory assertion of an intrinsic link between Islam and "fascist violence" would turn into a self-fulfilling prophecy.

28. See Bruno Latour, who calls this "the worst possible course" the West could have chosen for after 9/11, in his *War of the Worlds. What about Peace?* (Chicago: Prickly Paradigm Press, 2002), 4.

29. Stanley Fish, "Boutique Multiculturalism," in his *The Trouble with Principle* (Cambridge: Harvard University Press, 1999), 317.

30. See my "La nostalgie de l'ennemi chez Alain Finkielkraut et Carl Schmitt ou l'honneur perdu de l'adversaire politique," in *Bulletin trimestriel de la fondation Auschwitz* 88 (2005): 143–55.

31. H. Lübbe, "Staat und Zivilreligion: Ein Aspekt politischer Legitimität," in *Religion des Bürgers: Zivilreligion in Amerika und Europa* (Münster: Lit, 2004), 221. Lübbe defends a kind of "negative civil religion": "In this function, civil religion is precisely not a medium for the sacralization of the political system, but the latter's guarantee of liberality" (p. 209).

32. See on this Ignaas Devisch, *We: Jean-Luc Nancy and the Question of Community* (New York: State University of New York Press, forthcoming), esp. chap. 1.

33. Wendy Brown, *Regulating Aversion: Tolerance in the Age of Identity and Empire* (Princeton: Princeton University Press, 2006), 151.

34. For this development in France, see especially Gauchet, *La religion dans la démocratie*, 61–89.

35. See the Conclusion to Seyla Benhabib, *The Rights of Others: Aliens, Residents, and Citizens* (Cambridge: Cambridge University Press, 2004).

36. Maurice Blanchot, *The Unavowable Community*, trans. Pierre Joris (Barrytown, N.Y.: Station Hill, 1988; orig. 1983). Nancy's essay first appeared in French in 1982, in the journal *Aléa* (4); it was later expanded into *La communauté désoeuvrée*.

37. Marguerite Duras, *The Malady of Death*, trans. Barbara Bray (New York: Grove Press, 1986; orig. 1982).

38. Blanchot, *The Unavowable Community*, 31.

39. See: Nancy, "Changing of the World," *FT* 300–7 / *PD* 139–49; *TD*; and Maurice Blanchot, *Political Writings, 1953–1993*, trans. and introd. Zakir Paul (New York: Fordham University Press, 2010).

40. Blanchot, *The Unavowable Community*, 32.

41. See "Ex nihilo summum (Of Sovereignty)," in *CW* 10462: "If sovereignty is not a substance that is given, it is because it is the *reality* that the people must give themselves, insofar as it is not, itself, a substance or a given subject."

42. Blanchot, *The Unavowable Community*, 33.

43. Ibid., 33, 34.

44. See also "Nichts jenseits des Nihilismus," *PD* 159–67.

45. In full, the sentence reads: " EINEN SINN HINEINLEGEN—diese Aufgabe bleibt unbedingt immer noch übrig, gesetzt, dass keinen Sinn darin liegt" ("To establish a sense—this task definitely remains, provided there is no sense in it"; Friedrich Nietzsche, *Sämtliche Werke: Kritische Studienausgabe*, ed. Giorgio Colli and Massimo Montinari [Berlin: De Gruyter, 1980], 9 [48]; quoted by Nancy in *PD* 165n1).

46. See *PD* 162 and 165.

Winke: Divine Topoi in Nancy, Hölderlin and Heidegger
Hent de Vries

NOTE: An earlier version of this article appeared in *The Solid Letter: Readings of Friedrich Hölderlin*, ed Aris Fioretos (Stanford, Calif: Stanford University Press,

1999), 94–120. For this volume, the text his been reworked and shortened slightly. The epigraph can be translated "And nods are, from time immemorial, the language of the gods."

1. See Jean-François Courtine, "Les traces et le passage du Dieu dans les *Beiträge zur Philosophie* de Martin Heidegger," *Archivio di Filosofia* 1–3 (1994): 519–38, esp. 530; as well as Manfred Frank, *Der kommende Gott: Vorlesungen über die neue Mythologie* (Frankfurt a. M.: Suhrkamp, 1982), 1:245–342.

2. See the chapter with this title in *BP* 48–57 / *PF* 353–64.

3. Nancy shies away from Jean-Luc Marion's suggestion that it is precisely in this discovery of the structural insufficiency of the principle of reason—in the uncovering, that is, of a "principle of insufficient reason," culminating in the death of the ontotheological and moral conception of God—that theology, as the privileged discourse of difference or, rather, "distance," can take its chances and finally conquer its proper place. An elaboration of this view can be found in Marion's reading of Hölderlin. See *The Idol and Distance: Five Studies*, trans. Thomas Carlson (New York: Fordham University Press, 2001; orig. 1977), 81–136.

4. *Paronomasia* ("play on words") in this context refers to the juxtaposition of divine names that all sound alike but each give the divine a different meaning.

5. See Martin Heidegger, *Elucidations of Hölderlin's Poetry*, trans. and introd. Keith Hoeller (Amherst, N.Y.: 2000).

6. For how traditions of negative theology can and cannot be rephrased within a contemporary philosophical context, see also my "The Theology of the Sign and the Sign of Theology: The Apophatics of Deconstruction," *Flight of the Gods: Philosophical Perspectives on Negative Theology*, ed. Ilse N. Bulhof and Laurens ten Kate (New York: Fordham University Press, 2000), 165–94 (esp. in dialogue with Jacques Derrida); and, in the same volume, Laurens ten Kate, "The Gift of Loss: A Study of the Fugitive God in Bataille's Atheology, with References to Jean-Luc Nancy," 249–92.

7. Martin Heidegger, *Denkerfahrungen 1910–1976* (Frankfurt a. M.: Klostermann, 1983), 176.

8. Ibid., 178.

9. Ibid.

10. Ibid., 179.

11. Ibid.

12. On these matters, see also Jean Greisch, "Hölderlin et le chemin vers le sacré," in *Cahier de l'Herne: Heidegger*, ed. Michel Haar (Paris: L'Herne, 1983), 543–67; and Jean-Louis Chrétien, "La réserve de l'être," in the same volume, 233–60.

13. See Françoise Dastur, *Hölderlin: Tragédie et modernité* (Paris: Encre Marine, 1992), 25.

14. Friedrich Hölderlin, "Was ist Gott?" *Sämtliche Werke*, ed. Friedrich Beissner et al. (Stuttgart: Kohlhammer, 1943–85), 2; 1:210.

15. Martin Heidegger, ". . . Poetically Man Dwells . . . ," in *Poetry, Language, Thought* (New York: Harper & Row, 1971), 225.

16. Friedrich Hölderlin, "In lieblicher Bläue blühet," *Sämtliche Werke*, 2.2:991–92.

17. These lines figure prominently in a host of critical writings on Hölderlin and Heidegger's *Erläuterungen*. See, e.g., Maurice Blanchot, *The Space of* Literature, trans. Ann Smock (Lincoln: University of Nebraska Press, 1989; orig. 1955); Marion, *The Idol and Distance*, 122–23; Françoise Dastur, *Hölderlin: Tragédie et modernité*, 91; and also Beda Allemann, *Hölderlin und Heidegger* (Zurich: Atlantis, 1954), 169.

18. See Andrzej Warminski, *Readings in Interpretation: Hölderlin, Hegel, Heidegger* (Minneapolis: University of Minnesota Press, 1987), 47, 64.

19. Heidegger, *Elucidations*, 64.

20. Martin Heidegger, *Vorträge und Aufsätze* (Pfullingen: Neske, 1985), 144.

21. See, e.g., for such a problematization, Christopher Fynsk, *Heidegger: Thought and Historicity* (Ithaca, N.Y.: Cornell University Press, 1986), 222n33.

22. Martin Heidegger, *Beiträge zur Philosophie* (Frankfurt a. M.: Klostermann, 1994), 24. For Courtine, see "Les traces et le passage du Dieu," 529–30.

23. See Martin Heidegger, *Hölderlins Hymnen "Germanien" und "Der Rhein"* (Frankfurt a. M.: Klostermann, 1980), 54, 110.

24. See, for an analysis of (parts of) "On a Divine *Wink*," the following contribution in this book, by Laurens ten Kate.

25. See Courtine, "Les traces et le passage du Dieu," 533.

26. Ibid., 524n20.

27. It would seem, however, that, certainly in Nancy, the motif of radical finitude is at the same time inspired by the experience of a certain indelible elusiveness, a relation without relation (*religion*) or, at least, by a finitude that is experienced and thought as absolute, in the etymological sense of the word, that is, as that which *infinitizes* itself in the very measure with which we approach it.

28. Heidegger, *Elucidations of Hölderlin's Poetry*, 63; trans. modified. See also Heidegger's poem "Winke," in *Denkerfahrungen*, 162.

29. See also Jean Greisch, *La parole heureuse: Martin Heidegger entre les choses et les mots* (Paris: Beauchesne, 1987), 108, on a "weisendes Offenbarmachen," and 109: "Every donation of a sign refers in the final instance to an arche-sign, which Heidegger calls *Wink*."

30. Heidegger, *Denkerfahrungen*, 33.

God Passing By: Presence and Absence in Monotheism and Modernity
Laurens ten Kate
NOTE: Portions of this essay have been reworked from my earlier "Outside In, Inside Out: Notes on the Retreating God in Nancy's Deconstruction of Christianity," *Bijdragen: International Journal in Philosophy and Theology* 69, no. 3 (2008): 305–20; and "Intimate Distance: Rethinking the Unthought God in Christianity," *Sophia: International Journal for the Philosophy of Religion and Philosophical Theology* 47 (2008): 327–43.

1. Assmann first applied this concept in his *Moses the Egyptian: The Memory of Egypt in Western Monotheism* (Cambridge: Harvard University Press, 1997),

then again in *Of God and Gods: Egypt, Israel, and the Rise of Monotheism* (Madison: University of Wisconsin Press, 2008), e.g., 84–85.

2. See on this esp. chap. 2 of *Moses the Egyptian*, "Suppressed History, Repressed Memory: Moses and Akhenaten," 23–54, where Assmann presents these first inventions of monotheism (Egyptian, then Hebrew) and of the distinction vital to it as "counter-religions" (e.g., 24–25)

3. Assmann, *Of God and Gods*, 3.

4. See, on the relation between mono- and polytheism, Aukje van Rooden's and Alena Alexandrova's articles in this volume.

5. The Hebrew word *thora* actually does not mean "law" but rather "pointing toward," "indication"; it has an aspect of promise that is conveyed by Martin Buber and Franz Rosenzweig in their German translation of the Jewish Bible, Tenach. They present the Torah as *Bücher der Weisung* (*Books of Teaching;* but *Weisung* also means to point in a direction, to indicate, like the Jewish original). See *Die fünf Bücher der Weisung* (Heidelberg: Lambert Schneider, 1976; orig. 1925–28). The emphasis on distance already becomes clear in the very first verse of Genesis, where God's initial act of creation is described not as the creation of the world or the universe (as some translations have it) but of a distinction: "In the beginning God created the heavens and the earth." The concept of distinguishing and separating plays an important role in the ensuing story of the creation in its first version, that of Gen. 1 and 2:1–4.

6. See, for closer analyses of the issue of monotheism's iconoclasm, Alena Alexandrova's contribution to this volume. See also her "The Auto-Deconstructive Image: Of Vestigal Places," in *Bijdragen: International Journal in Philosophy and Theology* 69, no. 3 (2008): 321–36.

7. For a valuable account of the problem of monotheism dealt with as a modern problem, see Jürgen Manemann, ed., *Jahrbuch Politische Theologie*, vol. 4, *Monotheismus* (Münster: LIT, 2002).

8. Assmann, *Of God and Gods*, 87.

9. Although Nancy attempts a deconstruction of monotheism in general in *Dis-Enclosure*, he concentrates almost entirely on the Judeo-Christian traditions, and within these especially on Christianity. He explicitly maintains that the self-deconstruction of monotheism pertains to Islam as well, and he makes some preliminary distinctions between the three religions of the Book (see, e.g., the Preamble to this volume). However, without anticipating the "long exposition" a deconstruction of Islam would require, one could at least mention three features of the Quranic theology that resemble the complexities of the Mosaic distinction (leaving aside the fact that the beginnings of Islam were influenced considerably by Judaism and Christianity): (1) Allah stands at a great distance from the world; (2) Islam is a radically ethical religion, like its fellow monotheisms, stressing human action on earth instead of the activity of God; (3) The ban on images has been taken to the extreme in Islam, suggesting the absence of the divine in this world.

10. For a different view on the relation between construction and deconstruction in Nancy, see Marc De Kesel's contribution to this volume.

11. See also EG 76, where Nancy speaks of the "unthought in Christianity that is only to be understood as 'coming.'"

12. Outside Christianity, in the sense Nancy formulates it in EG: "that what has not mingled with it," and, I would add, never can mingle with it according to a logic of presence.

13. See also my "Outside In, Inside Out," 318n32.

14. The double meaning of *retreat* should be kept alive: retreat as withdrawal and as dealing with (treating) something/someone *again* (re-), in other words, readdressing. It indicates a turning away as well as a turning toward. The French word *retrait* contains the same contradictory meanings; however, in the German *Auszug/Entzug* the second meaning is lost. See also on the meanings of retreat the Introduction to this volume.

15. Christianity does not oppose atheism. It forms no counterforce against the "disenchantment of the world" but accompanies it or, as Karl Löwith would argue, has actually led to it. See, e.g., Karl Löwith, *Christentum und Geschichte* (Düsseldorf: Pädogischer Verlag Schwann,1955).

16. See, on the idea of an absence within presence, an outside within the inside, or transcendence within (or rather, *as*) immanence, Frans van Peperstraten's essay in this volume.

17. See also on this passage Ian James's contribution to this volume and my "Outside In, Inside Out," 314–16.

18. The last sentence (my translation) does not appear in BT, since this translation is based on an earlier version of UJ.

19. See on this also *GI* 37/75, where Nancy distinguishes between the "absence *of* the thing" and the "absence *within* the thing"—the latter absence being written as *absense* as well. See also Alena Alexandrova's contribution to this volume.

20. See, for an analysis of this chapter and esp. of the relation designed by Nancy between faith and act ("work") Frans van Peperstraten's article further on in this part.

21. This passage was added by the author to the English edition of *La déclosion*; it does not appear in the French original.

22. Let me mention two of the many other themes treated by Nancy within the context of a deconstruction of monotheism and Christianity that all touch upon this crucial structure. First, Nancy's rethinking of the meaning of death and resurrection in the Christian gospels and in theology stresses that the life "revived" by the resurrection—whether speaking of the story of Lazarus (John 11) or of Christ's own resurrection—is not a liberation from death, nor is it opposed to it. The opposition of presence and absence, life and death, is radically undone here. The "truth" of the raising of Lazarus, Nancy explains in "Blanchot's Resurrection," "resides in the simultaneity of death and a life within it that does not come back to life, but that makes death live qua death. Or yet again: the true Lazarus lives his dying as he dies his living" (*D* 91–92/138). A similar

understanding of the resurrection can be found in *NT*, with regard to Christ. See also in this volume the contributions by Marc De Kesel, Daniela Calabrò, and Boyan Manchev. Second, measuring the importance of a particular concept of experience, in Nietzsche ("experience at a heart") and in Bataille ("inner experience"), Nancy remarks that this experience opens up a "being" that is "neither a being nor a nonbeing, but existing nevertheless. Neither God nor humanity, but yet a world as that *in* which an *outside* can open itself, and become experience. This experience is an 'experience at a heart,' . . . an experience which is that heart itself beating with the beating of the inside/outside through which it ex-ists and, in ex-isting, senses and feels itself as the interval between the within and the without" (*D* 80/123).

23. See the chapter "A Faith That Is Nothing at All," a reading of G. Granel, "Loin de la substance: Jusqu'où?," in *Études philosophiques* 4 (1999), 535–44.

24. Nancy quotes from "Loin de la substance," 535.

25. See, for a more detailed reading of Nancy's chapter on Granel, Michel Lisse's and Ian James's contributions to this volume.

26. See Jacques Derrida, *Speech and Phenomena* (Evanston, Ill.: Northwestern University Press, 1973; orig. 1967).

27. See, e.g., *BSP* 200–201n53/83n1.

28. See ibid.; here Nancy refers to paragraphs 55–58 of Husserl's *Cartesianische Meditationen* (The Hague: Martinus Nijhoff, 1950).

29. The semantic domain of German *Wink* includes hinting at something and beckoning someone or nodding; the possible translation "wink (of the eye)" covers part of the meanings in German. Nancy deals with the problems and possibilities of the translation of this German word at length in the opening section of "On a Divine *Wink*." See on this also Hent de Vries's contribution to this volume; he translates *Wink* as "nod."

30. Martin Heidegger, *Beiträge zur Philosophie (Vom Ereignis)*, in *Gesamtausgabe*, vol. 65 (Frankfurt a.M.: Klostermann, 1994). Nancy focuses on two citations from the *Beiträge*. The first is from chap. 256, "Der letzte Gott" (409): "The last god: his occurring is found in the sign [*im Wink*], in the onset and absence of an arrival [*dem Anfall and Ausbleib der Ankunft*], as well as in the flight of the gods that are past and their hidden metamorphosis" (translated in *D* 104/155). The second is from chap. 255, "Die Kehre im Ereignis" (407): "The event must need the being there [*Dasein*] and, being in need of it, the event should open it toward the calling and in this way bring it before the passing by of the last God."

31. Heidegger, *Beiträge*, 407.

32. "On a Divine *Wink*" was originally Nancy's contribution to a conference on Derrida's work in Coimbra in 2003.

33. Heidegger, *Beiträge*, 409.

34. Nancy refers here to Heidegger's play with the German *Ereignis*, in which the words (*zu-*)*eignen* ("appropriate") or *eigen* ("own, self, proper") are present.

Thinking Alterity—In One or Two? Nancy's Christianity Compared with Lyotard's Judaism

Frans van Peperstraten

NOTE: For a related article on this subject, see my "Displacement or Composition? Lyotard and Nancy on the *Trait d'union* between Judaism and Christianity," *International Journal for the Philosophy of Religion* 65, no. 1 (2009): 29–46. Available online at: http://www.springerlink.com/openurl.asp?genre = article&id = doi:10.1007/s11153-008-9177-6.

1. "The Judeo-Christian (on Faith)" in *Dis-enclosure* reproduces, with slight emendations, the essay as published in *Judeities: Questions for Jacques Derrida*, ed. Bettina Bergo, Joseph Cohen, and Raphael Zagury-Orly (New York: Fordham University Press, 2007), 214–33. It thus contains a number of additions Nancy apparently made for his presentation at the conference on which *Judeities* was based but lacks the footnotes in the French *La déclosion*.

2. This book, which was co-authored with Eberhard Gruber, originally appeared as *Un trait d'union, suivi de "Un Trait, ce n'est pas tout"* (Sainte-Foy, Québec, and Grenoble: Le Griffon d'argile and Presses Universitaires de Grenoble, 1993); "D'un trait d'union" was later included in Jean-François Lyotard, *Misère de la philosophie* (Paris: Galilée, 2000), 133–51, but a letter from Lyotard to Gruber in the earlier book was not. The English edition, *The Hyphen: Between Judaism and Christianity*, trans. Pascale-Anne Brault and Michael Naas, (New York: Humanity Books, 1999), includes both texts. Hereafter, this work will be referred to as *TH*, with page numbers to the English edition followed by page numbers of the French original in *Misère de la philosophie*; where no second page is given, the text does not appear in *Misère*.

3. I must limit myself to Lyotard, but this discussion ought to be placed within a much wider context. First of all, although Nancy's "The Judeo-Christian" takes off with a quote from Lyotard, the essay as a whole is primarily a reaction to Derrida's "Faith and Knowledge: The Two Sources of 'Religion' at the Limits of Reason Alone" (in *Religion*, ed. Jacques Derrida and Gianni Vattimo [Cambridge: Polity Press, 1998], 1–78). In his *On Touching—Jean-Luc Nancy*, trans. Christine Irizarry (Stanford, Calif.: Stanford University Press, 2005), Derrida questions Nancy's deconstruction of Christianity. Furthermore, Blanchot, in his *The Unavowable Community*, trans. Pierre Joris (Barrytown, N.Y.: Station Hill Press, 1988), had already delivered a critique of Nancy by appealing to Levinas. The works of Jean-Luc Marion and Michel Henry also play an important role in the discussion on Christianity in France. For these matters, see Ian James, *The Fragmentary Demand: An Introduction to the Philosophy of Jean-Luc Nancy* (Stanford, Calif.: Stanford University Press, 2006), chaps. 3 and 4.

4. See *TH* 13/135 for the phrase quoted by Nancy.

5. See *D* 34/54 for the second definition, which does not deviate far from the first.

6. Huub van de Sandt (in "James 4, 1–4 in the Light of the Jewish Two Ways Tradition 3, 1–6," *Biblica* 88, fasc. 1 (2007), argues that James's letter is

dependent on a Jewish "Two Ways" doctrine, related to the *Derekh Erets* tradition. This is clear from the fact that James opposes wisdom from above to earthly wisdom (James 3:15–17) and Abraham's friendship with God (James 2:23) to friendship with the world (James 4:4). As we shall see, in Nancy's interpretation this dualism of the "Two Ways" becomes a tension within one world.

7. Peter J. Tomson (in *"If This Be from Heaven . . . "*: *Jesus and the New Testament Authors in their Relationship to Judaism* [Sheffield: Sheffield Academic Press, 2001], 340) observes that James's letter "has had difficulties being accepted by the orthodox mainstream" of Christianity because of "a scarcity of clear Christological formulations, a consistent emphasis on obedience to the law and an explicit plea for justification by works and not by faith alone."

8. This passage does not appear in the French original of *D*.

9. According to Nancy, this "other James," namely, Derrida, "is another Judeo-Christian" (*D* 46/70).

10. The Greek word *Christos* means "the anointed." It was used to designate priests, prophets, and kings, but especially the Messiah. In Hebrew, the word for "Messiah" also means "anointed."

11. See also, on this, Nancy's Preamble to this volume.

12. For other texts in which Lyotard contrasts Judaism and Western culture, see: "Figure forclose," *L'écrit du temps* (March 1984; orig. 1968); "Jewish Oedipus," in Lyotard, *Driftworks*, ed. Roger McKeon (New York: Columbia University Press, 1984; orig. 1970), 35–55; "On a Figure of Discourse," in *Toward the Postmodern*, ed. Robert Harvey and Mark S. Roberts (Alantic Highlands, N.J.: Humanities Press, 1993; orig. 1972); *Pacific Wall*, trans. Bruce Boone (Venice, Calif.: Lapis, 1989; orig. 1979); "Discussions, ou: Phraser après 'Auschwitz,'" in *Les fins de l'homme: À partir du travail de Jacques Derrida*, ed. Philippe Lacoue-Labarthe and Jean-Luc Nancy (Paris: Galilée, 1981), 283–310; *The Differend: Phrases in Dispute*, trans.Georges van den Abbeele (Minneapolis: University of Minnesota Press, 1988, orig. 1983); *Heidegger and "the jews,"* trans. Andreas Michel and Mark Roberts (Minneapolis: University of Minnesota Press, 1990; orig. 1988); "Survivant: Arendt," in *Leçons d'enfance* (Paris: Galilée, 1991), 59–87; and *Soundproof Room*, trans. Robert Harvey (Stanford, Calif.: Stanford University Press, 2001; orig., 1998).

13. See Exod. 20.

14. Elisabeth Weber, in conversation with Lyotard, in her *Questioning Judaism: Interviews*, trans. Rachel Bowlby (Stanford, Calif.: Stanford University Press, 2004), 107–8; trans. modified. See Gershom Scholem, *The Kabbalah and Its Symbolism*, trans. R. Manheim (New York: Shocken Books, 1965), 30.

15. The etymology of the word *religion* has been debated for centuries. Two etymological Latin sources are generally put forward: (1) *re-legere*, "to read together again, to reread, to reconsider carefully, to go over again"; and (2) *re-ligare*, "to bind, to bond, to return to bondage, to unite." The second explanation is more customary; it is also the one most suited to Christianity, to the belief in a fixed bond between signifier and signified. The first, by contrast, is better

suited to Judaism: because the "bond" is unstable, we are thrown back into the task of endless rereading.

The Excess of Reason and the Return of Religion: Transcendence of Christian Monotheism in Nancy's *Dis-Enclosure*
Donald Loose

1. See also: "Indeed, we must not forget that this sentence from the Preface to the *Critique of Pure Reason*—'I have had to suppress knowledge in order to make room for belief'—provides an opening for belief within the limits of reason" (*D* 144/209).

2. Nancy refers here to Anselm's proof of the existence of God and, in particular, its formulation of a *maius quam cogitari possit* ("something greater than can be thought").

3. I borrow the term *meta-critique* from Boyan Manchev, "Jean-Luc Nancy: La déconstruction du christianisme," in *Critique*, March 2007, 170.

4. "Omnem nostrum intellectum transcendit." See Nicholas of Cusa, *De docta ignorantia*, 1.4. See also W. Beierwaltes, *Platonismus im Christentum* (Frankfurt a.M.: Klostermann, 1998).

5. Augustine, *Confessiones*, ed. and trans. Henry Chadwick (Oxford: Oxford University Press, 1991), 10.7.11.

6. Jan Assmann, *Die Mosaische Unterscheidung oder der Preis des Monotheismus* (Munich: Hanser, 2003); see also idem, *Moses the Egyptian: The Memory of Egypt in Western Monotheism* (Cambridge: Harvard University Press, 1997), and *Monotheismus und Kosmotheismus: Ägyptische Formen eines "Denkens des Einen" und ihre europäische Rezeptionsgeschichte* (Heidelberg: Winter, 1993).

7. Thomas Aquinas, *De Veritate*, q. 1 a. 1.

8. See: H. Gouhier, *Fénelon Philosophe* (Paris: Vrin, 1977); L. Devillairs, *Fénelon: Une philosophie de l'Infini* (Paris: Cerf, 2007); and R. Spaemann, *Reflexion und Spontaneität: Studien über Fénelon* (Stuttgart: Kohlhammer, 1963).

9. J. Le Brun, the editor of Fénelon's *Oeuvres complètes* in the Pléiade edition (Paris: Gallimard, 1983–97), has outlined the continuation of this theme within Western philosophy in *L'amour pur, de Platon à Lacan* (Paris: Seuil, 2002).

10. See Manchev, "Jean-Luc Nancy," 177: "Nancy's thought emerges as a radical thinking of finitude. . . . The program of a deconstruction of Christianity is thus entirely governed by the demand of a thinking that is *infinitely finite*."

11. Assmann, *Die Mosaische Unterscheidung*.

12. In this way, *vera religio dei veri* is a continuous process of falsification. See Serge Margel, *Superstition: L'anthropologie du religieux en terre de chrétienté* (Paris: Galilée, 2005).

13. Assmann views the distinction between knowing and believing as an effect of anticosmotheistic monotheism in *Die Mosaische Unterscheidung*. Such a distinction is only possible following the separation of God and world.

14. Immanuel Kant, *Critique of Pure Reason*, B 25 and 28.

15. Ibid., *Critique of Pure Reason*, B 352, and *Prolegomena* (Akademie ed., 4:373).

16. In premodern philosophy, and particularly in the major syntheses of the thirteenth and fourteenth centuries, e.g., by philosopher/theologians such as Thomas Aquinas, transcendence is first of all the transgression of all categories by what are referred to as "transcendental concepts" (*transcendentalia*), which are therefore present not just in one specific category but in all categories. As a result, such *transcendentalia*—*ens, unum, verum, bonum*—are characterized by a universal presence and therefore are immanently present in the corresponding part of reality referred to by each categorical proposition.

17. Kant, *Critique of Pure Reason*, B 671.

18. Ibid., B 365.

19. In his own way, Derrida refers to a particular demarcation of this relationship in *Eyes of the University: Right to Philosophy 2*, trans. Jan Plug et al. (Stanford, Calif.: Stanford University Press, 2004; orig. 1990), 54. He reverses the relationship of the Kantian concentric circles of rational religion and revealed religion: "Around the same center, the inside circle is that of revealed or historical religion, while the outside circle is that of rational religion." On the one hand, the philosopher thus delineates the entire religion, but, on the other hand, he is also able to remain at the margins of the outer circle, which has nothing to do with religion.

20. See also Maurice Blanchot, *The Writing of the Disaster*, trans. Ann Smock (Lincoln: University of Nebraska Press, 1986; orig. 1980), 50: "Desire remains in relation to the distantness of the star, entreating the sky, appealing to the universe." Desire (Latin: *desiderium*) refers to the star, (Latin: *siderum*; Greek: *aster*). The disaster is to be without a guiding star, without any perspective or orientation. In this context, Blanchot writes about this desire as an "undesirable impossible," which "remains" as such. It is as if the illusion that Kant expresses in the Introduction to the *Critique of Pure Reason* resurfaces here: "The light dove, in clear flight cutting through the air the resistance of which it feels, could get the idea that it could do even better in airless space" (A5; *Critique of Pure Reason*, ed. and trans. Paul Guyer and Allen W. Wood [Cambridge: Cambridge University Press, 1998]).

21. Jacques Derrida, *The Gift of Death*, trans. David Wills (Chicago: University of Chicago Press, 1995), 29–30.

22. The debate about the tension between the absolute alterity at play within Christianity, as well as its historical facticity and significance, can already be seen in the eighteenth century. Fénelon warned against the ethereal illusion of pure contemplation that would free itself of any specific figuration or figure. That view held that one should take a pure phantasm without any content as the subject matter for contemplation, so as no longer to be able to make a distinction between God and nothing. According to Fénelon, one thereby destroys Christianity under the veil of purification. See Fénelon, *Oeuvres complètes* 1:1068.

23. Nancy has been explicitly confronted with this fundamental question about God's existence as a being and as a concrete figuration, that is, confronted with the inevitable return of this question as it is posed time and again, e.g., by children. See his address to children entitled "In Heaven and on Earth" (*NT*

71–99). In the following discussion, the children show that they actually do face the question that Nancy had attempted to show is not the question. See also Elie During, "Le ciel, Dieu, le divin: jeux interdits," In *Critique*, 2006, 175: "The children are not satisfied. This is because they are, in a spontaneous way, metaphysicians."

24. Blanchot, *The Writing of the Disaster*, 5.

25. Ibid., 92.

26. Ibid., 4.

27. Maurice Merleau-Ponty, *Signs*, trans. and introd. Richard C. McCleary (Evanston, Ill.: Northwestern University Press, 1964), 35.

"My God, my God, why hast Thou forsaken me?" Demythologized Prayer, or the Poetic Invocation of God

Aukje van Rooden

NOTE: An earlier version of this essay appeared as "A Demythologised Prayer? Religion, Myth and Poetry in Nancy's Deconstruction of Christianity," *Bijdragen: International Journal in Philosophy and Theology* 69, no. 3 (2008): 285–304.

1. This statement reiterates Gauchet's description of Christianity as "*a religion for departing from religion.*" See Marcel Gauchet, *The Disenchantment of the World: A Political History of Religion* (Princeton, N.J.: Princeton University Press, 1999; orig. 1985).

2. Although the translator of this essay renders the French title " 'Prière démythifiée' " as " 'Prayer Demythified,' " in the text itself, he consistently translated the same phrase as "prayer demythologized." I shall use the latter translation, which echoes the English translation of Adorno's *Quasi una Fantasia*, where the phrase appears for the first time.

3. Christianity is, however, less radically monotheistic than the other monotheistic religions, since it disputes the idea of a wholly transcendent God by claiming his incarnation in a human body. Nevertheless, this incarnation is at the same time conceived as an absenting from presence.

4. Theodor W. Adorno, "Music and Language: A Fragment," in *Quasi una Fantasia: Essays on Modern Music*, trans. Rodney Livingstone (London: Verso, 1998; orig. 1978), 2; my emphasis. This phrase of Adorno is cited by the poet Michel Deguy in his *Sans retour* (2004), which in turn is cited in " 'Prayer Demythified.' "

5. See esp. Jean-Luc Nancy, "Nothing But the World:. An Interview with *Vacarme*," in *Rethinking Marxism* 19, no. 4, (2007): 521–35. For a further elaboration of this task, see the contribution of Ignaas Devisch and Kathleen Vandeputte to this volume.

6. See also "There is no God because God does not belong to the 'there is': his name names precisely the category of that which would be subtracted from the 'there is' " (*SW* 156/236).

7. For Nancy's analysis of the question "What is God?" see DP.

8. One could also say, with Nancy, that it is a question of "praying without prayer" (*D* 133/195).

9. See also, for Nancy's view of the relation between *logos* and *muthos*, chap. 2 of the 2004 film *Der Ister* (ed. David Barison and Daniel Ross), starring Bernard Stiegler, Jean-Luc Nancy, Philippe Lacoue-Labarthe and Hans-Jürgen Syberberg.

10. Nancy comes back to this question of *muthos* in "Un commencement: Post-face à Lacoue-Labarthe, *L'allégorie*'" (Paris: Galilée, 2006). There he distinguishes between *mythology* and *myth*, thereby calling for a "myth without mythology," which corresponds to the self-deconstructive movement described above.

11. Sometimes a third etymological source is mentioned, that of *relegere* ("to collect, to gather").

12. See Walter Benjamin's early text "Two Poems of Friedrich Hölderlin" (1914–15), in *Selected Writings*, vol. 1: 1913–1926 (Cambridge: Harvard University Press, 1996), 35. In this text, Benjamin claims that Hölderlin's poetry is *mythical* rather than *demythologized*. What he understands by "mythical" is nevertheless analogous to what Nancy declares to be demythologized. Furthermore, in "Un commencement," Nancy distinguishes between the mythological and the mythical, though without referring to Benjamin's analysis.

13. See, e.g.: "'art' is merely that which takes as its theme and place the opening [*frayage*] of sense as such along sensuous surfaces, a 'presentation of presentation,' the motion and emotion of a coming" (*SW* 135/207). See also *M1* 34/63.

14. For an analysis of Nancy's poetic ontology, see the Anne O'Byrne's essay in this volume.

15. Briefly, I would say, as does Blanchot in *The Book to Come*, that this ritual accompaniment forms the essence of art or poetry: "Literature begins with writing. Writing is the totality of rites, the overt or subtle ceremony, by which, independently of what one wants to express and of the way in which one expresses it, this event is announced: that what is written belongs to literature, that the one who reads it is reading literature" (Maurice Blanchot, *The Book to Come*, trans. Charlotte Mandell [Stanford, Calif.: Stanford University Press, 2002; orig. 1959], 205–6.

Literary Creation, Creation ex Nihilo
Michel Lisse

NOTE: An earlier version of this essay appeared in French in *Mythe et création: Théorie, figures*, ed. E. Faivre d'Arcier, J.-P. Madou, and L. Van Eynde (Brussels: Publications des Facultés universitaires Saint-Louis, 2005), 13–24. I am grateful to Aukje van Rooden, whose remarks and suggestions have been both pertinent and subtle, and who has led me to nuance or develop certain passages in my argument.

1. Thus the master's program in literary studies at the Université du Québec, in Montréal, includes "courses in creation" that provide theoretical, critical, and technical means for students who want to conceive and write a literary work.

2. Nancy has expressed regret that Derrida's death made a discussion on the deconstruction or dis-enclosure of Christianity impossible (see *D* 176–77n15/

24–25n1). I imagine that this discussion would have treated such matters as the undeconstructible (from which Nancy takes pains to distance himself; see *D* 176n12/20n2) or the messianic (which Derrida developed, nonetheless strictly distinguishing it from messianism, whereas Nancy displays a great wariness in relation to the "messianic . . . mode"; *D* 4/12). The discussion between two friends would doubtless have occasioned an intense confrontation concerning Heidegger. The most sensitive point might have been Nancy's rapprochement of *différance* and Heidegger's ontic-ontological difference (see EE 96). It seems necessary to begin a reading of *différance* by taking the following question into account: Is not "the determination of différance as the ontico-ontological difference . . . still an intrametaphysical effect of différance?" (Jacques Derrida, *Margins of Philosophy*, trans. Alan Bass [Chicago: University of Chicago Press, 1982; orig. 1972], 22).

3. Cf.: "The paradigm of the given, structured, and animate universe—the same one that will be called a *mythology*, so that a *physiology* and a *cosmology* may be substituted for it—has ceased to function. . . . Gods are departing into their myths" (*D* 15/28).

4. Cf. *D* 24/39.

5. Cf. DI 33.

6. On this topic, see *CW* 68–69/88–89.

7. Maurice Blanchot, *The Book to Come*, trans. Charlotte Mandell (Stanford, Calif.: Stanford University Press, 2002; orig. 1959), 229.

8. Ibid., 229.

9. Perhaps this verb should be read as an active translation of the Heideggerian thesis *"der Mensch ist weltbildend"* (Man is world-forming; (Martin Heidegger, *The Fundamental Concepts of Metaphysics: World—Finitude—Solitude*, trans. William McNeill and Nicholas Walker (Bloomington: Indiana University Press, 1995; orig. 1983), 185. This is another occasion when it would be interesting to compare Nancy's reading of this thesis with that of Derrida. See: Jacques Derrida, *Of Spirit: Heidegger and the Question*, trans. Geoffrey Bennington and Rachel Bowlby (Chicago: University of Chicago Press, 1989), chap. 6; idem, *The Animal That Therefore I Am*, trans. David Wills (New York: Fordham University Press, 2008), chap. 4 (which looks anew at the question of ontological difference); and idem, "Rams," trans. Thomas Dutoit, in Derrida, *Sovereignties in Question*, ed. Thomas Dutoit and Outi Pasanen (New York: Fordham University Press, 2005), 163.

10. Cf.: "Thus Christianity is *in* the element of sense, in both senses, significative and directional, of the world. Christianity is par excellence the conjunction of both senses: it is sense as tension or direction toward the advent of sense as content. Consequently, the question is less that of the sense of Christianity than that of Christianity as a dimension of sense, a dimension of sense that—and this is the point to be analyzed—is at once the opening of sense and sense as opening" (*D* 147/213).

11. Cf.: "In the first place, we might say that the *nihil* is posited. . . . *ex nihilo* means: undoing any premise, including that of nothing. That means: to empty

nothing [rien] (cf. *rem*, the thing) of any quality as principle. That is creation" (*D* 24–25/39).

12. Is there a proximity with Heidegger, who holds *Denken* and *Dichten*, "thinking" and "poetry," to be parallels which only meet at infinity? See Martin Heidegger, *On the Way to Language*, trans. Peter D. Hertz (New York: Harper and Row, 1971).

13. Gérard Granel, "Far from Substance: Whither and to What Point?," *D* 163–74.

14. In the same way, prayer allows an outside, toward which it is turned, to come about (*advenir*); prayer is an *address*: "recognition of the fact that its saying is deleted in going toward what it says (will never say)" (*D* 136/198). On the question of prayer, literature, and myth in the deconstruction of Christianity, see Aukje van Rooden's text in this volume.

The God Between
Anne O'Byrne

1. My thanks to Aukje van Rooden for her many insightful comments on earlier drafts of this essay.

2. Julia Kristeva, *Black Sun: Depression and Melancholia*, trans. Leon S. Roudiez (New York: Columbia University Press, 1989), 8.

3. See Hannah Arendt, *The Human Condition* (Chicago: University of Chicago Press, 1958), 8.

4. Ludwig Wittgenstein, "Lecture on Ethics," in *Culture and Value*, ed. G. H. Von Wright (Oxford: Blackwell, 1966), 28–33.

5. See Grace Jantzen's comments on the rejection of pantheism, e.g., in *Becoming Divine* (Manchester: Manchester University Press, 1998), 266–70.

6. Jacques Derrida, *Margins of Philosophy*, trans. Alan Bass (Chicago: University of Chicago Press, 1982), 18.

7. Cf. the thought of de-severance (*Entfernung*) in Martin Heidegger, *Being and Time*, trans. John Macquarrie and Edward Robinson (New York: Harper & Row, 1962; orig. 1927), 138–44.

8. See Jürgen Habermas, "Technology and Science as 'Ideology,'" in *Toward a Rational Society: Student Protest, Science, and Politics* (Boston: Beacon Press, 1971), 81–122.

9. Mark Poster works through this problem with considerable insight in a slightly different context in "Critical Theory and Technoculture: Habermas and Baudrillard," in *Baudrillard: A Critical Reader*, ed. Douglas Kellner (Oxford: Blackwell, 1994), 68–88.

10. See Anne O'Byrne, "Utopia Is Here: Revolutionary Communities in Baudrillard and Nancy," in *Subjects and Simulations: Thinking the Ends of Representation* (New York: Rowman and Littlefield, forthcoming). The article is also available at http://people.hofstra.edu/Anne_O'Byrne/Utopia_is_Here.pdf. See also Jean Baudrillard, *Simulacra and Simulation*, (Ann Arbor: University of Michigan Press, 1994).

11. Nancy addresses the question of technology repeatedly. Particularly relevant to this point are his essays "Creation as Denaturation: Metaphysical Technology," in *CW* 77–90/103–35, and "War, Right, Sovereignty—Technē," in *BSP* 101–43/126–68.

12. See, for an account of this structure of interiority and exteriority in the context of the artwork, *M1* 54/95–96: "The eye of the girl [in an engraved depiction of a bearer of offerings from Pompeii] . . . is nothing less than *entirely exposed interiority*, but at the point at which it no longer even refers to itself as to some content or some latent presence, having become on the contrary *the patency of its very latency* and thus irreconcilable with any interiority."

13. I am particularly grateful to Aukje van Rooden for suggesting this approach and for directing me to specific passages in Nancy's work, including this one: "What is making? To posit within being" ("Making Poetry," *M2* 7/ *R* 14).

14. See Plato, *Timaeus*, 29a, in *The Collected Dialogues*, ed. Edith Hamilton and Huntington Cairns (Princeton, N.J.: Princeton University Press, 1961).

15. See Plato, *Republic*, 10.596–97.

16. Plato, *Symposium*, 205b.

17. See Plato, *Timaeus*, 41d.

18. Plato, *Republic* 10.603b.

19. See Plato, ibid., 3.415a-d.

20. See Plato, *Charmides*, 163b-c.

21. Friedrich Schlegel, "Athenaeum Fragments," 430, in *Friedrich Schlegel's Lucinde and* The Fragments, ed. and trans. Peter Firchow (Minneapolis: University of Minnesota Press, 1971), 236.

22. Novalis, *Bluthenstaub*, in *Schriften*, ed. Paul Kluckhohn and Richard Samuel (Stuttgart: Kohlhammer, 1960, 2:463. Quoted in *LA* 49/70.

23. Nancy writes elsewhere: "Allow me to lend authority to this proposition by referring to my book *The Speculative Remark (One of Hegel's Bon Mots)*, where I sought to demonstrate how the dialectic itself undecides itself, or functions only by means of decisions taken elsewhere. The *Aufhebung* is the upside down, decided, and even twice-decided figure of the undecidable" (*DS* 10n9/ 13n.d).

The Immemorial: The Deconstruction of Christianity, Starting from "Visitation: Of Christian Painting"
Daniela Calabrò

1. Maurice Blanchot, *The Infinite Conversation*, trans. Susan Hanson (Minneapolis: University of Minnesota Press, 1993), 317. According to Blanchot, our relationship with this "immemorial memory" is our most difficult and radical challenge. See also Maurice Blanchot, *The Unavowable Community*, trans. Pierre Joris (Barrytown, N.Y.: Station Hill Press, 1988).

2. Jacques Derrida, *Aporias*, trans. Thomas Dutoit (Stanford, Calif.: Stanford University Press, 1993), v.

3. Nancy frequently comes back to Rimbaud. See, e.g., *A Finite Thinking* and *Concealed Thinking*.

4. See Blanchot's chapter "The Sharing of the Secret," in *The Unavowable Community*, 19–21.

5. Roberto Esposito, *Terza persona* (Turin: Einaudi, 2007), 159. Esposito refers consecutively to Maurice Blanchot, *The Space of Literature*, trans. and introd. Ann Smock (Lincoln: University of Nebraska Press, 1982), 73, and *The Infinite Conversation*, trans. with a Foreword by Susan Hanson (Minneapolis: University of Minnesota Press, 1993), 381.

6. Blanchot, *The Infinite Conversation*, 303.

7. For kenosis and the "atheization" of thought, that is to say, the deconstruction of Christianity, see: Marcel Gauchet, *The Disenchantment of the World: A Political History of Religion*, trans. Oscar Burge (Princeton, N.J.: Princeton University Press, 1999; orig. 1985); Jacques Derrida and Gianni Vattimo, eds., *Religion* (Cambridge: Polity, 1998; orig. 1995); Gianni Vattimo, *Belief*, trans. Luca D'Isanto and David Webb (Stanford, Calif.: Stanford University Press, 1999; orig. 1996]; Gérard Granel, "Far from Substance: Whither and to What Point?" *D* 163–74; Giorgio Agamben, *The Time That Remains: A Commentary on the Letter to the Romans*, trans. Patricia Daley (Stanford, Calif.: Stanford University Press, 2005; orig. 2000); and Alfonso Galindo Hervás, *La soberanía: De la teología política al comunitarismo impolitico* (Madrid: Res publica, 2003).

8. On the theme of resounding and the unheard of, see Enrica Lisciani Petrini, *Risonanze: Ascolto, Corpo, Mondo* (Milan: Mimesis, 2006).

9. See Roberto Esposito, "Chair et corps dans la déconstruction du christianisme," in *Sens en tous sens: Autour des travaux de Jean-Luc Nancy*, ed. Francis Guibal and Jean-Clet Martin (Paris: Galilée, 2004), 153–64.

10. On this theme, see LP and also Mauro Carbone and David Levin, *La carne e la voce* (Milan: Mimesis, 2003).

11. Translation by Aukje van Rooden.

Incarnation and Infinity
Ian James

1. Jacques Derrida, *On Touching—Jean-Luc Nancy*, trans. Christine Irizarry (Stanford, Calif.: Stanford University Press, 2005), 220; trans. modified.

2. Ibid., 59; trans. modified.

3. Ibid., 59.

4. For a detailed account of Nancy's understanding of "dis-enclosure," see "Re-opening the Question of Religion," the introduction to this volume.

5. Derrida would perhaps appeal to the Judaic tradition, and specifically to the concept of the "Messianic" (as borrowed from Benjamin) to locate a deconstructive resource within the Western theological tradition. See, e.g., his thinking of the Messianic in relation to Marx in *Specters of Marx: The State of the Debt, the Work of Mourning, and the New International*, trans. Peggy Kamuf (New York: Routledge, 1994; orig. 1992), 65–66, 73–75, 167–69.

6. Derrida, *On Touching*, 244.

7. Ibid., 137; trans. modified.

8. Ibid.,111; trans. modified. Touch, it becomes clear in *Le toucher*, is bound up with the question of originary intuition within philosophy (i.e., that which is

primordially "given" within consciousness). It also organizes the phenomenological language of affection. Within Husserlian phenomenology, for instance, affection can be understood as the affective allure or force that inhabits the intentional structure of consciousness in such a way that perceived phenomena and the system of horizonal and referential implications drawn in their wake impose themselves on, or "touch," perceptual consciousness.

9. Derrida, *On Touching*, 41. Derrida also remarks: "along with touch, it is everywhere a question of 'being,' of course, of beings, of the present, of its presence and its *presentation*, its *self-presentation*" (7; see also 95).

10. Ibid., 99–100; trans. modified.

11. Ibid., 101; trans. modified.

12. Ibid., 99–103.

13. Jean-Louis Chrétien, *The Call and the Response*, trans. Anne A. Davenport (New York: Fordham University Press, 2004).

14. Derrida, *On Touching*, 245.

15. Ibid., 247.

16. Derrida cites Maurice Merleau-Ponty and Henri Maldiney on this point, ibid., 244. Nancy also continues the tradition (dating back to Aristotle) of thinking sensation or "sensing" (*sentir*) as structurally self-reflexive; see, e.g., *L* 8.

17. Derrida, *On Touching*, 247.

18. Ibid., 248.

19. Ibid., 254; trans. modified.

20. Ibid.; trans. modified.

21. Ibid., 255; trans. modified.

22. Ibid., 254.

23. Ibid., 248; trans. modified.

24. Ibid., 261–62. For an account of Nancy on the question of technics and ecotechnics, see Ian James, *The Fragmentary Demand* (Stanford, Calif.: Stanford University Press, 2006), 143–51 and idem, "Art, Technics," in *Thought's Exposure, Oxford Literary Review* 27 (2007): 83–102.

25. Derrida, *On Touching*, 262; trans. modified.

26. Ibid., 119.

27. The passages of Saint Paul in question are Philippians 2:5–11.

28. Nancy's early work on Kant in *DS* is strongly influenced by Granel's *L'équivoque ontologique de la pensée kantienne* (Paris: Gallimard, 1970).

29. For an extended discussion of Nancy's thinking of embodiment, see James, *The Fragmentary Demand*, 105–8, 114–51.

30. For Hegel, "bad" infinity is "bad" in the sense that the infinite extension or regression of the finite into infinity is ultimately incoherent on a logical level. Thus the "true" or "good" infinite, which is actual within the finite, does not "go on forever"; it is ultimately a more coherent thought and is thus infinity of reason.

31. Nancy remarks that this difference from Derrida's "indeconstructible" "will have to be more firmly established later on" (*D* 176n12/20n2).

32. Derrida, *On Touching*, 254.

33. Alain Badiou, *Being and Event*, trans. Oliver Feltham (New York: Continuum, 2006), 143.

34. See ibid., 142 and 143.

35. See ibid., 142.

36. Ibid., 143.

37. Ibid., 145 and 151–60.

38. In *The Creation of the World*, Nancy suggests, however, that he is attempting to think the "nothing" of creation not in terms of the Heideggerian "nothing" of ontological difference but rather as the Nietzschean "nothing" of origin (*CW* 68–69/87–91).

39. Badiou, *Being and Event*, 165.

40. The term *infinity* has a central place both in Nancy's "Christian" texts (e.g., *Noli me tangere*) and in his texts treating the question of sense and sensing (e.g., *Listening*). Just as in *Noli me tangere* the story of Christ's resurrection is read as an affirmation of "an infinite raising" (*une infinie levée*) of "finite life" (*NT* 112n33/39n2), so in *Listening* the faculty of listening is taken as paradigmatic of the "infinite referral" (*renvoi infini*) (*L* 8/25) or "infinite rebound" (*rebond infini*) (*L* 22/45) of the self-reflexive structure of sensing, which is the opening of the world to perception. To this extent, Nancy's account of Christianity as a religion of presentation in withdrawal and his postphenomenological account of the sense of the world and of the reflexivity of sensing are intimately bound together by the concept of "actual" or "good" infinity.

41. Derrida, *On Touching*, 254.

Ontology of Creation: The Onto-aisthetics of Jean-Luc Nancy
Boyan Manchev

1. I use the term *aisthetic* with reference to its etymology—from the Greek work *aisthesis*, "sensible experience," out of which Alexander Baumgarten coined the term *aesthetics*. This neologism has a central role in my recent work and has clear ontological dimensions.

2. I have introduced these views elsewhere; see Boyan Manchev, "La métamorphose du monde: Jean-Luc Nancy et les sorties de l'ontologie négative," *Europe* no. 960, April 2009.

3. In Blanchot's words, in a paragraph entitled "The Question of Art," creation is "the least divine of the god's functions, the one which is not sacred, which makes of God a laborer six days of the week, the demiurge, the 'jack of all trades'" (Maurice Blanchot, *The Space of Literature*, trans. Ann Smock [Lincoln: University of Nebraska Press, 1982; orig. 1955], 219).

4. In "Atheism and Monotheism," Nancy writes: "*ex nihilo* means: undoing any premise, including that of nothing. That means: to empty *nothing* [rien] (cf. *rem*, the thing) of any quality as principle. That is creation" (*D* 24–25/39).

5. I have elsewhere described the ontological thinking in the Hegelian-Heideggerian tradition as *ontologies of negativity* or *negative ontologies*. In the simplest terms, these are ontologies that have their basis in a constitutive negativity, which is the transposition to the conceptual level of the experience of finitude.

6. See Jacques Derrida, "Force of Law: The 'Mystical Foundation of Authority,'" *Cardozo Law Review* 11 (1990): 919–1045; idem, "Faith and Knowledge: The Two Sources of 'Religion' within the Mere Limits of Reason," in *Religion*, ed. Jacques Derrida and Gianni Vattimo (Cambridge: Polity Press, 1998), 1–78; and Giorgio Agamben, *Homo Sacer: Sovereign Power and Bare Life*, trans. Daniel Heller-Roazen (Stanford, Calif.: Stanford University Press, 1998).

7. See Derrida's comment: "Let us merely note for now that, in it, a certain 'deconstruction' ironically recognizes the signature of God himself—or at least of the 'creator's power'. In truth deconstruction = creation"(Jacques Derrida, *On Touching—Jean-Luc Nancy*, trans. Christine Irizarry [Stanford, Calif.: Stanford University Press, 2005; orig. 2000), 327n47.

8. See Boyan Manchev, *La métamorphose et l'instant* (Strasbourg: La Phocide, 2009) and *L'altération du monde* (Paris: Lignes, 2009).

9. Gilles Deleuze, *Spinoza: Practical Philosophy*, trans. Robert Hurley (San Francisco: City Lights Books, 1988; orig. 1981), 122–30.

10. One could reread several texts with this in mind, particularly Jacques Derrida, "Plato's Pharmacy" and "Dissemination" (on the subject of mime), in *Dissemination*, trans. Barbara Johnson (Chicago: University of Chicago Press, 1983; orig. 1972), as well as "Le ventriloque," by Jean-Luc Nancy, in *Mimèsis des articulations* (Paris: Galilée, 1975).

11. Plato, *The Collected Dialogues*, ed. Edith Hamilton and Huntington Cairns, trans. Benjamin Jowett. (Princeton, N.J.: Princeton University Press, 1961), *Cratylus*, 403e–4a.

12. Jacques Derrida, *Speech and Phenomena and Other Essays on Husserl's Theory of Signs*, trans. David B. Allison (Evanston, Ill.: Northwestern University Press, 1973; orig. 1967), 102.

13. Jean-Luc Nancy, "The Free Voice of Man," in *Retreating the Political*, ed Jean-Luc Nancy and Philippe Lacoue-Labarthe, English. version ed. Simon Sparks (London: Routledge, 2007), 131.

14. For Nancy's complex relationship with Spinoza, see "On the Soul" (*C* 129–30/118–20).

15. According to Antonio Negri, "Matter is itself revolutionary" (A. Negri, *Du retour: Abécédaire biopolitique—Entretiens avec Anne Dufourmantelle* [Paris: Calmann-Lévy, 2002], 136).

Distinct Art
Alena Alexandrova
NOTE: An earlier version of this text, entitled "The Auto-Deconstructive Image: Of Vestigial Places," appeared in *Bijdragen: International Journal in Philosophy and Theology* 69, no. 3 (2008): 321–36.

1. Similar themes appear in virtually all the essays included in *M1, GI, C, CW*, and "The Look of the Portrait," in *M2*. Footnote 4 in "The Image—The Distinct" reads: "But in the second direction [the direction of what Nancy identifies as the "sacrificial image," sacrifice understood as an image, the Eucharistic "sacred species"], sacrifice deconstructs itself, along with all monotheism. The

image—and with it, art in general—is at the heart of this deconstruction" (*GI* 140n4/15n1).

2. The difference between these two religious modes is a central theme Nancy develops in a number of essays, see: "Atheism and Monotheism" (*D* 14–28/27–46), "A Deconstruction of Monotheism" (*D* 29–41/47–64), "The Look of the Portrait" (*M2* 220–47), and "Of Creation" (*CW* 57–74/ 56–102).

3. For a detailed analysis of demythologization with regard to poetry, see the contribution by Aukje van Rooden in this volume.

4. For a discussion of this issue, see the contribution by François Raffoul in this volume.

5. For a detailed account of this issue, see Part I of this volume.

6. "Thou shalt not make unto thee any graven image, or any likeness of any thing that is in heaven above, or that is in the earth beneath, or that is in the water under the earth. Thou shalt not bow down thyself to them, nor serve them: for I the LORD thy God am a jealous God, visiting the iniquity of the fathers upon the children unto the third and fourth generation of them that hate me" (Exodus 20:4–6, King James Version).

7. See Hans Belting, *Likeness and Presence: A History of the Image Before the Era of Art*, trans. Edmund Jephcott (Chicago: The University of Chicago Press, 1994), 7: "For the Jews, Yahweh was visibly present only in the written word. No image resembling a human being was to be made of him, since it would then resemble the idols of the neighboring tribes. In monotheism, the only way for the universal God to distinguish himself was by invisibility."

8. A similar observation is made by Alain Besançon, for Islam: "the association (*shirk*) between God and any external notion of his essence, any person (as among Christians), and a fortiori any matter, is perceived with horror as an attack on unity, as a return to polytheism. It is the very idea of God that rules out representations of him. . . . 'Absolute' means, among other things, 'having no hollow parts,' the negation of any mixture and any possible division into parts; 'dense,' opaque, like a cliff without fissures" (*The Forbidden Image: An Intellectual History of Iconoclasm*, trans. Jane Marie Todd [Chicago: University of Chicago Press, 2000], 78).

9. This theme resonates with a moment in modernism that, in accordance with the Kantian aesthetic of disinterestedness, postulates the absolute autonomy of the artwork from practical, social, or religious issues. However, this autonomy embodies a paradox. First, this high modernist moment is associated historically with the bourgeois instrumentalization of life. Second, the postulate of the autonomy of the artwork becomes the figure of art's own destruction. Absolute autonomy means the rejection of a representational regime, and it merges the excess and the absence of signification. As a result, in its absolute freedom art does not signify any more, or rather, it signifies its own end.

10. This is why the first Christian images to be considered unconditionally authentic—*acheiropoieta*, or not produced by a human hand, appear as miraculously circumventing all the operations of mimesis and their implications. For a

detailed analysis of this type of image, see Marie-José Mondzain, *Image, Icon, Economy: The Byzantine Origins of the Contemporary Imaginary*, trans. Rico Franses (Stanford, Calif.: Stanford University Press, 2005), 176–209.

11. Jean-Luc Marion also makes this claim. He explains that the impoverishment of the contemporary art image, in the sense that it is no longer based on a mimetic operation, is similar to the monotheistic tenet of the invisibility of God. See Jean-Luc Marion, *The Crossing of the Visible*, trans. James K. A. Smith (Stanford, Calif.: Stanford University Press, 2004), 63.

12. For a discussion of the notion of divine places, see the contribution by Hent de Vries in this volume.

13. See Georges Didi-Huberman, *Confronting Images: Questioning the Ends of a Certain History of Art*, trans. John Goodman (University Park: Pennsylvania State University Press, 2005), 211–12.

14. Ibid., 184.

15. Ibid., 211.

16. See Georges Didi-Huberman, *Fra Angelico: Dissemblance and Figuration*, trans. Jane-Marie Todd (Chicago: University of Chicago Press, 1995), 6.

17. Ibid., 27, 30.

18. Ibid., 7.

19. Ibid., 10.

The Dis-enclosure of Contemporary Art: An Underpinning Work
Federico Ferrari
NOTE: The quote from Nancy under which this text runs is from *GI* 10–11/ 27–28.

On Dis-enclosure and Its Gesture, Adoration: A Concluding Dialogue with Jean-Luc Nancy
Jean-Luc Nancy and the Editors

1. Marcel Gauchet, *The Disenchantment of the World*, trans. Oscar Burge (Princeton, N.J.: Princeton University Press, 1997), 4, trans. modified.

2. Jan Assmann, *Violence et monothéisme* (Paris: Bayard, 2009). For a further discussion of Assmann's work on monotheism, see also the Preamble and Laurens ten Kate's contribution to this volume.

3. Marlène Zarader, *Heidegger et les paroles de l'origine* (Paris: Vrin, 1986), and idem, *The Unthought Debt: Heidegger and the Hebraic Heritage*, trans. Bettina Bergo (Stanford, Calif.: Stanford University Press, 2006; orig. 1990).

4. Friedrich Nietzsche, *The Antichrist*, trans. R. J. Hollingdale (Harmondsworth: Penguin, 1972; orig. 1888), fr. 39.

5. See ibid., fr. 32.

6. Immanuel Kant, *Religion Within the Boundaries of Mere Reason*, trans. Allen Wood and George Di Giovanni (Cambridge: Cambridge University Press, 1998; orig. 1793–94), 188; trans. modified.

7. Sigmund Freud, Lecture 32, "Anxiety and Instinctual Life," in *The Standard Edition of the Complete Psychological Works of Sigmund Freud*, ed. and trans. James Strachey (London: The Hogarth Press, 1964), 22:95; trans. modified.

8. Jean-Christophe Bailly, *Adieu: Essai sur la mort des dieux* (Paris: L'Aube, 1993).

9. Translation taken from Karl H. Worner, "Arnold Schoenberg and the Theater," *The Musical Quarterly* 48, no. 4 (October 1962): 444–60.

10. See Henri Matisse, *Matisse on Art*, ed. Jack D. Flam (Berkeley: University of California Press, 1995), 48.

Contributors

Alena Alexandrova completed her doctoral dissertation at the University of Amsterdam on how contemporary art critically reappropriates religious motifs. At present she teaches at the Dutch Art Institute, Arnhem, and at the Gerrit Rietveld Academy, Amsterdam. Among her published essays is *"Death in the Image: The Post-Religious Life of Christian Images,"* in *Religion: Beyond a Concept*, ed. Hent de Vries (New York: Fordham University Press, 2008).

Daniela Calabrò is Research Professor in Theoretical Philosophy at the University of Salerno. She is the author of *L'infanzia della filosofia: Saggio sulla filosofia dell'educazione di Maurice Merleau-Ponty* (Turin: Utet, 2002) and *Dis-piegamenti: Soggetto, corpo e comunita in Jean-Luc Nancy, con un'intervista al filosofo*, which contains Jean-Luc Nancy, *"58 indici sul corpo"* (Milan: Mimesis, 2006). She is also the editor of *Il peso di un pensiero, l'approssimarsi* (Milan: Mimesis, 2009).

Ignaas Devisch is Professor of Ethics, Philosophy, and Medical Philosophy at Ghent University and lecturer in philosophy at the Artevelde University College. He has published on the sociopolitical writings of Nancy; an English translation of his book *We: Jean-Luc Nancy and the Question of Community* is forthcoming.

Federico Ferrari teaches Contemporary Philosophy and Art Theory at the Brera Academy of Fine Arts in Milan. His most recent books are: *Lo* *spazio critico: Nota per una decostruzione dell'istituzione museale* (Rome: Luca Sossella, 2004) and *Sub specie aeternitatis: Arte ed etica* (Reggio Emilia: Diabasis, 2008). With Jean-Luc Nancy, he has published: *Nus sommes: La peau des images* (Strasbourg: Klincksieck, 2006) and *Iconographie de l'auteur* (Paris: Galilée, 2005).

Ian James completed his doctoral research on the fictional and theoretical writings of Pierre Klossowski at the University of Warwick in 1996. Since then he has been a fellow and lecturer in French at Downing College, University of Cambridge. He is the author of *Pierre Klossowski: The Persistence of a Name* (Oxford: Legenda, 2000), *The Fragmentary Demand: An Introduction to the Philosophy of Jean-Luc Nancy* (Stanford, Calif.: Stanford University Press, 2006), and *Paul Virilio* (London: Routledge, 2007).

Laurens ten Kate is Associate Professor in the Philosophy of Religion and Theology at the University of Humanistic Studies, Utrecht. With Ilse N. Bulhof, he co-edited *Flight of the Gods: Philosophical Perspectives on Negative Theology* (New York: Fordham University Press, 2001) and, with Jean-Luc Nancy, he has published "'Cum' Revisited: Preliminaries to Thinking the Interval," in *Intermedialities: Philosophy, Arts, Politics*, ed. H. Oosterling and E. P. Ziarek (Lanham, Md.: Lexington Books, 2010).

Marc De Kesel teaches philosophy at Artevelde University College, Ghent, and is Senior Researcher at the Radboud University, Nijmegen. He is the author of *Eros & Ethics: Reading Jacques Lacan, Séminaire VII* (Albany: State University of New York Press, 2009).

Michel Lisse is Research Associate at the Belgian Fonds National de la Recherche Scientifique and Professor at the Catholic University of Louvain-la-Neuve. He is the editor of several volumes, including *Passions de la littérature: Avec Jacques Derrida* (Paris: Galilée, 1996) and, with Marie-Louise Mallet and Ginette Michaud, Jacques Derrida's *Séminaire La bête et le souverain*, vol. 1: *2001–2002* (Paris: Galilée, 2008), and vol. 2: *2002—2003* (Paris: Galilée, 2010). Among the books he has authored are: *L'expérience de la lecture 1: La soumission* (Galilée: Paris, 1998) and *L'expérience de la lecture 2: Le glissement* (Paris: Galilée, 2001).

Donald Loose is Associate Professor of Philosophy at Tilburg University and Thomas More Professor at Erasmus University, Rotterdam. He has published on Kant, the political philosophy of Claude Lefort, and the issue of religion in the public domain.

Boyan Manchev is Associate Professor of Philosophy at the New Bulgarian University in Sofia and Visiting Professor at Sofia University and the Universität der Künste, Berlin. He is a former Director of Program and Vice President of the International College of Philosophy in Paris, Associate Professor of Philosophy at the New Bulgarian University in Sofia, and Guest Professor at Sofia University. He is a member of the editorial committee of the journal *Rue Descartes* (Paris) and of the editorial board of the journal *Altera* (Sofia). His publications include *L'altération du monde: Pour une esthétique radicale* (Paris: Lignes, 2009); *La métamorphose et l'instant* (Paris: La Phocide, 2009); and *The Body-Metamorphosis* (Sofia: Altera, 2007).

Jean-Luc Nancy is Distinguished Professor of Philosophy at the Université Marc Bloch in Strasbourg, France. His most recent books to appear in English are: *God, Justice, Love, Beauty: Four Little Dialogues*; *The Truth of Democracy*; *On the Commerce of Thinking: Of Books and Bookstores*; and *The Fall of Sleep* (New York: Fordham University Press, 2011, 2010, 2009, and 2009).

Anne O'Byrne is Associate Professor of Philosophy at Stony Brook University. She is the author of *Natality and Finitude* (Bloomington: Indiana University Press, 2010) and the co-translator, with Robert Richardson, of Jean-Luc Nancy, *Being Singular Plural*.

Frans van Peperstraten is Associate Professor of Philosophy at Tilburg University. His writing focuses on the relationship between art and politics, mostly starting from a discussion of the works of Kant, Hölderlin, Heidegger, Lyotard, and Lacoue-Labarthe.

François Raffoul is Associate Professor of Philosophy at Louisiana State University. He is the author of *Heidegger and the Subject* (New York: Prometheus, 1999), *À chaque fois mien* (Paris: Galilée, 2004), and *The Origins of Responsibility* (Bloomington: Indiana University Press, 2010). He has co-edited several volumes, including *Disseminating Lacan* (Albany: State University of New York Press, 1996), *Heidegger and Practical Philosophy* (Albany: State University of New York Press, 2002), *Rethinking Facticity* (Albany: State University of New York Press, 2008), and *French Interpretations of Heidegger* (Albany: State University of New York Press, 2008). He is the co-translator of Jean-Luc Nancy, *The Creation of the World, or Globalization*.

Aukje van Rooden is Research Associate in Textual Culture and Contemporary Philosophy at the Research Institute for History and Culture at Utrecht University. She completed a doctoral dissertation at Tilburg University on the entwining of politics and literature within myth, with a particular focus on the work of Jean-Luc Nancy.

Kathleen Vandeputte is Assistant at the Department of Performing Arts and Film at Ghent University, where she is preparing a dissertation on the significance of difference and *sensus communis* in contemporary political philosophy.

Hent de Vries holds the Russ Family Chair in the Humanities and is Professor of Philosophy at The Johns Hopkins University. He is also Professor Ordinarius of Systematic Philosophy and the Philosophy of Religion at the University of Amsterdam and Program Director at the International College of Philosophy, Paris. He is the author of *Minimal Theologies: Critiques of Secular Reason in Adorno and Levinas* (Baltimore: Johns Hopkins University Press, 2005), *Religion and Violence: Philosophical Perspectives from Kant to Derrida* (Baltimore: Johns Hopkins University Press, 2002), and *Philosophy and the Turn to Religion* (Baltimore: Johns Hopkins University Press, 1999). Among the volumes he has co-edited are, with Lawrence E. Sullivan, *Political Theologies: Public Religions in a Post-Secular World* (New York: Fordham University Press, 2006), and, with Samuel Weber, *Religion and Media* (Stanford, Calif.: Stanford University Press, 2001) and *Violence, Identity, and Self-Determination* (Stanford, Calif.: Stanford University Press, 1998). Most recently, he has edited *Religion: Beyond a Concept* (New York: Fordham University Press, 2008).

Theo W. A. de Wit is Assistant Professor as well as Extraordinary Professor at Tilburg University, where he teaches social ethics and political philosophy. He has published on Carl Schmitt, Walter Benjamin, Jacob Taubes, and Alain Finkielkraut, and on the issues of solidarity, religion and politics, toleration, and humanism and religion.

Index

Page numbers in bold indicate particularly important or thorough entries.

177–78, 204, **218–19**, **247–53**, 255,
258–60, 264–65, 268, 270, 295, **353**,
355–59, 363, 367–69, 371, 373–74,
377–78, 380
Descartes, René, 204, 208, 215, 217, 312,
316
désoeuvrement, 26, 149, 262, 293, 349
destruction/*Destruktion*, 48, 50, **54–56**,
63, 106, 135, 230, 248, 295, 310, 316,
319, **321**, **355**, 381
Devillairs, L., 370
dialectic, 52, 99, 101, 112, 118, 121, 126,
147, **158–60**, 166, 175, 212, 222, 225,
227, 232, 262–63, 271, 291, 309, 376
diaspora, 14, 110, 324, 326
Dichten/Dichtung, 118–21, 126, 196, 200,
375
Didi-Huberman, Georges, 285–88, 382
différance, 54, 74, 236, 244, **288**, 374, 392
difference, 53, 57, 65, 68–69, 113–14,
117, 131, 133, 140, 173–74, 223,
226–28, **271**, 294, 358, 363; indifference, 15, 117, 125, 207, 299;
ontological difference, 219, 374, 379;
sexual difference, 225
Dikè/-dicy, 88–90
Diognetus, 358
Dionysius the Areopagite (Pseudo-
Dionysius), 37, 113, 165
Dionysus, 67, 181, 235, 276
disassemble/assemble, 14, 24, **56–58**, 111,
133, **147–48**, 152, **165–66**, 169,
173–74, 177–78, 293, 355
Discourse of the Syncope, The (Jean-Luc
Nancy), 206, 213, 226–27
dis-enclosure 4, 6, 8, 13, 16–17, 19, 25,
28, **54**, 72, **164–67**, 169, 172–73,
176, 179, 181, 186, 188, 199, 208,
229, 234, 239, 243, 245, **248–49**, 255,
258, 295, 297, 302, 304, 307–8, 320
disintegration, 5, **47–49**, 53, 179, 323
distance/distancing, 17, 125, 131, 166,
220, 233, 247, **291–95**, 297, 302, 314,
357, 363; of God, 6, 9, 25, 30, 38, 114,
133, **137**, 141, 170, 325, 329, 349,
365
distensio, 53, **56–58**, 165, 167
distinct, the, 26, 62, 115, 205, 216–18,
220, 257, 276, 279, 283, **286–87**, 292,
294

divine place/*topos*, 26, 110, 113, 115, 121,
125, 127, 269
donation, 35, 85, 364
Dostoevsky, Fyodor, 295, 347
Duquoc, Christian, 360
Duras, Marguerite, 104, 362
Duve, Thierry de, 335

Eckhart, Meister, 13, 113, 262, 306
éclat (brilliance, radiance), 9, 125, 208,
292
eclosure, 58–59, 62, 208
Eco, Umberto, 336
ecstacy/*ek-stasis*, 147, 195, 219, 234
Ego sum (Jean-Luc Nancy), 213
Elizabeth (mother of John the Baptist),
235, 287–88
emptiness/emptying. *See* void
enclosure, 54, 176, 179, 247
end, 3, 6, 12, 61, 76, 90, 93, 96, 99, 105,
156, 166, 168, 179, 199, 205, 209,
217, 223, **230–33**, 239, 258, 264, 271,
278, 280, 294–96, 298, **300–301**, 312,
319–20, 339, 381; of Christianity/of
religion, 22, 26–27, 44, 47–48, **50–51**,
61, **136–39**, 167, **179**, 263, 272, 293,
337
Erasmus, 136
erection, 11, **66–68**, 227
ergon, 149, 223, 262
eschatology/*eschaton*, 53, 76, 78, 95, 179,
239, 265
esotericism, 20, 114, 298
Esposito, Roberto, 233, 361, 371
estrangement, 111, 155, **157–62**
eternal life, 2, 76, 216, 238
eternity, 91–92, 95, 238, 265, 329
ethics/*ethos*, 48, 79, 94, 100, 157, **161**,
176, 210, 234, 310, 313, 359, 365
event/*Ereignis*, 35, 37–38, 56, 114, 136,
138–39, **142–44**, 161, 207, 231–33,
235, 239, **254**, **256**, **258–59**, **264–65**,
288–89, 292, 319, 325, 331, 347, 356,
367, 373
exceptional, 84, 307, **339–42**
excess, 10, 45, **54**, **85–88**, 98, 105, 111,
149, **163–64**, **169–70**, **173–74**, 176,
212, 238, 247, 255, 294, 303, 381
exclamation, 190, 195, **332–34**, 341
exhaustion, 37, 54, 87, 103, 230, 239; of

technē, 267
technics/technology, 10, 33, **47–49**, 95,
    119–20, 220, 252, 299, 307, 311,
    320–21, **338–39**, 348–49, 360, 376,
    378; ecotechnics, 252
teleology/*telos*, 91, 101, **171–72**, 239, 251,
    271, 311, 321
theological turn in phenomenology, **34–36**
Theseus, 180–81
Thom, René, 265
Thomas Aquinas, 204, 251, 259, 371
Tomson, Peter J., 369
Torah, 365
touch, 40, 63, 67, 68, 141, 159–60, 168,
    211–12, 214, **220–22**, **235–38**, 247,
    249–53, 255, 258, 259–60, 270–71,
    294, **357**, 377–78
transcendence, 25, 32, **35**, 47, 82, 102,
    111, 127, 165, **167**, **169–73**, 175–76,
    179, 230, 233, 251, 259, 271, 280,
    306, 314, 324, 371
transcendentalia, 175, 371
transimmanence, 82
transitivity, 207, 218, **251**
Trieb, 4, 18, 322, 346
Trinity, 9, 27, 38, 110, 174, 328–29
Tutankhamen, 339

universality, 20, **37–38**, 52, **101**, 172,
    211, 224, 231–32, 239, 277–78, 371,
    381
un-world, 47–48

Vattimo, Gianni, 34, 349, 352
Verbum caro factum est (Jean-Luc Nancy),
    253–55
Veyne, Paul, 345

"Visitation: Of Christian Painting" (Jean-
    Luc Nancy), 30, 188, 229, 287
Voegelin, Eric, 95, 360
voice, 20, 104, 134, **156–59**, 161, 214,
    235
void, **12**, 25, 29, 32, **50–51**, **55–59**,
    57–58, 60, 62, 77–78, 82, 95, 98, 110,
    116, 124, **138–39**, 148, 154, 167–68,
    170–72, 176, **192**, 195–96, 199–200,
    203, 205–6, 211, 213, 218–19, 233,
    244, **254–58**, 260, **262–63**, 265,
    270–72, 279, 284–85, 292–93, 295,
    302, 307, 311, 314, 324, 331, 337,
    355, 357, 374, 379; ontological, 139,
    144, 256–57
Voltaire. 46
Vries, Hent de, 36

Wahl, Jean, 117
Ward, Graham, 353
Weber, Elisabeth, 369
Whitehead, Alfred North, 348
Wink, **112–13**, **127–31**, 264, 301, 367
with/*cum*, 9, **19–21**, 26, 148; being with,
    74, 161, 219, 221–22, 225–26, 358
Wittgenstein, Ludwig, **3**, **80–81**, 113,
    216, 313, 346, 375
work(s), **148–54**, 157–58, 161–62
world: opening of, 3, 7–8, 16, **18**, 28, 60,
    62, 74, 143, 153, 205, 216, 218, 258,
    279, 307, 379; origin of, 82, 133, 311.
    See also sense
Worner, Karl H., 383

Zarader, Marlène, 309, 382
Zeus, 276, 329
Žižek, Slavoj, 37, **38**, 354